Ubiquitous and Pervasive Knowledge and Learning Management:

Semantics, Social Networking and

New Media to Their Full Potential

Miltiadis D. Lytras
University of Patras, Greece

Ambjörn Naeve
KMR Group, Royal Institute of Technology, Sweden

IDEA GROUP PUBLISHING
Hershey • London • Melbourne • Singapore

Acquisition Editor:	Kristin Klinger
Senior Managing Editor:	Jennifer Neidig
Managing Editor:	Sara Reed
Assistant Managing Editor:	Sharon Berger
Development Editor:	Kristin Roth
Copy Editor:	April Schmidt and Lanette Ehrhardt
Typesetter:	Jamie Snavely
Cover Design:	Lisa Tosheff
Printed at:	Yurchak Printing Inc.

Published in the United States of America by
Idea Group Publishing (an imprint of Idea Group Inc.)
701 E. Chocolate Avenue
Hershey PA 17033
Tel: 717-533-8845
Fax: 717-533-8661
E-mail: cust@idea-group.com
Web site: http://www.idea-group.com

and in the United Kingdom by
Idea Group Publishing (an imprint of Idea Group Inc.)
3 Henrietta Street
Covent Garden
London WC2E 8LU
Tel: 44 20 7240 0856
Fax: 44 20 7379 0609
Web site: http://www.eurospanonline.com

Library of Congress Cataloging-in-Publication Data

Ubiquitous and prevasive knowledge and learning management : semantics, social networking and new media to their full potential / Miltiadis Lytras and Ambjörn Naeve, editors.
    p. cm.
  Summary: "This book presents an alternative view to ubiquitous and pervasive knowledge, architectural frameworks, and methodological issues, and introduces some of the major techniques and tools developed in the domain of ontology building, analysis, and semantic Web"--Provided by publisher.
  Includes bibliographical references and index.
  ISBN 978-1-59904-483-5 (hardcover) -- ISBN 978-1-59904-484-2 (softcover) -- ISBN 978-1-59904-485-9 (ebook)
  1. Ubiquitous computing. 2. Mobile computing. I. Lytras, Miltiadis D., 1973- II. Naeve, Ambjorn.
  QA76.5915.U257 2007
  004--dc22
                           2006033757

British Cataloguing in Publication Data
A Cataloguing in Publication record for this book is available from the British Library.

All work contributed to this book is new, previously-unpublished material. The views expressed in this book are those of the authors, but not necessarily of the publisher.

Dedication

To Theodora, Dimitris, Chara and Katerina
And to Ursula and Ylva

Ubiquitous and Pervasive Knowledge and Learning Management:
Semantics, Social Networking and New Media to Their Full Potential

Table of Contents

Foreword

¤✳¤✳¤✳

What was your childhood dream?

¤✳¤✳¤✳

Just take a look around.

We are living the dreams from a couple of decades back or even some from a century or more ago. Some of the dreams that come to mind are (forgive me for my bias toward TV programs from the 1970s):

- Almost everyone is carrying a cell phone now and can call anyone, anytime, wherever he or she might be. Video-call-capable 3G cell phones are already commercially available.

  When I watched the original "Star Trek" TV series, I really wanted to have one of those communicators (although, in retrospect, it is already too bulky). I also watched a science fiction show, "Ultra Seven," in Japan when I was a kid and there was a wristwatch-type device capable of audiovisual communication. Or you might recall Dick Tracy's wrist radio from the 1940s, 1950s, and 1960s if you were born in the United States.

- A computer can beat the best chess player in the world, although it came a little bit (three decades or so) later than Herbert Simon's forecast, made in 1957 that "within 10 years, a computer would routinely beat the world's best player."

- Walking robots are commonplace in Japan, although bipedal walk-ing robots were deemed extremely difficult just ten years ago. There was a Japanese cartoon, "Atomic Boy," in which a very powerful boy robot is walking, aside from his capabilities of intelligent conversations and flying. Now walking robots are commodities in Japan, and DIY kits are even available for kids to make a walking robot of their own.

- I am using a Bluetooth headset and voice recognition on a cell phone to make phone calls through reasonably natural interactions. It really makes me feel futuristic. Fortunately, my phone is much more obedient than HAL in "2001 - A Space Odyssey."

The list goes on and on, and you must have your own dream list from your child-hood. Technology has, in one way or another, made happen much of what we could once but dream.

Dreams and their realizations: Is this a coincidence?

No, of course not. We are creatures driven by dreams and visions. Especially since my childhood years in the 1970s, dreams and visions come animated in full color, leaving us strong and enduring impressions. Science fiction and cartoons, though fiction, need their own set of (meta-) physical rules, frameworks, and world-views consistent within themselves, in order to be convincing and interesting. As such, we consciously or unconsciously work toward realization of those dreams and visions. Sure, we have failed more than once and some research has led us to dead ends, but strong visions have prevailed in the end.

¤✳¤✳¤✳

The research area of ubiquitous and pervasive computing is uniquely close to our everyday life. This area has also been vision-driven from its inception. Mark Weiser has eloquently articulated a vision with disappearing computers woven into the fabric of everyday life, and this vision has effectively defined the research area.

These characteristics of the area will give the research a very strong impact on everyday life when realized. Sometimes the impact will be so profound that it can even change its initial assumptions and the ground and environment on which it stands.

¤✳¤✳¤✳

When you read this book, you will find many innovative ideas that will change how you learn, both inside and outside classrooms, with access to information based on your context, anytime and anywhere you are.

Then I begin to wonder ... what happens next?

When we get a GPS navigation system in our car, we do not have to remember directions and struggle with maps anymore. Instead, we just (literally) tell the destination to the navigation system and then we can enjoy a more efficient and much safer drive, simply by following the directions given by the navigation system.

I envision the time when we have frictionless access to any information we want anytime and anywhere. Then, it would change not only *how* we learn things, but also, significantly, *what* we learn in the classroom. There is even the potential that the whole meaning of learning will be redefined. It would be much less about specific knowledge or even how to find the knowledge, but more about training on how to use the knowledge (or perhaps something else I can not even imagine now).

You, the reader, will benefit most by also asking yourself "what happens next" after each chapter of this book. These questions will lead you to the next big vision for the future that drives your research. After all, you, as well as the authors of this book, are privileged to pursue your own dreams and visions through research.

Naturally, my question for you after you have read this book is:

¤❋¤❋¤❋

What is your dream now?

¤❋¤❋¤❋

Ryusuke Masuoka

Dreamer & Director, Trusted System Innovation Group

Fujitsu Laboratories of America, Inc.

Dr. Ryusuke Masuoka is a director with Fujitsu Laboratories of America, Inc. at College Park, Maryland, USA. He is also an adjunct professor of UMIAC, University of Maryland, USA. Since joining Fujitsu Laboratories Ltd. in 1988, he has conducted research into neural networks, simulated annealing, and agent systems. Results from all of those areas of research have lead to products from Fujitsu. Specifically, recent research on agent systems has paved the road to an agent system software product, INTERSTAGE AGENTPRO. After moving to Fujitsu Laboratories of America, Inc., in March of 2001, he has engaged in researches on pervasive/ubiquitous computing, Semantic Web, and bioinformatics, from which task computing resulted.

Preface

Ubiquitous and Pervasive Knowledge and Learning Management is the third book of our series. The initial goal was in the first year of the series to provide the state-of-the-art in Knowledge and Learning Management according to our perception for the key technological enablers that in the next years will influence critically the domain. In fact, we wanted to deliver our strategic point of view for the new era of Knowledge and Learning Management.

We started by providing, in *Intelligent Learning Infrastructure for Knowledge Intensive Organizations: A Semantic Web Perspective,* the Semantic Web insights for Knowledge and Learning Management. One year after this publication the evolution of Semantic Web, its adoption in business and industry, supports our argumentation that the future of Knowledge and Learning Management will have a critical Semantic Web dimension.

In the second book of the series, the *Open Source for Knowledge and Learning Management: Strategies Beyond Tools*, we wanted to concentrate on the evolution of the free and open source software (FOSS). Through an excellent combination of themes we wanted to initiate the scientific debate for the benefit of all the citizens and the governments of the knowledge society. Thanks to the contributing authors, this second edition is really a reference book for the area.

The third book is the one you hold in your hands. *Ubiquitous and Pervasive Knowledge and Learning Management: Semantics, Social Networking and New Media to Their Full Potential* analyzes how mobile and wireless networks, and ubiquitous and pervasive computing in general, support a new generation of knowledge and learning management systems aiming to provide services beyond time or geographical borders.

We are really happy. We feel that we have done a great job in this first year. Our edition strategy was from the beginning to develop reference books for big audiences. It is quite strange to realize that especially in academia after a few years the people you can collaborate with are the most competitive to you. This is why you have to open up your mind and ask for collaborations by admitting your limited capacity to deliver more meaningful and greater results. We are really grateful to all the contributing authors of our editions because we share the same beliefs.

In this journey we wanted to go beyond the typical scholar books flavor. We wanted to develop three books that give answers to significant questions but also set new challenges for critical thinking about the deployment of knowledge and learning management for the common wealth.

Having a huge network of collaborations, and being part of big networks of excellence in knowledge and learning management, Semantic Web, open source, ubiquitous and pervasive computing, we tried to create synergies that the audiences of the books could exploit. In business strategy a major lesson is to be able to understand that the pair *explore and exploit* is a key adoption mechanism. In these three edited books we have explored the state of the art for knowledge and learning management as affected by three critical and in fashion technological evolutions: Semantic Web, open source, ubiquitous and pervasive computing.

But in parallel we have tried also to promote the discipline. In a parallel process, we are more than happy that we undertook and delivered, or are currently developing, a great number of special issues in prestigious journals. We mention just a few of them.

Special issues planned to be published in 2007:

1. **IEEE Transactions on Knowledge and Data Engineering:** Special Issue on *Knowledge and Data Engineering in the Semantic Web Era* (Guest Editors: Gottfried Vossen, Miltiadis Lytras, and Nick Koudas)

2. **IEEE Transaction on Education:** Special Issue on *Open Source for Engineering Education: Pedagogical strategies beyond tools* (Guest Editors: Miltiadis Lytras and Walt Scacchi)

3. **IEEE Internet Computing:** Special Issue on *Semantic Based Knowledge Management Systems* (Guest Editors: John Davies, Miltiadis Lytras, and Amit Sheth)

4. **Computers in Human Behavior:** Special issue on *Advances of Knowledge Management and the Semantic Web for Social Networks* (Guest Editor: Miltiadis Lytras)

5. **International Journal of Technology Management:** Special issue on *Knowledge Management in the Health, Pharmaceutical and Clinical Sectors* (Guest Editors: Miltiadis Lytras, Ambjörn Naeve, Constantine Makropoulos, and Vipul Kashyap)

6. **Journal of Knowledge Management:** Special issue on *Competencies Management: Integrating Semantic Web and Enhanced Learning approaches for effective Knowledge Management* (Guest Editors: Miltiadis Lytras, Miguel Angel Sicilia, and Ambjörn Naeve)

7. **International Journal of Knowledge and Learning:** Special Issue on *Knowledge Society: A roadmap for government consultation* (Guest Editors: Miltiadis Lytras, Thomas Devenport, and Larry Prusak)

8. **International Journal of Knowledge and Learning:** Special Issue on *Knowledge and Learning Technologies for National Educational Systems: New Horizons for open minds* (Guest Editors: David Jonassen, Albert Angehrn, Miltiadis Lytras, and Ambjörn Naeve)

9. **International Journal of Knowledge and Learning:** Special Issue on *Learning and Interacting in the Web: Social Networks and Social Software in the Web 2.0* (Guest Editors: Sheizaf Rafaeli, Stephen Downes, Miltiadis Lytras, and Ambjörn Naeve)

10. **International Journal of Knowledge and Learning:** Special Issue on *Empirical Surveys on the Adoption of ICTs in Schools: From Wishful Thinking to Constructivist Learning and Beyond* (Guest Editors: Griff Richards, Dragan Gasevic, Weihong Huang, and Miltiadis Lytras)

11. **International Journal of Teaching and Case Studies:** Special Issue on *Information Systems: The new research agenda the emerging curriculum and the new teaching paradigm* (Guest Editors: John Carroll and Miltiadis Lytras)

12. **International Journal of Teaching and Case Studies:** Special Issue on *Teaching Knowledge Management: Integration into Curriculum, Teaching Strategies and Teaching Case Studies* (Guest Editors: Dov Te'eni, Nick Bontis, and Miltiadis Lytras)

13. **International Journal of Teaching and Case Studies:** Special Issue on *Teaching Semantic Web: Integration with CS/IS Curriculum and Teaching Case Studies* (Guest Editors: Dov Te'eni, Nick Bontis, and Miltiadis Lytras)

14. **IJ of Management in Education:** Special Issue on *Exploiting Information and Communication Technologies for Effective Management of Education: Towards Interactive Managerial and Leadership Styles in Schools* (Guest Editors: Miltiadis Lytras, and Maria Mantziou)

Already Published

1. Naeve, A., Lytras, M., Nejdl, W., Balacheff, N., & Hardin, J. (2006). Advances of Semantic Web for e-learning: Expanding learning frontiers. *British Journal of Educational Technology, 37*(3). http://www.blackwellsynergy.com/toc/bjet/37/3?ai=2ez&ui=18sh2&af=H

2. Lytras, M., Iyer, L., & Tsakalidis, A. (2006). Exploiting knowledge management for ubiquitous e-government in the Semantic Web era. *Electronic Government, an International Journal (EG), 3*(1). http://www.inderscience.com/browse/index.php?journalID=72&year=2006&vol=3&issue=1

3.   Gutiérrez de Mesa, J.A., Rodríguez-García, D., & Lytras, M. (2005, October). Ubiquitous computing. *Upgrade, Digital journal of CEPIS* (Council of European Professional Informatics Societies) (vol. VI). http://www.upgrade-cepis. org/issues/2005/5/upgrade-vol-VI-5.html

4.   Lytras, M., Sicilia, M.A., Kinshuk, & Sampson, D. (2005). Semantic and social aspects of learning in organizations. *The Learning Organization Journal, 12*(5). http://www.emeraldinsight.com/Insight/viewContainer.do?containerType=Iss ue&containerId=22676

5.   Lytras, M., Sicilia, M.A, Davies, J., & Kashyap, V. (2005). Digital libraries in the knowledge era: Knowledge management and semantic Web technologies. *Library Management, 26*(4/5). http://www.emeraldinsight.com/Insight/view-Container.do?containerType=Issue&containerId=22447

6.   Sampson, D., Lytras, M., Wagner, G. & Diaz, P. (2004). Ontologies and the semantic Web for e-learning. *Educational Technolgy and Society Journal, 7*(4). http://www.ifets.info/issues.php?id=25

7.   Lytras, M., Naeve, A., Pouloudi, N. (2005). Knowledge management technologies for e-learning. *International Journal of Distance Educational Technologies, 3*(2). http://www.idea-group.com/journals/toc.asp?ID=498&volume=V ol%2E+3%2C+No%2E+2

For the second year of the Knowledge and Learning Society series, we emphasize the applications domains of knowledge and learning management. In fact, we want to provide our strategic point of view for the kind of applications that the technological enablers of knowledge and learning management as described in the first three editions will be realized. Thus, four more editions have been scheduled for late 2007:

-   **Knowledge Management Strategies: A handbook of applied technologies** (Editors: Miltiadis D. Lytras, Meir Russ, Ronald Maier, and Ambjörn Naeve)

-   **Technology Enhanced Learning: Best practices** (Editors: Weihong Huang, Dragan Gasevic, and Miltiadis D. Lytras)

-   **Knowledge and Networks: A social networks perspective** (Editors: Stephen Downes and Miltiadis D. Lytras)

-   **Semantic Web Engineering for the Knowledge Society** (Editors: Jorge Cardoso and Miltiadis D. Lytras)

Currently, we are preparing for the third year of the series, targeting specific pillars of the knowledge society. Although the final decision has not been made, we are thinking of five more editions along the following themes:

- Digital culture and e-tourism in the knowledge society
- European Union R&D strategy: Lessons learned from a knowledge management perspective
- Sustainable development in the knowledge society
- Politics of the knowledge society
- E-banking and e-finance
- Labor policies in the knowledge society
- Decision making under uncertainty: A knowledge and learning management perspective

We live in an era in which we have modified our traditional assumptions for the provision of information technology supported services. In fact, we live in an era where the information highways enabled by information networks provide unforeseen opportunities for knowledge dissemination.

The traditional simplification of IT, namely the knowledge representation / knowledge retrieval, two-fold approach has gained new insights from the ubiquitous and pervasive computing.

We do believe that this edition contributes to the literature. We invite you to be part of the exciting knowledge and learning management community, and we look forward to your comments, ideas and suggestions for future editions.

August 2006
Miltiadis D. Lytras
Ambjörn Naeve

Structure/Edititng Strategy/Synopsis of the Book

When dealing with ubiquitous and pervasive computing, it makes no sense to try to be exhaustive, not only because of the fast pace in technologies that support ubiquitous computing, but mostly because of the many aspects of the domains. Moreover, when you are trying to investigate the new insights of ubiquitous and pervasive computing to knowledge and learning management, then the mission becomes even more complex.

This is why from the beginning we knew that our book should be selective and focused. In simple words, we decided to develop a book with characteristics that would help readers follow several paths through the contents. We also decided to open the book to large audiences. While we could pursue through our excellent contacts and great network of collaborators a publication aiming to promote the discipline, we decided it would be most significant (from a value-adding perspective) to develop a reference book. And this is what we made with the support of great contributors: a reference book for Ubiquitous and Pervasive knowledge and learning management providing an excellent starting point for further studies in the topics.

Having already the experience of the edition of *Intelligent Learning Infrastructure for Knowledge Intensive Organizations: A Semantic Web Perspective* and getting feedback from hundreds of researchers from all over the world, we decided to keep the same presentation strategy. We have tried, and we think we have succeeded, in developing a book that has three characteristics:

- It discusses the key issues of the relevant research agenda.
- It provides practical guidelines and presents several technologies.
- It has a teaching orientation.

The last characteristic is a novelty of our book. Very often, editions seem like a compilation of chapters but without an orientation to the reader. This is why every edited chapter is accompanied by a number of additional resources that increase the impact for the reader.

In each chapter we follow a common didactic-learning approach:

- At the beginning of each chapter authors provide a section entitled **Inside Chapter**, which is an abstract-like short synopsis of their chapter.

At the end of each chapter there are some very interesting sections, where readers can spend many creative hours. More specifically, the relevant sections are entitled:

- **Internet Session:** In this section authors present one or more Web sites relevant to the discussed theme in each chapter. The short presentation of each Internet session is followed by the description of an **Interaction**, where the reader (student) is motivated to have a guided tour of the Web site and to complete an assignment.
- **Case Study:** For each chapter, contributors provide "realistic" descriptions for one case study, that readers must consider in order to provide strategic advice.
- **Useful Links:** Authors refer to Web sites, with content capable of exploiting the knowledge communicated in each chapter. We decided to provide these links in every chapter, even though we know several of them will be broken in the future, because their synergy with the contents of the chapter can support the final learning outcome.

- **Further Readings:** These refer to high quality articles available both on the Web and electronic libraries. We have evaluated these resources as being of significant value to readers.

- **Essays:** Under this section a number of titles for assignments are given. In the best case, essays could be working research papers. The general rule is that we provide three to six titles for essays, and in their abstract title readers can find an excellent context of questioning.

The edited book consists of 11 chapters. We will try in the next paragraphs to give an overview of the contents and also to explain the strategic fit of each chapter to our vision.

In Chapter I, *Pervasive Computing: What is it anyway?,* Emerson Loureiro, Glauber Ferreira, Hyggo Almeida, and Angelo Perkusich (Federal University of Campina Grande, Brazil) give an excellent introduction to pervasive computing providing the rich picture of the domain.

In fact, they introduce the key ideas related to the paradigm of pervasive computing. They discuss in depth pervasive computing concepts, challenges, and current solutions by dividing it into four research areas. Such division makes it possible to understand what is really involved in pervasive computing at different levels. They provide readers with introductory theoretical support in the selected research areas, giving an excellent introduction for the exploitation of pervasive computing for knowledge and learning management.

In Chapter II, *"Neomillennial" Learning Styles Propagated by Wireless Handheld Devices,* Edward Dieterle, Chris Dede, and Karen Schrier (Harvard Graduate School of Education, USA) give fresh ideas and innovative ways for the exploitation of ubiquitous and pervasive technologies for learning. According to their strategic point of view, as the digital-aged learners of today prepare for their post-classroom lives, educational experiences within classrooms and outside of schools should reflect advances both in interactive media and in the learning sciences. Two recent research projects that explore the strengths and limitations of wireless handheld computing devices (WHDs) as primary tools for educational innovations are Harvard University's Handheld Devices for Ubiquitous Learning (HDUL) and Schrier's Reliving the Revolution (RtR). These projects provide rich data for analysis using their conceptual framework, which articulates (a) the global proliferation of WHDs, (b) society's movement toward "ubiquitous computing," (c) the potential of WHDs to enable sophisticated types of instructional designs, and (d) WHD's fostering of new, media-based learning styles.

In Chapter III, *Mobile Education: Lessons Learned,* Holger Nösekabel (University of Passau, Germany) encourages readers to apply their critical thinking. He initiates an interesting debate by acknowledging that mobile education, comprising learning, teaching, and education-related administrative services delivered via mobile technologies, has incited several projects and discussions in the last years.

When reviewing these projects, it becomes apparent that most of them are technology-driven, and only a few were formally evaluated at the end. However, certain lessons, chances, and obstacles can be identified which may be helpful for further development in this sector.

One critical issue is the distribution of costs for mobile services. As both educational institutions and students act on a limited budget, it is necessary to choose an infrastructure which meets the requirements of the users and addresses all relevant obstacles. Consequently, there is no single ideal technological alternative, but each project needs to make a situational choice.

Readers will really value this chapter, and Nösekabel's critical point of view will give significant answers to several questions.

In the same line with Nösekabel's work, Chapter IV, *Ubiquitous Applications in Education,* by Kostas Kolomvatsos (National & Kapodistrian University of Athens, Greece) deals with issues directly connected to ubiquitous computing, such as its features, types of devices used, and pedagogical goals. The advantages and disadvantages of ubiquitous environments are fully examined and some initiatives are presented and discussed.

In Chapter V, *Using Multimedia and Virtual Reality for Web-Based Collaborative Learning on Multiple Platforms,* Gavin McArdle, Teresa Monahan, and Michela Bertolotto (University College Dublin, Ireland) discuss the benefits that 3D environments offer the e-learning community. They outline how this type of system emerged and describe some currently available systems using these new technologies. In particular, they describe in detail a virtual reality environment for online learning developed in their research group and the features it provides. They also discuss the extension of this system to a mobile platform so that users have anytime, anywhere access to course materials. Finally, they put forward some thoughts on future technologies and discuss their possible contribution to the development of a truly ubiquitous and pervasive learning environment. We fully agree with their point of view that future e-learning systems will be much different from the text-based monolithic systems that currently dominate the market.

In Chapter VI, *Using Emotional Intelligence in Personalized Adaptation,* Violeta Damjanovic (Salzburg University, Austria) and Milos Kravcik (Open University Nederland, The Netherlands) provide significant insights for the critical theme of adaptation in ubiquitous and pervasive learning environments. The process of training and learning in Web-based and ubiquitous environments brings in a new sense of adaptation. With the development of more sophisticated environments, the need for them to take into account the user's traits, as well as user's devices on which the training is executed, has become an important issue in the domain of building novel training and learning environments. This chapter introduces an approach to the realization of personalized adaptation. Because they are dealing with the stereotypes of e-learners, having in mind emotional intelligence concepts to help in adaptation to the e-learners real needs and known preferences, they have called this system eQ. It stands for using of the emotional intelligence concepts on the Web.

In Chapter VII, *Accessing Learning Content in a Mobile System: Does Mobile Mean Always Connected?*, Anna Trifonova (University of Trento, Italy) points out an important functionality of a ubiquitous mobile system, and more specifically its application in the learning domain. This functionality is the possibility to access the learning material from mobile devices, like PDAs (personal digital assistants) during their off-line periods and the technique to approach it, called hoarding. The chapter starts with an overview of a concrete mobile learning system, Mobile ELDIT, to give a clear idea of when and how this problem appears and why it is important to pay attention to it. Later, a description of the development approaches for both general and concrete solutions are discussed, followed by a more detailed description of the important hoarding steps.

In Chapter VIII, *A Choreographed Approach to Ubiquitous and Pervasive Learning,* Sinuhé Arroyo and Reto Krummenacher (Digital Enterprise Research Institute, Innsbruck, Austria) introduce a conceptual choreography framework and show its tremendous interest for ubiquitous and pervasive applications. Choreography is the concept of describing the externally visible behaviour of systems in the form of message exchanges. As information about various sensors, services, and user applications have to be integrated in ubiquitous and pervasive environments to provide seamless assistance to users, it is indispensable that means to map heterogeneous message exchange patterns and vocabularies are provided. The authors' aim is to give the reader an understanding of the principles and technologies underlying the choreography framework of **SOPHIE**: semantic descriptions of message exchange patterns are used to overcome heterogeneity in communication regardless of the concrete application domain.

In Chapter IX, *Semantic Knowledge Mining Techniques for Ubiquitous Access Media Usage Analysis,* John Garofalakis, Theodoula Giannakoudi, Yannis Panagis, Evangelos Sakkopoulos, and Athanasios Tsakalidis (University of Patras, Greece) present an information acquisition system which aims to provide log analysis dealing with ubiquitous access media by use of semantic knowledge. The lately emerging figure of the Semantic Web, the ontologies, may be used to exalt the Web trails to a semantic level so as to reveal their deeper usage info. The presented architecture, intended to overcome mobile devices' trail, duplicates problems and detect semantic operations similarity of server Web services, which are often composed to provide a function. The references that supplement the chapter provide publications that mainly discuss log file mining and analysis and semantic similarity. Useful technology-used URL resources are also provided.

In Chapter X, *To Ease the Dilemma of Help Desk: The Application of Knowledge Management Techniques in Manipulating Help Desk Knowledge,* Nelson Leung and Sim Kim Lau (University of Wollongong, Australia) describe the development of help desk, ranging from help desk structures to support tools. This chapter also discusses the application of knowledge management techniques in the development of a proposed conceptual knowledge management framework and a proposed re-distributed knowledge management framework. While the conceptual knowledge management framework proposes a standard methodology to manage help desk knowledge, the proposed redistributed knowledge management framework allows simple and routine enquiries to be re-routed to a user self-help knowledge management system. The proposed system also enables help desk to provide technical knowledge to user 24 hours a day, 7 days a week. Regardless of time and geographical restrictions, users can solve their simple problems without help desk intervention simply by accessing the proposed system through portable electronic devices.

In Chapter XI, *Discursive Context-Aware Knowledge and Learning Management Systems,* Caoimhín O'Nualláin, Adam Westerski, and Sebastian Kruk (DERI Galway, Ireland) look at the research area of discursion and context-aware information as it relates to the user. Much research has been done in the area of effective learning, in active learning, and in developing frameworks through which learning can be said to be achieved with some possibility of being measured (i.e., networked learning and Bloom's Taxonomy). Having examined many such frameworks, they found that dialogue plays a large part, and in this chapter they specifically examine dialogue in context of the user's background and social context. They provide a quality discourse analysis model which achieves in more detail a picture of the user's actual level of knowledge.

Acknowledgments

We finalized this book, *Ubiquitous and Pervasive Knowledge and Learning Management*, in early July 2006—Ambjörn in Stockholm and Miltiadis in Monemvassia, a lovely Greek village.

So the time has come for us to express our deepest appreciation and respect to the more than 20 contributors of this edition. Their knowledge, expertise, and experience are evident in every line of this edition. It sounds typical, but it is the ultimate truth. Every edition is just an outlet, where the world of ideas is seeking a fertile ground. And this ground is not self-admiring. It requires the interest and insights of people. Hence our second deepest thank you goes to our readers in academia, industry, government, and in society in general.

It is also typical to acknowledge the publishers and all the supporting staff in all the stages of the book production. In Idea Group Inc., we have found more than just publishers and excellent professionals. We have found great supporters of a shared vision to develop books/editions and knowledge for a highly demanding society. Mehdi, Jan, Kristin, and Meg, please accept our warmest compliments for your encouragement and inspiration. You prove to us every day that IGP is not only a high quality publishing organization but also a community that cares for its people.

Our deepest appreciation and respect to Ryusuke Masuoka, Fujitsu Laboratories of America, Inc., USA, for his excellent foreword.

Last but not least, we would like to thank by name a few colleagues that in various ways have motivated us to work toward our human vision for the deployment of information technologies in our society. In our academic life we have a clear motto. We want to make important things happen, and due to our intrinsic motivation to be of good will and very optimistic guys, we really love people who encourage others, and people who say "go on and we stand by you."

Miltiadis:

My warmest compliments and thank you go to Gottfried Vossen and Gerd Wagner, who supported me in my vision to establish AIS SIG on Semantic Web and Information Systems. I also feel blessed to have Miguel-Angel Sicilia as a great friend and collaborator. I will also never forget the support of Professors Kinshuk and Demetrios Sampson at the beginning of my wonderful journey.

In my Greek academic world, my thinking has been deeply affected by Professors Athanassios Tsakalidis, George Pavlidis, Georgios Vassilacopoulos and Georgios Doukidis, to whom I express my heartfelt thank you.

My deepest appreciation and a great thank you also to Amit Sheth, who accepted my invitation to serve as the editor in chief of the International Journal on Semantic Web. I learn every day from Amit, and mostly I learn that leading academics are hard working people helping and encouraging younger guys to follow their achievements.

My colleagues that stand by me in Research Academic Computer Technology Institute, Patras, ELTRUN, in the Department of Management Science and Technology in Athens University of Economics and Business and in the American College of Greece, for their encouragement and continuous motivation.

Finally, I would like to thank especially Efstathia/Maria Pitsa (University of Cambridge), Nikos Korfiatis (Copenhagen Business School), and Martin Papadatos (University of Cambridge) for their great support in all the recent initiatives.

Ambjörn:

First of all, I want to express my gratitude to my PhD students and programmers that have made my work as the head of the Knowledge Management Research group so effective and enjoyable: Matthias Palmér, Mikael Nilsson, Fredrik Paulsson, Henrik Eriksson, Jöran Stark, Jan Danils, Fredrik Enoksson, and Hannes Ebner. Without their commitment to excellence, the KMR-group would not have managed to establish itself on the international research scene.

My very special thank you to Mia Lindegren, the director of Uppsala Learning Lab, with which the KMR-group collaborates closely. Without the unwavering support of Mia, the KMR-group would not have existed in its present shape.

I also want to acknowledge my deep gratitude to Jan-Olof Eklundh, Yngve Sundblad, and Nils Enlund at KTH. Over the years—and against all odds—they have provided "incubator environments" that have enabled the growth of the unacademic and controversial discipline of knowledge management at KTH.

I am also grateful to Cherlie Gullström, Alex Jansson, and Mets Erixom for being instrumental in establishing our new centre of excellence, the Centre for Sustainable Communications, her at KTH.

Over the next 10 years, CSC will provide a stimulating and challenging environment for applying "globalised knowledge management" from a sustainability perspective.

My sincerest thank you to Janiche Opsahl, Agneta Sommansson, and Krister Widell of the Swedish Educational Broadcasting company (UR). They have had the courage to apply some of the KMR-tools in a sharp industrial setting, which has given us invaluable feedback and practical experience with knowledge management problems of the real world.

Moreover, I want to express my gratitude to the members of the PROLEARN network of excellence, who have been instrumental in establishing our collaboration with leading European actors in Technology Enhanced Learning and Knowledge Management. Prominent among them are: Wolfgang Nejdl, Peter Scott, Kevin Quick, Erik Duval, Martin Wolpers, Ralf Klamma, Amine Chatti, Katherine Maillet, Milos Kravcik, Marcus Specht, Daniel Burgos, Rob Koper, Alexander Karapidis, Gustaf Neumann, Bernd Simon, Fridolin Wild, Barbara Kieslinger, Margit Hofer, Borka Jerman-Blasic, Tomaz Klobucar, Constantin Makropolous, Vana Kamtsiou, Dimitra Pappa. Tapio Koskinen, Anna-Kaarina Kairamo and Pertti Yli-Luoma.

Finally, just like Miltiadis, I am grateful for the friendship and collaboration of Miguel-Angel Sicilia, who is constantly using his network to bring us into interesting proposals.

Geja sou filaraki, we made it!

Chapter I

Pervasive Computing:
What is it Anyway?

Emerson Loureiro, Federal University of Campina Grande, Brazil

Glauber Ferreira, Federal University of Campina Grande, Brazil

Hyggo Almeida, Federal University of Campina Grande, Brazil

Angelo Perkusich, Federal University of Campina Grande, Brazil

Abstract

In this chapter, we introduce the key ideas related to the paradigm of pervasive computing. We discuss its concepts, challenges, and current solutions by dividing it into four research areas. Such division is how we were able to understand what really is involved in pervasive computing at different levels. Our intent is to provide readers with introductory theoretical support in the selected research areas to aid them in their studies of pervasive computing. Within this context, we hope the chapter can be helpful for researchers of pervasive computing, mainly for the beginners, and for students and professors in their academic activities.

Inside Chapter

The recent advances in hardware and wireless technologies have leveraged the creation of the first experimental pervasive computing scenarios. Due to the belief that these scenarios will be an integral part of future living, research in this field is increasing at a fast pace. Therefore, theoretical and mainly practical studies are of great use as a way of supporting this belief.

Performing such studies, however, implies identifying the intricacies behind pervasive computing. Although its concept is quite simple, understanding these intricacies is a task which scatters across different research fields. Computer networks, distributed and cognitive systems, software engineering, and user interface design are some of these fields.

Therefore, in this chapter our main objective is to identify and discuss, at an introductory level, some of these intricacies. More specifically, we define four major research areas in pervasive computing, namely pervasive networking, context awareness, pervasive systems development, and pervasive computing middleware. Based on this view, we then take the reader on a journey through the universe of pervasive computing, discussing concepts, challenges, and current solutions.

Introduction

Today, computing is facing a significant revolution. There is a clear migration from the traditional desktop-based computing to the ubiquitous era, where computing will be spread all around us and seamlessly integrated into our lives. It is this new stage of computing that researchers have named pervasive computing. We can say that it is the accomplishment of the so-called concept of *calm technology* (Weiser & Brown, 1995), or as Weiser (1993) has said, it "envisions computation primarily in the background where it may not even be noticed" (p. 1). Not surprisingly, these ideas require us to view computers in a totally different way, not only as something we log onto, work on, and log out of when we are finished (Saha & Mukherjee, 2003). Instead, we should see a computer as a portal to a repository of computational resources, making use of them to work on the background and fulfill tasks according to our needs and preferences.

Pervasive computing, also known as ubiquitous computing (Weiser, 1991), has been recognized as the third wave in computer science, following the mainframe and the personal computer ages. Therefore, even if not fully conceived, pervasive computing will be the prevailing paradigm of the 21st century. Observing the graph shown in Figure 1[1], one can see the sales associated with ubiquitous computing devices follow a fast exponential growth. As more and more facilities, or services,

Figure 1. Sales of mainframes, personal computers, and ubiquitous computing devices

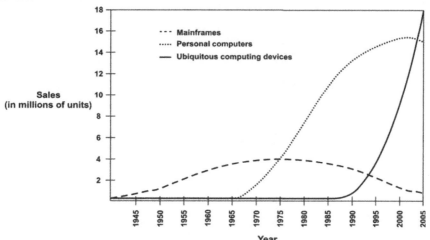

will be available for users of such devices, this growth, even that in a lower rate, will be expected to continue. After all, it is not for nothing that academy and mainly industry are so confident on the pervasive computing paradigm.

Getting a ride on this new trend, the purpose of this chapter is to conduct the reader behind the scenes of pervasive computing, introducing the main concepts and challenges involved in it. The structure of the chapter is illustrated in Figure 2. We start with a first glance at pervasive computing by describing a sample scenario in order to provide the reader with the general concepts. It is presented as an overview of the technological advances that have leveraged the development of pervasive systems, as well as the challenges imposed by pervasive computing scenarios. In the Pervasive Networking section, we present two key concepts for pervasive environments, mobility and host discovery. The notion of context and its importance to pervasive computing will be outlined in the Context in Pervasive Computing section. Next, we present some methods that have been used for developing pervasive systems. More specifically, some techniques that application developers need in order to deal with the inherent characteristics of software for pervasive computing are discussed. Based on this discussion, we then outline in the Middleware for Pervasive Computing section the main features that should be presented by a pervasive computing middleware and how they can aid the development of pervasive applications. Additionally, some pervasive computing middleware solutions are presented. We conclude the chapter by summarizing the actual state of pervasive computing research, and also discuss possible future directions.

Figure 2. Overview of the chapter

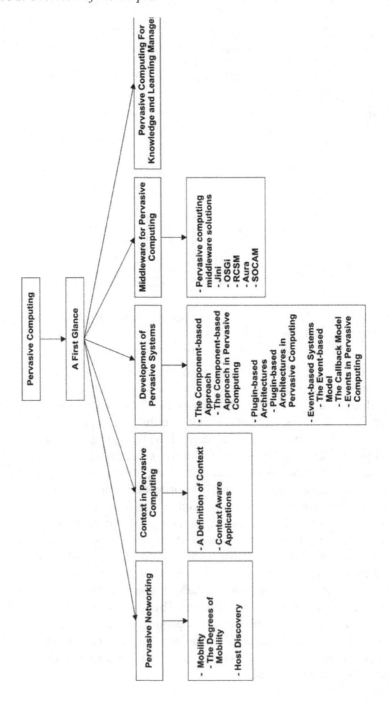

A First Glance at Pervasive Computing

Imagine yourself porting a mobile device, like a handheld, while walking through a shopping mall. Now imagine you are very interested in having a cappuccino. You think it is a pity there is no place in this mall offering cappuccinos. Fortunately, your handheld "knows" that you like cappuccino, and it becomes aware that the shopping mall has just opened a coffee shop. And guess what? Cappuccinos are sold there. Based on this information, your mobile device notifies you about this news, and now you can have your desired cappuccino. While you are savoring it, you are reminded of that book you are interested in. Without hesitation, you take your device out and check to see if any store in the mall has such a book to offer. When the search is finished, you find out that two bookstores are selling the book you want. The search returns all the information you need, such as the price of the book in both stores, discounts, and payment options. With such information at hand, you select the offer best suited for you and request the book. From your mobile device, you provide all the information to complete the purchase. Now, all you need to do is go to the bookstore and get your brand new book.

Wonderful, is it not? Just by porting a mobile device you were able to savor a cappuccino and buy the book you wanted. And both tasks were completed in a very natural way, as if computing had been fully woven into our lives. This is a typical example of a pervasive computing scenario. First introduced by Mark Weiser in his seminal paper (Weiser, 1991), pervasive computing is part of an evolution chain consisting of distributed systems and mobile computing (Satyanarayanan, 2001). It envisions a world where computing and applications are embedded in everyday objects. Clothes, televisions, air conditionings, and cars are examples of such objects. They will be capable of seamlessly interacting with each other in order to perform tasks on behalf of the users by taking intelligent actions or making available relevant information at the right place and at the right time.

Weiser affirmed that pervasive computing can be achieved through three major technologies: cheap and low-power devices, a network infrastructure for communicating these devices, and pervasive applications. At the time this was said, hardware technology was not fully available to support pervasive computing. Wireless networking, as we have today, was neither available nor deployed in mobile devices. Consequently, pervasive applications could not be developed.

This started to change with the introduction of more powerful mobile devices, such as the current smart cellular phones and handhelds, that allowed for the development of more complex applications for such devices. Also, the embedding of wireless networking technologies, like Bluetooth (Bray & Sturman, 2000) and Wi-Fi (Reid & Seide, 2002), on mobile devices has promoted the availability of mobile applications. These technologies have permitted us to give the first steps toward the vision of pervasive computing. This has caused a rush for the first solutions in the field, and many works with this purpose have been developed. Oxygen (*http://www.oxygen.lcs.mit.edu*), Aura (Garlan, Siewiorek, Smailagic, & Steenkiste, 2002), Smart Space (Stanford, Garofolo, Galibert, Michel, & Laprun, 2003), Portolano (Esler, Hightower, Anderson, & Borriello, 1999), and Wings (Loureiro, Bublitz, Barbosa, Perkusich, Almeida, & Ferreira, 2006) are some examples of works related to the branch of pervasive computing.

However, a long road is still ahead. Despite the hardware advances in the last years, there are still a new set of problems associated with software systems for pervasive environments. For pervasive computing to become a true reality, applications need to have full access to the information about the users and the environments in which they are situated. This is in a broad sense what has been named *context*, although many variations for the concept exist nowadays. The current lighting condition, temperature level, and the number of users around a mobile device are some examples of the information associated with the word *context*. The great challenge that remains within this scope is how to model context information, and mainly how to effectively exploit it. The effective use of context information is one of the key issues to achieve Weiser's vision of invisible computing (Satyanarayanan, 2001). Still, acting on behalf of users requires pervasive systems to be ready for changes in their interests. Changes in the local and remote resources available should also be considered, as they are important for achieving such pervasiveness.

Going down to the networking level, we find that mobility and host discovery are two important features for pervasive environments. Whereas the former allows embedded applications to perform their tasks uninterruptedly; that is, even when the user is moving through different networks, host discovery permits a device to discover network hosts, and also to be discovered by them. Due to the discovery

Table 1. The introductory literature that has been used and their main contributions

Reference	Main Contribution
(Weiser, 1991)	
(Weiser, 1993)	Overview of pervasive computing
(Saha & Mukherjee, 2003)	
(Satyanarayanan, 2001)	Challenges brought on by pervasive computing
(Weiser & Brown, 1995)	The concept of calm technology
(Garlan, Siewiorek, Smailagic, & Steenkiste, 2002)	
(Stanford, Garofolo, Galibert, Michel, & Laprun, 2003)	
(Esler, Hightower, Anderson, & Borriello, 1999)	Some current solutions for pervasive computing
(Loureiro, Bublitz, Barbosa, Perkusich, Almeida, & Ferreira, 2006)	

of such hosts, a device is then able to query for the information and resources they share, informing the user about the most relevant ones.

It is clear the preceding challenges need to be first well understood and solved. Only then can dependable pervasive systems emerge. Therefore, from this point on, we start delineating such challenges, as well as mentioning some of the current solutions for them. However, if any of the introductory ideas are not clear enough, the reader can refer to the literature presented in Table 1, where we indicate the contribution of references used throughout the first two sections.

Pervasive Networking

Pervasive networking is about the plumbing involved in the communication of devices in pervasive computing environments. Therefore, studies within this area range from the design and energy consumption techniques of wireless interfaces to the development of high level protocols, such as routing and transport ones. At this high level, mobility and host discovery play fundamental roles as enablers of pervasive environments. Research in these areas has considerably advanced, and as a result, some practical solutions are already available today. Therefore, in this section we present a review of the concepts associated with mobility and host discovery.

Mobility

You probably receive your mail at your residence, right? Now, consider that you are moving to a new house. Among other concerns, you would probably want to change the mailing address associated with correspondences like your credit card bill. In this case, you must notify your credit card company that you have just moved, and that consequently your mailing address has changed. Either you do this or your credit card bill will be delivered to the old address, which is not a desirable situation.

A scenario similar to the above one is basically what happens in computing environments enhanced with mobility. In other words, mobility must allow a device to change its physical location and still be capable of receiving network packages from the other hosts. Note that, by physical location, we are referring to the network a device is connected to. Therefore, moving through different networks is what requires a node to have its address changed.

Mobility is certainly a fundamental element for pervasive environments. The possibility for providing users with *on the move* networking enables applications to work in the background by invisibly searching for some relevant content. However, the use of mobility in computing systems inherently leads them to face a set of new and challenging problems, which can be grouped in the following way (Satyana-rayanan, 1996):

- **Resource poverty of mobile computing devices:** It is a fact that mobile devices are resource-poor when compared to personal computers. Processor speed and memory/disk capacities are considerably higher in static computers than in mobile ones. Therefore, software for mobile computing need to be well designed in order to save processor usage and storage space.

- **Energy restrictions:** Static computers are plugged to some energy network, which is theoretically an unlimited source of energy. Mobile devices, on the other hand, depend on limited capacity batteries. Therefore, techniques for saving energy should be applied in mobile applications.

- **Variability of wireless links:** Wireless connectivity is still highly variable in terms of performance and reliability. Whereas some buildings provide high-bandwidth and reliable wireless connections, others may provide considerably less bandwidth and reliability. This can be even worse in an open environment, where connection may be shared by lots of users. Undoubtedly, these changes in wireless connectivity need to be addressed in pervasive computing systems by, for example, implementing some network congestion control algorithm.

- **Security of wireless connections:** Due to the broadcast nature of wireless links, they are easier to eavesdrop with than wired ones. Therefore, if security is already an important feature of fixed networks, for wireless ones it is an even more important feature.

The Degrees of Mobility

The different degrees of mobility have a direct impact over the topology of a network. The more mobile are the network nodes, the more flexible the network needs to be. In the case of Ethernet networks, for example, nodes are too static. Therefore, only in sporadic situations is it necessary to change the network address of a node. Consequently, the network topology does not necessarily need to be flexible. In this case, protocols like DHCP (dynamic host configuration protocol) seamlessly solve the problem of delivering new network addresses to nodes. At the other extreme, a network may be populated by highly mobile nodes. Such a level of mobility allows users to move around areas that, for various reasons, have no fixed network coverage. In these situations infrastructureless networks are more appropriate. That is, nodes should be capable of establishing connections with each other whenever needed. In this case, the network would be formed opportunistically as more and more mobile devices get together.

Within this context, as Sun and Savoula (2002) have already pointed out, three modes of communication can be distinguished when it comes to the degree of mobility: *nomadic, cellular*, and *pervasive communication*. In the first case, no connection is necessary when the device is migrating from one network to another. A typical example of the nomadic communication is a user who uses a notebook for connecting to a network both at work and at home. Note that there is no need to keep network connections while the users are moving from work to their house. Only when getting home should the notebook receive a new address for accessing the network. In the cellular communication mode, the network is organized in cells, where each cell is located adjacent to a set of others. All cells have a central element, which provides connectivity for the nodes within them. Therefore, a mobile device can move through different cells and maintain a connection with their central element, becoming thus accessible even when moving. Current mobile telephony networks are an example of this kind of communication, where the base stations act as the central elements. Finally, pervasive communication can be mainly characterized by the lack of a fixed network infrastructure different from the two previous ones. Therefore, nodes should establish connections directly with each other whenever they come close enough. These features are what characterize the so-called ad hoc networks (Chlamtac, Conti, & Liu, 2003), and will be of great importance in the deployment of pervasive computing environments.

Among the current solutions for mobility, we could cite Mobile IP (Perkins, 1997), GPRS (General Packet Radio System), and Bluetooth. Basically, Mobile IP and GPRS are mobility solutions respectively for IP and mobile telephony networks. Bluetooth, on the other hand, is a standard for short-range and low-cost wireless communication in an ad hoc way. Further description concerning these technologies can be found on the Web sites listed in the Useful URLs section.

Host Discovery

Putting it simply, host discovery is about finding other hosts in the network, and also being found by them. This apparently simple concept is of great importance for pervasive computing environments, and can be found in technologies such as Bluetooth and UPnP (Universal Plug and Play). As an example of its usage, consider the acquisition of context information in decentralized environments, such as the available services. By using host discovery, a device can, for example, find the available hosts in the environment and query them for the services they provide. This is the service discovery mechanism used by the Bluetooth technology.

Host discovery can be performed either by using a *notification*-based approach or a *query*-based one. In the former, a host is discovered when it notifies itself to the others. This requires the host to send its advertisement through the network, so that the others can be aware of it. Such advertisements contain information such as the

Figure 3. Host discovery approaches

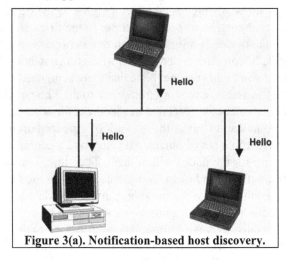

Figure 3(a). Notification-based host discovery.

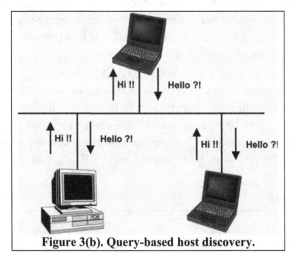

Figure 3(b). Query-based host discovery.

address, name, and description of the hosts. The advertising task can be executed a singe time (e.g., when the host joins the network) or periodically (e.g., each second). The notification-based host discovery is illustrated in Figure 3(a). On the other hand, the query-based approach, illustrated in Figure 3(b), is based on sending *discovery messages* and waiting for their responses, which contain information about the discovered hosts. Therefore, by retrieving the information contained in these responses, a host is able to contact the discovered hosts.

Context in Pervasive Computing

A fundamental functionality of pervasive computing applications is to present users with relevant information or services at the right place and in the right time, in a seamless way. Such information can be, for instance, a landmark for tourists to visit based on their preferences. In this process, two key inputs are involved: the needs and interests of the user and the information available both in the environment and in their devices. The former allows the applications to define what sort of information would be relevant to the user. The latter is the source from where such information will be retrieved. Let us get back to our first example, the one presented in the First Glance on Pervasive Computing section. In that case, your desire for a cappuccino and the book you wanted to buy were your needs and interests. Whereas the former could be acquired, for instance, by keeping historic information of your preferences, the information about the book has been explicitly provided by you. Based on both information, the application running in the handheld was able to determine what would be considered relevant information for you. By gathering information from the environment, the application decided that the opening of a new coffee shop and the bookstores in the surrounding area were relevant enough information to present you.

A Definition of Context

The preceding discussion should provide at least a first impression of what *context* really means. In pervasive computing literature, context has been defined in a number of ways. Some researchers have defined context by categorizing the different information associated with it. Gwizdka (2000), for example, identifies two types of context: *internal* and *external*. Internal context provides information about the state of the users, such as their current emotional state. External context, on the other hand, describes the environment on which a user is immersed, for example, informing about the current noise or temperature level. In the work of Petrelli, Not, Strapparava, Stock, and Zancanaro (2000), two types of context are identified: *material* and *social*. Material context is associated with location (e.g., at home), devices (e.g., a handheld, a cellular phone) or the available infrastructure (e.g., available networks). Social context, on the other hand, encapsulates the information about the current social state of the user, for example, in a meeting or a movie theater. Another work, by Schilit and Theimer (1994), defines three categories for grouping context information: *computing context*, *user context*, and *physical context*. A refinement of these categories is presented by Chen and Kotz (2000), through the addition of a fourth category, *time context*. The information associated with each category is presented as follows.

- **Computing context:** Network bandwidth, the cost involved in communication, and available resources, such as printers, displays, and workstations.

- **User context:** People in the vicinity and the location, profile, and current social situation of the user.

- **Physical context:** Lighting and noise levels, current temperature, and traffic conditions.

- **Time context:** Time of the day, day of the week, month and season of the year.

Note that the above ideas do not really define what is context, but instead try to give it a meaning by enumerating the sort of information that could be related. The problem in defining context in this way is that it may be hard to affirm whether some information can be considered context information or not. Additionally, a more general definition of context would certainly enable a better understanding of its role in pervasive computing. Therefore, for the purposes of this chapter, we consider a context as defined by Dey (2001, p. 45).

Context is any information that can be used to characterize the situation of an entity. An entity is a person, place, or object that is considered relevant to the interaction between a user and an application, including the user and applications themselves.

Context Aware Applications

Considering the current context for determining the actions that can be taken is very natural for us. We commonly use information such as the place we are at and the people around us to guide our actions. When we are in a movie theater, for example, we know how bothersome it is to speak loudly, and so most of us generally do not do so. In this scope, applications that make use of this kind of information are called *context aware applications*. Such applications, however, require functionalities for acquiring and interpreting the context information, and to choose and execute an action based on it. More precisely, three elements are involved throughout this process: *context acquisition, context representation*, and *context reasoning*.

Context acquisition concerns the way context information is obtained, namely *sensed*, *derived*, or *explicitly provided* (Mostéfaoui, Rocha, & Brézillon, 2004). Sensed context information is gathered from physical sensors, such as lighting or temperature ones. Derived context information is computed on demand, like the time of the day and the number of people around. Finally, when context information is explicitly provided, the user is responsible for providing it. An example of this acquisition can be viewed on applications which provide a form for users to fill in with their preferences (i.e., favorite kinds of books, movies, food, and entertainment).

Once acquired, context information needs to be made available to the interested applications. This implies that it must be represented in an agreed format, so that the interested applications can "understand" the information they received from the providers. As already pointed out by Held, Buchholz, and Schill (2002), the representation of the context should be *structured, interchangeable, composable/decomposable, uniform, extensible*, and *standardized*. Structuring is important for enabling applications to filter pieces of information from the context. Interchangeability is related to the possibility of applications to exchange context information with each other. Therefore, in order to provide this characteristic, a context representation must be serializable. Composition and decomposition enables to compose and decompose context information from different sources. This allows transferring only sub-parts of the information, for example, when it has been updated, to avoid sending the whole context representation. Uniformity claims that different kinds of context information (e.g., user's profile, device profiles, resource profiles) should be represented in a similar manner in order to ease interpretation by the applications which use them. As the number of terms and variables of a context is difficult to predict, even in quite restricted domains, extensibility is also a fundamental characteristic for context information representation. Finally, as devices and applications can come from different vendors, context information must be based on standards. This would certainly improve the exchanging of context information among pervasive computing applications. Current solutions for pervasive computing represent context in different ways; for example, using key-value pairs, XML documents (Boyera & Lewis, 2005; Ryan, 1999), object-oriented models (Henricksen, Indulska, & Rakotonirainy, 2002), and ontology-based models (Chen, Finin, & Joshi, 2003; Henricksen, Livingstone, & Indulska, 2004; Masuoka, Labrou, Parsie, & Sirin, 2003).

Considering that the context information is represented in a way that applications understand, it is possible to make use of this information and perform context reasoning. Basically, context reasoning is the use of contextual information for guiding the actions an application will take. As Satyanarayanan (2001) has already pointed out, the effective use of context information is a fundamental element in pervasive computing, as a means for achieving the invisibility feature envisioned by Weiser. The context reasoning mechanism of a pervasive computing system can be as simple as *if-then-else* statements, or as complex as rule-based (Nishigaki, Yasumoto, Shibata, Ito, & Higashino, 2005) and case-based methods (Ma, Kim, Ma, Tang, & Zhou, 2005). An important characteristic of context reasoning systems is the ability to deal with uncertain context information. As the information acquired by sensors (i.e., sensed context information) is prone to errors, applications should consider the quality of the acquired context information when performing their reasoning tasks. To this end, different approaches have been proposed using, for example, Bayesian networks (Gu, Pung, & Zhang, 2004a) and Fuzzy logic (Ranganathan, Muhtadi, & Campbell, 2004).

Development of Pervasive Computing Systems

Based on our discussion until now, it is easy to realize that the intrinsic features of pervasive computing have an impact on the way software is designed and developed. For example, adaptability, customization, and context sensitivity are some of the characteristics that are constantly associated with pervasive computing systems (Raatikainen, Christensen, & Nakajima, 2002). Different software engineering techniques have been used when dealing with them. In this way, we will now review some of these techniques, as well as how they can be applied in pervasive computing systems. More precisely, we will discuss how the component and plugin-based approaches can be used to provide such systems with adaptability and customization. In addition, we show how they can be aware of changes in the context, through the generation and notification of events.

The Component-Based Approach

Component-based software engineering addresses the development of systems as an assembly of components. More precisely, its focus is on the development of components as reusable entities, as well as on the maintenance and upgrade of systems through the customization and replacement of such components. The main advantages of this reuse and assembly-based paradigm is a more effective management of complexity, reduced time to market, increased productivity, and improved quality (Crnkovic, 2001).

In a general way, a component is a software implementation which can be executed in a logic or physical device and can be reused in several applications of the same domain (Bachman, Bass, Buhman, Dorda, Long, Robert, Seacord, & Wallnau, 2000). The well-defined interface of the component describes the services or events that implement its functionalities. Such interface enables encapsulation of the component's functionalities, reducing the coupling among them, and also improving the flexibility of the software design.

Because the components must be connected to assemble the application, it is necessary software to ensure the interaction among components, managing their service and event dependencies. Generally, such entity is implemented as a software framework. To guarantee the components will behave as expected by the framework, some interfaces, called *contracts*, are defined (see Figure 4). These contracts, which components are forced to implement, guarantee that the development of independent components satisfies certain standards, allowing the framework to use such components without being aware of their internal implementation details (Bachman et al., 2000).

Figure 4. Component-based architecture

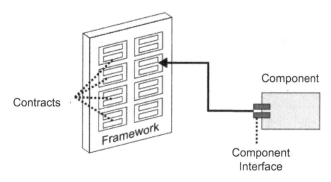

The Component-Based Approach in Pervasive Computing

Within the scope of pervasive computing, the application of the component-based approach is straightforward in the development and maintenance of software. Due to the dynamics and heterogeneity they present (e.g., different services available, several kinds of protocols, devices with different processing power, and storage capabilities), the reuse and flexibility characteristics of components are mandatory in pervasive computing software design. The combination of these features provides an efficient way for enabling an application to seamlessly adapt. This can be performed either by dynamically changing a component by an equivalent, or by assembling a new functionality to the application.

In this context, reuse is important, for example, due to the increasing number of technologies related to pervasive networking, such as Bluetooth, UPnP, Zeroconf (Guttman, 2001), and JXTA (Gong, 2001). Since such technologies are based on standard protocols, they can be implemented as software components in order to be reused in several applications. Reuse is not only interesting for communication technologies. Components can also be implemented for many other purposes, such as audio and video streaming and context information retrieval, and yet provide the same reuse feature.

Examples of pervasive computing systems which make use of the component approach include Aura (Garlan, et al., 2002), Runes (Costa, Coulson, Mascolo, Picco, & Zachariadis, 2005), and PCom (Becker, Handte, Schiele, & Rothermel, 2004).

Plug-in-Based Architectures

Applications based on the plug-in approach are characterized by having a functional core with well-defined hooks where extensions (i.e., plug-ins) can be dynamically

Figure 5. General view of a plug-in-based architecture

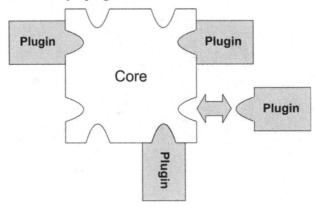

plugged (see Figure 5) (Mayer, Melzer, & Schweiggert, 2002). The functional core contains only the minimum set of functionalities the application needs to run. Plug-ins, on the other hand, are intended to enhance the application by adding features to it. Therefore, plug-in-based applications can be executed even when no extensions have been installed. Besides, features that are not in use can be safely removed, by plugging out the associated plug-in.

A more revolutionary view of plug-in-based architectures is to consider everything as a plug-in. In this new form of plug-in architectures, the application becomes a runtime engine for managing each plug-in's life cycle. As a consequence, end user functionalities are entirely provided by means of plug-ins. For such kinds of application, the extension of plug-ins through other plug-ins is thus a fundamental feature (Birsan, 2005).

Plug-in-Based Architectures in Pervasive Computing

The application of the plug-in approach in pervasive computing systems provides them with the needed characteristic of customization. From minimum, but functional software, users can gradually download specific plug-ins to their daily activities, choosing the ones which best supply their needs. Take as an example an environment filled with services of video streaming, delivered in *avi* format. Consider now a mobile device, with a video player installed, capable of receiving video streaming through the network and displaying it to the user. Such a player, however, can only decode *mpeg* formats, and the environment delivers video in *avi*. Once the user wants to play some movie available in the environment, the player has to transparently find out a way of playing *avi* video formats. Therefore, considering that Internet access is available in the environment, the video player can download an *avi* plug-in from a repository, install it, and play the required video in a transparent way. Note that, although the player did not know the user would ever need to receive a video stream in *avi* format, it was prepared for such situation, permitting it to fulfill the process smoothly.

It is interesting to note how the pure plug-in approach fits well when applied in pervasive computing. The plug-in runtime environment, obviously equipped with other features, like context sensitivity, can be mapped to a pervasive computing infrastructure. Applications would then be viewed as plug-ins, which could be extended by other plug-ins, and so on. Therefore, plug-ins, in this case, applications, could be installed in the user's device on demand, and be removed from it when no longer needed.

Within this scope, the fact that plug-ins can be removed without affecting its host application is also important for pervasive computing. Mobile devices are restricted concerning disk and memory capacity, and thus it would be helpful to remove non-used plug-ins in order to save some space.

Practical examples concerning the usage of the plug-in concepts in pervasive computing can be found in middlewares like Wings (Loureiro, et al., 2006), BASE (Becker, Schiele, Gubbels, & Rothermel, 2003), ReMMoC (Coulson, Grace, Blair, Duce, Cooper, & Sagar, 2005), and Plugin-ORB (dAcierno, Pietro, Coronato, & Gugliara, 2005).

Event-Based Systems

An event-based system is the one in which the communication among some of its components is performed by generating and receiving events. In this process, initially a component fires an event, and after that, such an event will be delivered to all the components interested in it. In an event-based system, a component can assume the role of *producer*, *consumer*, or both. The producer is responsible for generating and firing events. The consumer, on the other hand, is a component which registers itself for the occurrence of a particular event, and is notified when such event occurs.

The process of event notification can be performed in two ways: through the event-based or the callback cooperation models (Fiege, Mühl, & Gärtner, 2002). In the former, a key element is the *event service*. Such an element is responsible for receiving an event from a producer and forwarding it to consumers. To exemplify this process, we have presented an example, which is illustrated in Figure 6. In such a figure, we have six components (A, B, C, D, E, and F), the event service, and two kinds of events (X and Z). Some components act only as producers (components A and C) whereas others only as consumers (components B, D, and F). Finally, component E acts as both a producer and a consumer. The arrows in the figure indicate the flow of event announcements and notifications within the system. In the callback model, on the other hand, the consumer subscribes directly to the provider

Figure 6. Event delivery through the event service

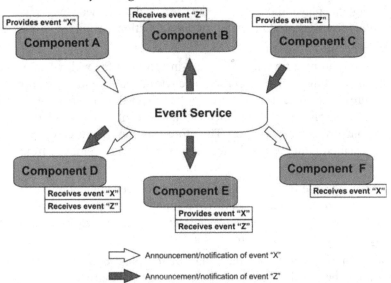

of the event. Therefore, the provider must keep track of the consumers for each event it provides. When some component is interested in various events, it must thus subscribe to each component providing the event. The so-called *Observer* design pattern (Gamma, Helm, Johnson, & Vlissides, 1995) is an abstraction of the callback event cooperation model.

The Event-Based Approach in Pervasive Computing

In the context of pervasive computing, the event-oriented approach can be very helpful in the notification of changes in the context. An example would be a user, located in a shopping mall, who is interested in book discounts. Applications dispersed in the environment could frequently deliver events associated with the discounts available in the mall. Through a handheld, the users could then register their interests on events associated, for example, with books discounts. As soon as one of such events is generated by some application, a centralized event service would be able to deliver the event to the user's handheld, which in turn would notify the user. The event could then provide the user with information such as the store offering the discounts and the associated books.

Another use of events in pervasive computing is for notifying applications about the battery level of a device. In this scenario, through the callback cooperation model, an application could specify a value associated with the remaining battery (e.g., 5%) and register itself to an event which is fired every time the battery level reaches such a value. In this way, an application could be notified when the device is about to be run out of energy, in order to save some critical data before the battery be completely consumed.

The event approach has been successfully used in the development of pervasive software systems. Maybe the best example we can cite is the UPnP specification. Its event mechanism, which uses the General Event Notification Architecture (GENA) (Cohen, Aggarwal, & Goland, 2000), permits the notification of changes in a device, such as the services that have been inserted or removed from it. Other examples include the Scooby (Robinson & Wakeman, 2003) and Solar (Chen & Kotz, 2002) pervasive computing middlewares.

Middleware for Pervasive Computing

The task of building pervasive computing applications can be too tedious if performed from scratch. In other words, the developer will need to deal with low level networking protocols, the way the context is acquired and monitored, notification of changes in the context, and methods for enabling flexibility in their applications. This, of course, deviates the attention of the developers to tasks that are not the purpose of the application. Instead, they should only concentrate on the application logic, that is, the tasks the application must perform. This is where middleware for pervasive computing comes in.

By providing a high level abstraction for application developers, middlewares can considerably speed up development time and also decrease the number of errors in software implementation (Mascolo, Capra, & Emmerich, 2002). Besides abstracting low level details, an ideal middleware should also provide the developer with robustness, efficiency, and security (Aldestein, Gupta, Richard, & Schwiebert, 2005).

These are, however, characteristics that should be presented by any kind of middleware, targeted at pervasive computing or not. From the discussion we have presented until now, it is clear that pervasive computing middleware should not stop at this point. Adaptability, for example, is part of any application in pervasive environments, and consequently, pervasive computing middlewares should present it. Take as an example the RPC (remote procedure call) protocols they use for invoking remote services available in the environment. Considering the diversity of such protocols (e.g., XML-RPC, RMI, SOAP), the middleware could be faced with situations in which it does not implement the RPC protocol used by a certain service. Middlewares for pervasive computing should be capable of transparently overcoming this problem, by downloading the specific RPC protocol implementation, installing it, and finally invoking the service. Moreover, middlewares for pervasive computing should naturally support the development of flexible applications on top of it. In other words, they should provide all the necessary tools for developers to build inherently adaptable applications. Based on our previous discussions, the component and plug-in-based approaches can be very effective, both for the middleware and the applications running over it.

Another characteristic is that pervasive computing middlewares need to provide a way for applications to retrieve information from the context, and also to be notified about changes related to it. In middlewares for traditional distributed systems this was not required, as the context on which they were executed was too static. Therefore, the sporadic changes in the context could be easily managed by the middleware, with no need to be exposed to the applications. As a result of the dynamics involved in pervasive environments, middlewares can not efficiently take decisions on behalf of applications (Mascolo et al., 2002). It is more reasonable, thus, to expose the context to applications and let them take their own actions. At this point, context representation and event notification are very useful for pervasive computing middlewares.

Pervasive Computing Middleware Solutions

Current solutions for pervasive computing middlewares have been focused on different aspects, such as service discovery, service composition, context sensitivity, and networking heterogeneity. These solutions range from general purposes middlewares, like Jini (Waldo, 1999) and Aura (Garlan, et al., 2002), to application domain specific ones, such as healthcare (Bardram & Christensen, 2001) and e-learning (Apostolopoulos & Kefala, 2003). Due to their importance in the development of pervasive computing applications, in this section we outline some of these solutions.

Jini

Jini is a middleware focused on service discovery and advertisement. Jini services are advertised in service catalogs through a Java interface. When the service catalog address is known a priori, Jini clients make requests directly to the service catalog in order to discover services. The service catalog returns a proxy for each discovered service, which is used by clients for remotely invoking it. If the service catalog address is not known, requests are performed in order to find it. As the service provider—and consequently its services—may not be available in the network, Jini implements a lease mechanism to help clients avoid finding unavailable services. Therefore, when providing a service, its provider receives a lease, which must be renewed at a specified time interval. If the lease is not renewed, the service is removed from the service catalog, and thus can no longer be found by Jini clients.

OSGi

The open services gateway interface (OSGi) is a specification supporting the development of Java service-based applications through the deployment of components known as *bundles* (Lee, Nordstedt, & Helal, 2003). A major advantage of the OSGi specification is that such bundles can be installed, uninstalled, and updated without the need to stop and restart the Java applications. In the scope of pervasive computing, this is a fundamental feature, as it enables pervasive computing systems to adapt themselves in a completely transparent way to their users.

The main idea behind OSGi is the sharing and discovery of *services*. In other words, bundles are able to advertise and discover services. When advertising a service, a bundle can define a set of key-value pairs, representing the service's properties. Such properties can thus be useful for other bundles, in order to discover the services they need. These advertisement and discovery processes are both performed through a registry, managed by the OSGi implementation. In this way, it is able to keep track of all services currently advertised and being used, thus enabling a bundle to be updated even when other bundles are executing and using its services.

RCSM

Reconfigurable context-sensitive middleware (RCSM) (Yau, Karim, Yu, Bin, & Gupta, 2002) addresses context-awareness issues through an object-based framework. The context-independent information of an application is implemented in programming languages such as C++ and Java. The context-sensitive information is implemented as an interface, using the context-aware interface definition language (CA-IDL). This interface has a mapping of what actions should be executed according to each activated context. In this way, the application logic is isolated from the context specification.

SOCAM

Service-oriented context-aware middleware (SOCAM) (Gu, Pung, & Zhang, 2004b) supports the development of context-aware services where ontologies are used for representing context information. There are two types of ontologies: *high-level ontologies* describe generic concepts which are domain-independent, such as person, activity, location, and device, and *domain-specific ontologies* define concepts which concern specific domains, such as vehicle and home domains.

Aura

The main focus of Aura is to minimize the distraction of users by providing an environment in which adaptation is guided by the user's context and needs. This project, developed at the Carnegie Mellon University, has been applied in the implementation of various applications, such as a wireless bandwidth advisor, a WaveLan-based people locator, an application which captures the user's intent in order to provide task mobility among different environments. All these applications use components provided specifically by the Aura project, as well as other components, such as the service registry functionalities provided by Jini and Coda (Satyanarayanan, 2002).

Current and Future Trends in Pervasive Computing Research

Undoubtedly, research in the pervasive computing field has considerably advanced. At the networking level, for example, wireless communication is already possible through technologies like Bluetooth, Wi-Fi, and Zigbee. Wi-Fi, although providing a data rate of up to 54 Mbps, has high energy consumption. Bluetooth and Zigbee consume considerably less energy than Wi-Fi, but provide less transmission rates, respectively of 1 Mbps and 250 Kbps at most. The tradeoff of these characteristics must then be analyzed when deploying a pervasive computing environment. Despite these advances, enhancements must still be achieved in this area. Among them, we could point out the power consumption of wireless interfaces. Are current solutions well suited for today's appliances? Can power consumption be improved? Or better, can the relation between power consumption and transfer rate of a wireless interface be improved? Considering this variability of power consumption and transfer rate in wireless interfaces, what would be an ideal configuration for the network and the appliances (i.e., the set of wireless interfaces in the environment and the devices) to minimize power consumption and maximize the transfer of data?

Mobility and ad hoc networking protocols have also been developed, like Mobile IP, GPRS, UPnP, and Zeroconf. The mix of wireless interfaces and these protocols have already leveraged the deployment of some experimental pervasive environments. One point to be considered in this scope is the degree of pervasiveness of such solutions. In other words, how seamless are they concerning configuration, initialization, and finalization? Do we need to start and stop them all the time? One could still think about the performance of these solutions in current mobile devices. Do they consume too much energy? If yes, how can they be improved?

When considering the context-awareness, undoubtedly some efforts have been made in specific application domains. As examples, we could cite tourist information, healthcare, sports, learning, multimedia, and intelligent houses. However, context is far from being used as it is intended. For example, some of the current solutions focus on discovering needed services, but do not well address the assembly of new functionalities based on the requirements of the users and the resources available. In this case, what sort of methods should be applied in order to improve this assembly? Is the context information represented in a reasonable way, so that it simplifies such assembly? Work in this area should involve more precise representation of the context, including the resources and the interests of the user, as well as more intelligent methods for better determining what is relevant to the users, and what is not. Determining what is relevant to the user also requires the application to be capable of capturing the user's preferences, needs, and different states (i.e., social, emotional, physical). User preferences are mostly acquired by providing forms which users fill in. However, how boring can it be for a user to update such forms? Considering that this is a boring task, are they willing to pay this price for some degree of pervasiveness? Concerning the needs of the user, they are commonly obtained explicitly; that is, the users provide to the system what functionality they are interested in. Can this acquisition be enhanced? Is it possible to draw a profile of the user from its reoccurring needs in order to enable pro-activity? What about the information concerning the states of the user? Is it reasonable to require the users to explicitly set them in their personal devices? Can this information be acquired in a different way, through sensors placed in the user's body for example?

Another point to be analyzed concerns the social impact pervasive computing may cause. Consider, for example, the way people will react to sensors that detect their presence and suggest actions for them. Will they be pleased for these suggestions or angry because there is always some boring gadget telling them what to do? One should consider also whether people will accept having sensors in their bodies for obtaining information like their health and emotional state. Will you? What about privacy and security? Many people are still mistrustful of checking their banking accounts through the Internet, what would they say about sharing personal information in an open environment inhabited by all kinds of people? Certainly, all these social factors are as important as technological ones, and thus, must be deeply investigated.

Pervasive Computing for Knowledge and Learning Management

As we have seen throughout this chapter, the evolution that has taken place in hardware and networking technologies, along with the dissemination of mobile devices like cellular phones, make pervasive computing the prevailing paradigm for the next computing systems. Within the scope of this trend, one of the aspects that pervasive computing can greatly contribute is knowledge management, mainly when we consider the increased demand for learning independently of time and place (Lytras, Pouloudi, & Poulymenakou, 2002). The use of information technology (IT) in the context of knowledge management is already commonplace. As already stated by Marwick (2001), many different IT solutions can be used for this purpose, with the goal of enabling knowledge to be acquired, created, and disseminated by transforming it from tacit to explicit forms and vice-versa. One of the great advantages of IT, in this case, is the possibility to transpose the barriers of time and space. Based on this, it is not hard to realize how pervasive computing can aid in further transposing such barriers. With pervasive computing technology, members of an organization are able to establish meetings, anytime and anywhere, with the goal of sharing their knowledge. In this scenario, video and audio over the Internet could be used to give the impression that the members are in a real meeting. Therefore, people from organizations geographically distributed would not need to travel to meet each other. Another use of pervasive computing technology is for the generation of reports with the intent of disseminating someone's knowledge. With the possibility of having Internet connection whenever needed, members of an organization could prepare reports about a specific topic and then distribute them to the others, no matter where they are. Within this process, any needed document, either internal or external to the organization, could also be accessed, enabling knowledge to be acquired, created, and disseminated in a ubiquitous way.

Due to this possibility of extending the limits of knowledge acquisition, creation, and dissemination, it is not surprising to see the first solutions trying to combine pervasive computing and knowledge management. An example is the work of Will, Lech, and Klein (2004), which proposes a tamagotchi-based solution for supporting mobile workers in finding relevant information for the work they perform. Basically, this solution works by enabling a mobile device to interact with information suppliers in a seamless way, through a continuous and proactive matching between the information they provide and the one needed by the mobile workers. Another work in this category is the p-learning Grid, also known as the pervasive learning Grid (Liao, Yang, & Hsu, 2005). As its name indicates, the p-Learning Grid is targeted to support mobile learners in pervasive environments. The overall idea of this work is to represent learning objects (LOs) using Grid services (Foster, Kesselman, Nick, & Tuecke, 2002), distributing them among several connected computers (i.e., Grid infrastructure). In this way, through such an infrastructure, LOs can be dynamically discovered by client devices, using, for example, the current learning needs of users. Other solutions in this field include the work of Amman, Bright, Quirchmayr, and Thomas (2003) and the GetSmart system (Marshall, Zhang, Chen, Lally, Shen, Fox, & Cassel, 2003).

Conclusion

In this chapter, we have discussed some concepts surrounding pervasive computing. We have provided the reader with a high level understanding of the pervasive computing paradigm at different levels, and thus we have ranged from networking to software engineering issues. By using this approach, we presented a broad vision related to pervasive computing to aid researchers, students, and professors in research and teaching activities.

Based on the concepts we have discussed, it is possible to conclude that the application of pervasive computing in the real world is still in its beginning. Many efforts have still to be made in order to bring the primary vision of pervasiveness to real life. One could ask whether such vision will really be conceived. This is, for now, a question which is still unanswered. Answering it will require deep theoretical and, mainly, practical studies. This is what researchers should focus on, and thus, this work has been an introductory theoretical contribution to this end. We believe the concepts presented here will be summed up in other works, and also be useful when developing real world applications, with the intent of reaching a reasonable vision of pervasive computing.

References

Aldestein, F., Gupta, S.K.S., Richard, G.G., & Schwiebert, L. (2005). *Fundamentals of mobile and pervasive computing*. McGraw-Hill.

Amann, P., Bright, D., Quirchmayr, G., & Thomas, B. (2003). Supporting knowledge management in context aware and pervasive environments using event-based co-ordination. *In Proceedings of the 14th International Workshop on Database and Expert Systems Applications*, Prague, Czech Republic.

Apostolopoulos, T.K., & Kefala, A. (2003). A configurable middleware architecture for deploying e-learning services over diverse communication networks. In V. Uskov (Ed.), *Proceedings of the 2003 IASTED International Conference on Computers and Advanced Technology in Education* (pp. 235-240). Rhodes, Greece. Acta Press.

Bachman, F., Bass, L., Buhman, C., Dorda, S.C., Long, F., Robert, J., Seacord, R., & Wallnau, K. (2000). *Technical concepts of component-based software engineering* (vol. 2). Pittsburgh, PA. EUA: Carnegie Mellon Software Engineering Institute. Retrieved October 10, 2006, from http://www.sei.cmu.edu/pub/documents/00.reports/pdf/00tr008.pdf

Bardram, J.E., & Christensen, H.B. (2001). Middleware for pervasive healthcare: A white paper. In G. Banavar (Ed.), *Advanced topic workshop: Middleware for mobile computing*, Heidelberg, Germany.

Becker, C., Handte, M., Schiele, G., & Rothermel, K. (2004). PCOM: A component system for pervasive computing. In *Proceedings of the 2nd IEEE International Conference on Pervasive Computing and Communications* (pp. 67-76). Orlando, FL: IEEE Computer Society.

Becker, C., Schiele, G., Gubbels, H., & Rothermel, K. (2003). BASE-A micro-broker-based middleware for pervasive computing. In *Proceedings of the First IEEE International Conference on Pervasive Computing and Communications* (pp. 443-451). Fort Worth, USA: IEEE Computer Society.

Birsan, D. (2005). On plug-ins and extensible architectures. *ACM Queue, 3*(2), 40-46, 197-207.

Boyera, S., & Lewis, R. (2005, May 2). *Device independence activity*. Retrieved October 10, 2006, from http://www.w3.org/2001/di

Bray, J., & Sturman, C.F. (2000). *Bluetooth: Connect without cables*. Prentice Hall.

Chen, H., Finin, T., & Joshi, A. (2003). An ontology for context-aware pervasive computing environments. *Knowledge Engineering Review, 18*(3), 197-207.

Chen, G., & Kotz, D. (2000). *A survey of context-aware mobile computing research* (Tech. Rep. No. TR2000-381). Hanover: Dartmouth College.

Chen, G., & Kotz, D. (2002). *Solar: A pervasive computing infrastructure for context-aware mobile applications* (Tech. Rep. No. TR2002-421). Hanover: Dartmouth College.

Chlamtac, I., Conti, M., & Liu, J.J.N. (2003). Mobile ad hoc networking: Imperatives and challenges. *Ad hoc Networks, 1*(1), 13-64.

Cohen, J., Aggarwal, S., & Goland, Y.Y. (2000, September 6). *General event notification architecture base: Client to arbiter*. Retrieved October 10, 2006, from http://www.upnp.org/download/draft-cohen-gena-client-01.txt

Costa, P., Coulson, G., Mascolo, C., Picco, G. P., & Zachariadis, S. (2005). The RUNES middleware: A reconfigurable component-based approach to network embedded systems. In *Proceedings of the 16th Annual IEEE International Symposium on Personal Indoor and Mobile Radio Communications* (pp. 11-14). Berlin, Germany.

Coulson, G., Grace, P., Blair, G., Duce, D., Cooper, C., & Sagar, M. (2005). *A middleware approach for pervasive grid environments*. Paper presented at the Workshop on Ubiquitous Computing and E-research, Edinburgh, Scotland.

Crnkovic, I. (2001). Component-based software engineering: New challenges in software development software. *Software Focus, 4*, 127-133.

dAcierno, A., Pietro, G.D., Coronato, A., & Gugliara, G. (2005). Plugin-orb for applications in a pervasive computing environment. In *Proceedings of the 2005 International Conference on Pervasive Systems and Computing*. Las Vegas, Nevada: CSREA Press.

Dey, A.K. (2001). Understanding and using context. *Personal and Ubiquitous Computing, 5*(1), 4-7.

Esler, M., Hightower, J., Anderson, T., & Borriello, G. (1999). Next century challenges: Data-centric networking for invisible computing (The Portolano Project at the University of Washington). In *Proceedings of the 5th International Conference on Mobile Computing and Networking* (pp. 24-35). Seattle, Washington: ACM Press.

Fiege, L., Mühl, G., & Gärtner, F.C. (2002). Modular event-based systems. *The Knowledge Engineering Review, 17*(4), 359-388.

Foster, I., Kesselman, C., Nick, J., & Tuecke, S. (2002). Grid services for distributed system integration. *Computer, 35*(6), 37-46.

Gamma, E., Helm, R., Johnson, R., & Vlissides, J. (1995). *Design patterns: Elements of reusable object-oriented software*. Addison-Wesley Professional.

Garlan, D., Siewiorek, D., Smailagic, A., & Steenkiste, P. (2002). Project Aura: Toward distraction-free pervasive computing. *IEEE Pervasive Computing, 1*(2), 22-31.

Gong, L. (2001). JXTA: A networking programming environment. *IEEE Internet Computing, 5*(3), 88-95.

Gu, T., Pung, H.K., & Zhang, D.Q. (2004a). A Bayesian approach for dealing with uncertain contexts. In G. Kotsis (Ed.), *Proceedings of the 2nd International Conference on Pervasive Computing,* Vienna, Austria. Austrian Computer Society.

Gu, T., Pung, H.K., & Zhang, D.Q. (2004b). Toward an OSGi-based infrastructure for context-aware applications. *IEEE Pervasive Computing, 3*(4), 66-74.

Guttman, E. (2001). Autoconfiguration for IP networking: Enabling local communication. *IEEE Internet Computing, 5*(3), 81-86.

Gwizdka. J. (2000). *What's in the context?* (Position Paper for Workshop on the What, Who, Where, When, Why, and How of Context-Awareness). The Hague: The Netherlands.

Held, A., Buchholz, S., & Schill, A. (2002). Modeling of context information for pervasive computing applications. In *Proceedings of the 6th World Multiconference on Systemics Cybernetics and Informatics*, Orlando, Florida.

Henricksen, K., Indulska, J., & Rakotonirainy, A. (2002). Modeling context information in pervasive computing systems. In F. Mattern & M. Naghshineh (Eds.),

In *Proceedings of the First International Conference on Pervasive Computing* (pp. 167-180). Zurich, Switzerland: Springer-Verlag.

Henricksen, K., Livingstone, S., & Indulska, J. (2004). Towards a hybrid approach to context modeling, reasoning, and interoperation. In *Proceedings of the First International Workshop on Advanced Context Modeling, Reasoning, and Management,* Nottingham, UK (pp. 54-61). ACM Press.

Lee, C., Nordstedt, D., & Helal, S. (2003). Enabling smart spaces with OSGi. *IEEE Pervasive Computing, 2*(3), 89-94.

Liao, C. J., Yang, F. C., Hsu, K. (2005). A service-oriented approach for the pervasive learning grid. *Journal of Info. Science and Engineering, 21*(5), 959-971.

Loureiro, E., Bublitz, F., Barbosa, N., Perkusich, A., Almeida, H., & Ferreira, G. (2006). A flexible middleware for service provision over heterogeneous networks. In *Proceedings of the 4th International Workshop on Mobile Distributed Computing*, Niagara Falls, New York. IEEE Computer Society. (Accepted for publication)

Lytras, M., Pouloudi, A., & Poulymenakou, A. (2002). Knowledge management convergence: Expanding learning frontiers. *Journal of Knowledge Management, 6*(1), 40-51.

Ma, T., Kim, Y.D., Ma, Q., Tang, M., & Zhou, W. (2005). Context-aware implementation based on CBR for smart home. In *Proceedings of IEEE International Conference on Wireless and Mobile Computing, Networking and Communications,* Montreal, Canada (pp. 112-115). IEEE Computer Society.

Marshall, B., Zhang, Y., Chen, H., Lally, A., Shen, R., Fox, E., & Cassel, L. (2003). Convergence of knowledge management and e-learning: The GetSmart experience. In *Proceedings of the Joint Conference on Digital Libraries,* Houston, Texas (pp. 135-146). IEEE Computer Society.

Marwick, A.D. (2001). Knowledge management technology. *IBM Systems Journal, 40*(4), 814-831.

Mascolo, C., Capra, L., & Emmerich, W. (2002). Mobile computing middleware. *Advanced Lectures on Networking* (pp. 20-58). Springer-Verlag.

Masuoka, R., Labrou, Y., Parsia, B., Sirin, E. (2003). Ontology-enabled pervasive computing applications. *IEEE Intelligent Systems, 18*(5), 68-72.

Mayer, J., Melzer, I., & Schweiggert, F. (2002). Lightweight plug-in-based application development. In M. Aksit, M. Mezini, & R. Unland (Eds.), *Revised Papers from the International Conference on Objects, Components, Architectures, Services, and Applications for a Networked World,* Erfurt, Germany (pp. 87-102). Springer-Verlag.

Mostéfaoui, G.K., Rocha, J.P., & Brézillon, P. (2004). Context-aware computing: A guide for the pervasive computing community. In F. Mattern & M. Naghshineh

(Eds.), *Proceedings of the 2004 IEEE/ACS International Conference on Pervasive Services,* Beirut, Lebanon (pp. 39-48). IEEE Computer Society.

Nishigaki, K., Yasumoto, K., Shibata, N., Ito, M., & Higashino, T. (2005). Framework and rule-based language for facilitating context-aware computing using information appliances. In *Proceedings of the First International Workshop on Services and Infrastructure for the Ubiquitous and Mobile Internet* (pp. 345-351). Columbus, Ohio: IEEE Computer Society.

Perkins, C.E. (1997). Mobile IP. *IEEE Communications, 35*(5), 84-99.

Petrelli, D., Not, E., Strapparava, C., Stock, O., & Zancaro, M. (2000). Modeling context is like taking pictures. In *Proceedings of the Workshop on Context Awareness.* The Hague: The Netherlands

Raatikainen, A.K., Christensen, H.B., & Nakajima, T. (2002). Application requirements for middleware for mobile and pervasive systems. *Mobile Computing Communication Review, 6*(4), 16-24.

Ranganathan, A., Muhtadi, J.A., & Campbell, R.H. (2004). Reasoning about uncertain contexts in pervasive computing environments. *IEEE Pervasive Computing, 3*(2), 62-70.

Reid, N.P., & Seide, R. (2002). *Wi-Fi (802.11) network handbook.* McGraw-Hill.

Robinson, J., & Wakeman, I. (2003). The scooby event based pervasive computing infrastructure. In *Proceedings of the Postgraduate Networking Conference,* Liverpool, UK.

Ryan, N. (1999, August 6). *ConteXtML:* Exchanging contextual information between a mobile client and the FieldNote server. Retrieved October 10, 2006, from http://www.cs.kent.ac.uk/projects/mobicomp/fnc/ConteXtML.html

Saha, D., & Mukherjee, A. (2003). Pervasive computing: A paradigm for the 21st century. *Computer, 36*(3), 25-31.

Satyanarayanan, M. (1996). Fundamental challenges in mobile computing. In *Proceedings of the 15th Annual ACM Symposium on Principles of Distributed Computing* (pp. 1-7). Philadelphia: ACM Press.

Satyanarayanan, M. (2001). Pervasive computing: Vision and challenges. *IEEE Personal Communication, 8*(4), 10-17.

Satyanarayanan, M. (2002). The evolution of coda. *ACM Transactions on Computer Systems, 20*(2), 2-25.

Schilit, B., & Theimer, M. (1994). Disseminating active map information to mobile hosts. *IEEE Network, 8*(5), 22-32.

Stanford, V., Garofolo, J., Galibert, O., Michel, M., & Laprun, C. (2003). The NIST smart space and meeting room projects: Signals, acquisition, annotation and metrics. In *Proceedings of the 2003 IEEE Conference on Acoustics, Speech, and Signal Processing,* Hong Kong, China. IEEE Computer Society.

Sun, J.Z., & Savoula, J. (2002). Mobility and mobility management: A conceptual framework. In *Proceedings of the 10ᵗʰ IEEE International Conference on Networks* (pp. 205-210). Singapore: IEEE Computer Society.

Waldo, J. (1999). The Jini architecture for network-centric computing. *Communications of the ACM, 42*(7), 76-82.

Weiser, M. (1991). The computer for the 21ˢᵗ century. *Scientific American, 265*(3), 94-104.

Weiser, M. (1993). Ubiquitous computing. *Computer, 26*(10), 71-72.

Weiser, M., & Brown, J.S. (1995). Designing calm technology. *PowerGrid Journal, 1*(1). Retrieved October 10, 2006, from http://www.ubiq.com/weiser/calmtech/calmtech.htm

Will, O.M., Lech, C.T., & Klein, B. (2004). Pervasive knowledge discovery: Continuous lifelong learning by matching needs, requirements, and resources. In *Proc. of the 4ᵗʰ International Conf. on Knowledge Management*, Graz, Austria.

Yau, S.S., Karim, F., Yu, W., Bin, W., & Gupta, S.K.S. (2002). Reconfigurable context-sensitive middleware for pervasive computing. *IEEE Pervasive Computing, 1*(3), 33-40.

Endnote

[1]   Courtesy of the Xerox Palo Alto Research Center - http://www.ubiq.com/hypertext/weiser/UbiHome.html

Appendix I: Internet Section: Ubiquitous Computing Grand Challenge

The Ubiquitous Computing Grand Challenge is a community of researchers from different parts of the world targeting ubiquitous computing (*http://www-dse.doc.ic.ac.uk/Projects/UbiNet/GC*). Their research is focused at different levels of ubiquitous computing, from social to technological. With this purpose, this community has been proposing a set of, as they call it, *foothill projects,* within the scope of ubiquitous computing. This community still provides a mailing list used by their members to discuss the projects and directions of the community, among other adjacent topics. The registration to the list is open.

Interaction

Select one of the foothill projects presented on the Ubiquitous Computing Grand Challenge Web site and prepare one of the following items:

1.   A research paper with at least 3000 words, without counting images, or
2.   A presentation at least 40 minutes long.

Both the paper and the presentation should present in what way the selected project contributes to the ubiquitous computing research, the state of the art, and practical applications. Remember that it could be helpful to access the mailing list, for example, to generate some interesting discussion concerning the selected foothill project.

Appendix II: Case Study

A Usual Day with Pervasive Computing

At half past six in the morning, Jessica's alarm clock wakes her up, as programmed. As soon as she gets off the bed, the curtains of the bedroom are automatically opened and the alarm clock stops yelling. Within one hour, she dresses for work, takes her breakfast, gets her stuff, and leaves.

When arriving at work, a camera positioned at the entrance of the parking lot recognizes Jessica and her car, and thus, the gates are automatically opened. She greets the gateman and enters. At this point, her car automatically selects the best parking options. She chooses one of them, and leaves the parking lot.

Jessica is about to enter the company when a sensor in the entry of the building detects her presence, and by knowing the elevator she usually takes to go up, warns her that it is on maintenance. Based on the number of people waiting at each elevator, it suggests the best option for Jessica.

Finally, Jessica gets to her office, and at this moment environmental conditions, like lighting or air conditioning levels or curtains opening, are automatically adjusted according to her preferences. Furthermore, a coffee machine, which knows that Jessica usually drinks a cup of coffee in the morning, greets her and asks if she would like some. She has a meeting within a few minutes, but she thinks she has enough time to taste her daily coffee. Then, through a voice command, Jessica orders the machine to prepare it. After finishing the coffee, she then leaves the room for another day of work.

Late in the night, Jessica gets ready to return home. When leaving the parking lot, her car informs her that the usual way she takes home is too congested and it automatically provides an alternative route.

On her way home, she receives a phone call on her cellular phone. As she is currently driving, the phone redirects the caller's talk to an audio output located in the car. Jessica can use an available microphone to talk to the caller by forwarding the audio streaming to the cellular phone. Therefore, the focus on the driving is not compromised.

When she gets home, the mail box identifies her and notifies her about the three letters left in it. She takes the correspondences and enters her home, when again the environment is adjusted according to her preferences. Furthermore, the answering machine detects her presence and automatically informs her of missed calls. Through a voice command, Jessica starts listening to each message left. She then finds a message by her mother, asking her to return the call as soon the she gets home. Jessica stops listening to the missed calls and orders the answering machine to dial her mother's number through her cellular phone. After talking to her, Jessica has dinner and finally gets ready to sleep. She lies down on her bed, and automatically the air conditioning is turned on, the curtains are closed, and the alarm clock is set to wake her up in the morning to have one more usual day with pervasive computing.

Questions

1.   What other pervasive computing features would be helpful for Jessica's daily activities? For each feature provide a detailed description of how it would be fit into the above scenario.

2.   Do you think the current society is ready for this kind of technology? Explain your answer.

3.   Considering the hardware and software technologies we have today, identify/ describe issues of creating the pervasive computing scenario described.

Appendix III: Useful URLs

UPnP Forum Web site

http://www.upnp.org

Wi-Fi Alliance

http://www.wi-fi.org

Bluetooth Special Interest Group

https://www.bluetooth.org

What is General Packet Radio Service?

http://www.gsmworld.com/technology/gprs/intro.shtml

Zigbee Alliance

http://www.zigbee.org

Home Networking with Zigbee

http://www.embedded.com/showArticle.jhtml?articleID=18902431

Mobile IP for IPv4

http://www.ietf.org/html.charters/mip4-charter.html

Zero Configuration Networking (Zeroconf)

http://www.zeroconf.org

OSGi Alliance

http://www.osgi.org

Appendix IV: Further Reading

Banavar, G., & Bernstein, A. (2002). Software infrastructure and design challenges for ubiquitous computing applications. *Communications of the ACM, 45*(12), 92-96.

Gupta, R., Talwa, S., & Agrawal, D.P. (2002). Jini home networking: A step toward pervasive computing. *Computer, 35*(8), 34-40.

Kallio, P., Niemelä, E., Latvakoski, J. (2004). *UbiSoft—pervasive software*. Retrieved October 10, 2006, from http://www.it.lut.fi/kurssit/04-05/010651000/Luen-not/T2238.pdf

Kindberg, T., & Fox, A. (2002). System software for ubiquitous computing. *IEEE Pervasive Computing, 1*(1), 70-81.

Landay, J.A., & Borriello, G. (2003). Design patterns for ubiquitous computing. *Computer, 36*(8) 93-95.

Milanovic, N., & Milutinovic, V. (2003). Ad hoc networks and the wireless Internet. In V. Milutinovic & F. Patricelli (Eds.), *Mastering e-business infrastructure* (pp. 255-335). Kluwer Academic Press. Retrieved October 10, 2006, from http://informatik.hu-berlin.de/~milanovi/chapter6.zip

Plymale, W.O. (2005). Pervasive computing goes to school. *EDUCAUSE Review, 40*(1), 60-61.

Tarkoma, S., Balu, R., Kangasharju, J., Komu, M., Kousa, M., Lindholm, T., Mäkelä, M., Saaresto, M., Slavov, K., & Raatikainen, K. (2004). *State of the art in enablers of future mobile wireless Internet. HIIT Publications*. Retrieved October 10, 2006, from http://www.hiit.fi/publications/pub_files/fc-state-of-the-art-2004.pdf

Weiser, M. (1994). The world is not a desktop. *Interactions, 1*(1), 7-8.

Weiser, M., Gold, R., & Brown, J.S (1999). The origins of ubiquitous computing research at PARC in the late 1980s. *IBM Systems Journal, 38*(4), 693-696.

Appendix V: Possible Paper Titles/Essays

- Pervasive computing: a utopia of human mind or a promising paradigm for everyday life?
- Social impacts of pervasive computing
- Bringing pervasiveness to the real world: practical applications of pervasive computing
- Dealing with privacy of context information in pervasive computing systems
- The impact of pervasive computing on software development

Chapter II

"Neomillennial" Learning Styles Propagated by Wireless Handheld Devices

Edward Dieterle, Harvard Graduate School of Education, USA

Chris Dede, Harvard Graduate School of Education, USA

Karen Schrier, MIT Alumni, USA

Abstract

As the digital-aged learners of today prepare for their post-classroom lives, educational experiences within classrooms and outside of schools should reflect advances both in interactive media and in the learning sciences. Two recent research projects that explore the strengths and limitations of wireless handheld computing devices (WHDs) as primary tools for educational innovations are Harvard University's Handheld Devices for Ubiquitous Learning (HDUL) and Schrier's Reliving the Revolution (RtR). These projects provide rich data for analysis using our conceptual framework, which articulates (a) the global proliferation of WHDs; (b) society's movement toward "ubiquitous computing;" (c) the potential of WHDs to enable sophisticated types of instructional designs; and (d) WHD's fostering of new, media-based learning styles. In this chapter, our primary focus is the last of these four themes.

Chapter Framework

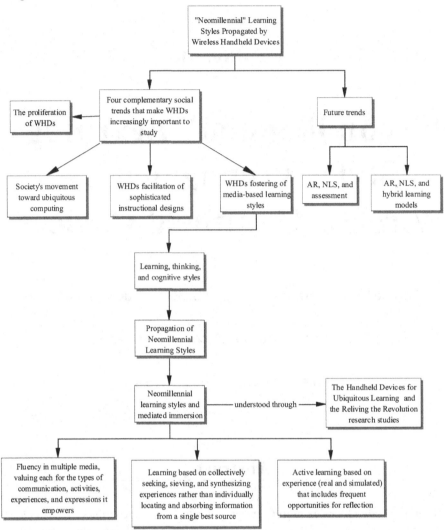

Introduction

In the latter half of the twentieth century, first generation handheld computers left research laboratories and entered the marketplace (Polsson, 2005). Driven by advances in software, hardware, and networking, mobile computing has now moved beyond single purpose functionality (e.g., cellphones, gaming devices, personal digital assistants) to evolve and converge into a new generation of wireless handheld devices (WHDs) that combine the affordances of personal information managers, telephony, wireless Internet connectivity, and global positioning systems (GPS). Familiar to users, computationally powerful, and often wirelessly networked, such devices routinely travel with students and educators into academic settings, making them ripe for utilization as part of formal and informal learning experiences.

Harnessing WHDs as powerful tools with which to think and learn provided the impetus for Harvard University's *Handheld Devices for Ubiquitous Learning* (HDUL) research project. Similarly, Schrier's study at MIT, *Reliving the Revolution* (RtR), designed and assessed a specific historical curriculum, analyzing WHDs as potential tools to facilitate learning. Collectively, these studies offer compelling models for this chapter's analysis of WHDs in an array of learning situations. Whereas HDUL offers a broad review of how WHDs can be used for teaching and learning in a university setting, RtR provides a deep investigation of a participatory simulation implemented using WHDs. To interpret our findings, we use a conceptual framework that incorporates the proliferation of WHDs, ubiquitous computing, instructional design, and media-based learning styles. After unpacking the first three themes of our four-part conceptual framework, we will focus the rest of the chapter on the fourth, media-based learning styles propagated and supported by WHDs. Finally, we consider the implications of our findings for the learning sciences, policy, and educational practice.

Background

Nascent handhelds introduced in the late 1980s and early 1990s (e.g., Apple's *Newton*, Nintendo's *Game Boy*) have evolved considerably, gaining sophisticated computational and connectivity capabilities, morphing into smart phones, PDA-phone hybrids, and next generation handheld gaming devices (e.g., Sony's *Playstation Portable, Nintendo DS*). Beyond technical advancements are four complementary social trends that make WHDs increasingly important to study (Dieterle & Dede, 2006a, 2006b): (a) the proliferation of WHDs, (b) society's movement toward "ubiquitous computing," (c) WHDs facilitation of sophisticated instructional designs based on situated and distributed perspectives on learning, and (d) WHDs fostering of media-based learning styles.

The Proliferation of WHDs

Access and ownership of WHDs are expanding among all demographics and cultures throughout the world, especially among adolescents and young adults (Rheingold,

2002; Roberts, Foehr, & Rideout, 2005). A recent report, *Wireless Industry Indices: 1985-2005*, issued by the Cellular Telecommunications Industry Association (2005), illustrates this trend with cellular telephones, one of the first and most pervasive WHDs. In June 1985, the United States accounted for an estimated 200,000 wireless subscribers. Ten years later, the number of subscribers increased to just over 28 million. In June 2005, wireless subscriptions rose to just under 195 million; described another way, approximately 6 in 10 U.S. citizens hold a cellular telephone subscription. Similar growth trends in cellular telephony are taking place globally and, in some instances, more intensively than in the U.S. In Italy, the United Kingdom, and Taiwan, for example, the ratio of activated cellphones to residents is greater than one-to-one (International Telecommunication Union [ITU], 2005). Globally, the number of mobile phones surpassed 2 billion in mid-2005 (ITU, 2005).

Among U.S. teenagers, as Lenhart, Madden, and Hitlin (2005) have found, almost half report owning a cell phone, with a greater percentage of older teens owning a phone (nearly three in five teens aged 15-17) than younger teens (nearly one in three teens aged 12-14). More than four out of five teenagers report owning at least one personal media device, such as a cell phone, desktop, laptop, or handheld computer (Lenhart et al., 2005), and more than half own at least one handheld gaming device (Roberts et al., 2005).

As a result, students and instructors are increasingly likely to own one or more WHDs—often for reasons other than education—and to bring such devices to class. Through regular interaction and personalization, WHDs become more personally meaningful (Turkle, 2005) than traditional pedagogical tools such as graphing calculators, which are designed for academic exercises, but not much else (Perkins, 1992). Given the pervasiveness of WHDs, educators must understand the strengths and limitations of these devices as evocative objects with which to think and learn.

Society's Movement toward "Ubiquitous Computing"

"Ubiquitous computing" provides contextually specific, dynamic, and temporally aware media and tools that participate seamlessly and almost unnoticed as integral parts of our daily activities. As powerful computational devices such as WHDs pervade our physical surroundings, users can obtain ever-present connectivity and access to capture, process, send, and receive information through multiple devices anytime and anywhere. Recent research on the ubiquitous computing interface has led to the development of ambient technology systems that support elder care networks (Consolvo, Roessler, & Shelton, 2004); objects, such as chemical carboys, that assess and make decisions about their environments (Strohbach, Gellersen, Kortuem, & Kray, 2004); and noninvasive WHDs that coordinate destination and geospatial information to support navigation through public transportation systems (Patterson, Liao, Gajos, Collier, Livic, & Olson, 2004). However, as engineering and computer scientists continue to wrestle with the challenges of constructing ubiquitous computing environments (Satyanarayanan, 2001), the primary implementation barriers for the adoption of new learning devices are neither technical nor economic, but psychological, organizational, political, and cultural (Dede, 2001).

The affordances and psychosocial limitations of a tool, not just its construction, must be examined critically before, during, and after integrating that tool into a learning environment. If used improperly, for example, the mobility of WHDs can also be a barrier to learning. The personal nature and small size of handhelds may hinder collaboration by isolating users from meaningful social interactions (Mandryk, Inkpen, Bilezikjian, Klemmer, & Landay, 2001). On the other hand, Danesh and colleagues (2001) posit that the mobility of these devices can enhance inter-group collaboration: *"Children can walk around, maintaining the flexibility of interacting with many other children, rather than limiting their collaboration to those on the computer beside them"* (p. 88). Moreover, these devices support social interactivity, are sensitive to shifts in context, enable individualized scaffolding, and facilitate cognition distributed among people, tools, and contexts (Klopfer, Squire, & Jenkins, 2003).

WHDs Facilitation of Sophisticated Instructional Designs

Recent advances in the science of how people learn focus on the situated and distributed nature of cognition as applied to thinking, learning, and doing in workplace and community settings (Borgnakke, 2004; Engeström & Middleton, 1996; Wenger, 1998; Wenger, McDermott, & Snyder, 2002). Cognition is viewed as situated within both a physical and a psychosocial context and as distributed between a person and his or her tools (National Research Council, 2000; Sternberg & Preiss, 2005). Knowing, doing, and context are seen as intertwined and interdependent (Dede, Whitehouse, & Brown-L'Bahy, 2002). The learner's environment is essential to the learning process, since the context can alter, improve, and support certain types of performances, approaches to problems, or learning activities.

When used in conjunction with constructivist learning principles (Brooks & Brooks, 1993) and guidelines for differentiating instruction (Tomlinson, 1999), handhelds have the potential to change both what and how we teach and learn. Untethered by cords, cables, and power sources, WHDs provide resources so that students can effectively solve problems in the environment where they would typically occur. As Staudt (2005) explains:

Teachers will guide student learning experiences and, particularly in our standards-based environment, will align learning experiences to meet those standards. What the new technology [of WHDs] allows is for students to meet those standards in individual ways, collect personally meaningful data, and use it to gain understanding of a large inquiry process that begins to replicate the thinking and learning process of real work or advanced study. (p. 2)

Predetermined learning experiences are replaced with students following their own trails of interest, scaffolded by teachers, peers, and tools. Instead of receiving piecemeal information, students are supplied with relevant conditions and authentic problems to help them focus on large ideas while socially constructing deep understandings. As a result, students can navigate their own self-defined learning paths, engage with multiple modalities with varying degrees of complexity, make new contextually relevant connections, reformulate ideas and preconceived notions, and create their own conclusions.

WHDs Fostering of Media-Based Learning Styles

Technological advances are reshaping the learning styles of many students (Dede, 2005), in part because of progress in three complementary human-computer interfaces (Dede, 2002). First, the *world-to-the-desktop* interface currently dominates human-computer interactions. Typically facilitated through laptop and desktop computers connected to the Internet, this interface provides access to distant experts and archives and enables collaborations, mentoring relationships, and virtual communities-of-practice. *Multi-user virtual environments* (MUVEs), the second interface, are commonplace to gamers (i.e., players of Sony's *EverQuest* and id software's *Doom*). Participants use avatars (i.e., digital representations of themselves) to guide action within this interface and to interact with computer-based agents and digital artifacts in a 3-D virtual context. For example, Harvard University's *River City Project* (*http://muve.gse.harvard.edu/rivercityproject*) is exploring the MUVE interface for learning scientific inquiry and 21st century skills (Nelson, Ketelhut, Clarke, Bowman, & Dede, 2005). *Ubiquitous computing*, a third human-computer interface, imbues computation and interconnectivity in countless devices on varying scales of connectivity and interactivity (Greenfield, 2006; Weiser, 1993). Digital information superimposed onto the real world can be supported by ubiquitous computing, generating augmented realities, examples of which are described in greater detail later in the chapter. Augmented reality blends the physical and virtual world so that, as Oblinger (2006) describes, "sometimes we are interacting with the real world and sometimes with the virtual world," leading to hybrid environments created by the juxtaposition of the two worlds. Utilizing the affordances of this human-computer interface amplifies the five senses (e.g., seeing microorganisms, hearing inaudible phenomenon), while distorting time (i.e., looking into the past or future, speeding up or slowing down simulated phenomena) and space, at least partially within the real world rather than a purely virtual context.

"Millennial" learning styles are media-based shifts in the learning process that stem primarily from extensive use of the world-to-the-desktop interface (Howe & Strauss, 2000; Tapscott, 1998). For example, by its nature, the Internet rewards critically comparing multiple sources of information, individually incomplete, and collectively inconsistent. This predicament encourages learning based on seeking, sieving, and synthesizing, rather than on assimilating a single validated source of knowledge as from books, television, or a professor's lectures.

The growing prevalence of MUVE and ubiquitous computing interfaces supported by virtual environments and WHDs is fostering a media-driven shift to what Dede (2005) terms "neomillennial" learning styles (NLS). The crucial factor leading to the incorporation of neomillennial characteristics into millennial learning styles is that the world-to-the-desktop interface is not psychologically immersive, while, in contrast, virtual environments and augmented realities induce a strong sense of "presence." "Immersion" is the subjective impression that one is participating in a comprehensive, realistic all-encompassing experience (Witmer & Singer, 1994). Today, immersion in virtual environments and augmented realities shapes and supports participants' learning styles beyond what using sophisticated computers and telecommunications have generated thus far, with multiple implications for K-12 education.

Other researchers and scholars have contributed to advancing the first three themes of our four-part framework. Few studies, however, have explored the fourth component of NLS, the focus of this chapter. We use findings from the HDUL and RtR research projects to further illuminate media-driven shifts in students' learning preferences and strengths and to explicate how WHDs can support their preferred pathways of learning.

Overview of the Handheld Devices for Ubiquitous Learning (HDUL) Research Study

During the 2003-2004 and 2004-2005 academic years, HDUL integrated WHDs into eight diverse courses at both the Harvard Graduate School of Education (HGSE) and the Harvard Extension School (HES). Participants in HDUL included faculty and graduate students in education, many of whom were seasoned teachers and researchers who did not have prior experience with educational usage of handhelds. Course subjects included distributed learning, math methods, online learning, qualitative methods and interviewing, science methods, teaching with emerging technologies, team learning, and technology and assessment. Class sizes varied from approximately 20 to 50 students.

Seeking to maximize both students' and professors' experiences, the HDUL team—comprised of faculty, students and staff from HGSE—strove to guarantee that participants: (a) had appropriate opportunity to use the handhelds, (b) recognized and comprehended the affordances of the devices (Dieterle, 2005a, 2005b), and (c) through authentic tasks and activities, were motivated to take advantage of the device's capabilities. Based on individual experiences in relation to the assigned task (e.g., using WHDs in the field to collect survey information from participants), students spent a subsequent class in a facilitated discussion about their perceptions of the strengths and limitations of handheld computers for learning, teaching, and researching in that subject area.

HDUL research demonstrated that WHDs can be highly useful as (1) portable research assistants and (2) traveling conduits for online learning (Dede & Dieterle, 2004; Dieterle & Dede, 2006b). As research assistants, WHDs enabled users to: (a) capture what users have learned through various educational software packages designed for formative and summative assessments, (b) retain and project learners' opinions in real-time during face-to-face, whole-class discussions, (c) conduct surveys in the field, and afterwards aggregate data to be analyzed by the whole class, (d) log and analyze real-time data through probeware and calculation software that makes use of a menu-driven interface, and (e) record interviews digitally and capture digital images.

As traveling conduits for online learning, WHDs serve as tools that enhance thinking and as vehicles through which information can pass between individuals and their surroundings. For example, students enrolled in a distributed learning course completed *Environmental Detectives* (Klopfer et al., 2003), an augmented reality game using WHDs. Working in groups, participants role-played as environmental scientists investigating a toxic spill on the MIT campus. As students explored the augmented environment, their WHD alerted them to virtual characters that they can interview and site-specific data to determine whether the spill has contaminated ground and surface water. After collecting field data, students analyze their data to provide an informed decision to the president of the university.

Barriers and insights encountered in scaling up the use of WHDs include:

1. Logistics for use of the WHDs. Straightforward procedures for checking out and returning equipment streamlined distribution and collection of hardware; otherwise, equipment would likely have been lost or underutilized, and scheduling conflicts would have led to frustration and disinterest in the HUDL project.
2. Effective instructional design. To maximize experiences, implementation design requires that participants have appropriate access, understanding, and motivation to take advantage of the device's affordances.
3. Instructors' perceptions of new technologies. The instructors' beliefs affected the students' initial perceptions. A lack of advocacy of new technologies by instructors could lead to an initial lack of interest in students.

4. Lack of connections between "online learning" and learning with Internet-connected WHDs. Participants, even after rich experiences with WHDs, do not automatically make these connections and associate online learning strictly with laptop and desktop computers connected to the Internet. Some participants exhibited characteristics of functional fixedness: the tendency to limit an object to a pre-established belief system, which inhibits the usage and thinking of the same object in novel ways (Dieterle & Dede, 2006b).

5. Teachers' concerns about students' use of the WHD technology. Teacher-participants shared concerns regarding: (a) new technologies, especially those their students have already mastered, (b) students engaging in off-task behaviors, and (c) students using computational devices without an understanding of the underlying domain knowledge.

Overview of the "Reliving the Revolution" (RtR) Research Study

During the 2004-2005 academic year, Schrier (2005) developed and tested "Reliving the Revolution" (RtR) as a model for using WHDs in augmented reality games to teach historic inquiry, effective collaboration, media fluency, decision-making, and critical thinking skills. RtR enables participants to traverse the present-day site of the Battle of Lexington, equipped with WHDs, to "relive" this historic battle from the American Revolution through the eyes of one of four historic figures present at the battle. Participants use their WHDs to collect information or "evidence" to determine who fired the first shot in the battle, a source of continued debate in American history. GPS-enabled WHDs provide participants location-based "virtual" information on the social, historical, economic, geographic, and political processes relevant to both the Battle of Lexington and the American Revolution.

Evidence comes from two sources. First, participants can encounter virtual historic figures (e.g., Paul Revere), called non-playing characters (NPCs), in preprogrammed locations. NPCs provide evidence that explains their perception of what happened at the battle. Second, virtual game items and descriptions of buildings help participants evaluate their evidence and gain a deeper understanding of their location and the context for the battle. Each user receives evidence tailored to his or her alter ego's background and social status. For example, a "virtual" spy for the British Regulars would provide very different information to a Minuteman soldier than he would to a British soldier.

After participants collect various forms of evidence from fragmentary, inconsistent, and possibly biased sources, RtR scaffolds the reasoning and procedural skills required of a historian so that participants working in pairs can interpret data to construct an overall historical narrative and can provide an evidence-based opinion about which side fired the shot that initiated the battle. After immersing themselves in the simulated events leading up to and following the gunshot, the roles come together and, using the evidence collected and stored in their WHDs throughout the game, collectively debate what they think happened at the Battle of Lexington.

Although designed for junior high, high school, and college-aged students, field tests suggest that RtR appeals to an even wider range of ages. Schrier did not design RtR as a standalone, teacher-proof educational experience; rather, she created it as an innovation that a teacher could integrate into a broader history curriculum while acting as a guide, mentor, and resource for the simulation. Having this type of scaffolding is particularly important during the third part of RtR (i.e., the debate period). A teacher, for example, can pose additional questions and ensure that alternative views are considered.

Schrier's analysis of RtR's effectiveness suggests that properly designed WHD-enabled augmented reality-based participatory simulations can enhance the learning of: (1) historical figures, sites, and issues, (2) historical methodology and the limits to understanding the past, and (3) alternative views of the past, the construction of new versions of history, and critiques of authoritative interpretations. Participants practiced critical thinking skills such as managing and navigating information, deeply evaluating evidence, finding creative solutions, framing and subdividing problems, and devising thoughtful arguments. Most importantly, the participants were excited, engaged, and enthusiastic.

Participants applied the concepts they learned to other disciplines and critiqued their own preconceived notions and beliefs. Schrier's results suggest that this learning occurs in RtR in part because of the following affordances for WHDs in supporting neomillennial learning styles:

1.   **Collaboration:** WHDs' portability and size increased collaboration among participants, which concomitantly enhanced opportunities for reflection. Participants greatly enjoyed working as a team and learning from each other.

2.   **Authenticity:** WHDs granted access to an authentic "practice field" (Klopfer et al., 2003) for solving problems and implementing real-world contexts and tools.

3.   **Role-playing:** WHDs enabled participants to play as and experiment with unique roles, and then to share those identities with others.

4.   **Mobility:** WHDs encouraging participants to explore a physical site and experience interactions between the real and virtual worlds.

5.   **Self-directed learning:** WHDs' functionality allowed participants to control their navigation of the game, and discover new information at a pace with which they were comfortable.

Propagation of Neomillennial Learning Styles

Learning, Thinking, and Cognitive Styles

Sternberg and Zhang (2001) differentiate learning styles, thinking styles, and cognitive styles thusly: *learning styles* characterize "how one prefers to learn about," *thinking styles* characterize "how one prefers to think about material as one is learning it or after one already knows it," and *cognitive styles* characterize "ways of cognizing [i.e., knowing, perceiving, and recognizing] the information." (p. vii) Collectively, they are qualitatively different from one another and distinct from *abilities*: the natural or acquired skills and talents that result in being able to do something. "Abilities," as Renzulli and Dai (2001) explain, "are not the only thing important for successful learning, and surely not the only contributing factor for the development of cognitive and learning styles" (p. 31). For example, a student may have the ability to navigate the Internet and read a newspaper to find information, but might prefer learning about her favorite professional athletes by watching sports television shows, receiving Rich Site Summary (RSS) feeds on her blog, or getting Short Message Service (SMS) text updates on her cell phone.

Building on Sternberg's (1997) approach to styles, Biggs (2001) notes that, "Preferences are a matter of degree, not of category, so that individuals may have a profile of styles, with one or more dominant" (p. 79). Although abilities may overlap with preferred pathways for establishing new connections and assimilating new information, they do not necessarily have to align. Performance on a given task is amplified when a person's dominant style coincides with his or her abilities, but typically erodes when the two do not overlap (Biggs, 2001). For educators, designers, researchers, and policymakers, it is clear that aligning styles and opportunities for learning is paramount.

Of the learning, thinking, and cognitive styles aforementioned, learning styles are the most activity-oriented and of the greatest utility to educators. Keefe (1979) defines learning styles as "cognitive, affective, and physiological behaviors that serve as relatively stable indicators of how learners perceive, interact with, and respond to the learning environment." Three learning styles widely accepted as standards include: sensory-based (e.g., visual, auditory, kinesthetic); personality-based, measured using instruments such as the Myers-Briggs inventory; and aptitude-based, which draws on categorizations such as Gardner's multiple intelligences (Gardner, 1983). As discussed earlier, Dede (op cit) proposes a fourth style: media-based learning.

The Millennials and Millennial Learning Styles

During their formative years, Millennials—the cohort born after 1982—have had unprecedented access to a broad range of media in the United States (Roberts et al., 2005) and abroad. Especially profound are their gains in access to interactive media (e.g., video game consoles, computers) and information and communication technologies (e.g., instant messenger). Pervasive availability of interactive media has helped contribute to nearly 9 in 10 U.S. teens regularly accessing the Internet and more than half going online daily (Lenhart et al., 2005). More interesting than access is what millennials do once they go online. Of those who access the Internet, four in five play online games, three in four gather news, and just under one in three seek out health information (Lenhart et al., 2005). Besides consuming information, nearly three in five U.S. teenagers contribute to the content of the Internet by creating blogs and Web pages, posting original artwork, stories, and photos, and remixing existent content in novel ways (Lenhart & Madden, 2005).

Raines (2003) has argued that the learning preferences of the millennial cohort are geared toward entertainment, excitement, experiential activities, structure, team-work and the use of technology. Their communication preferences, as Raines (ibid) continues, are characteristically electronic, goal-focused, motivational, positive, respectable, and respectful. Today's students are accustomed to negotiating among various media sources and working in "a digital environment for communication, information gathering, and analysis" (Oblinger, 2004, p. 2). Whereas Raines connects these characteristics to those born after 1982, we and other scholars (e.g., Dede and colleagues, 2007) assert that these qualities are observable to varying degrees in learners of all ages who make extensive use of modern interactive media.

Neomillennial Learning Styles and Mediated Immersion

What learning styles might these media-based lifestyle shifts induce? Research on educational MUVEs and augmented reality learning experiences suggests that the following may emerge as cross-age learning styles:

1. Fluency in multiple media, valuing each for the types of communication, activities, experiences, and expressions it empowers.

2. Learning based on collectively, seeking, sieving, and synthesizing experiences rather than individually locating and absorbing information from a single best source.

3. Active learning based on both real and simulated experiences that includes frequent opportunities for reflection.

In the sections that follow, we consider each of these themes as they relate to work conducted in HDUL and RtR, delving deeply into the first of these three neomillennial learning styles and providing summary examples of the other two. Discussion of other neomillennial learnings styles—such as (a) expression through nonlinear, associational webs of representations and (b) co-design of learning experiences personalized to individual needs and preferences—will be addressed in future works. Mediated immersion likely has other influences on learning styles yet to be discovered, but these initial findings have a variety of implications for strategic planning, investment, and professional development at all levels of education.

1.   Fluency in multiple media, valuing each for the types of communication, activities, experiences, and expressions it empowers.

Fluency in multiple media goes beyond millennial learning styles, which center on working within a single medium best suited to one's style and preferences. In contrast, the majority of U.S. teenagers tend to use multiple media at any given time. Roberts et al.'s (2005) research finds that more than half of 7th–12th graders report accessing at least one additional medium either "most of the time" or "some of the time" when watching TV (53%), reading (58%), listening to music (63%), and using a computer (65%). In contrast to multitasking, "the proportion of kids who say they 'never' use other media in response to these questions ranges from a low of 12% when listening to music to a high of 19% when watching TV" (p. 36). This is also reinforced by a recent report issued by the Pew Internet and American Life Project investigating when and how kids use IM, e-mail, cellphones, and telephones (Lenhart et al., 2005).

In Dede's "Learning Media that Bridge Distance and Time," HGSE students explore various immersive technologies (e.g., groupware, threaded discussion sites, videoconferencing, virtual environments, WHDs) as vehicles for socially constructing knowledge. As Dede, Whitehouse, and Brown-L'Bahy (2002) report, students' learning styles tend toward distributed interaction across multiple media and feel their learning experiences are lessened by only engaging in activities and media found in traditional classroom settings.

From our HDUL research, 20 future math teachers in a graduate course on teaching mathematics compared and contrasted WHDs to TI graphing calculators as tools for computation, modeling, and visualization. A week prior to a whole class discussion, participants checked out WHDs (i.e., Toshiba e750 Pocket PCs) and were instructed to focus on the general functionality of the devices and the computation, spreadsheet, and visualization capabilities of Microsoft's *Pocket Excel* and MRI Graphing Calculator software, a calculation application that makes use of a menu-driven interface. In general, participants shared concerns about the learning curve that must be overcome with the WHDs they investigated. While they felt that teachers would need detailed professional development to understand and properly utilize the instructional functionality of the devices, they felt that students would easily navigate them. As one future math teacher stated:

I think sometimes when you look at students, they gravitate toward this [type of device]. They grew up on Game Boys. They walk around with cell phones taking pictures of each other, so maybe they have greater patience. Maybe they're willing to fumble through this even more so than we as teachers.

This description is characteristic of a shift in the classroom and highlights the malleability and adaptability associated with NLS, in which tech-savvy students have surpassed their more technologically limited teachers. Although some in the test group expressed initial frustration with the devices, others suggested it was no more challenging to master than a graphing calculator interface when both are new and unfamiliar.

Indeed, graphing calculators support the understanding of expressions and equations (National Research Council, 2001) and, as tools for thinking with data, graphing calculators facilitate the visualization and analysis of data (National Research Council, 2000). Correspondingly, about 7 in 10 U.S. high school students use calculators almost everyday (U.S. Department of Education, 2000). Despite reports by some of using graphing calculators outside of math and science classrooms (e.g., Parker & Mills, 2004), such instances force graphing calculators beyond their core competencies of computation and visualization, resulting in very limited utility. WHDs, on the other hand, include the functionality of graphing calculators and go beyond being task-oriented and school-specific. For example, using WHDs with *Pocket Excel* helps bridge the gap between what kids are using at school and what they might potentially use in the outside world. As one math methods participant stated, "They're not going to use a graphing calculator to do finance." By using a WHD and Excel "You've done two things: you've taught them new math, and you've also given them that skill that they're going to need when they get to college or the world place" (focus group discussion, December 2, 2003). These uses, and others described later in the chapter demonstrate how teachers and students will likely find everyday use and functionality for their WHDs beyond formal educational pursuits inside of school settings.

With RtR, Schrier sought to design an educational experience that would spark novel connections and perspectives through the interplay of multiple media sources. Such a seamless integration of text and images with the physical world could potentially support and enhance students' neomillennial multimodal learning styles. Thus, while playing RtR, participants used WHDs to retrieve location-based graphical and textual information on the Battle of Lexington, the historic site of Lexington,

Figure 1. Two examples of the types of information supplied to participants via WHDs

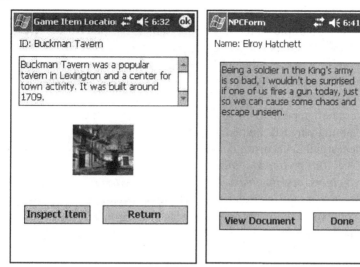

and the historic figures involved in the battle, as well as evidence about who might have fired the first shot and initiated the battle. Figure 1 shows screen captures of the types of information participants received.

For example, participants encountered "virtual" historic figures who offered visual documents, such as diary entries, letters, maps, and newspaper articles. Participants inspected these images to consider their validity and, when necessary, compared them to other images and texts they received. Participants also used their WHDs to access photographs and descriptions of physical monuments or buildings that were involved in the battle and are still present in current-day Lexington. This activity encouraged participants to inspect thoroughly the physical structures and sites at Lexington, to support their hypotheses about who fired the first shot. Results of trials of RtR suggested that the opportunity for multimodal learning and thinking helped the participants better absorb, interpret, and recall the information, as well as enjoy learning it.

As an illustration, participants would consider the type of media (diary entry, testi-monial, photograph) when assessing bias and validity of data. They would also pull apart the visual and textual elements of the evidence, such as the tone or language of a testimonial, to consider whether a source was trustworthy or reliable. Moreover, participants would look at how the virtual data and physical world complemented or contradicted each other. For example, when participants read Captain John Parker's words first on their WHDs and then on a monument on the actual Lexington Com-mon, they felt the corroborating evidence bolstered Parker's character and made his testimony more believable The confluence of both virtual and corresponding physical information further motivated participants to delve more deeply into the historic site, to think more creatively about the virtual evidence, and to compare their reflections with others.

The interaction with multiple modes of information also helped participants better navigate, categorize, remember, and integrate content. Stopping to read virtual information at a physical site and then interpreting the information to understand its relationship to other virtual or physical information helped participants recall specific details more easily. In fact, when comparing, sharing, and corroborating evidence, participants would often point to the physical location where they retrieved virtual evidence. Explaining why RtR helped him learn about the Revolutionary War better than how he learned in his history classroom, a student remarked, *"I re-learned U.S. History One...this recapped it and I relearned it and now I know more about history. ... the pictures, and the items [helped make it clearer]."* This participant's experience demonstrates the interrelation of activity, concept, and culture via physical and social contexts for knowing and understanding (Brown, Collins, & Duguid, 1989), which traditional classrooms tend to overlook.

By situating RtR as an authentic experience, the participant is able to comprehend the nature and significance of concepts that before were abstract and unconnected. These findings suggest that continued experience with games and simulations like RtR could produce similar effects. In RtR the inclusion of multiple media added more depth and complexity to the participants' conception of the historic period, their reconstruction of the historic moment, as well as to their own interpretations of what happened at Lexington. Multimodal learning helped the participants better synthesize and articulate arguments, make novel connections, and analyze sources.

2.   Learning based on collectively seeking, sieving, and synthesizing experiences rather than individually locating and absorbing information from a single best source.

Collective learning goes beyond millennial learning styles in preferring communal learning in diverse, tacit, situated experiences to the solo integration of divergent, explicit information sources, as well as in valuing knowledge distributed across a community and a context as well as within an individual.

Examples of this neomillennial learning style from HDUL research included:

1.   Graduate students in a distributed learning course investigated MIT's (2005) *Virus*, in which participants simulate the spread of infectious disease with WHDs to determine the causes, distribution, and control of disease in populations. Participants completed multiple rounds of play, repeating the same

5-10 minute simulation with the same parameters, using facilitated reflection between games. Instead of a linear transmission of information, participants heuristically and socially constructed meaning.

2. Participants in an online learning course brought their WHDs into the field, and each participant conducted surveys of approximately 10 participants and collected results using Microsoft's *Pocket Excel*. Afterward, participants uploaded their data from the WHD, the datasets were aggregated, and participants analyzed the resulting collective database as an entire class. Surveys generally take place in the field, over the phone, online, or through the mail (Fowler, 2002), wherein researchers typically wait until they return to their desktop or laptop computers to begin analysis. Although analysis with WHDs is not as detailed or thorough as is possible with laptops or desktop computers, the strength of using WHDs for rapid and rudimentary evaluation of data in the field enables formative shifts in research approaches. An additional strength of WHDs is the power to quickly expand dataset samples. In this class implementation, 12 student participants independently surveyed approximately 10 random participants with their WHDs. On aggregation of the data, the collective sample size expanded to 120 participants.

Through the processes outlined in both examples, HDUL participants learned that real world phenomena are complex, multiple perspectives exist, and "truth" is often a matter of how meaning is constructed.

Similarly, RtR encourages participants to seek, incorporate, sift through, and synthesize information from multiple sources, as well as to rely on each other to collectively interpret, edit, and categorize information. While gathering evidence the participants worked in pairs and played one of four historic roles. Each role received different—complementary or contradictory—information from virtual people, digital items, and the physical environment, compelling participants to depend on each other to get a more detailed and holistic view of the full situation. The distinctiveness of each role provided an impetus for the participants to collect and analyze deeply their evidence, knowing they would have to share and contribute their findings and insights with the group during the debate period. The relatively compact space of the game and the mobility and size of the WHD, allowed for verbal exchanges of evidence among the various roles. Participants could ask each other for advice, share discoveries, and make connections based on serendipitous exchanges. The WHDs also further enabled the physical sharing of information, because participants could literally "beam" evidence from one WHD to another, and they could hand over WHDs to other roles to show them relevant evidence. The WHD was small enough to be passed around in groups, shown to other individuals for comparison or corroboration of evidence, and carried to specific locations for further inspection of an area.

During the debate period, the participants shared and compared their unique evidence and collaboratively drew conclusions. Thus, the game encouraged participants to not only access and gather information, but also to discuss, analyze, and question material, as well as to rely on the collective intelligence of the group. Said one participant in the game trial, comparing this learning experience to what she normally does in her middle school history class: *"A history class is like data, but this was like data and then you had to interpret or analyze it on top of it."*

Thus, game play elements (such as the inclusion of roles, the collective debate, the role-specific evidence and mini-objectives), coupled with the use of WHDs, supported and encouraged the participants' negotiation of multiple sources of information and creation of a distributed learning community, which further led to the consideration of alternative perspectives on the Battle of Lexington. Said a participant in the game trials: *"I learned about all the different sides. Normally you would just think of the American soldiers and the British soldiers, slaves, the wives, the people at the bar, the Minutemen, there are people frustrated here for personal reasons, patriotic reasons, you get a sense of the different roles of that time period."* While playing the game, the participants began to have a more complex, nuanced understanding of the various points of view of the historic moment of the Battle of Lexington. They did not just interpret the tensions involved in the battle as a simple dichotomy, but as a more multidimensional social issue with "many different factors" involved, as another participant noted. The participants became more aware of subtle variations in views and the spectrum of agendas for the people involved in the Battle of Lexington, while also challenging assumptions and preconceived notions about the past, in part because they were authentically "doing history" within a community of practice. Results of RtR suggest that creating WHD activities where students can distribute intelligence and problem solving, while considering multiple views, sources, and opinions, can support and enhance neomillennial learning styles and may lead to deeper understanding and engagement.

3. Active learning based on experience (real and simulated) that includes frequent opportunities for reflection.

   This type of active learning goes beyond millennial learning styles in valuing immersive frames of reference that begin with experiential participation, and then infuse guidance. Drawing parallels between interpersonal interactions facilitated by media and how people interact, Reeves and Nass (1996) have demonstrated that engagement with various forms of media are *"fundamentally social and natural, just like interactions in real life"* (p. 5).

Examples of this neomillennial learning style from HDUL research include:

1. Participants in a team learning course and a technology and assessment course used WHDs and WiFi connectivity to complete online Likert Scale surveys and answer open-ended questions in "thought grabbing" exercises. Immediately after participants submitted their responses, the data were aggregated and displayed on a computer projector in real time to facilitate immediate class discussion of the findings.

2. Participants explored the use of WHDs in science using Data Harvest's (2005) probeware to collect and analyze data in real-time. Participants explored and discussed various examples of probeware (e.g., temperature probe), the benefits of probeware for teaching and learning science (Staudt, 2001; Thornton, 1999), and a software interface for processing information.

Through iterative thought grabbing and data analysis experiences, participants continuously reflect on and reevaluate their understanding of complex concepts and ideas with fellow students toward deeper understandings.

Results of RtR suggested that the game encouraged active, participatory, and reflective learning through appropriate pedagogy surrounding the affordances of WHDs. Throughout the game, participants were continually invited to act like historians, rather than passively receiving historic information or accepting an institutionally-vetted narrative of the past. Participants needed to actively collect evidence, analyze evidence, and formulate hypotheses. The combination of game play, content, and WHD mobility, interactivity, and ease of use helped compel participants to discover new information, explore a historic site, and create their own novel narratives of the past. The participants' newly formed sense of entitlement to construct their own interpretations and conclusions is echoed in one participant's statement that "Reliving the Revolution" differs from other games. She said, *"You had to research and then figure something out for yourself. It wasn't like a set like 'you have to click on this conclusion now.' You have to come up with whatever."*

The participants in the Redesign trial especially enjoyed being able to physically walk around and learn, rather than sitting passively in a classroom. This is reflected in the following conversation between two participants in the study:

Participant 1: *Yeah, if we sat in a classroom and did this and I would walk away and be like "Yeah, okay."*

Participant 2: *But when you are actually moving around to do it....I think it's definitely more interesting to do it this way than to sit in the classroom.*

9

Results also suggested that RtR motivated reflective learning through the sharing of findings and ideas with other participants. Playing a role as a pair helped the participants more deeply consider the information they gathered; they needed to collaboratively digest, discuss, and draw conclusions about each piece of information. They could gain immediate feedback for their mini-hypotheses and conjectures from their peers. Collaborating as a role also helped participants practice critical skills such as decision-making and teamwork: the participants needed to work together to decide which virtual historic figure to find next, how to analyze the evidence they received, or whether they should trust some data and not other information. For instance, one participant said she *"liked playing with others because you could get corrected and get new ideas,"* while another commented *"if you talk things out, you can remember them better than just writing them down."*

The collaborative debate period of RtR also encouraged active, reflective learning. Participants were constantly brainstorming collectively, asking other roles about the documents and testimonials they gathered, questioning authorial intentions and pointing out biases, and evaluating each other's conclusions. For example, during the debate, one participant would offer a hypothesis and a few pieces of evidence, such as a diary entry or a testimonial, and then another participant would counter with a contradictory piece of evidence or offer supporting evidence. Finally, the participants would incorporate each other's versions of the past to create a collective interpretation of who fired the first shot at Lexington, while simultaneously reflecting on their process in creating this narrative.

In the following exchange from the debate period of a game trial of RtR, participants explained how they reached their conclusions about who fired the first shot:

Participant 1 (British soldier): *There wasn't one piece of evidence, but it was the mentioning of one name over and over again. Like you can never really trust one firsthand account, because of course they are going to be biased by their side. But if you get like four or five people mentioning Edward Mitchell [a British soldier], it kind of leads you to believe that he did something.*

Participant 2 (Slave/Minuteman): *Like whenever we found a British person, they were too busy to talk to people, they were only busy looking for something and doing something.*

Participant 1 (British soldier): *Well that could have just been you, since you are a slave and a minuteman soldier, they wouldn't have talked to you anyway. (looking through her handheld) Because a lot of British soldiers talked to us because we are British. Like this guy said, "Those Lexington Minutemen asked for it. The Minutemen were out for revenge. They should surrender."*

Copyright © 2007, Idea Group Inc. Copying or distributing in print or electronic forms without written permission of Idea Group Inc. is prohibited.

Participant 3 (Loyalist): *Yeah, we found a hat that had been marched on. So that probably means that...the British were in pursuit, that they probably came here looking for a fight, and they were willing to pursue it.*

Participant 4 (Loyalist): *That they were prepared to pursue it.*

Thus, the participants did not just collect and offer evidence, but they reflected on the challenges in constructing their argument and explained the rationales for their decisions. The participants explored deeply each other's arguments by exposing possible biases or offering contradictory or supportive evidence. Throughout the debate, all of the participants were actively engaged, by explaining their ideas, listening to others' opinions, or searching through their WHDs to find compelling evidence to share with the group.

In RtR, the WHDs, together with appropriate levels of guidance, constraints, and scaffolding, motivated the participants to direct their own learning, take responsibility for completing the game's tasks, and reflect on their participation as historians and game players. This seemed to enhance and complement the participants' neomillennial learning style of active, participatory, self-guided learning.

Future Trends

Innovations that use WHDs to leverage NLS, such as HDUL and RtR, will shape and change what and how students learn. As we explore the implications of NLS for learning, we must also consider future effects NLS will have on policy and educational practice. Although an array of future trends could be considered, in this chapter we forecast NLS in relation to issues of assessment and hybrid learning models, as these important topics are generalizable from HDUL and RtR to similar projects.

AR, NLS, and Assessment

Salomon and Perkins (2005) describe three levels by which technology affects thinking and learning. The most straightforward and immediate results of a technology's influence on thinking, learning, and doing are the *effects with* a technology, which result in expanded cognitive capacity and amplified perception while a technology is coupled with an activity. After considerable experience with a technology, users exhibit the *effects from* a technology, the residual impact of a technology when it is no longer present. The most profound effects are the *effects through* a technology, which fundamentally reorganize cognitive activity. Brown and Thomas (2006) describe this type of effect as, "learning to be... as opposed to learning about." (p.120) Schrier's RtR and HDUL's investigation of *Environmental Detectives* illustrate WHD-enabled innovations that develop NLS in support of participants of various ages as they acquire *through* technology the reasoning and procedural skills of historians and environmental scientists, respectively.

How can we measure sophisticated effects such as these? As Sheingold and Frederiksen (1994) have noted, *"to change our expectations about what students should know and be able to do will involve also changing both the standards by which student achievements are judged and the methods by which student's accomplishments are assessed."* Accurately assessing effects with, from, and through technology requires measurement methodologies and objectives that match our evolving expectations for students' educational outcomes, as well as new ways in which they learn. Russell (2006) identifies, *"A major challenge to assessing the impact of technology on student learning is identifying learning measures that are aligned with and sensitive to the types of learning that may occur when students work with computers"* (p. 185). Many current assessments, however, measure what students have learned from technology (i.e., *effects from* a technology), not what students are capable of doing with access to technology (Perkins, 1993) or through technology.

Educational MUVES such as *River City* (Ketelhut, Dede, Clarke, Nelson, & Bowman, in press) and intelligent tutoring systems (ITSs) (Anderson, Corbett, Koedinger, & Pelletier, 1995) have the ability to record and store every user action and utterance. WHDs that support AR do not yet have the capacity to keep as detailed records of student activities, but hybrid simulations that shift between virtual and real-world experiences, such as RtR and *Environmental Detectives*, can create rich histories of students' learning processes. Parallel to MUVEs and ITSs, WHDs can use a data-tracking system that generates log files stored in a relational database (Ketelhut et al., in press). Designers can collect, store, and retrieve information on the activities of each team of students as they participate in the simulation, a feature impossible to replicate in purely face-to-face learning. The level of detail in these records is extensive: the logs indicate exactly where students went, with whom they communicated, what virtual artifacts they activated, and how long each of these activities took. This richly varied store of data can couple with other types of student learning products to develop novel, performance-based assessments of complex performances such as NLS or learning disciplinary reasoning and procedural skills. Such performance-based instruments "gauge a person's understanding at a given time" and *"ask the person to do something that puts the understanding to work,"* with the intention that *"what learners do in response [to the assessment activity] not only shows their level of current understanding but very likely advances it"* (Perkins, 1998, p. 41).

AR, NLS, and Hybrid Learning Models

As information and communication technologies advance, various forms of "hybrid" learning models are now emerging. For example, "distributed learning" is a term used to describe educational experiences that combine the use of face-to-face teaching with synchronous and asynchronous mediated interaction (Dede et al., 2002). This "hybrid" or "blended" instructional strategy distributes learning across a variety of geographic settings, across time, and across various interactive media. Millennial learning styles flow in part from the different ways in which each type of medium shapes its messages and its users. As an illustration, some students silent in face-to-face instructional settings "find their voice" in one or another type of mediated discussion.

AR enables another type of "hybrid" learning: immersive simulations that combine the real world and the virtual world. We speculate that, parallel to distributed learning, students in such virtual/real hybrid models experience forms of learning and engagement different than either purely real or purely virtual simulations. Designing successful hybrid learning conditions requires a balance between the experiences encountered in the real world and the information overlaid on the real world. Learning that positively transfers from one situation to a novel situation is reliant on a learner's ability to *discriminate* important and trivial features of the new situation (Sternberg & Frensch, 1993), whether in the real world or the virtual world. Simulations and models necessarily must selectively reduce the complexity of the real world in order to provide learning experiences that are not confusing, but still capture the core of knowledge and skills involved. Preserving too much complexity can reduce a learner's ability to differentiate what is significant and what is insignificant. Instead of filtering out information, augmented realities weave information into surroundings that enhances the senses, time, and space. Critical to AR design is determining how much information to include, which sense to engage, and how long the experience should last. Maximizing learning opportunities in hybrid environments, therefore, requires scaffolds that help filter the real world while enhancing it through AR, as learners *learn to be* instead of *learn about*.

As Norman (1993) cautions about all new technologies, before hybrid learning models are introduced and studied in practice *"it isn't always obvious just which parts are critical to the social, distributed nature of the task, [and] which are irrelevant or detrimental."* As this form of learning model becomes available, much work will be needed to determine how to best blend real world and virtual experiences. Research is needed to deeply understand the affordances and psychosocial limitations of hybrid learning models based on AR technologies.

Conclusion

Overall, as the findings in this chapter illustrate, WHDs support emerging media-driven learning styles, which Dede has dubbed "neomillennial" because they go beyond the popular conception of millennial learning styles. Contributing to NLS are (a) WHDs proliferating among all demographics, (b) "ubiquitous computing" gradually infusing WHDs into many aspects of everyday life, and (c) WHDs' potential to enable sophisticated types of instructional designs based on situated and distributed theories of learning. Examples from Harvard's HDUL and Schrier's RtR advance evidence for NLS in three distinct ways.

First, fluency in multiple media, often used concurrently, is characteristic of NLS. Each medium, moreover, is valued for the types of communication, activities, experiences, and expressions it empowers, evading functional fixedness and over-reliance on one preferred medium. From our HDUL research, future math teachers explored the expanded functionality of WHDs as tools for computation, modeling, and visualization, compared to the limited academic purposes of graphing calculators. In RtR, WHDs' integration of text and images with the physical world engaged multimodal learning and encouraged analyzing and comparing different types of media, supporting NLS.

Second, NLS captures learning based on collectively seeking, sieving, and synthesizing experiences rather than individually locating and absorbing information from a single best source. Although HDUL participants individually gathered survey data with their WHDs, the total data sample was expanded when these individual datasets were aggregated, allowing participants to unpack and analyze the observed phenomena as a whole class and draw conclusions collectively. Disparate evidence from virtual people, digital items, and the physical environment caused RtR participants to sift through and synthesize information from multiple sources. No single role provided a complete or fully accurate account of what happened at Lexington. Afterward, participants relied on one another to collectively interpret, edit, and categorize information in determining who might have fired the first shot and initiated the battle. Providing opportunities for collective learning and multiple sources of data helps to enhance NLS.

Third, NLS value active learning based on experience (real and simulated) that includes frequent opportunities for reflection. HDUL participants used WHDs to complete exercises that summarized and displayed perceptions and beliefs. Similarly, HDUL participants used WHDs and probeware to collect and analyze scientific data in real-time. By making this information visible, participants were provided opportunities to reflect on and reevaluate their understanding of complex concepts and ideas with fellow students. Through the facilitation of the instructor, participants reexamined their meaning making by reflecting on prior knowledge, observations, and explanations put forth by peers, moving toward deeper and more complete understandings. Results from RtR show participants were motivated to reflect on their learning through the sharing of findings and ideas with other participants. Participant pairs considered evidence and drew conclusions; collaborating as a role supported critical skills such as decision-making and teamwork. By planning for NLS, educators, researchers, and designers have the opportunity to harness WHDs inside and outside of formal and informal learning environments creatively.

As evidenced by this chapter, handheld devices enabled by wireless connectivity have the ability to engage neomillennial learning styles in people of all ages. Although HDUL and RtR provide rich contexts for exploring NLS, additional work is needed to more fully understand immersive learning that blends the real and virtual worlds.

References

Anderson, J.R., Corbett, A.T., Koedinger, K.R., & Pelletier, R. (1995). Cognitive tutors: Lessons learned. *Journal of the Learning Sciences, 4*(2), 167-207.

Biggs, J. (2001). Enhancing learning: A matter of style or approach? In R.J. Sternberg & L-F. Zhang (Eds.), *Perspectives on thinking, learning, and cognitive styles* (pp. 73-102). Mahwah, NJ: Lawrence Erlbaum Associates.

Borgnakke, K. (2004). Ethnographic studies and analysis of a recurrent theme: Learning by doing. *European Educational Research Journal, 3*(3), 539-565.

Brooks, J.G., & Brooks, M.G. (1993). *In search of understanding: The case for constructivist classrooms*. Alexandria, VA: Association for Supervision and Curriculum Development.

Brown, J.S., Collins, A., & Duguid, P. (1989). Situated cognition and the culture of learning. *Educational Researcher, 18*(1), 32-42.

Brown, J.S., & Thomas, D. (2006). You play World of Warcraft? You're hired! *Wired, 14*(4), 120.

Cellular Telecommunications Industry Association. (2005). *Wireless industry indices: 1985-2005*. Washington, DC: Cellular Telecommunications Industry Association.

Consolvo, S., Roessler, P., & Shelton, B.E. (2004). The CareNet display: Lessons learned from an in home evaluation of an ambient display. In N. Davies, E.D. Mynatt, & I. Siio (Eds.), *UbiComp 2004: Ubiquitous Computing. Sixth International Conference Proceedings* (pp. 1-17). New York: Springer.

Danesh, A., Inkpen, K., Lau, F., Shu, K., & Booth, K. (2001). *Geney™: Designing a collaborative activity for the Palm™ handheld computer.* Paper presented at the Conference on Human Factors in Computing Systems, Seattle, Washington.

Data Harvest. (2005). *Data harvest homepage.* Retrieved October 10, 2006, from http://www.dataharvest.com/index.htm

Dede, C. (2001). Creating research centers to enhance the effective use of learning technologies. *Testimony to the Research Subcommittee, Science Committee, U.S. House of Representatives,* Washington, DC.

Dede, C. (2002). Vignettes about the future of learning technologies. In 2020 visions: Transforming education and training through advanced technologies. (pp. 18-25). Washington, DC: U.S. Department of Commerce.

Dede, C. (2005). Planning for "neomillennial" learning styles: Implications for investments in technology and faculty. In J. Oblinger & D. Oblinger (Eds.), *Educating the net generation* (pp. 226-247). Boulder, CO: EDUCAUSE Publishers.

Dede, C., & Dieterle, E. (2004). *Ubiquitous handhelds: Sifting knowledge through our fingertips.* Paper presented at the Harvard Graduate School of Education Technology in Education Open Seminar, Cambridge, Massachusetts.

Dede, C., Dieterle, E., Clarke, J., Ketelhut, D., & Nelson, B. (in press). Media-based learning styles: Implications for distance education. In M.G. Moore (Ed.), *Handbook of distance education* (2nd ed., pp. 339-352). Mahwah, NJ: Lawrence Erlbaum Associates.

Dede, C., Whitehouse, P., & Brown-L'Bahy, T. (2002). Designing and studying learning experiences that use multiple interactive media to bridge distance and time. In C. Vrasidas & G.V. Glass (Eds.), *Distance education and distributed learning* (pp. 1-30). Greenwich, CT: Information Age Publishing.

Dieterle, E. (2005a). *Handheld devices for ubiquitous learning: An overview.* Retrieved October 10, 2006, from http://gseacademic.harvard.edu/~hdul/whd-overview.htm

Dieterle, E. (2005b). *Handheld devices for ubiquitous learning: Getting to know your wireless handheld device.* Retrieved October 10, 2006, from http://gseacademic.harvard.edu/~hdul/getting-started.htm

Dieterle, E., & Dede, C. (2006a). *Straightforward and deep effects of wireless handheld devices for teaching and learning in university settings.* Paper presented at the 2006 American Educational Research Association Conference, San Francisco.

Dieterle, E., & Dede, C. (2006b). Building university faculty and student capacity to use wireless handheld devices for learning. In M. van 't Hooft & K. Swan (Eds.), *Ubiquitous computing in education: Invisible technology, visible impact* (pp. 303-328). Mahwah, NJ: Lawrence Erlbaum Associates.

Engeström, Y., & Middleton, D. (Eds.). (1996). *Cognition and communication at work*. Cambridge University Press.

Fowler, F.J. (2002). *Survey research methods* (3rd ed.). Thousand Oaks, CA: Sage Publications.

Gardner, H. (1983). *Frames of mind: The theory of multiple intelligences*. New York: Basic Books.

Howe, N., & Strauss, W. (2000). *Millennials rising: The next great generation*. New York: Vintage Books.

International Telecommunication Union. (2005). *The Internet of things*. Geneva, Switzerland: International Telecommunication Union.

Keefe, J.W. (1979). Learning style: An overview. In *NASSP's student learning styles: Diagnosing and prescribing programs* (pp. 1-17). Reston, VA: National Association of Secondary School Principals.

Ketelhut, D., Dede, C., Clarke, J., Nelson, B., & Bowman, C. (in press). Studying situated learning in a multi-user virtual environment. In E. Baker, J. Dickieson, W. Wulfeck, & H. O'Neil (Eds.), *Assessment of problem solving using simulations*. Mahwah, NJ: Lawrence Erlbaum Associates.

Klopfer, E., Squire, K., & Jenkins, H. (2003). *Augmented reality simulations on handheld computers*. Paper presented at the 2003 American Educational Research Association Conference, Chicago.

Lenhart, A., & Madden, M. (2005). *Teens content creators and consumers*. Washington, DC: Pew Internet & American Life Project.

Lenhart, A., Madden, M., & Hitlin, P. (2005). *Teens and technology: Youth are leading the transition to a fully wired and mobile nation*. Washington, DC: Pew Internet & American Life Project.

Mandryk, R.L., Inkpen, K.M., Bilezikjian, M., Klemmer, S.R., & Landay, J.A. (2001). *Supporting children's collaboration across handheld computers*. Paper presented at the Conference on Human Factors in Computing Systems, Seattle, Washington.

National Research Council. (2000). *How people learn: Brain, mind, experience, and school* (expanded ed.). Washington, DC: National Academy Press.

National Research Council. (2001). *Adding it up: Helping children learn mathematics*. Washington, DC: National Academy Press.

Nelson, B., Ketelhut, D., Clarke, J., Bowman, C., & Dede, C. (2005). Design-based research strategies for developing a scientific inquiry curriculum in a multi-user virtual environment. *Educational Technology, 45*(1), 21-27.

Norman, D.A. (1993). *Things that make us smart: Defending human attributes in the age of the machine*. Reading, MA: Addison-Wesley.

Oblinger, D.G. (2004). The next generation of educational engagement. *Journal of Interactive Media in Education, 8*, 1-18.

Oblinger, D.G. (2006). *Listening to what we are seeing.* Paper presented at the 2006 Technology, Colleges, and Community Worldwide Online Conference, Honolulu, Hawaii.

Parker, M., & Mills, B. (2004). Graphing calculators: Handheld technology in non-traditional classes. *Media & Methods, 41*(2), 15.

Patterson, D.J., Liao, L., Gajos, K., Collier, M., Livic, N., Olson, K., et al. (2004). Opportunity knocks: A system to provide cognitive assistance with transportation services. In N. Davies, E.D. Mynatt, & I. Siio (Eds.), *UbiComp 2004: Ubiquitous Computing..Sixth International Conference Proceedings* (pp. 433-450). New York: Springer.

Perkins, D. (1992). *Smart schools: Better thinking and learning for every child.* New York: Free Press.

Perkins, D. (1993). Person-plus: A distributed view of thinking and learning. In G. Salomon (Ed.), *Distributed cognitions: Psychological and educational considerations* (pp. 88-110). Cambridge University Press.

Perkins, D. (1998). What is understanding? In M.S. Wiske (Ed.), *Teaching for understanding: Linking research with practice* (pp. 39-57). San Francisco: Jossey-Bass Publishers.

Polsson, K. (2005). *Chronology of handheld computers.* Retrieved October 10, 2006, from http://www.islandnet.com/~kpolsson/handheld/

Reeves, B., & Nass, C.I. (1996). *The media equation: How people treat computers, television, and new media like real people and places.* Stanford, CA: CSLI Publications.

Renzulli, J.S., & Dai, D.Y. (2001). Abilities, interests, and styles as aptitudes for learning: A person-situation interaction perspective. In R.J. Sternberg & L-F. Zhang (Eds.), *Perspectives on thinking, learning, and cognitive styles* (pp. 23-46). Mahwah, NJ: Laurence Erlbaum Associates.

Rheingold, H. (2002). *Smart mobs: The next social revolution.* Cambridge, MA: Perseus Publishing.

Roberts, D.F., Foehr, U.G., & Rideout, V. (2005). *Generation M: Media in the lives of 8-18 year-olds.* Washington, DC: Henry J. Kaiser Family Foundation.

Russell, M. (2006). *Technology and assessment: The tale of two interpretations.* Greenwich, CT: Information Age.

Salomon, G., & Perkins, D. (2005). Do technologies make us smarter? Intellectual amplification with, of and through technology. In R.J. Sternberg & D. Preiss (Eds.), *Intelligence and technology: The impact of tools on the nature and development of human abilities* (pp. 71-86). Mahwah, NJ: Lawrence Erlbaum.

Satyanarayanan, M. (2001). Pervasive computing: Vision and challenges. *IEEE Personal Communications, 8*(4), 10-17.

Schrier, K.L. (2005). *Revolutionizing history education: Using augmented reality games to teach histories.* Unpublished master's thesis, Massachusetts Institute of Technology, Cambridge.

Sheingold, K., & Frederiksen, J. (1994). Using technology to support innovative assessment. In B. Means (Ed.), *Technology and education reform: The reality behind the promise* (pp. 111-132). San Francisco: Jossey-Bass.

Staudt, C. (2001). Curriculum design principles for using probeware in a project-based learning setting: Learning science in context. In R. Tinker & J. Krajcik (Eds.), *Portable technologies: Science learning in context. Innovations in science education and technology* (pp. 87-102). New York: Kluwer Academic.

Staudt, C. (2005). *Changing how we teach and learn with handheld computers.* Thousand Oaks, CA: Corwin Press.

Sternberg, R.J. (1997). *Thinking styles.* Cambridge University Press.

Sternberg, R.J., & Frensch, P.A. (1993). Mechanisms of transfer. In D.K. Detterman & R.J. Sternberg (Eds.), *Transfer on trial: Intelligence, cognition, and instruction* (pp. 25-38). Norwood, NJ: Ablex Publication Corporation.

Sternberg, R.J., & Preiss, D. (Eds.). (2005). *Intelligence and technology: The impact of tools on the nature and development of human abilities.* Mahwah, NJ: Lawrence Erlbaum Associates.

Sternberg, R.J., & Zhang, L.-F. (Eds.). (2001). *Perspectives on thinking, learning, and cognitive styles.* Mahwah, NJ: Laurence Erlbaum Associates.

Strohbach, M., Gellersen, H.-W., Kortuem, G., & Kray, C. (2004). Cooperative artefacts: Assessing real world situations with embedded technology. In N. Davies, E.D. Mynatt & I. Siio (Eds.), *UbiComp 2004: Ubiquitous Computing. Sixth International Conference Proceedings* (pp. 250-267). New York: Springer.

Tapscott, D. (1998). *Growing up digital: The rise of the net generation.* New York: McGraw-Hill.

Thornton, R.K. (1999). *Using the results of research in science education to improve science learning.* Paper presented at the 1999 International Conference on Science Education, Nicosia, Cyprus.

Tomlinson, C.A. (1999). *The differentiated classroom: Responding to the needs of all learners.* Alexandria, VA: Association for Supervision and Curriculum Development.

Turkle, S. (2005). *The second self: Computers and the human spirit* (20th anniversary ed.). Cambridge, MA: MIT Press.

U.S. Department of Education. (2000). *For mathematics, how often do you use a calculator for classwork?* Retrieved October 10, 2006, from http://nces.ed.gov/nationsreportcard/NAEPdata/getdata.asp?subj=MAT&grade=12&sample=R2&scale=MC&jud=NT&yrlist=20002&id=M812001&dispMissing=1

Weiser, M. (1993). Some computer science issues in ubiquitous computing. *Communications of the ACM, 36*(7), 75-84.

Wenger, E. (1998). *Communities of practice: Learning, meaning, and identity.* Cambridge University Press.

Wenger, E., McDermott, R.A., & Snyder, W. (2002). *Cultivating communities of practice: A guide to managing knowledge.* Boston: Harvard Business School Press.

Witmer, B.G., & Singer, M.J. (1994). *Measuring immersion in virtual environments.* Alexandria, VA: U.S. Army Research Institute for the Behavioral and Social Sciences.

Appendix I: Case Study: Ms. Clarke's 7ᵗʰ Grade Class Visits an Augmented Zoo

To provide insight and make concrete the design and research heuristics we discuss in this chapter, we provide the following vignette to help educators, designers, and researchers plan for NLS.

Ms. Clarke passed out WHDs to her middle school science class as they traveled to the nearby city zoo to study variation in form and function of legs, eyes, ears, and teeth of different animals. Some kids preferred to use their own personal devices, which were repurposed for the day's activities; others were content to use the school's devices. While the majority of the students had previously worked with handhelds, many had not, but found the interface similar enough to navigate easily through standard applications (e.g., a Web browser, a word processor, a spreadsheet).

On arrival, students disbanded into random groups to explore various exhibits. As Brian, Diane, and Jody, a trio of seventh graders, set off to find the panda exhibit, they activated their devices and quickly found the zoo's interactive Web site. Pulling up a map of the zoo, Brian noticed a series of small, slowly moving dots, which he assumed to be his classmates, and one that began pulsing, which he assumed represented him. Built into each of the devices was a GPS receiver that showed the location of all the students. Since Brian was only interested in his teammates' locations, he designated them with a different color. Ms. Clarke, prior to arrival, had enabled the devices to show only the members of the class while ignoring everyone else in the zoo with similar devices. This feature also allowed her to keep track of everyone in the class, whom they were with, which exhibits they went to visit, and for how long.

As Brian leaned over to show Diane the flashing dot on his handheld screen, Diane was ready to show Brian and Jody that she had figured out how to use the device to locate all of the animal exhibits at the zoo, including the pandas. Hearing this news, the three set off and quickly found themselves in front of the panda exhibit. After reading the standard placards, Jody mentioned that she had visited the zoo's panda exhibit online prior to their trip. As Ms. Clarke requested, each kid then used their device to capture at least one digital picture of various animals and record a brief audio summary of their initial thoughts and reflections of the animal's mobility, reach and grasp, vision, hearing, and eating habits. After collecting panda information together, the trio split up and each explored different animals throughout the zoo. Periodically, they used VoIP and SMS to communicate and share findings they found particularly interesting.

At the crocodile exhibit, Diane used her WHD to simulate the audio and visual senses of a saltwater crocodile—the largest living crocodilian species—above and below water. Diane was struck by the animal's keen sight and hearing, especially at night and underwater. The feature she liked best, however, allowed her to construct her own crocodilian species. As she manipulated the dimensions of her super croc, she realized how and why nature selectively determines proportions and functions. The first eight crocodiles she constructed immediately died because they were either too heavy, couldn't swim, or weren't able to eat nourishing foods. Based on her deepened understanding of why a saltwater crocodile looks, acts, and moves the way it does, she saved the new species' parameters and added them to the class database. Diane looked forward to the class discussions of the database, as it would give her a chance to reexamine her and other's discoveries.

As the visit ended, each of the participants transferred their images, audio files, and other data to a remote server via FTP for later use. As the participants traveled away from the zoo, Ms. Clarke asked what students would like to do with their collected information, having several plans in mind, but encouraging students to debate their own ideas. After some discussion, Jody suggested a collective digital diary that could be shared online with friends, family, and next year's group. This, when put to a vote, won by a landslide.

In this case study, we provide a vignette in which a group of middle school students visit a local zoo augmented with virtual data and experiences.

Questions

1. Based upon your understanding of neomillennial learning styles, what are the strengths and limits of the type of learning in this vignette?

2. In what ways could the learning environment better address neomillennial learning styles?

3. How would this case be similar and different if WHDs were removed from the story?

4. What other ways could the WHDs have been used to support critical inquiry, and to apply the students' learning to other disciplines?

Chapter III

Mobile Education:
Lessons Learned

Holger Nösekabel, University of Passau, Germany

Abstract

Mobile education, comprising learning, teaching, and education related adminis-trative services delivered via mobile technologies, has incited several projects and discussion in the last years. When reviewing these projects, it becomes apparent that most of them are technology driven, and only a few were formally evaluated at the end. However, certain lessons, chances and obstacles can be identified which may be helpful for further development in this sector. One critical issue is the dis-tribution of costs for mobile services. As both educational institutions and students act on a limited budget, it is necessary to choose an infrastructure which meets the requirements of the users and addresses all relevant obstacles. Consequently, there is no single ideal technological alternative, but each project needs to make a situational choice.

Introduction

Technological progress continually creates new opportunities for creating, storing, and disseminating knowledge. One aspect is the utilization of new technologies for learning and teaching: e-learning. Recent endorsements in this sector were *mobile devices*, which can increase mobility, flexibility, and personalization compared to traditional, PC-based approaches. The term "e-learning" was thus extended to "*m-learning,*" or "*mobile education.*"

Mobile education covers three distinct but interconnected areas in which mobile devices may be implemented: learning, teaching, and administration. A major focus in the past was placed on learning activities, mobile learning or m-learning, as the term itself was derived from e-learning. Teaching and administrative tasks were either omitted or understood as learning tasks. Consequently, m-learning can either be understood as a subclass of e-learning or as a distinct area of research (Nösekabel, 2005).

After establishing a framework by clarifying what will be termed as mobile education in this chapter, a survey of m-education projects establishes the state of the art. Selected projects are grouped into high school and university projects, as the didactic requirements for these educational institutions are different. Universities, for example, allow their students a higher degree of self-determination and self-direction in learning.

The results of this comparison are compiled into a *SWOT analysis*, which is used to point out experiences, obstacles, and chances for existing and future mobile education projects. Both the analysis and the strategic recommendation focus on mobile infrastructures, end user devices, and educational processes.

Figure 1. Chapter overview

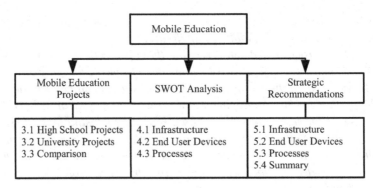

Mobile Education

Defining *m-education* is the focus of the following discussion, which helps identify relevant projects which are then analysed. First, a restriction should be placed on the devices used for educational purposes. Devices need to be mobile, as stated by Lyytinen and Yoo (2002), which means they must have a high degree of mobility but only a low degree of embeddedness. This would include mobile phones, personal digital assistants, and other devices (e.g., MP3 players), but excludes laptops, as laptops are only portable and cannot be used easily while in motion. Another factor is that laptops do not have the same technical restrictions as mobile devices; thus, services and experiences from e-learning are mostly applicable and do not require a new view on these issues. The restriction also excludes pervasive and ubiquitous devices (Dourish, 2001), which are both highly embedded and could be subject to research in "pervasive" or "ubiquitous education."

Second, m-education addresses—as already mentioned—learning, teaching, and administration, affecting not only students, but lecturers and possibly administrative staff alike. One result for the selection of projects is that so called *"classroom applications"* (Myers, 2001) using mobile devices are also included in the survey. These *"classroom applications"* run on mobile devices, often in combination with a non-mobile PC or laptop. They foster interaction between students and teachers, for example, by offering the ability to conduct polls or to remotely annotate presentation slides as a group.

Third, a network connection is not permanently required when using mobile education. This allows the inclusion of applications where data are transmitted to a mobile device via a stationary PC, for example, during synchronisation. Further included are Java applets (J2ME MIDlets) on mobile devices, which possibly make use of a network connection only during installation over the air or during data transmissions.

These various aspects are covered by several definitions, even though most authors define "Mobile Learning," not "Mobile Education." Nyiri, for example, reasons that the primary purpose for mobile devices is interpersonal communication, and, therefore m-learning is learning *"[...] as it arises in the course of person-to-person mobile communication"* (2002, p. 123). Communication aspects are also mentioned by Hummel and Hlavacs (2003). Constructivistic learning theories emphasise that communication is a decisive element in the learning process, supporting this kind of definition. However, there are mobile devices which are designed for *personal information management (personal digital assistants – PDAs)* and coordination. Clarke and Flaherty (2002) therefore include the aspect of collaboration, defining m-learning as *"[...] an approach to teaching and learning that utilizes wireless technologies to communicate and collaborate in an educational context"* (p. 68).

Sharma and Kitchens (2004) additionally include the notion of context, stating that learning content should be specifically prepared for a learner in a given situation.

Lehner, Nösekabel, and Lehmann follow a more technical approach and define mobile education as *"[...] any service or facility that supplies a learner with general electronic information and educational content that aids in the acquisition of knowledge, regardless of location and time"* (2004, p. 24).

Introducing mobile technologies into learning-related processes primarily results in an increased flexibility for both learners and instructors. Depending on the underlying learning theories, support for a learning process can be assumed. Mobile behaviouristic learning, for example, allows the learning loop of information presentation, question, answer, analysis, and feedback to be initiated at any time and in any place. Constructivistic approaches, on the other hand, benefit from increased spatial flexibility, which allows teachers to employ real-life locations and scenarios in the learning process.

The effect of technology on learning with regard to flexibility is shown in Figure 2. In a space-time matrix, where the amount of flexibility is differentiated, physical participation in a course or class always requires a person to be at a specific place at a specific time. With synchronous learning, for example by transmitting the course via video, students no longer are required to be at a certain place. Thus, spatial flexibility is gained. However, non-mobile computing still has requirements regarding network connectivity, power supply, and physical transportation of hardware equipment. As a result, synchronous e-learning is not as flexible as synchronous m-learning.

Learning can also take place outside predetermined times, for example when students visit the library. In this case, the place is fixed (the physical location of the library), but the time is more flexible compared to a course participation. Restrictions, such

Figure 2. Comparison of non-electronic, electronic, and mobile learning

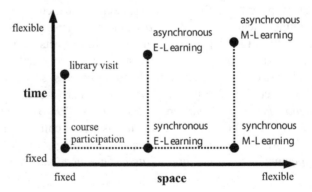

as opening times, may still exist, prohibiting greater flexibility. Electronic resources, such as e-books, recorded lectures, or other learning materials, can be accessed with a PC without these restrictions. Again, however, a non-mobile PC must be present, which is not always the case. Mobile technologies, on the other hand, provide greater time and space flexibility, as these devices can be carried around and are readily available.

To demonstrate the use of mobile technologies in educational processes, a set of exemplary *educational tasks* will serve as a background for discussion, and key elements will be extended in the SWOT analysis. Table 1 lists positive and negative aspects when supporting certain tasks with mobile technologies. In order to overcome limitations or problems, enabling factors may provide solutions.

One typical learning task is using various learning materials: presentation slides, audio or video recordings, images, or text. With mobile technologies, these materials can be accessed without spatial or temporal restrictions, but currently mobile devices often lack the ability to display more complex materials satisfactorily. A

Table 1. Effect of mobile technologies for educational tasks

Educational task	Positive aspects	Negative aspects	Enabling factors
Access to learning material	Ubiquitous access to content anywhere, anytime; utilization of short free time periods	Device limitations (display size, computing power); bandwidth or memory requirements	Mobile hardware advancements; fast and inexpensive network access; dedicated mobile content
Planning of educational activities	Integrated *Personal Information Management* (PIM); group coordination and collaboration	Support for common data exchange format required; network connectivity	Conformity to standards; inexpensive network access
Giving lessons	New teaching methods possible (classroom applications); increased cooperation	Device limitations (display size, input methods); change to teaching process	Mobile hardware advancements; didactic integration of mobile services
Communication	Direct and immediate communication; ability to communicate when necessary	Many messages to few experts; information overload; additional communication channel	Communication etiquette; unified messaging to combine different communication channels
Activities regarding curriculum	Real-time access to information; individuality through personal device	Security risks when device is stolen or damaged; device limitation (display size, input methods)	Improved security technologies; mobile hardware advancements
Management of resources	*M-Payment* could allow monetary transactions; flexible initiation of transaction	Integration of backend management system required; security risks	Interoperability through open interfaces, data exchange, or middleware; *M-Payment*

short term solution to this problem would be to create learning materials suited for mobile device. In the long run, hardware advancements could lift these limitations. A second learning task is planning educational activities, where mobile device offer *personal information management* (PIM) services to manage contacts and appointments. Exchanging this kind of information, however, is sometimes hindered by proprietary implementations or interpretations of standardized data formats.

Giving lessons is a teaching task which can be supported with mobile technologies, for example by implementing *classroom applications* as described before. Since this requires changes to the teaching process, it could be met with resistance. Consequently, a didactic integration into existing processes is necessary. Another teaching task regards the communication between students and teachers. With mobile technologies, communication is direct and immediate (via SMS, MMS, mobile e-mail, instant messaging, etc.) and popular recipients, for example experts and teachers, may face a high number of incoming messages. Unified messaging and the adherence to communication etiquette can help to channel or reduce the information load.

Administrative tasks include, among others, activities concerning student curricula and resource management. With mobile technologies, a real-time, individualized access to information and a flexible initiation of transactions is possible. Both require a technical integration of backend systems and high standards regarding privacy and data security. Improvements in mobile security technologies and data exchange/middleware are thus enabling factors in this area.

Curtis, Williams, Norris, O'Leary, and Soloway (2003) list several positive effects which were observed in projects after introducing handheld computers in classrooms. Students had equitable access to IT, motivation increased, collaboration among students was easier, and learning environments could be individualized and organized.

In summary, mobile technologies can provide additional flexibility and increased motivation, although it should be noted that these effects are not compulsory and the results depend on the integration of mobile devices into existing activities. The technologies also offer an opportunity to enhance or alter educational processes. In the following section, projects in the area of mobile education will be presented to give an overview of similarities, differences, and trends.

Mobile Education Projects

For the survey, a total of 30 *mobile education projects* were analyzed regarding infrastructure, devices, and educational processes (Nösekabel, 2005; Lehner, Nösekabel, & Bremen, 2004; Lehner, Nösekabel, & Lehmann, 2004). Ten of these projects were

Table 2. Project information URLs

Project	URL for information
Ballard High School	http://ballard.seattleschool.org/
Consolidated Highschool District 230	http://www.d230.org/Handheld/default.htm
Hartland Farms Intermediate	http://www.oetc.org/handhelds.html
King Middle School	http://www.pcmag.com/article2/0,4149,15154,00.asp
Gymnasium Landau a. d. Isar	http://www.gymnasium-landau.de/wissen/journada/jo-ziele.htm
MobiSkoolz	http://www.mobiwave.com/
Palm Education Pioneers	http://www.palmgrants.sri.com/
RAFT Project	http://www.raft-project.net/
Anglia Polytechnical University	http://www.ultralab.ac.uk/
Berlin Univ. der Künste	http://www.campus-mobile.de/
Wirtschaftsuniv. Wien	http://nm.wu-wien.ac.at/palm.shtml
Carnegie Mellon University	http://www.cmu.edu/computing/handheld/index.html
Cornell University	http://mobile.mannlib.cornell.edu/
East Carolina University	http://www.ecu.edu/handheld/
Harvard Medical School	http://www.theanswerpage.com/
Kentucky Migrant Project	http://www.migrant.org/
Purdue University	http://www.purdue.edu/UNS/html4ever/010724.Chan.pda.html
Stanford School of Medicine	http://mednews.stanford.edu/stanmed/2001fall/mobilemed.html
Stanford University	http://palm.stanford.edu/
University of North Carolina	http://aa.uncwil.edu/numina/
University of Michigan	http://hi-ce.org/
University of South Dakota	http://www.usd.edu/pda/
University Twente	http://usa.nfia.nl/publish/su2001news.pdf
Wake Forest University	http://www.palm.com/us/enterprise/studies/study9.html

initiated at high schools, and 20 of them at universities. For further information on these projects, consult the corresponding URL provided in Table 2.

A first differentiation separates the projects based on the implemented infrastructure: local transmission of files, for example via synchronization, wireless local access via WLAN, or wireless remote access via a cellular network. File transmissions include sending and receiving data and information as well as applications, which are installed on the device. These transmissions may occur with the help of a data cable, which connects the mobile device to a stationary PC, or with a wireless connection (an infrared interface or Bluetooth). WLAN, typically used to describe wireless networks based on IEEE 802.11 standards, may also include other local wireless technologies like Hiperlan, although IEEE 802.11b and 802.11g networks were implemented most often. Cellular networks encompass all digital mobile phone networks, for example GSM, HSCSD, GPRS, and IMT-2000.

A second differentiation determines whether the projects used PDAs, mobile phones or other mobile devices. PDAs, or handheld computers, are operated with a stylus on a touch sensitive display, or with a small hardware keyboard (Hansmann, Merk, Nicklous, & Stober, 2003). They can be equipped with WLAN and Bluetooth access. Mobile phones, on the other hand, have smaller displays, which are not touch sensitive, and some models are equipped with an alphanumerical hardware keyboard. They connect to cellular networks, and an increasing number features Bluetooth connectivity. Smart phones combine mobile phones and PDAs into one device. They offer a touch sensitive display with cellular network connectivity, sometimes extended with WLAN. For the following analysis, smart phones are either included in the "PDA" or in the "Mobile" section. Other mobile devices include appliances with no or small displays, and some can connect to a WLAN network. Examples include MP3 players, digital cameras, or portable game consoles.

A third differentiation examines which of the three educational processes (learning, teaching, and administration) are covered by the project implementation. Learning processes include all activities pursued by a learner to gain knowledge or skills, whereas teaching processes include all activities by a lecturer to aid this acquisition process. Both processes interact with one another, and both depend on their underlying didactic model. Administrative processes focus on activities concerning the curriculum of a learner, for example registering for tests or enrolling in courses.

High School Projects

Table 3 summarizes the findings for high school projects. File transfers are used by all but one project, whereas wireless transmissions via WLAN or cellular networks were implemented in only four projects. It can also be noted that wireless technologies were used by only one project exclusively.

A similar result is apparent with regard to the mobile devices used. All projects targeted PDAs as an end user device; again only one project used mobile phones. Considering that these projects piloted a new form of education, most of them focused on the learning process, where immediate benefits could be expected. Two projects additionally used mobile devices to support teaching activities, and three other projects allowed users to perform administrative tasks with their end device.

Table 3. Infrastructure, end user devices and processes in high school projects

Project	Infrastructure			End User Device			Process		
	File	WLAN	Cell	PDA	Mobile	Other	Learn	Teach	Admin
Ballard High School	x			x			x		x
Cons. HS District 230	x	x		x			x		
Hartland Farms Inter.	x			x			x		
King Middle School	x			x			x		
Gym. Landau a. d. Isar	x	x		x			x		x
Lessenger Elementary	x			x			x		
Mead Elementary	x			x			x		
MobiSkoolz	x		x	x			x	x	
Palm Educ. Pioneers	x			x			x		x
RAFT Project		x	x	x	x		x	x	
Total	**9**	**3**	**2**	**10**	**1**	**0**	**10**	**2**	**3**

University Projects

In the next table, the same analysis is presented for university projects. Even though the results are more diverse compared to high school projects, a few observations can be made. First, once again most projects preferred file transfer to wireless transmission. In contrast to high school projects, those institutions that chose to implement wireless networks did not offer file transfer as an additional option—except for one case. Second, PDAs were a common end device in university projects, although a few projects supported the use of mobile phones. Third, almost all projects tried to improve learning and administration processes, while only three targeted the teaching process.

Comparison

When contrasting *m-education projects* at high schools and universities, three differences can be seen:

1. Unlike high schools, universities install and use wireless networks. This is motivated by the facts that university students spend more time between classes

Table 4. Infrastructure, end user devices and processes in university projects

Project	Infrastructure			End User Device			Process		
	File	WLAN	Cell	PDA	Mobile	Other	Learn	Teach	Admin
Anglia Polytechnical Univ.			x	x	x		x		
Berlin Univ. der Künste			x		x				x
Wirtschaftsuniv. Wien	x			x			x		
Carnegie Mellon University		x		x			x	x	
Columbia Sch. of Nursing	x			x			x		x
Cornell University	x			x					x
East Carolina University	x			x			x		
Harvard Medical School	x			x			x		
Kentucky Migrant Project			x	x			x		
Purdue University		x		x					x
Stanford Sch. of Medicine		x		x			x	x	
Stanford University	x			x					x
University of Michigan	x			x	x	x	x		
Univ. of North Carolina	x	x		x			x	x	
University of Buffalo	x			x					x
University of Minnesota	x			x			x		
University of South Dakota	x			x			x		x
University Twente			x		x		x		x
Wake Forest University	x			x			x		x
Total	**12**	**4**	**4**	**17**	**4**	**1**	**14**	**3**	**9**

on a campus, and university campuses tend to be larger than school campuses, with higher computer literacy and usage at universities.

2.   High schools focus on PDAs; universities tend to support mobile phones. PDAs are easier to use and are able to hold larger amounts of data than mobile phones. They are therefore better suited for learning purposes. University projects, on the other hand, strive not only to support learning, but also to target a larger and readily available hardware base.

3.   Administrative and organisational information is more common at university projects. Students at universities have more freedom in learning compared to students at high schools. Furthermore, they need to acquire all information themselves, which can be a time consuming task if there is no central

information repository. To remedy these factors, support for administrative and organisational tasks becomes more relevant at universities than at high schools.

It should be noted that some projects were initiated in cooperation with PDA device manufacturers, which additionally explains the high number of projects using PDAs. Taking the implemented functions into consideration, it is possible to identify those which were available in most projects:

- **Access to learning material:** Theoretically, this function is relatively easy to implement if there is already an e-learning platform: access to learning materials can be achieved by transferring the electronic documents to a mobile devices, for example by providing a URL. The problem is that mobile devices often lack the software to present certain media formats, and small display sizes limit legibility. As a result, learning material should be designed with a possible mobile use in mind.

- **Carrying out knowledge assessments:** Knowledge assessments can be carried out as part of a classroom application, or as a method for self assessment. The latter can be implemented easily with various technologies (J2ME stand-alone quiz applications, WAP-based questionnaire) if multiple-choice answers are allowed. Development of a *classroom application* is more complex and depends on the available devices and network infrastructures in the classroom.

- **Communication between students and lecturers:** Communication is the main function of mobile devices. One way to enable synchronous communication is to insert a WTAI (Wireless Telephony Application Interface) link in WAP pages, which, when clicked, dial the provided phone number (Larsson, 2000). J2ME application can also access mobile device functions (Schmatz, 2004). Depending on the number of supported communication protocols and their complexity (e.g., AIM/ICQ, E-mail, voice calls, SMS, MMS, fax, newsgroups) communication services are moderately hard to implement.

- **Information about courses and events:** Lecturers can inform students via push or pull methods. Push methods actively inform users about new information, while pull methods require the user to query this information regularly. Pull services are relatively easy to implement, as course information and events are usually published in text form which can be presented without problems. Push services are more complex, as they could require additional technologies, such as SMS gateways.

- **Enrol for courses and exams:** With these functions, students can use mobile devices to enrol for courses or exams. Technically, such services are not complex. They need, however, a connection to administrative backend systems. This creates potential security and legal risks that must be addressed.

- **Querying dates and examination results:** Similarly, students could be informed with push or pull methods about examination results. Again, this requires a connection to systems containing sensitive personal data, creating security and legal issues.

- **Reservation of resources (e.g., lab places, books, PCs):** An educational institution possesses a number of resources where access to them needs to be managed. Specific books or technical equipment are not available in unlimited numbers, and thus students and lecturers must make reservations for them in advance. If those reservations are already stored in a database, mobile access to these is easily granted. Users can then make reservations or check their status.

- **Information about external data (public services, events):** It is also possible to include external data and services in a m-education system. Depending on the complexity and openness of the service, such an inclusion can be difficult. For example, if an external service is Web-based and financed with online advertising, the provider is not interested in allowing direct access to his database. In this case, one common solution is to pass the input of the mobile interface to the Web-based service and parse the resulting HTML page. This technique, however, is technically and legally problematic.

Some of these services were mobile extensions to existing functions accessible via a PC. Other functions were created with both wireless and wired usage in mind. Only a few services, primarily communication and collaboration functions, were usable exclusively with mobile devices. As the discussion shows, most functions can be implemented with medium effort (depending on the complexity approximately 3-6 person months per function) but their integration into existing technical and organizational frameworks needs additional attention. The following SWOT analysis provides decision support by presenting strength and weaknesses of various directions when planning and designing mobile education services.

SWOT Analysis

The *SWOT analysis* was developed to identify strengths, weaknesses, opportunities, and threats (SWOT) as internal and external factors, and to help create adequate strategies for an organization. Even as it was originally intended for use in a business environment, it has also been applied in educational contexts (Balamuralikrishna, & Dugger, 1995, Gorski, 1991; Rosenberg, 2001). Criticism has resulted in further developments (Novicevic, Harvey, Autry, & Bond, 2004; Valentin, 2001); however, a SWOT analysis can provide initial insights, which can then be refined. The following SWOT analysis examines mobile education in general, not a specific project or institution. Additional factors must thus be taken into account when planning to implement a mobile education system. Again, the SWOT analysis will be structured along the three key factors from the presented projects:

1. Infrastructure
2. End user devices
3. Processes

Each of these factors will be analysed regarding internal, external, favourable, and unfavourable effects. The result is then assigned to the appropriate SWOT quadrant.

Infrastructure

A favourable, internal factor arising for mobile education from the *infrastructure* is flexibility. Learners and lecturers have the ability to access information and carry out educational processes regardless of location and time. The gained flexibility is even higher than with traditional, PC-based e-learning, as this requires a stationary desktop computer.

While flexibility is a favourable factor, interoperability between different technical infrastructures currently is unfavourable. Content and information can be distributed over multiple infrastructure channels, for example a video lecture can be broadcast via WLAN or via a cellular network, and course information are available via file transfer, cellular push (messaging) or WLAN. But switching between infrastructure technologies with a single device is problematic, as technical details of data transmissions are different. This is also due to interface limitations in end user devices (only smart phones can be used for file transfers, WLAN, and cellular networks).

External factors, which are determined by network providers, contain market demand as a favourable factor, and costs as an unfavourable factor. Market demand results from both users and infrastructure providers looking for ways to utilize mobile networks. Furthermore, increased workforce mobility and life long learning can be seen as drivers for mobile learning.

Costs for infrastructures cover several elements. First, the m-education provider (the educational institution offering mobile services) needs to install required hard- and software, resulting in initial costs. Second, the provider has to cover recurring costs caused by network data traffic and maintenance. Third, m-education users also need to purchase dedicated hardware in order to connect to the network, and, fourth,

Table 5. Range and cost structures for infrastructure technologies

infrastruct. technology	typical end user device	range	costs for provider		costs for user	
			initial	recurring	initial	recurring
File	PDA	short	low	none	none	none
WLAN	PDA	medium	high	low	medium	none
Cell. (pull)	mob. phone	high	low	none	none	high
Cell. (push)	mob. phone	high	low	high	none	none

bear recurring costs for data traffic. Not all of these costs occur simultaneously, but rather depending on the chosen technology, and not all costs are distributed evenly among the participants.

Table 5 summarizes the three infrastructure technologies with regard to range, and costs for both provider and user. Cellular connections are divided into pull services (when a user actively requests data) and push services (when a user is informed by an m-education provider, for example with a SMS) as their cost structures vary. It should be noted that the range applies during an exchange of data. File transfers require the mobile device to be physically close to the transmitting source device, and after the transfer the data can be used on the mobile device without any further restrictions. However, the data can only be as current as the most recent transfer, decreasing timeliness of information (Lehner, Nösekabel, & Lehmann, 2004).

File transfers incur very few costs, as they are based on wired or wireless personal area networks. m-education providers only need to implement a distribution channel for information and content, which can then be transferred by the users to their already available devices. Costs for data transfer are, in this case, negligible.

WLAN requires an initial installation of access points (based on either IEEE 802.11 or Bluetooth technology), and users need to be equipped with hardware enabling them to utilize the wireless network. Costs for data transfer are, again, negligible, although there are costs for maintaining the hardware.

In order to use cellular networks, the provider has to create an appropriate service, for example a WAP site, or a SMS gateway. As this kind of infrastructure primarily targets mobile phones as an end user device, it can be assumed that most users already possess an adequate device. By differentiating between pull and push technologies, the resulting cost structures for a provider and a user can be taken into account. When users pull desired information (e.g., from a WAP site), they are charged for the data connection. If the information is pushed to the users (e.g., with a SMS), the sender is charged for each data transmission.

End User Devices

A favourable, internal factor of mobile education is the availability of appropriate *mobile devices* (Le Bodic, 2003), although PDAs are not as common as mobile phones. Therefore, most projects using PDAs as the end user device made arrangements for lending or sponsoring, reducing the initial costs for users. Other mobile devices, such as portable multimedia players, can be either popular (MP3 player) or uncommon (DVD player).

Unfavourable factors are technical limitations imposed by mobile devices. Even as technological progress—an external, favourable factor—increases computing power and battery life with each device generation, physical limitations, such as screen size and cumbersome input methods, remain. Not all of these limitations can be overcome, though. The screen size, for example, is dependent on the overall size of the device, which is limited due to mobility considerations.

One drawback of short development cycles in device development is a lack of standard conformity, an external, unfavourable factor. As a result, interoperability can be hindered, if implementations are not compatible to standards. Such an incompatibility can occur when either a standard is not yet defined, is unspecific, or when a manufacturer explicitly decides not to follow it. One example is the case of "Smart Messaging," a system developed by Nokia in the late 1990s to extend the capabilities of SMS. With "Smart Messaging," messages could contain multimedia content and text formatting. In 2001, the official 3GPP "Enhanced Messages Service" (EMS) was formally standardized and Nokia abandoned "Smart Messages" in favour to EMS (Dornan, 2002).

Processes

As mobile devices are personal devices, *educational processes* can address each user individually, making this a favourable, internal factor. Individual data for a learner encompasses—among others—learning progress, courses taken, personal preferences, and administrative data. It should be noted that such a system requires a high level of technical integration and security, on a level not always achievable with wireless networks (Sikora, 2001). An unfavourable, internal factor is caused by the already mentioned limitations of mobile devices, and extra effort has to be taken to produce content which is usable on a wide range of these devices. For example, long text, detailed graphics, or complex animations are difficult to read on small screens. Multimedia files take up too much memory, although in these cases streaming technologies can provide a solution.

Opportunities arise when mobile education services are didactically integrated into teaching and learning processes, resulting in added flexibility for both the learner and the lecturer. However, such integration builds on the willingness of all users to adapt such services, and resistance to change poses a threat.

Strategic Recommendations

Table 6 summarizes the aforementioned factors, contrasting strengths, weaknesses, opportunities, and threats. Based on these factors, a number of strategies can be deducted for implementing a mobile education service. Again, the discussion will revolve around feasible choices for an infrastructure and for end user devices, and which processes should be integrated.

Before engaging in a mobile education project, a decision on whether to implement a mobile education system or not has to be made. This decision should be part of an e-learning strategy (Back, Bendel, & Stoller-Shai, 2001; Rosenberg, 2001) for several reasons. First, mobile services should extend an e-learning system, which provides a basic data and content infrastructure. Non-mobile e-learning systems also offer easier and faster access for lecturer and administrative staff, who are usually working at a stationary PC. Second, an e-learning strategy defines the framework for mobile services, for example which functions should be implemented, or who should be responsible—organizationally and financially. Third, it is possible that the strategy already contains statements regarding the choices for an infrastructure, for end user devices, or for didactic processes (e.g., when the support for lecturers is explicitly demanded, or when it is part of the e-learning strategy to equip each student with a PDA).

As a result, the following recommendations should always be adapted to the specific requirements of the implementing institution. They can present various options

Table 6. SWOT factors for mobile education

	favourable factors	unfavourable factors
internal factors	Strengths 1. flexibility 2. availability 3. individuality	Weaknesses 1. interoperability 2. technical limitations 3. effort
external factors	Opportunities 1. market demand 2. technological progress 3. didactic integration	Threats 1. cost 2. standard conformity 3. resistance to change

which may then be discussed, but they should not be understood to be an optimal solution for every project.

Infrastructure

The choice for an *infrastructure* must consider the cost situation, the range required, and the targeted end user devices. Basically, the lower the costs, the shorter the achievable range. Under certain conditions, costs could be considered under long-term aspects. For example, when the mobile education system is implemented within the scope of a project and funding would include infrastructure costs. Then it is important how the cost structure will evolve after funding has expired, and users are required to bear their own costs. In the long run, a decrease in data transmission costs might be expected due to market demand—already some mobile network providers offer data flat rates for WAP pages today.

When initiating a mobile education system, several paths can be taken. If no infrastructure exists and funding is limited, transferring files via synchronization or personal area networks (e.g., Bluetooth or IR transmission) reduces initial costs and does not require extensive knowledge of mobile technologies, but it does provide first experiences and feedback from users. Such systems can later be upgraded by including wireless networks (WLAN or cellular) for extended coverage.

Another option in this situation is offering a cellular network-based service, for example a WAP service. Public wireless networks provide network connectivity, and the costs are carried by the users. As a result, acceptance will most likely be low. Cellular networks could extend file transfers; they should not be the only way to access the system.

With the success of i-mode in Japan, additional business models for mobile services have been discussed and established. Educational institutions function as content and service providers in these mobile value chains, theoretically allowing them to charge users for their learning content and services. I-mode network providers (Japans NTT DoCoMo, or a licensee) handle the billing, so content providers are not required to charge each user individually (Barnes & Huff, 2003; Sharma & Nakamura, 2003). Therefore, it would be possible to create revenue with e-learning content and services, assuming that a demand for these exists. Creating content for i-mode requires only basic knowledge of Internet technologies, as pages are implemented using cHTML (compressed HTML), which is a subset of HTML. Some browsers in i-mode phones are also able to render XHTML.

If sufficient funding exists, an educational institution could opt for installing a campus-wide wireless LAN. Such a WLAN is more attractive for universities than for high schools, as the number of privately owned mobile devices (especially laptops) is higher, campuses are usually larger, and students work at less determined times and places. Similarly, if a WLAN already exists at the campus, a mobile education system should include it as a distribution channel.

Should an infrastructure and additional funding be available, another strategy could be to subsidize network connectivity for users. This might include wireless network traffic via cellular networks or hardware (e.g., PDAs, WLAN cards, or mobile phones). Such incentives can lead to an increased acceptance of the mobile education system.

End User Devices

The cost factor also affects the type of usable *mobile devices*. Short range, cost efficient infrastructures primarily target PDAs as end user devices. Most students and staff do not have such a device, and additional costs would be incurred for purchasing or lending a device. Again, this factor could be absorbed within a project or by a hardware sponsor. Mobile phones, on the other hand, are widespread and therefore are an attractive target base. However, they have technical limitations which must be taken into account.

When end user devices are issued by the educational institution, organizational tasks increase effort for and, possibly, resistance by teachers. Purchasing, keeping track of, and supporting mobile devices are additional challenges for teachers and lecturers. If damaged, devices have to be replaced, which may incur costs for either the student or the organization. Small devices are also prone to loss or theft. Curtis et al. (2003) argue that students, after having proven able to utilize their devices carefully and adequately, should be allowed to keep their devices provided by the school even outside the classroom. When mobile services target devices which are already owned by the students, this issue is less of a problem.

Device support is determined by the availability of the device, the infrastructure, and the implemented services. Providing access to mobile phones allows a higher number of users to employ the mobile education system, increasing acceptance. Push services, like SMS information, can be adopted intuitively without extensive training. Complex services, for example WAP sites or video streaming, create usability challenges ranging from device configuration to GUI design.

These complex services are easier to implement for PDAs and smartphones, as display capabilities (higher resolution, touch sensitive screen, etc.) allow intuitive usability design. Furthermore, multimedia content can be shown in a higher quality. PDAs can also be extended with external devices, such as probes, graphic cards for beamer connection, or GPS. They are more versatile than traditional mobile phones, but this added versatility has to be exploited by offering appropriate services.

Processes

Availability of mobile education systems is the key factor for anytime, anywhere learning. Students are given the ability to engage in *educational processes* regardless of time and place. Weiss (2002) notes that mobile usage patterns focus on retrieving a specific answer within a short time frame ("hunting"), instead of browsing through data provided by the system. As a result, m-education should reflect this behavioural pattern by offering short learning segments, and the ability to query personalized information.

All educational processes benefit from the achievable individuality mobile devices can provide. Since each mobile device is—as a personal item—usually associated with a single user, processes can be automatically adapted to individual preferences. From a usability viewpoint, this benefit is also a requirement. Display size and input limitations prohibit extensive user interaction with the system. Therefore, users should be presented the functions they are most likely to choose in a manner that reduces navigational efforts and speeds up transactions.

Extending the idea of adaptation to a technical level leads to the concept of "transcoding" (Sharma & Nakamura, 2003). Multimedia content can be created once, and will then be transcoded from this single source to the capabilities and requirement of a specific device and network. Thus, the need for producing identical information in varying formats, sizes, and for different bandwidths is eliminated and replaced by a (semi) automatic conversion process.

For mobile education, this means that multimedia educational content—audio and video lectures, slides, or pictures—only have to be created once by the lecturer. This content is then available, without further modifications, for PC-based and PDA- or mobile phone-based e-learning systems. For textual content, where automatic adaptation from a source text is not feasible, a multi channel delivery approach is possible. Here, the length and depth of a text is tailored to the end user device. A short summary is available for mobile phones, a longer text for PDAs, and the full text for PCs. Apparently, with such a solution mobile devices can only be an addition to existing e-learning efforts, and not a replacement.

Usually, at educational institutions the number of students is considerably higher than the number of lecturers and teaching staff. Therefore, learning-oriented services are relevant to the largest user group and could include access to learning material and self tests. Teaching-oriented services (e.g., Myers, 2001) primarily focus on support during lectures, as the preparation of content—including the production of multimedia data—requires the capabilities of stationary PCs. Furthermore, teaching staff is less mobile than students, reducing the need for mobile solutions. Administrative-oriented services depend on a connection to existing systems. Since these systems contain sensitive material, security is an essential factor for such services. Several security approaches are available (Dornan, 2002; Hansmann, Merk, Nicklous, & Stober, 2003; Sharma & Nakamura, 2003), but not all might be available for a specific wireless technology mix.

Summary

Currently, there is not a single combination of mobile technologies which would fit the needs of all mobile education projects. Both the choice for an infrastructure and end user device depend on the specific situation. Also, some infrastructures (e.g., WLAN) can be used more flexibly than others, as they offer access to a larger variety of device types. As a result, many projects start with applications that are easy to implement and cost-effective to distribute. J2ME programs with educational purpose provide a good starting point to get familiar with the characteristics of mobile services development. Other approaches may include adapting an existing Web-based e-learning system for mobile access, either through file transfer (using Plucker or AvantGo), i-mode, or WML.

With regard to processes, it is probably best to start with learning-oriented processes, from which a large number of users can benefit. Mobile classroom applications can also be implemented easily, especially when they are not dependent on or connected with the mobile education system. This way, dependencies can be reduced, and introduction of new technologies is alleviated. Mobile learning, in its simplest form, can be achieved by offering short audio clips of lectures for download as MP3 files. Students can then transfer these audio files to their portable MP3 player or burn them on a CD as a type of audio book. Other means include converting lecture notes to e-books, which can be read on a PDA.

Table 7 summarizes possible software choices for each infrastructure—end user device combination. Since this sector continually develops, the items in the table are not meant to be exhaustive. Furthermore, not all devices in a category support

Table 7. Mobile technology matrix

	File transfer	WLAN	Cellular network
Mobile phone	Applications (J2ME) Multimedia download		SMS WAP i-mode Multimedia streaming AvantGo
PDA	Applications Multimedia download Plucker/AvantGo	HTML WAP Multimedia streaming Plucker/AvantGo	HTML WAP Multimedia streaming Plucker/AvantGo
Other	Multimedia download	Multimedia streaming	Multimedia streaming

all software solutions: not all mobile phones are yet capable of playing audio- or video-files, and only certain handsets can use i-mode. Personal area network connectivity, such as Bluetooth, is mainly used to transfer data directly between devices. Thus, they can be included in the "file transfer" column.

"Multimedia" comprises, as a generic term, educational content in various formats: for example, audio, video, animations, pictures, e-books. "Plucker" and "AvantGo" are applications which store HTML pages on the mobile device and let the user browse them off-line. AvantGo is available for some mobile phone models and can be synchronized over a wireless network.

Table 8 lists examples for m-education software solutions. Not included are multimedia applications (e.g., video or audio players). A discussion of these can be found in Lehner, Nösekabel, & Bremen (2004) and in Nösekabel (2005). The list is by no means exhaustive, but shows the wide range of available software solutions. Most m-learning approaches make use of stand-alone application that are installed on a mobile device, and they either already contain learning content or retrieve them via a wireless network connection. With ImagiProbe, a hardware/software combination is also included in the list. ImagiWorks offers various probes (e.g., for temperature measurement) that can be connected to a mobile device. The software records and analyzes data collected with the hardware probe, and results can be shared with other users.

If possible, a new mobile education system should be organizationally integrated into an existing e-learning system. Some e-learning systems already offer mobile access to their services and content, such as Stud.IP and Blackboard. This access

Table 8. Exemplary software solutions for mobile education

Product	URL	Infrastr.			Devices			Processes		
		F	W	C	P	M	O	L	T	A
Mobile Learning Engine	www.elibera.com			x		x		x		
AvantGo	www.avantgo.com	x	x	x	x	x		x		
Plucker	www.plkr.org	x	x	x	x			x		
Stud.IP	www.studip.de		x		x	x		x		x
Blackboard	www.blackboard.com		x		x	x				x
Pebbles	www.pebbles.hcii.cmu.edu		x		x				x	
Hi-CE	www.hi-ce.org	x			x			x	x	
Hot Lava	www.hotlavasoftware.com	x	x	x	x	x		x		
Four.OStudent	www.fourostudent.net	x			x					x
ImagiProbe	www.imagiworks.com	x			x			x	x	

is mostly, but not exclusively, based on WML. Such additional modules are easy to integrate into the existing system. However, they require a specific combination of infrastructure and end user devices. If this combination is feasible for a specific project, then these models could be the best way to implement mobile services for e-learning. Furthermore, they could be the only solution, if the existing system is not accessible and does not provide interfaces for data exchange.

Future Trends

Technological progress will increase both device and network capabilities, and demand for data services may lead to an attractive pricing structure. Already a few network operators offer flat rates for WAP data transmission, although these are restricted to WML pages and do not include HTTP traffic or other downloads. Should this change, mobile services in general, and mobile education specifically, will be more attractive than they are today.

Additionally, an increased adoption of learning objects (Dodero, Aedo, & Diaz, 2002; Rosenberg, 2001; Wagner, 2005; Wiley, 2002) would solve some content related issues. Learning objects are small units of information or instruction, and they can be assembled into structures of a higher order, for example, courses. Learning objects are scalable and each of these objects can be created for mobile deployment, taking device capabilities and limitations into account. Learners can then decide which learning objects they require and transfer them to their mobile devices. If a learning path or another connection between learning objects is defined, succeeding objects can be suggested to the student. As a result, data transmission and memory requirements are reduced because only needed learning objects are retrieved.

Another area which has received limited research so far is mobile edutainment. Edutainment combines entertainment applications (e.g., games) with an educational background. Software for stationary PCs is already well established, especially with learning content appropriate for children. For mobile devices, however, few concepts exist (Bellotti, Berta, De Gloria, & Margarone, 2003; Feix, Göbel, & Zumack, 2004; Ströhlein, 2004). This could prove to be a potential market gap, as mobile phones and mobile entertainment products (ring tones, themes, and games) are popular among younger users.

Conclusion

Both the survey and the SWOT analysis show that costs are a deciding factor for m-education projects. Costs are primarily determined by the infrastructure, which is also limiting the supported devices (e.g., only very few mobile phones can be used in WLANs). Furthermore, both the providing institution and the users act on a limited budget. As a result, file transfers, which incur low costs to both the provider and the user, are a popular choice.

Regarding end user devices, a dependency on industrial partners can be observed. Since mobile phones are the devices mostly available to students, supporting them would ensure a large, although technically somewhat limited, user base. Additionally, users are already competent in operating their devices. PDAs offer more capabilities, but have to be provided through partnership programs because they are not as widespread as mobile phones or laptops among students. A problem is that mobile phones are less suitable for a file transfer infrastructure than PDAs.

Most projects initially focused on supporting learning processes. This can be considered to be feasible, as immediate benefits are likely to be gained here. Lecturers and administrative staff are also working at stationary PCs and would be unable to realise the full potential of a mobile solution. However, employing mobile services in the teaching process has proven to be viable. Offering mobile access to administrative data requires additional efforts concerning security.

One important factor is the combination of technical and pedagogical aspects. Systems providing only a technical solution without sensible pedagogical integration do not address the needs of learners and thus reduce acceptance. Mobile technologies are therefore only a part of the solution. *"Technology in and of itself may not guarantee better learning. But when effectively deployed, technology can help focus attention while attracting and maintaining a learner's interest"* (Wagner, 2005, p. 48). All in all, there is no immediate pressure to implement mobile education services. Still, if an e-learning infrastructure has already been successfully established, a next step could consist of planning and extending this infrastructure with mobile services. In this case, it is important to select an appropriate wireless infrastructure in order to create a significant additional value for the users. If the costs outweigh the perceived benefit, usage of the system will remain low.

An important aspect of any e-learning or m-education system is thus the alignment with pedagogical theories and practices. Technology-driven projects are useful for discovering new potentials and possibilities. Long-term solutions, however, require an integrated and interdisciplinary approach.

References

Back, A., Bendel, O., & Stoller-Shai, D. (2001). *E-learning im unternehmen. Grundlagen – Strategien – Methoden – Technologien.* Zurich, Switzerland: Orell Füssli.

Balamuralikrishna, R., & Dugger, J.C. (1995). SWOT analysis: A management tool for initiating new programs in vocational schools. *Journal of Vocational and Technical Education, 12*(1), 1-5.

Barnes, S.J., & Huff, S.L. (2003). Rising sun: iMode and the wireless Internet. *Communication of the ACM, 46*(11), 79-84.

Bellotti, F., Berta, R., De Gloria, A., & Margarone, M. (2003). MADE: Developing edutainment applications on mobile computers. *Computers & Graphics, 27*(4), 617-634.

Clarke, I., & Flaherty, T.B. (2002). mLearning: Using wireless technology to enhance marketing education. *Marketing Education Review, 12*(3), 67-76.

Curtis, M., Williams, B., Norris, C., O'Leary, D., & Soloway, E. (2003). *Palm handheld computers – A complete resource for classroom teachers.* Eugene: International Society for Technology in Education.

Dodero, J.M., Aedo, I., Diaz, P. (2002). Participative knowledge production of learning objects for e-books. *The Electronic Library, 20*(4), 296-305.

Dornan, A. (2002). *The essential guide to wireless communications applications: From cellular to WiFi* (2nd ed.). Upper Saddle River, NJ: Prentice Hall.

Dourish, P. (2001). *Where the action is: The foundations of embodied interaction.* MA: MIT Press.

Feix, A., Göbel, S., Zumack, R. (2004, June 24-26). DinoHunter: Platform for mobile edutainment applications in museums. In *Proceedings of the Second International Conference on Technologies for Interactive Storytelling and Entertainment* (pp. 264-269). Berlin, Germany: Springer.

Gorski, S.E. (1991). The SWOT team: Focusing on minorities. *Community, Technical, and Junion College Journal, 63*(3), 30-33.

Hansmann, U., Merk, L., Nicklous, M.S., & Stober, T. (2003). *Pervasive computing* (2nd ed.). Berlin, Germany: Springer.

Hummel, K.A., & Hlavacs, H. (2003, January 6-12). Anytime, anywhere learning behavior using a Web-based platform for a university lecture. In *Proceedings of the SSGRR 2003 Winter Conference*, L'Aquila (pp. 1-6).

Larsson, M. (2000). Wireless telephony application: Telephony in WAP. In M. van der Heijden & M. Taylor (Eds.), *Understanding WAP* (pp. 65-96). Boston: Artech House Publishers.

Le Bodic, G. (2003). *Mobile messaging technologies and services: SMS, EMS, and MMS*. Chichester: John Wiley & Sons.

Lehner, F., Nösekabel, H., & Bremen, G. (2004). *M-learning und M-education – Mobile und drahtlose anwendungen im unterricht*. Passau: Research Report Business Computing W-08-04.

Lehner, F., Nösekabel, H., & Lehmann, H. (2004). Wireless e-learning and communication environment – WELCOME at the University of Regensburg. *E-service Journal, 2*(3), 23-41.

Lyytinen, K., & Yoo, Y. (2002). Issues and challenges in ubiquitous computing. *Communications of the ACM, 45*(12), 63-65.

Myers, B.A. (2001). Using handhelds and PCs together. *Communications of the ACM, 44*(11), 34-41.

Nösekabel, H. (2005). *Mobile education*. Berlin, Germany: GITO.

Novicevic, M.M., Harvey, M., Autry, C.W., & Bond, E.U. (2004). Dual-perspective SWOT: A synthesis of marketing intelligence and planning. *Marketing Intelligence & Planning, 22*(1), 84-94.

Nyiri, K. (2002, August 29-30). Towards a philosophy of m-learning.In *Proceedings of the IEEE International Workshop on Wireless and Mobile Technologies in Education* (pp. 121-124), Växjö.

Rosenberg, M.J. (2001). *E-learning. Strategies for delivering knowledge in the digital age*. New York: McGraw-Hill.

Schmatz, K.-D. (2004). *Java 2 micro edition*. Heidelberg, Germany: dpunkt.verlag.

Sharma, S.K., & Kitchens, F.L. (2004). Web service architecture for m-learning. *Electronic Journal on e-Learning, 2*(1), 203-216.

Sharma, C., & Nakamura, Y. (2003). *Wireless data services – Technologies, business models and global markets*. Cambridge University Press.

Sikora, A. (2001). *Wireless LAN - Protokolle und anwendungen*. Munich, Germany: Addison-Wesley.

Ströhlein, G. (2004). HistoBrick: Mobile edutainment into descriptive statistics. *I-com, 3*(2), 53-56.

Valentin, E.K. (2001). SWOT analysis from a resource-based view. *Journal of Marketing Theory and Practice, 9*(2), 54-69.

Wagner, E.D. (2005). Enabling mobile learning. *EDUCAUSE Review, 40*(3), 40-53.

Weiss, S. (2002). *Handheld usability*. Chichester: John Wiley & Sons.

Wiley, D.A. (2002). Connecting learning objects to instructional design theory: A definition, a metaphor, and a taxonomy. In D.A. Wiley (Ed.), *The instructional use of learning objects* (pp. 3-23). Bloomington: Association for Educational Communications and Technology.

Appendix I: Internet Session: Summarize Mobile and Wireless Learning Approaches

Interaction

The Web site lists several resources regarding learning with mobile technologies. Compile and compare typical definitions of mobile and wireless learning (*http://www.E-Learningcentre.co.uk/eclipse/Resources/mlearning.htm*). What are key differences and similarities? Use the strategic discussion in this chapter to apply it to one project of your choice from the Web site. Would you have suggested another kind of implementation? If so, which, and why?

Appendix II: Case Study

Enhancing an Existing E-Learning Solution with Mobile Services

A university with approximately 16,000 students on a single but spacious campus possesses an established Web-based e-learning portal. Although usage of the system is not compulsory, over 8,000 students have registered with the system, which provides learning material in the form of audio and video recordings, and lecture slides. Multimedia files can be streamed or downloaded, and slides are available as PDFs.

Plans of the university are to enhance the current system by offering mobile services. The existing portal is open sourced, and the underlying data model is well documented. Wireless access points have been installed at hot spots on the campus (e.g., cafeterias, larger classrooms). There is no further funding for additional infrastructure measures—including mobile devices—and currently no knowledge about writing mobile applications exists, although there is know-how about Internet technologies like HTML and PHP.

The university is well equipped with PCs and laser printers which are grouped in several pools all over the campus. A survey has shown that most students own a mobile phone, but no PDA. In the past, the university has cooperated loosely with a company offering mobile marketing services via SMS. Even though the financial funds of the company are very limited, it has signalled interest in a joined project should the opportunity arise.

Questions

1. What strategy (infrastructure, end user devices, and processes) of implementing mobile education services would you recommend and why?
2. Which key factors could result in success or failure of a mobile education project at the university?
3. Which other current (mobile and non-mobile) technologies could be integrated into the system to provide learning services?

Appendix III: Possible Paper Titles/Essays

*   Mobile learning and education: Benefits and limitations
*   Embedding mobile devices in learning processes
*   Mobile education and e-learning strategies
*   Location based services for mobile education
*   Mobile edutainment: Concepts and implementations

Chapter IV

Ubiquitous Computing Applications in Education

Kostas Kolomvatsos,
National & Kapodistrian University of Athens, Greece

Abstract

With the development of technology, new roads have been opened in education. An interesting idea is to use computers in teaching and learning procedure. Students will have the opportunity to gain access to information resources in a timeless and limitless way. Teachers will be able to transform their classes in a student-centered environment, avoiding the drawbacks of the traditional teacher-centered model. In this direction, ubiquitous computing has significant advantages. Ubiquitous means that computational devices are distributed into the physical world, giving us boundless access to communication and information channels. Now, knowledge can be built based on collaboration, communication, experimentation, and on students' experiences. Research has shown positive impacts on learning. This chapter deals with issues directly connected to ubiquitous computing, such as its features, types of devices used, and pedagogical goals. The advantages and disadvantages of ubiquitous environments are fully examined and some initiatives are referred.

Inside Chapter

With this effort we try to cover the subject of ubiquitous or pervasive computing in education. We present important issues related to it. The first is the features of this technology. It is important to see and understand them. We also describe the connection means in a pervasive environment. Devices are basic elements of such systems because all educational activities are based on them. Devices vary from those with small screens to those with larger screens. Another separation may be given based on their computational capabilities. We also deal with the pedagogical goals that must be implemented. It is a crucial part of such efforts because the desired result is to assimilate and efficiently teach the students. We describe the advantages and disadvantages of the referred technology. As we will see, ubiquitous computing offers a lot of interesting advantages, but on the other hand, there are open issues that must be taken into consideration. The last part is devoted to the description of some initiatives that take or took place in universities and schools. We describe some platforms that may be used to construct learning environments, most of which originated in the USA. Of course, there are common characteristics between these attempts, but their number is large enough to force us to describe only a few. These were randomly selected.

Introduction

New technologies have brought many changes in teaching, and of course in learning. Traditional classrooms are being transformed in order to utilize the advantages of the technology.

Ubiquitous computing (also known as "Pervasive," "Ambient," "1 to 1," or "one to one") is about distributed computing devices in the environment, with which users are able to gain access to information resources. These devices can be wearable computers, or sensors and computers embedded in everyday objects. On the other hand, ubiquitous computing involves the necessary infrastructures needed to support pervasive computing applications.

Ubiquitous computing integrates technology into the environment, giving the opportunity to users to utilize it anytime and anywhere. It differs from traditional systems where the user is bonded to a computer in a specific place. Now it is possible for a user to utilize the technology without the restriction of place or time.

Ubiquitous computing may provide significant advantages in the application domain of education. It can offer continuous access to a wide range of software, or the Internet, to all students, as well as teachers. As we will see below, the main targets of using pervasive techniques in education are efficiency in teaching and learning, equality between all students as to access to technology, regardless of their economical state, increased student engagement with their lessons, and different approaches according to the students' needs (Bonifaz & Zucker, 2004).

This chapter is organized as follows. The next section gives information about the examined technology, and the third section describes its basic features. In the fourth section, a full description of the means that are being used in order to help a user connect and utilize ubiquitous facilities is given. The fifth section describes the pedagogical goals of the use of pervasive computing, and in the sixth section, the advantages and disadvantages of the emerged technology are given. In the seventh section, we outline some initiatives in this research area, and in the eighth section, we give a specific case study. Finally, our conclusions are depicted in the last section.

Background

Ubiquitous computing environments are different from what one traditionally finds in most school settings. It offers to all students and teachers continuous access to a wide range of software, electronic documents, the Internet, and other digital resources for teaching and learning. These initiatives' goals include increasing economic competitiveness, reducing inequities in access to computers and information between students from wealthy and poor families, and raising student achievement through specific interventions. Other reasons cited for supporting laptop initiatives include improving classroom culture, increasing students' engagement, making it easier to differentiate instruction according to students' needs, and solidifying home-school connections (Bonifaz & Zucker, 2004).

The UK government and Scottish executives have listed a number of priorities for ubiquitous education for the 14+ age range. This list is discussed in Smith (2002) and Sutherland (2002). According to authors, the priorities posed are:

- Widening participation of students
- Increasing the diversity of students in education
- Quality and standards through the use of ubiquitous computing
- Employability in students' life
- Accessibility to various resources through the emerged technology
- The globalization of learning and the emergence of alternative HE (Higher Education) suppliers
- Provision of education in more accessible forms on a part-time basis

- Employers wanting more workplace learning
- Professionalisation of teaching
- Student awareness of quality teaching and pastoral care
- Increasing IT literacy of younger students and higher students' expectations
- Staff handling larger groups

Similar priorities have been posed in other countries recognizing the need to change the traditional educational model that has important disadvantages. To this target, the International Society for Technology in Education (ISTE) published a list (ISTE, 2002) with the most commonly referred conditions to create a learning environment for the use of technology. These factors are:

- **Shared vision:** This means that the commitment to technology is systemic and continual. Also, there is a proactive leadership and administrative support for the entire system.

- **Access:** Teachers must have limitless access to current technologies, software and telecommunications networks.

- **Skilled educators:** The educators that are called to instruct students, who use the technology in their tasks, must be skilled and familiar with the technology and with its use in the teaching procedure. Hence, learning will be more efficient.

- **Professional development:** Educators must have consistent access to professional development in support of technology use in teaching and learning.

- **Technical assistance:** Educators and students must have limitless technical support for maintaining and using the technology. Usually a technical helpdesk is established in order to meet these needs.

- **Content standards and curriculum resources:** Teachers must be knowledgeable in their subject and up to date with the content standards and teaching methods in their courses.

- **Student-centered teaching:** Ubiquitous access to technology drives the transformation of the traditional teacher-centered system to student-centered. Educators' methodologies must comply with these new requirements.

- **Assessment:** There must be continuous assessment of the effectiveness of technology for learning. All the problems and the progress of each program must be recorded and encountered in the programs' implementation.

- **Community support:** The community and every school's partners must provide expertise, support, and resources.

- **Support Policies:** There must be policies for financing, accessing in networks, and rewards structures that must be in place to support technology in learning.

  As we can see, there is an intention to use ubiquitous computing to help students learn in a more productive way. Ubiquitous access to technology by teachers and students has the capacity to transform not only the physical learning environment, but also the learning process, the role of students, and the role of teachers (Fullan, 1999).

Results of some 1 to 1 computing initiatives have shown:

- Improved writing skills.
- Increased student motivation and interest in school.
- Students that are more engaged in their learning.
- Teachers increasingly utilizing project-based and hands-on curriculum and teaching methods.
- Increase of math and science scores in the eighth grade.
- Children born since 1980 process information differently than children born before 1980. They learn best with multisensory input.

A case study is presented later in this chapter. It can be very helpful because it depicts valid results taken from questionnaires and interviews.

There are several research efforts in the field of ubiquitous computing in education. Especially with the spread of the wireless and handheld technology, these efforts become more intensive due to the advantages it can offer to learning process. Current research focuses on the impact of pervasive computing in teachers and students (Bayon et al., 2002). As for the teachers, the goal is to make them use effectively the new technology in their lessons' design in order to produce a student-centered class (Becker & Riel, 2000). This is the basic characteristic of constructivist theory, where students learn based on their collaboration and experimentation. Students build their knowledge based on their experiences and their research.

Regarding students, researchers study the effect ubiquitous learning has on them in terms of when and how they use the technology, how much the technology affects their behaviour, and how the new attempt is received by parents and the school community (Diggs, 2004). Interviews and observations have shown positive effects on students and this way of learning is accepted from the entire school community. There is an enhanced motivation, collaboration, and communication between students. This is also supported in Vahey, Enyedy, and Gifford (2002).

The research results are very optimistic, but there must be careful design and systematic observation to achieve the ultimate goal, which is more productive student learning.

Features

The use of ubiquitous computing in education has characteristics very important in learning. An educational policy can be based on these features in order to achieve a high level of learning. These features are:

- **Information Access:** Students have access to their documents, and also to various information sources from everywhere. All students may search the information needed in order to complete a task. Of course, the initiative is on them. They pose questions and take the results. The final step is to combine the results and extract the final conclusion.

- **Time and Place Immediacy:** This feature is allocated in the place and time in which the information can be reached. Whenever and wherever a student needs to access information is feasible. There are no limits in time or in place. This has the advantage of easy and useful access to resources, increasing the productivity of the work.

- **Interactivity:** Students are able to interact with teachers or experts with a synchronous or asynchronous communication. Hence, they have the opportunity to approach other people's knowledge, without the one teacher's limitation, of the traditional system. They may search, find, and pose questions to specific domain experts, and afterward combine the answers to effectively build their knowledge.

- **Student Activation:** A system in which all students have their own device and work by themselves demands activation. Every student has to work and learn, experimenting with software and searching to find the information needed to complete specific tasks.

- **Adaptability:** Learners can get the right information at the right time and at the right place. In this direction, the Intelligent Agent technology may be very useful. Intelligent software may learn from the owner's habits or instructions and work as its representative, searching and find information. Even further, this software can be used to adapt the information presented to the users based on their learning style.

Connection Means

When computers first arrived in educational environments, they brought a lot of challenges in the form of space for electrical cords, attachments, peripherals, and other entanglements (McKenzie, 2001). It is obvious that in recent years there was a 'blast' in wiring and cabling in school networks.

The ultimate goal of ubiquitous computing in education is the use of a computer for all students and teachers. This means that we need a more flexible way to connect all the devices. The development of the technology in the domain of wireless radio connections, which gives a high speed communication channels, can give us a means to efficiently interconnect devices in large areas.

We believe that a wireless connection will be more appropriate and efficient than a wired network where the users will be bound to specific spots in the area. Using wireless connection, students may have access from anywhere. They may have access in the cafeteria, in the library, in the class or outside.

In McKenzie (2001) authors provide a list of advantages of the wireless technology. They are:

- Ease of movement
- Relaxed fit
- Strategic deployment
- Flexibility
- Cleanliness
- Low profile
- Convenience
- Simplicity
- Speed (especially nowadays)

Synoptically, we can say that the greatest advantage of wireless technology is that it offers continuous access to the networks from anywhere in school. One can see a "wireless" scenario in Figure 1. All the devices can connect to access points and thus can have access to all the network resources. It can be implemented with either infrared rays or wireless Ethernet (e.g., 802.11b, or 802.11g with greater speed). Unfortunately, infrared rays have a disadvantage because they do not penetrate opaque objects. Hence, they may only be used in the classroom. On the other hand, wireless ethernet offers access to the network at a high rate, at any time or place.

The devices that can be used for wireless access vary, from a device with small screen and limited computational capabilities, like Blackberry RIM, to a device

Figure 1. A wireless network example

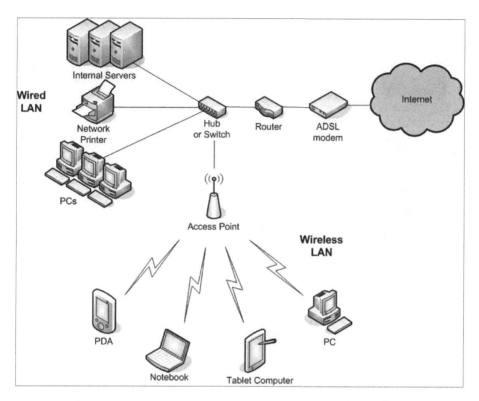

with larger screen and increased computational capabilities, like a laptop (Deters, 2001). Some pictures of these devices are shown in Figure 2.

The first kind of device usually allows simple interactions, like message passing, and so forth, but on the other hand, its use is very easy, even for a beginner. It may be used to help beginners enter into this new technology.

Bigger devices like Palm computers, Pocket PCs, or laptops offer increased computational capabilities, giving users the opportunity to utilize more complex software. They have greater memory size and a more powerful processor, and they comprise miniaturization of a desktop machine.

The most important matter with respect to devices and their software is compatibility, because students working in groups must exchange messages, files, or even more programs. Their devices must be compatible in order to facilitate the communication between them. Otherwise, there will be a significant problem that may be critical to the entire effort.

Figure 2. Portable devices: (1) Laptop, (2) small $100 laptop (3) PocketPC, (4) BlackBerry RIM, (5) handheld laptop, (6) palm computer

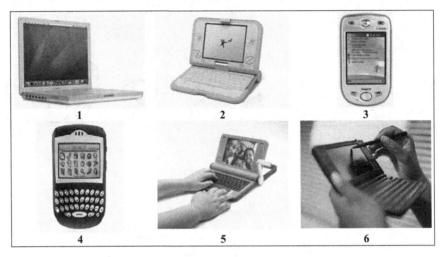

Pedagogical Goals

Today's generation of students looks at technology as part of their everyday environment. It is important to understand the difference between today's life in school in contrast to the past, where students only occasionally used computers. In the future, pupils will own a handheld device, which will be their partner to complete tasks. This means that these devices must be used in a correct manner in order to help them in the learning procedure.

To fully meet the students' needs, technology should be pervasive—always available. In one-to-one learning, each student has access to a wireless laptop to use at school or at home, enabling communication and collaboration among peers and teachers, and connecting parents to their children's learning. Educators are provided digital tools to create learning plans, manage educational content, track student progress, and more.

The most important point is that full attention to learning methodologies, with the help of the digital world, must be given. Technology is the mean to learning. A possible mistake will be to pay attention in technology rather than learning. For this reason, policy makers must grapple with several issues concerning appropriate and effective integration of computers into schools (Eagleton, 1999). In the referred list, one can distinguish financial, equality, curricular, and literacy issues.

The ultimate goal of such efforts is to improve the assimilation ability of the students. To this target, there are two critical factors. The first is teachers and their ability to transform their teaching. Teachers must know how to utilize the technology in their courses. They must apply new educational techniques oriented to the use of technology. This procedure needs careful design. It is useless to leave children to play for hours or aimlessly browse the Web. A specific scope must be posed.

The other factor is students. Research indicates that constant exposure to multiple, overlapping sights and sounds has affected the neural pathways of the brains of digital kids (Apple Education—*http://www.apple.com/education*). In fact, some researchers contend that multisensory input helps kids learn, retain, and use information better. However, the use of technology does not mean that all the students would do their learning with computers. For this reason, it is crucial what type of technology will be distributed to students. Students must be driven to collaborate with their classmates, to use learning software for their courses, to use their devices for communication, or to research with resources useful to complete their tasks. They build their knowledge by experimenting and testing their ideas based on their experiences. The true value of technology for learning lies not in learning to use technology, but in using technology to learn (Educational Research Service, 2001). A technology-using attitude must be cultivated in students in order to enhance their achievement and engagement.

Moreover, computers may help in the direction of the relevancy of schooling (Muir, 2005). Children always wander if what they learn in school may be useful in their future. Laptop initiative makes learning to appear more relevant to life's requirements. This is because students, with the help of technology, learn based on projects that allow students to use their own learning style. A typical project may be the searching for information in the network and the configuration of it to cover their needs. Hence, students see the connection between things they learn and their use in real life.

Furthermore, computers are an object that can be used in many ways related to the personal needs of each student. For example, some students may learn better by searching for information, as we described, while others may need multimedia information in order to assimilate the concepts. It is obvious that in such cases the most appropriate and efficient way for learning is working in groups, where all the students can contribute.

Thus, careful design of courses from the teachers' side may offer significant advantages in learning procedure. Unfortunately, many classrooms do not work that way. Pencil, paper, lecture, textbook, review, and test are still the norm. However, there are important attempts that show us the road to the ubiquitous computing revolution. Some of these tries are presented in *Ubiquitous Computing Initiatives*.

In summary, ubiquitous computing environments provide portability, flexibility and efficiency for collaborative learning projects (Sottilo, 2003). Teachers have the ability to integrate computers to every aspect of teaching and learning.

Advantages – Disadvantages

In this point, it is necessary to describe all the advantages and disadvantages of the emerged technology. It is critical to identify these issues because it is a key to the road of the embodiment of computers in the learning procedure.

Some advantages are:

- **Teaching efficiency:** With the use of ubiquitous computing, teaching style has to change. Teachers must adapt their methods to the new environment. This active environment gives the opportunity for students to build their knowledge on their own. Therefore, it is imperative that teachers change their lessons plan in order to reflect the new situation. They will have the convenience to adjust the lessons to each student's needs and the lessons' goals. Educators can now implement a broader range of new approaches to learning that are proven to be more effective. Also, teachers must encourage and support their students more vigorously, due to the different nature of teaching.

- **Learning efficiency:** One of the most important findings in past years is that student engagement is one of the most critical factors to learning achievement. It is obvious the traditional teaching method has significant drawbacks for its efficiency. A teacher-centered class does not provide the opportunity for students to learn to build their knowledge through collaboration or experiments. Ubiquitous computing offers an environment where students use their devices to access a class from anywhere, collaborate with other students, experiment with appropriate software, and pose questions to their classmates or their teacher. This method is more productive because the knowledge is built on students' experiences. Students are more active in the course and their engagement is compulsory in order to achieve the goals that are posed to them. Hence, the traditional model is transformed to a student-centered model, where the teacher becomes a consultant to their students. The procedure that we described reflects the method of constructivist pedagogy.

- **Access to technology:** Today, there are many computers in schools placed at labs, but students do not have limitless and timeless access to them. Consider the scenario where all the students have their own device to access teaching resources either from their class or from their homes. In this scenario, all the students are fluent with the use of technology. This is a very attractive idea because in such a class students are technologically equal. This equality can be allocated in the use of technology. In past years, there was a gap in technology access that translated into inequalities in different fields among people. This is known as "Digital Divide" (Digital Divide.org, 2005). Now, each student has a device and limitless access to digital information augmenting their productivity. The new technology gives more opportunities to students from previously disadvantaged groups. Also, research has shown that giving students a personal device can make learning more efficient (Vahey et al., 2002). Students become more autonomous and self-directed in their learning.

- **Easy to use:** Today's children are familiar with technology, especially with games. Gameboys™, Playstations™, and even computers are used for gaming. Thereby, it is easy to provide learning devices to students for their use. Of course, instructions must be given to them for the right use of the tools in order to avoid problems from inappropriate use, as we see below. Students want personal devices that, like a toy, are easy to operate.

- **Productivity:** With the emerged technology students can raise their productivity. This is because they build their knowledge based on techniques that are proven by research to give better results. Students become active, taking initiatives and working with their own pace. Also, the interaction with classmates of whom they share common interests plays an important role in the learning process. Finally, we must note that in such cases experimentation is another factor that builds knowledge. Students have boundless access to the Internet or to specific software, and may perform their own tasks with their devices or search information in various resources, such as the Internet or digital databases, and so forth.

- **Portability:** Students, during their time spent in schools, must be familiarized with tools, software, and devices that differ due to the different architecture of each computer. Computers are used mainly in labs devoted to a specific lesson. They spend significant time learning the use of each device and applications that detaches them from the actual learning activity. With their personal devices, they can focus on the learning procedure without worrying about the differences between various tools and applications. They can connect to the network from any place at any time.

Just like all the other domains of technology, ubiquitous computing has some drawbacks. These drawbacks must be taken into consideration by educational policy makers, and by the implementers of this technology, in order to anticipate and avoid problems that may appear in the implementation phase.

- **Cost:** Initiatives such as ubiquitous computing in education, where every student will have their own device in order to perform tasks, have a cost, detected at two points. The first is the financial cost. The provision of a big amount of devices is very costly, but, of course, their prices are reduced as the technology evolves, making them affordable. On the other hand, there is cost in the transformation of the traditional system into the new. A lot of things must change, such as the lesson plan, the teaching style, and the assessments model. This requires much effort from the teachers and the policy makers. It is important to note that the new model requires a careful design of all the teaching parts because in this environment students will be able to act freely.

- **Teachers' Expertise:** This kind of program needs teachers' expertise with the technology and with the design of the new kinds of lessons. Teachers must be fluent with this type of education. There is a fear that they will not know how to use the technology and how to design their lessons. Also, there is a possibility that they may not use the technology in their teaching methodology in an appropriate way. A solution to these problems is to further educate teachers in coping with the new situation.

- **Inappropriate use of Technology:** There is a fear that students may use the electronic devices with which they are provided inappropriately. For this reason measures must be taken. A lot of programs have the mechanisms to control the network access in order to avoid problems. Firewalls are in the front line of security. With them the administrators can check the traffic and discover the cases that are dangerous to students, and even more, to the system.

- **Equipment damage:** Devices are basic elements in ubiquitous computing environments. They are means for access in information sources. Also they are used for communication purposes. Communication and collaboration are the keys to succeed with the pedagogical goals we described in *Pedegogical Goals*. Hence, problems will arise when technical inefficiencies occur. In such cases, technical support is important for the program's success; otherwise the participants' faith may be unsettled.

All these advantages and disadvantages must be taken into consideration from the policy makers, and a specific policy must be set up according to each case's characteristics.

Ubiquitous Computing Initiatives

This section will present some initiatives and tools originating from all over the world. Of course, it is impossible to present all the efforts. A full list of the schools that apply the laptop initiative is available at *http://etc.usf.edu/L4L/A-Review.html*. Additional information about all programs in each state of the United States is given at *http://www.k12one2one.org/initiatives.cfm?initID=97*. We present some of them, in order to describe basic characteristics of ubiquitous computing in education. We must note that most of them originate in the United States, where first attempts appeared in the late 90s. Tools for a learning environment's construction are also presented. All these initiatives are being held in elementary schools or universities. The common characteristic between them is that the majority use portable devices (see *Connection Means*) with wireless access to the network. On their Web sites, evaluations are given for every one of the programs in order to discern their results and identify the advantages and disadvantages. However, it is commonly the conviction that the use of a computing environment in which the students complete their tasks, offers positive remarks in learning procedure, augmenting the enhancement and engagement of the pupils.

Ulysses

This is an effort from the University of Laval, in Quebec, Canada (Mantha, 2001). All the students and teachers are provided with a laptop. In the academic year 2001-2002, there were approximately 1800 laptops in the school. Students and teachers invested money to buy the devices. In Ulysses, the laptop is to a large extent a communication tool, and thus there is a need to be able to connect to the network. The connection is established in the classrooms, in the cafeteria, in hallways, and so forth. For financial reasons, the system uses wired connections to the network. There are 17 wired classrooms, of which 11 have the U shape. There are 6 classrooms with movable tables with network connections on the periphery of the room, allowing the grouping of tables for team work. In every classroom there is a console in which one can find a computer and multimedia tools. An intranet was developed to store all the material needed for courses, like exercises, examples, and so forth. Tools used for communication are e-mail, forums, course management utilities, and Athena. Athena is a tool with which the instructor is able to poll the class in a small amount of time and get the students' opinion about a question. The answers can be short texts, yes/no or a selection in a multiple choice question. Also, the instructor can display the answers on the projection surface at the front of the class. This capability may be very useful in the teaching process.

For user support, two helpdesks were set up. There is a technical helpdesk and a pedagogical. The first is responsible for hardware and software problems. Common issues encountered are computer parts replacement, systems configuration, network connection parameterization, or systems and applications installation. The second helpdesk is responsible for answering questions concerning the use of technology from teachers and students in a pedagogical setting. There are a lot of means to access this support center. One can get support from the desk, from the Web site, over the phone, or via e-mail. This center can help tutors find and apply new means of uses of technology in their lessons.

eFusion

This system consists of an initiative of the University of Illinois that originated in the spring of 2002 (Peiper, Warden, Chan, Capitanu, & Kamin, 2005). eFuzion is an interactive classroom learning environment where all students and teachers have access to computing devices inside and outside the class. During the lesson, educators present their notes and examples with the help of presentation tools that eFusion provides. Consequently, teachers send their notes to students' devices through a wireless network and students may make their remarks in presentations and store them for future access. The system supports interactive newsgroups and communication tools that give the opportunity for students to communicate with their instructors or their assistants and take answers during a lecture or asynchronously at a later time.

The most important part of the system is the facility for incorporation of active learning exercises into the lectures, giving instructors a mean to see the comprehension level of the learners in real time. As we understand, it is about a system that has the ability to facilitate teachers to diagnose their students' needs in a real-time manner during lectures. This is a critical factor because, based on results taken from quizzes or other forms of questions, instructors may change the teaching methodology in order to achieve a better comprehension level.

WIL/MA Toolkit

This is a toolkit written in Java and initiated by the University of Mannheim *(http://www.lecturelab.de/UCE_4.html)*. It is a client-server application, where a server provides connection management, user management, and service management. The first supports the establishment of a connection to the users and gives the capability for administrators to monitor the entire communication in and out from the server. The second is used for user identification and authentication. Finally, the service management unit is responsible to inform users of what services are available and also to control data flow.

The system is based on wired connections, but in order to avoid extensive use of cables, students are able to connect to the network with wireless LAN. The devices used by the students are PocketPCs. On the other hand, teachers are able to publish their material, which can be presentations, slides, or files, and furthermore, they can broadcast image and voice to remote places. During their lectures, teachers can also use tools like call-in (spontaneous questions), or quiz and feedback (from the students in real time). Asynchronous tolls are messaging and chat/forum channels.

University of Texas

In 2002, the University of Texas initiated a requirement for all teacher education students to obtain a prescribed laptop and software for use throughout their academic preparation (Resta & Tothero, 2005). The goal is the preparation of a new generation of teachers who would be able to use new tools and practices in their teaching. This program's vision is to prepare the future teachers to enhance their future students to learn in technologically rich classrooms. Its official name is LIFE (Laptop Initiative for Future Educators).

All the students are provided with laptops and software that meet specific requirements, and wireless access to network in their classrooms or throughout the building. The involvement with the technology creates two critical needs. The first is the need to train the students to use the new hardware and software tools. For this reason, in the start of every semester, workshops are offered to familiarize new students with the systems and applications. The second is the need for technical support. For this, a Students Laptop Helpdesk was established. It provides equipment, supplies, and instruction for both students and teachers.

Maine Public Schools

This is one of the first programs that try to embody ubiquitous computing in education and is considered the single largest 1 to 1 educational technology program in the world *(http://www.maine.gov/portal/education/educ_tech.html)*. It is a project of the Maine Department of Education. Every 7th and 8th grade student and teacher has a wireless laptop with a rich set of software. Students have the capability to work with word processing, spreadsheet creation, movie processing, e-mail clients, Internet browsing, and other multimedia software. Also, students can take laptops to their home, where they can have access to the network. There are now 37.000 laptops in Maine's 239 middle level schools. Additionally, there is a small group of educators, educational technologists producing research, documentation, evaluation, and advocacy of 1 to 1 learning. Evaluations have shown that student engagement and attendance are up and behaviour referrals are down (Silvernail, Harris, Lane, Fairman, Gravelle, Smith et al., 2003). The most prominent result is that parents can see this positive effect on their children's behaviour. The key to the success of this program is to focus on the initiatives as a computer enhanced learning procedures and not merely as technical training. The technology initiatives must focus on teaching and learning, and not on technology, in order to be successful (Schacter, 1995).

Recently, there was an agreement to upgrade the hardware and software tools. The most important change is the wireless network transition to Airport Extreme 801.11g, giving a 54 Mbps speed and improving performance.

Vermont Public Schools

This is an initiative developed by the Vermont Department of Education *(http://www. k12one2one.org/www.oakgrove.k12.vt.us)*. Vermont teachers and students have access to ubiquitous technology, which is available on an "as needed" basis. The results of the first year of the program were:

- Teachers were more comfortable with implementing more technology integrated lessons.
- Students were better organized.
- Students created better quality work.
- Students experimented with various tools.
- An impact on student learning because of the full access to the technology.

All the teachers and students are provided with laptops, with which they can have access to the network and to various software tools. They may process text, databases, spreadsheets, video, music, or even more images. Finally, Web browsing and communication tools are available.

New Hampshire Schools

This attempt concerns all the 7th grade students in six of the state's neediest schools *(http://www.nhadvantage.com/laptop.htm)*. Approximately 400 students participated in the program the first year. All these students are provided with a laptop and wireless network access. Additionally, cameras, printers, and videoconferencing tools are available to students and teachers. Teachers can control the children's laptops during classes while students do their assignments. The analysis of the results concerning the first year evaluation indicates many of the most frequently cited benefits of 1 to 1 computing, such as: increased involvement with technology from both teachers and students, increased student engagement, achievement, and motivation, and improved interactions between teachers and students.

Talbot County Public Schools

This is a laptop initiative in which all pupils hold a portable device with which they can cope with school tasks. This project has four goals, which are:

- Increased student achievement
- Effective technology for instruction
- Increased student engagement in the learning process
- Improved educational access for and participation by high-risk students and their parents

The program's drift derives from classroom observations, teacher competencies identified by National Education Technology Standards (NETS) for teachers, lesson plans that utilize technology, and examining students' work and performances.

Computers were provided to each ninth grade student at the beginning of the 2005-06 school year *(http://www.tcps.k12.md.us/index.php?page=1_to_1_laptop_initiative)*. Teachers were given extensive training on the computers and on instructional software.

Students have access to network from any place, in school or at home. Also, a helpdesk is available to students for technical and insurance issues.

Alexandria City Public Schools

The Alexandria City Public Schools High School Technology Integration Project provides a 1 to 1 computing environment for all students in grades 9-12 *(http://www.acps.k12.va.us/tip/index.php)*. A laptop is provided to each student, who has the opportunity to keep the device for the duration of the school year. Students have access to a wireless network with which they can access resources and material useful for their tasks. A set of applications is installed on laptops that is useful for common tasks like word processing, as well as a variety of teaching material and applications. Teachers can leave their material in a students' server, enhancing the electronic exchange of information. In this server, students have personal work folders where they can store their assignments. Printing support is available for students and teachers. Finally, we must note that for the program's support, there is a help desk that is responsible for repairing damages.

Hopkins Public Schools

This pilot program involves approximately 600 students and 30 staff members. The program's goals are to enhance student's achievement and engagement. Each student owns a laptop with which to complete his or her assignments. Teachers can give their files and presentations in electronic mode *(http://weblogs.hopkins.k12.*

mn.us/onetoone/). Students having wireless access can take the material and, using software like office, Web browsing tools, database, video, music, image processing, and communication software, can cope with their commitments. It is worthwhile to mention that students cannot have access to the Internet from their homes except in the cases that the family has its own Internet provider. Technical support is provided on a full-time basis.

Other Areas in the United States

There are laptop initiatives in 30 states in the United States *(http://www.k12one2one. org/initiatives.cfm?initID=97)*. These states are:

Alaska	Iowa
Arizona	Kansas
Arkansas	Maine
California	Massachusetts
Connecticut	Michigan
Florida	Minnesota
Georgia	Missouri
Illinois	New Hampshire
Indiana	New Jersey

These programs either came as district or school initiatives. Like the previously described examples, they are programs that offer wireless access from portable devices to their students and teachers. The goals and the characteristics of these programs are the same as we described in the previous cases.

Kaifu School – Hamburg

The project started in 1999 and lasted until 2003, and it is among the first in Europe *(http://www.hamburgmediaschool.com/pages/p118328_v1.html)*. Since then, the school chose to continue using portable devices in three classes. However, the entire effort is characterized as positive. All the students were provided with wireless laptops and specialized software. Students that continue this program are specialized in organizing themselves and in learning to use technology, which was the goal of the project.

Minervaskolan School

Since 1999, pupils in Minervaskolan have used laptops with wireless access to the network *(http://www.minervaskolan.se/)*. The program's technical specifications are similar to the others as we described. The most important is that from the project's evaluation students' non-attendance approaches to zero and scores to national tests are remarkable. Also, students' grades appear to be to a continuous increment advocating to the program's success. Now, Minervaskolan is one of the top schools in Sweden.

Case Study: The Maine Learning Technology Initiative – Teacher, Student, and School Perspectives, Mid-Year Evaluation Report

In this section, we synoptically show the results taken from the evaluation of the Maine learning technology initiative (Sirvenail et al., 2003). Three core areas are investigated: Teachers and teaching, students and learning, and schools and community. In order to derive useful conclusions for each area, specific questions were posed. The goal of these questions is to identify the impact, the use, and the obstacles of the technology. Therefore, there are three key questions.

- How are the laptops being used?
- What are the impacts of the laptops on teachers, students, and schools?
- Are there obstacles to full implementation of the initiative?

We give a short presentation of the evaluation results with regard to each core area.

The evidence in the area of teachers and teaching indicates that the majority of teachers use their laptops in lesson development and classroom instruction. They utilize their devices to prepare and present their lessons. Of course, they agree that the use of the merged technology has positive impacts on their teaching. Now, they are aware of up-to-date information critical to present a meaningful course. On the other hand, they see an obstacle to this effort concerning the technical support. They feel that technical problems and the lack of technical support sometimes limit the use of laptops. This is a critical factor for the program's success. They also felt that they need time to learn the new technology and its applications and professional development activities designed to help them in the teaching process. Of course, time must be given in order to overcome the limitations.

Students report that they use their laptops to complete tasks, to search for information sources, and to communicate with teachers and classmates. More importantly, they feel an increase in the benefits of their work, both in and out of school. The new technology has increased their interest in school activities, but there are some problems in coping with technical difficulties.

Positive impacts of the application of new technology in learning procedure are recognized from the school community. The difference in children's interest is visible to their parents. Financial matters are obstacles to this effort, but through creative solutions many schools find ways to minimize the overall cost.

As we have seen, there are many positive impacts in introducing these new technologies to education. Teaching focuses on students' generating a new environment, where learning comes from collaboration, experimentation, and research. At the same time there are obstacles, especially in technical support, that in time will be eliminated.

Conclusion

Ubiquitous computing changes the field of education. It offers a timeless access to information resources and allows learning methods that are difficult to apply in traditional classrooms. Research has shown it has positive impacts on students' learning. Also, a lot of advantages exist in teaching, and school communities see these positive impacts of the new technology.

In order to integrate computers in education smoothly, careful design is necessary. The focus must be on the pedagogy and not on technology. This is because the final goal is to accomplish a high level of learning. For this reason, we speak about technology enhanced learning, and not about technical training.

Ubiquitous or pervasive computing has significant advantages over traditional teaching methods, and we must work on them to reach the desired results.

References

Apple Computer, Inc. (n.d.). *Why 1 to 1 learning*. Retrieved October 11, 2006, from http://www.apple.com/education

Bayon, V., Rodden, T., Greenhalgh, C., & Benford, S. (2002, August 26-28). Going back to school: Putting a pervasive environment into the real world. *Pervasive*, 69-84. Zurich, Switzerland.

Becker, H., & Riel, M. (2000). *Teacher professional engagement and constructive-compatible computer usage* (Report No. 7). Irvine, CA: Teaching, Learning, and Computing. Retrieved October 11, 2006, from www.crito.uci.edu/tlc/findings/report7

Bonifaz, A., & Zucker, A. (2004). *Lessons learned about providing laptops for all students.* Retrieved December 18, 2006 from http://www.neirtec.org/laptop/LaptopLessonsRprt.pdf

Deters, R. (2001, May 19-23). Pervasive computing devices for education. In *Proceedings of the International Conference on AI and Education* (pp. 49-54), San Antonio, Texas.

Diggs, C. (2004, May). *The effect of palm pilots on student learning in the elementary classroom.* Retrieved October 11, 2006, from http://www.successlink.org/handheld/PalmInHand.pdf

Digital Divide.org (2005). *Digital divide: What it is and why it matters.* Retrieved December 18, 2006 from http://www.digitaldivide.org/dd/digitaldivide.html

Eagleton, M. (1999, April). *The benefits and challenges of a student-designed school Web site.* Retrieved October 11, 2006, from http://www.readingonline.org

Educational Research Service. (2001). *Does technology improve student achievement?* Retrieved October 11, 2006, from http://www.ers.org

Fullan, M. (1999). *Change forces: The sequel.* London: Farmer Press.

International Society for Technology in Education (ISTE) (2002). *Essential conditions to make it happen.* Retrieved December 18, 2006 from http://cnets.iste.org/students/s_esscond.html

Mantha, R.W. (2001, May 4-6). Ulysses: Creating a ubiquitous computing learning environment sharing knowledge and experience in implementing ICTs in universities. *EUA / IAU / IAUP Round Table*, Skagen, Denmark.

McKenzie, J. (2001, January). The unwired classroom: Wireless computers come of age. *The Educational Technology Journal, 10*(4). Retrieved October 11, 2006, from http://www.fno.org/jan01/wireless.html

Muir, M. (2005). *Laptops for learning: The Maine Learning Technology Initiative.* Joint publication in the Middle Level newsletters of Association of Childhood Education International (ACEI) and of the National Association of Elementary School Principals (NAESP).

Peiper, C., Warden, D., Chan, E., Capitanu, M., Kamin, S. (2005, June 27-29). eFuzion: Development of a pervasive educational system. In *Proceedings of the*

10ᵗʰ Annual SIGCSE Conference on Innovation and Technology in Computer Science Education (pp. 237-240). Caparica, Portugal.

Resta, P., & Tothero, M. (2005). Establishing a ubiquitous computing environment for teacher preparation students and faculty. In S. Powers & K. Janz (Eds.), *Ubiquitous and pervasive computing in higher education*. Terre Haute, Indiana: Indiana State University Curriculum Research and Development Center.

Schacter, J. (1995). *The impact of educational technology on student achievement. The Milken Exchange on Educational Technology*. Retrieved October 11, 2006, from http://www.mff.org/publications/publications.taf?page=161

Silvernail, D.L., Harris, W.J., Lane, D., Fairman, J., Gravelle, P., Smith, L., et al. (2003, March). *The Maine learning technology initiative: Teacher, student, and school perspectives mid-year evaluation report.* Maine Education Policy Research Institute.

Smith, T. (2002). *Strategic factors affecting the uptake, in higher education, of new and emerging technologies for learning and teaching.* York: Technologies Centre. Retrieved October 11, 2006, from www.techlearn.ac.uk/NewDocs/HEDriversFinal.rtf

Sottilo, S. (2003, May-June). *Pedagogical advantages of ubiquitous computing in a wireless environment.* The Technology Source Archives. Retrieved October 11, 2006, from http://ts.mivu.org/default.asp?show=article&id=1034

Stiles, M. (2002, September 10-11). Strategic and pedagogic requirements for virtual learning in the context of widening participation. In *Proceedings of the Nirtual Learning & Higher Education Conference,* Oxford, UK.

Sutherland, A. (2002). *Strategic factors affecting the uptake, in further education, of new and emerging technologies for learning and teaching.* Retrieved October 11, 2006, from http://www.techlearn.ac.uk/cgi-bin/docspec.pl?l=83

Vahey, P., Enyedy, N., & Gifford, B. (2000). Learning probability through the use of a collaborative, inquiry-based simulation environment. *Journal of Interactive Learning Research, 11*(1), 51-84.

Appendix I: Useful URLs

Ubiquitous Computing Information

http://nano.xerox.com/hypertext/weiser/UbiHome.html

Notes on Ubiquitous Computing

http://hci.stanford.edu/cs147/notes/ubicomp.html

Ubiquitous Computing Applications

http://www-lce.eng.cam.ac.uk/~kr241/html /101_ubicomp.html

Ubiquitous Computing Research Activities

http://ubicomp.teco.edu/index2.html

Ubiquitous Computing Evaluation Consortium

http://www.ubiqcomputing.org/ lit_review.html

Ubiquitous Computing Education

http://www.ubqed.info/

IEEE Pervasive Computing - A catalyst for advancing research and practice in ubiquitous computing

http://www.computer.org/portal/site/pervasive//

Chapter V

Using Multimedia and Virtual Reality for Web-Based Collaborative Learning on Multiple Platforms

Gavin McArdle, University College Dublin, Ireland

Teresa Monahan, University College Dublin, Ireland

Michela Bertolotto, University College Dublin, Ireland

Abstract

Since the advent of the Internet, educators have realised its potential as a medium for teaching. The term e-learning has been introduced to describe this Internet-based education. Although e-learning applications are popular, much research is now underway to improve the features they provide. For example, the addition of synchronous communication methods and multimedia is being studied. With the introduction of wireless networks, mobile devices are also being investigated as a medium to present learning content. Currently, the use of 3-dimensional (3D) graphics is being explored for creating virtual learning environments online. Virtual reality (VR) is already being used in multiple disciplines for teaching various tasks. This chapter focuses on describing some VR systems, and also discusses the current state of e-learning on mobile devices. We also present the VR learning environment that we have developed, incorporating many of the techniques mentioned above for both desktop and mobile devices.

Inside Chapter

E-learning has become an established medium for delivering online courses. Its popularity is mainly due to the convenience and flexibility it provides for users, allowing them to learn without time or location restrictions. Many different e-learning systems are currently available, the majority of which are text-based and allow users to contact the course tutor via electronic mail or discussion forums. These courses essentially offer access to a common pool of resources that allow users to gain knowledge and often qualifications. Researchers are now exploring new ways of making the online learning experience more engaging and motivating for students. Multimedia and communication technologies are being added, and together with 3D graphics, are fast emerging as a means of creating an immersive online learning experience. With the advent of mobile technologies, m-learning is showing promise as an accompaniment to online courses, offering the prospect of a modern and pervasive learning environment.

This chapter discusses the benefits 3D environments offer the e-learning community. We outline how this type of system emerged and describe some currently available systems using these new technologies. In particular, we describe in detail our own virtual reality environment for online learning and the features it provides. We discuss the extension of this system to a mobile platform so that users have anytime, anywhere access to course materials. Finally, we put forward some thoughts on future technologies and discuss their possible contribution to the development of a truly ubiquitous and pervasive learning environment.

Introduction

Distance learning has gone through a number of iterations since its introduction in the 1800s. The notion of distance learning grew mainly out of necessity, and helped to overcome geographical, economical, and cultural barriers that prevented people from partaking in traditional classroom-based education. Over the years a number of distance learning applications have emerged to address these issues. The evolution of such systems can be clearly linked to the technological developments of the time. This chapter focuses on giving a brief overview of the changes in distance learning from its inception to today, before concentrating on the distance learning technologies currently in use. We provide details of how the latest technologies and demand from students have led to the development of 3-dimensional (3D) e-learning systems. We also look to the future, suggesting what the next generation of technology can bring to distance learning. We pay particular attention to the need for ubiquitous and pervasive means of e-learning, and in doing so describe our own system, which uses state of the art technologies to deliver learning material to students both on a desktop computer and while they are on the move.

In the background section, we describe how distance learning has evolved from a simple postal service offered by universities to a sophisticated tool that utilises the convenience of the Internet. As the discussion progresses toward the introduction of 3D graphical environments to distance learning applications, the origins of 3D graphics and their uses are also presented. Multi-user environments for distance

Figure 1. Chapter overview

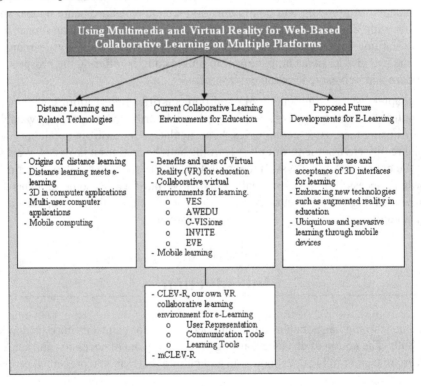

education is a major area of research at present, and so the latter part of the section provides a synopsis of the history of multi-user computer applications. We also present a brief discussion on the current uses of mobile technologies, which are now emerging as promising tools for e-learning.

In the main section of this chapter, we describe how recent technological advancements and requirements of students and tutors have led to a new breed of computer-based learning systems utilising the latest 3D graphics and communication tools. We detail a number of such systems outlining their strengths and weaknesses, in particular the system we are developing, which attempts to address some of these weaknesses. We describe how it uses the latest technologies to deliver a collaborative multi-user 3D learning system to students at fixed computer terminals and mobile devices. Finally we hypothesise how the current use of augmented reality (AR) technologies can be adapted to form a truly ubiquitous and pervasive learning environment. A summation and discussion of the chapter is provided in the concluding section.

Background

This section gives the reader an overview of how distance learning has evolved from its early days as correspondence courses to the modern Internet based learning solution. It also charts the progression of computer-based 3D and multi-user tools, hinting at how they can be combined to form a new type of distance learning system. This new learning paradigm is made all the more powerful when combined with the latest mobile technologies, and a short overview of this emerging technology is provided below. Figure 2 provides an overview of the literature reviewed in this chapter, while Figures 3 and 4 highlight the main points of discussion in each subsection.

A Brief History of Distance Learning

Distance learning is a form of education that has emerged out of necessity. It is not always possible for a student and instructor to be present at the same location at the same time. Distance learning is not a new concept, and has been in use since the 1800s. Today, it can take a wide variety of forms, including correspondence courses, video and radio broadcasts, and e-learning. One of the earliest forms of distance learning was a correspondence course. Traditionally, these courses were a form of home study. Students receive printed or written course material via the postal service, complete assignments, and return them to their tutor for appraisal. These courses were later augmented with different types of media. For example, the Open University (2005) offered lectures on audio and video cassettes in the 1980s.

Figure 2. Background

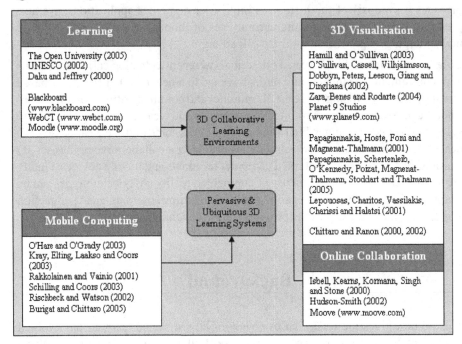

Figure 3. Progression of distance learning

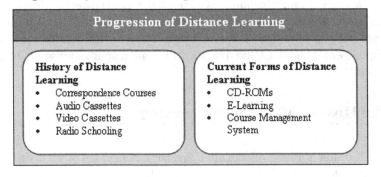

One major drawback of this form of distance education was the lack of interaction between student and teacher. Radio schooling provided a solution to this issue. Again, radio schooling is a form of home study, mainly used for primary and secondary education; pupils in remote locations can use a two-way radio to communicate with teachers and receive their assignments. This type of learning proved popular in Australia in the 1980s, and was particularly effective where large numbers of people lived in remote locations. Today it is being used in Africa to provide primary education for pupils in remote towns and villages (UNESCO, 2002). One of the key advantages radio schooling provided over the more traditional correspondence courses was the instant feedback between student and tutor. With the advancement of technology, this type of one-to-one distance education has now become much more attainable. Indeed, the advent and widespread growth of computer technology has introduced many additional communication and interactive features to distance learning, moving it forward into the realm of e-learning.

Distance Learning Meets E-Learning

E-learning is a term given to any form of learning which involves the use of an electronic medium to display learning material. Early forms of e-learning involved teachers demonstrating certain lessons to students through computer-based animations and simulations. CD-ROMs were then developed and soon became a popular accompaniment to textbooks. Students could use these CD-ROMs to further understand the book's content, and also as a study aid. Distance learning courses can also utilise this technology to distribute course material. The use of CD-ROMs means that the students' learning experience can be much more interactive and that learning content can be represented in different formats, including sound and video clips. For example, when studying historical events, news footage from the era can be displayed via the CD-ROM, helping to bring the learning material to life. CD-ROMs often provide interactive games (e.g., counting games) for younger students, helping them to improve their numerical skills. Automated quizzes provide instant feedback of a student's knowledge of a subject area. Daku and Jeffrey (2000) describe one such CD-ROM used for teaching, MATHLAB, a statistical application; it acts as a standalone tool for learning the functionality of MATHLAB. Experimental results have shown that students preferred learning using the CD-ROM rather than the traditional lecture/assignment format.

Over the last 10 years the popularity of the Internet as an information source has grown extensively. Its shear diffusion and convenience is ideal to disperse learning content for distance education. In general, Web sites are designed where tutors upload course material, including text, quizzes, and links to external knowledge sources. Registered students can then access this learning material and study it at their own pace. Course work can be submitted to the tutor using e-mail, and likewise students experiencing problems may contact tutors via e-mail. There are numerous examples of this type of distance learning system in use today. For example, the University of Colorado and the University of Illinois provide these kinds of courses. Indeed, many schools and universities now also use Web-based learning as an accompaniment to traditional classroom and lecture-based lessons.

Realising the importance and benefits of using the Internet for distance learning, much research is underway to improve the services and facilities that such learning portals can offer. Initially these Web sites were a mere bank of knowledge, simply providing the course material in HTML (Hyper Text Mark-up Language) format for students to access, read, and learn. Today, they are far more sophisticated. A number of successful companies have emerged which offer online course management tools for tutors to intuitively present course notes, lecture slides, and additional material online. All management, such as access rights and course registration, are provided by these applications. Blackboard (*www.blackboard.com*) is one such course management system, designed to facilitate teachers with the management of their online courses. It has been adopted as the e-learning platform by more than 2200 institutions, including Harvard University, the University of Maine, and the University College Dublin (Wikipedia, 2005). Web Course Tools (WebCT, *www.webct.com*) is another company involved in the provision of e-learning systems. Founded in 1995, it is currently the world's leading provider of e-learning systems, with institutes in over 70 countries relying on them for e-learning software. Like Blackboard, WebCT is an authoring environment for teachers to create online training courses. While these systems tend to be extremely costly, free systems with open source code have also been developed. Moodle (*www.moodle.org*) is one such learning system, which is in widespread use at institutions such as Dublin City University, University of Glasgow, and Alaska Pacific University, and looks like becoming the industry standard. Development of Moodle has been ongoing since 1999, and already it has a large user base. It offers a range of software modules that enable tutors to create online courses. One area that Moodle tries to address is the need for pedagogical support; this aspect is largely neglected in commercially available applications. In particular it promotes the notion of constructionist learning, where a student learns from his or her own experiences, resulting in a student-centred learning environment.

The current state of e-learning, and in particular distance learning, has been outlined above. Following the success of computers as a learning tool, much research is underway to enhance a user's learning environment. In particular, one area that is being researched is the use of 3D graphics in these systems. It is the examination of the use of 3D graphics and multimedia, combined with collaborative tools and mobile technologies within e-learning, that forms the focus of this chapter. The remainder of this section provides a brief description of the use of 3D graphics on computers, from their early days in computer games to its current role in visualisation. We also examine the emergence of 3D graphics on mobile devices such as personal digital assistants (PDAs). This section gives an insight into the previous use of collaboration tools and multi-user interaction on computers before the next section gives a detailed review of learning systems utilising these technologies.

3D, Collaborative, and Mobile Technologies

3D Computer Applications

For some time, 3D graphics have been an established means of entertainment, in particular within computer games. In 1993, ID Software released Doom, a first person shooter computer game. Like its predecessor Wolfenstein, 3D released in 1992, Doom was built using pseudo-3D, where images placed on a 2D plane give the impression of a 3D environment. The immersive game environment included advanced features such as stereo sound and multilevel environments with increased interaction for players. The popularity of these games and the 3D paradigm led to a succession of immersive 3D computer games using this formula, and ultimately led to the worldwide acceptance of this form of immersive environment. As technology improved, the complexity of the graphics used in such computers games increased. Today in games such as Half-Life, developed by Value Software, users take on roles of characters in stories with life-like scenes. Add-ons enable multi-user support for players to interact with each other in the game, although they may be geographically distant.

Another domain where 3D has been used for a long time is modelling; in particular engineering and architectural models can be effectively and efficiently modelled on a computer using 3D graphics. AutoCAD, developed by AutoDesk, is a computer aided drafting software application first developed in 1982 for use by mechanical engineers. It allows both 2D and 3D representation of objects to be rendered and has fast become the industry standard. This form of modelling objects enables designers

Figure 4. 3D, collaborative, and mobile technologies

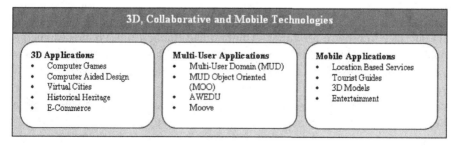

and customers to see how objects will look before they are built. Today property developers often produce 3D Virtual Reality (VR) models of houses in order to entice prospective buyers. This can be taken one step further as developers produce models of how new builds will affect the aesthetics of an area. Another area of interest in the research arena is that of modelling cities. Hamill and O'Sullivan (2003) describe their efforts in producing a large-scale simulation of Dublin City. The goal of their research is to allow users to navigate freely around the streets of Dublin. The city can be used as a test-bed for related work, such as simulating crowds in virtual environments (O'Sullivan, Cassell, Vilhjálmsson, Dobbyn, Peters, Leeson, et al, 2002). Zara, Benes, and Rodarte (2004) have produced a model of the old Mexican city of Campeche. This Internet-based application acts as a tourist aid and promotes the area as a tourist attraction. The area of urban modelling has much commercial interest. Planet 9 Studios (*www.planet9.com*), based in San Francisco and set up in the early 1990s, produces accurate and intricate 3D urban models for use in such diverse activities as homeland defence, military training, and tourism. It is tourism that has long been a driving force behind much of the development of the VR cities and has also led to a number of similar applications aimed at visitors and tourists. MIRALabs in Geneva have been investigating the area of virtual heritage. Much of this research focuses on enabling realistic models of historical sites to be created efficiently and in a means suitable for use on basic machines (Papagiannakis, Hoste, Foni, & Magnenat-Thalmann, 2001). Today, the work of MIRALab in the field of historical reconstructions involves the use of mixed realities; that is, augmenting real-world sites with VR 3D models of people and artefacts that would have once been there (Papagiannakis, Schertenleib, O'Kennedy, Poizat, Magnenat-Thalmann, Stoddart, et al, 2005). The benefits of using VR to host exhibitions in museums are outlined by Lepoursas, Charitos, Vassilakis, Charissi, and Halatsi (2001), where details on designing, such an exhibition, are also provided.

Several of the projects mentioned above use special features to allow users to interact with the environment. Often the environment acts as a 3D-Graphical User Interface (GUI) to access underlying information. E-commerce or purchasing products and services using Web sites on the Internet have long been popular. The number of people buying through this medium has increased dramatically over the last five years. According to Johnson, Delhagen, and Yuen (2003), online retail in the United States alone will have reached $229.9 billion by 2008, and so this is a natural area for researchers to investigate. While research has contributed to many improvements in this form of shopping, one area that is still emerging is the use of a 3D interface to browse for goods. Chittaro and Ranon (2002) have designed a virtual environment mimicking a traditional supermarket, where virtual products are placed on virtual shelves. Users navigate the store, selecting items they wish to purchase. They argue that this is a more natural way for consumers to shop online because it is more familiar to shoppers compared to lists of available items. These 3D department stores can be tailored and personalised to an individual user (Chittaro & Ranon, 2000). This can involve personalising the look and feel of the environment and user profiling to position relevant items in prominent positions. The extension of this 3D store paradigm to a multi-user platform is also discussed and proposed, where a number of shoppers are present in the one store. This, however, has drawbacks and provides difficultly in adapting the store for individuals. The next section provides a synopsis of the origins of multi-user computer applications and provides some details of their current uses.

Multi-User Applications

One of the earliest forms of multi-user interactivity using computers took the form of multi-user domains, known as MUDs. MUDs first appeared in 1978, and being primarily used for computer gaming purposes, quickly became popular. In a MUD, a text-based description of an environment is provided, with each user taking on the role of a character in that environment. Interaction with the system and with other users is achieved by typing commands in a natural language. Usually a fantasy game featuring goblins and other creatures, the purpose was to navigate through the virtual environment, killing as many demons as possible. While initially developed for entertainment, people saw the possibility of using this technology for other purposes, notably as a form of distance learning and as a means of virtual conferences. This move away from the use of MUDs for gaming led to the developments of a MOO (MUD Object Orientated) at the University of Waterloo in 1990. Again, MOO systems are text-based virtual environments, which were initially an academic form of a MUD. Isbell, Kearns, Kormann, Singh, and Stone (2000) discuss LambdaMoo, one of the longest running MOOs, created by Pavel Curtis in 1990. Today, it offers a social setting for connected users to engage in social interaction with similar functionality to that found in a chat room or online communities.

Improvements in technologies, along with increases in Internet connection speeds, have enabled a move away from the traditional text-based environments to more graphical-based communities. These communities, such as Active Worlds (Hudson-Smith, 2002), offer the same interaction as chat rooms. However, the rooms are designed as physical spaces complete with scenery and furniture. Each user is shown on-screen in the form of an avatar, a graphical representation visible to other users. A further extension of this type of environment is seen in the 3D online world of Moove (*www.moove.com*). Here, users maintain their own rooms in the 3D environment, which they can decorate to their own tastes and use to host chat sessions. Voice and video chat can also be used in many of the modern online 3D communities. In recent times, this type of 3D environment has been used for education, and this will be discussed later in this chapter.

Mobile Applications

In recent years, the use of mobile devices such as PDAs and cell phones has become prevalent, and this has led to a lot of research into providing applications on these devices. The widespread introduction of wireless networks has increased the use of these devices dramatically, and has helped fuel research in this area. People can now browse the Internet, send electronic mails (e-mails) and access their personal files while on the move. Many different applications have been developed for this mobile platform, the most popular of which utilise a global positioning system (GPS). These applications use a system of satellites and receiving devices to compute positions on the Earth, and therefore enable people to gain information relative to their position in the world. They are thus used mainly in providing location-based information to users, and in particular many tourist applications have been developed to help people find their way around foreign cities. For example, O'Hare and O'Grady (2003) have developed a context-aware tourist guide, which tracks a user's position and displays multimedia presentations for different attractions as the user approaches them. Their system uses images, videos, sound, and text to give the tourist information about the attraction. Kray, Elting, Laakso, and Coors (2003) developed an application to provide boat tourists with route instructions and information on services nearby.

A recent development in mobile technologies is the use of 3D graphics on these devices. Many large-scale 3D models have been successfully developed for use on laptop computers, but the challenge now is to extend these to smaller platforms, such as PDAs and even mobile phones. Rakkolainen and Vainio (2001) developed a Web-based 3D city model of Tampere and connected it to a database of relational information so that users can query the system about services available in the city. They customised it for mobile users by integrating a GPS receiver and have developed a fully working version for laptops. However, their 3D model is much too large to run on smaller devices such as PDAs, so they use only images and Web pages for these devices. Schilling and Coors (2003) have developed a system that provides a 3D map to help present route instructions to mobile users. In their model, landmarks and buildings of importance are visualised in detail through the use of textures, while less important buildings are rendered in grey. A user trial was carried out on a laptop running a mobile phone emulator. Results proved positive, with most users stating they would prefer to use the 3D maps than 2D paper maps and guidebooks. However, users did suggest that the 3D model should be more detailed and more realistic.

The major problem for extending these models to smaller mobile devices is their size in relation to processing power available, together with the users' desires for more detail and realism. Many researchers are exploring ways to achieve this using various culling techniques, parallelism, and information filtering (Burigat & Chittaro,

2005; Rischbeck & Watson, 2002). Smaller 3D models can, however, be displayed on smaller devices and are used in a variety of games on handheld devices and mobile phones, providing entertainment for their user. ParallelGraphics, a world leader in the provision of Web3D graphics solutions, describe uses of 3D for mobile devices, such as sales and marketing, real estate, and field maintenance.

The technologies presented in this section have been widely accepted by developers and computer users. As the next section shows, they have recently received attention from the educational research community. They show promise as a means of presenting learning material to students in an engaging and motivating way. A number of such systems using these technologies are presented in the following section before we discuss our own learning system, CLEV-R, which provides solutions to some of the issues that existing learning systems fail to address. In particular, the need for a range of communication and collaborative tools for both learning and socialising is dealt with. Also presented is a pervasive ubiquitous learning environment we developed for use on mobile devices as an accompaniment to the desktop system.

3D and Collaborative Virtual Environments for E-Learning and M-Learning

This section details the use of 3D as a learning aid. Firstly, we consider its use as a visualisation tool, and then discuss how multi-user technologies are being combined with 3D graphics to create effective online learning environments. We also discuss some current research into the provision of learning tools on mobile devices. Figure 5 provides an overview of the topics presented below.

3D Learning Tools

In addition to the uses of virtual reality (VR) and 3D graphics discussed in the previous section, these techniques have also been extended in various ways for use in education. The ability of these tools to model real-world objects and visualise complex data makes them an ideal learning tool. Users can explore these objects, interact with them, and discover their various features. Furthermore, the visualisation of complex data can greatly aid a person's comprehension of it. Thus, these models provide users with an intuitive way to learn about natural objects by presenting them in a visually appealing way. As such, many 3D resources for education have been developed, both for online and individual applications.

Scientific and engineering visualisations use VR to represent complex chemical structures and to present experimental data in a more visual manner in order to

Figure 5. 3D and collaborative virtual environments for e-learning and m-learning

3D and Collaborative Virtual Environments for E-Learning and M-Learning	
3D Learning Tools	**Collaborative 3D Learning Environments**
Virtual Laboratories: *Casher, Leach, Page & Rzepa (1998)* Introduction to laboratory equipment, displays complex chemical structures *Dalgarno (2002)* Introduce undergraduate students to laboratory procedures. **Medical Demonstrations:** *Ryan, O'Sullivan, Bell & Mooney (2004)* Teaching medical students through organ modelling. *Raghupathy, Grisoniz, Faurey, Marchalz, Cainy & Chaillouz (2004)* Preparing medical students to perform surgery. **Embodied Agents:** *Njholt (2000)* Demonstrate solving a problem for example, the Towers of Hanoi problem. *Rickel & Johnson (1997)* Demonstrate the use of a specific piece of equipment	**VES** *Bouras, Philopoulos & Tsiatsos (2001)* Interactive thematic rooms for teaching school children. **AWEDU** *Dickey (2003)* Web-based system where tutors can build an environment based on their requirements. **C-VISions** *Chee & Hooi (2002)* Interactive environment for teaching science and allowing students to conduct experiments **INVITE** *Bouras, Triantafiou & Tsiatsos (2001)* Supports collaborative on the job training for staff who may be geographically distant **EVE** *Bouras & Tsiatsos (2006)* Explores the used of shared training spaces for school children
Mobile Learning Environments	
European m-Learning Projects: *MOBIlearn* Research pedagogy in mobile learning environments *M-learning* Deliver learning content to young adults and particularly those who do not enjoy traditional education **3D Models:** *Lipman (2002)* Visualisation of structural steelwork models on construction sites *Zimmerman, Barnes & Leventhal (2003)* Teaching mobile users the art of origami	**Games:** *Ketamo (2002)* Teaches geometry to children in kindergarten who are experiencing difficulty with it *Göth, Hass & Schwabe (2004)* location-based game to help new students become familiar with the university *Luchini, Quintana & Soloway (2003)* Pocket PiCoMap – interactive tool that helps students to build concept maps

gain a better understanding of the results. Casher, Leach, Page, and Rzepa (1998) describe the use of VR for chemical modelling, and outline the advantages that animation can bring to these models. They also describe how a virtual laboratory can introduce students to various laboratory instruments. In addition, Dalgarno (2002) has developed a virtual chemistry laboratory that allows undergraduate students to become familiar with the layout of the labs, and also to learn about procedures to follow while in the laboratory. VR has more recently been introduced in the field of medical training. Its use varies from modelling different organs and allowing students to interact with them freely to developing training application for specific procedures. Examples include Raghupathiy, Grisoniz, Faurey, Marchalz, Caniy, and Chaillouz (2004), who developed a training application for the removal of colon cancer, and Ryan, O'Sullivan, Bell, and Mooney (2004), who explore the use of VR for teaching electrocardiography. The major advantage of using VR in medicine is that students can repeatedly explore the structures of interest and can interactively view and manipulate them. Real training cases can be hard to come by, and so this extra practice and experience can be invaluable. Also, patients are not put at risk by having inexperienced students carry out procedures on them.

3D models can also be particularly useful in teaching younger students. Many games have been developed using 3D images that the user must interact with in order to learn a certain lesson. Interactive models increase a user's interest and make learning more fun. 3D animations can be used to teach students different procedures and mechanisms for carrying out specific tasks. Some researchers have combined the benefits of 3D and software agent technologies to provide intelligent models to teach certain tasks. For example, Jacob is an intelligent agent in a VR environment that guides the user through the steps involved in solving the towers of Hanoi problem, as described by Nijholt (2000). By following the directions of Jacob, the users learn how to solve the problem themselves. Likewise, STEVE, described by Rickel and Johnson (1997, 1999), is an intelligent agent that has been developed for use in naval training to show individuals or groups of students how to operate and maintain complex equipment. STEVE can demonstrate certain tasks and then observe while users carry out these tasks, correcting them when mistakes are made.

Collaborative 3D Learning Environments

VR also allows for the development of complete virtual environments that users can "enter" and navigate through as if it was a real environment. The most immersive of these environments require the user to wear a head mounted display and tracking gloves, while other VR environments are displayed on desktop computers, where users interact through the mouse and keyboard. As shown in the previous section, virtual environments like these have evolved from computer games, but are fast emerging in other areas such as e-commerce, chat-rooms, and indeed education.

E-learning in particular is an ideal target for the development of an immersive VR environment. Here an entire VR environment is designed where all the learning takes place. This kind of system represents a shift in e-learning from the conventional text-based online learning environment to a more immersive and intuitive one. Since VR is a computer simulation of a natural environment, interaction with a 3D environment is much more intuitive than browsing through 2D Web pages looking for information. These environments tend to be multi-user, exploiting the notion of collaborative learning where students learn together. The benefits of collaborative learning have been researched extensively and are outlined in Laister and Kober (2002) and Redfern and Naughton (2002). The main advantage of this type of learning is that users no longer feel alone or isolated. This feeling of isolation can be particularly prevalent in online learning, where students do not attend actual classes or lectures. Thus, multi-user learning environments have proven very popular for online learning. The VES, AWEDU, C-VISions, EVE, and INVITE systems all concentrate on developing collaborative learning environments using VR to further immerse students in their learning. The following paragraphs outline the main features of these systems before we discuss our own research and what it has to offer.

In 1998, Bouras, Fotakis, Kapoulas, Koubek, Mayer, and Rehatscheck (1999) began research on virtual European schools (VES), the goal of which was to introduce computers to secondary school students and encourage teachers to use computers in the classroom. VES uses 3D to provide a desktop immersive environment. A different room in the 3D environment is used for each school subject, and these themed rooms provide information about the specific subject in the form of slide shows and animations, as well as links to external sources of information. The VES project was carried out in conjunction with book publishers, and these publishing houses provided much of the content that is displayed in the environment. VES is an example of a multi-user distributed virtual environment (mDVE). In an mDVE, more than one person can access the environment at the same time, and users are aware of one another. In the VES environment users can "talk" to each other using text chat facilities. The evaluation of VES took the form of questionnaires, which students and teachers completed. The results, which are presented in (Bouras, Philopoulos, & Tsiatsos, 2001) show that navigation in the 3D environment was difficult, the user interface was old fashioned, and there was not enough content to keep students amused and entertained. These points were taken on board and the system was improved. When launched, VES was used in 4 countries and had the cooperation of more that 20 publishers.

The Active Worlds Universe, a very popular and powerful Web-based VR experience, is a community of thousands of users that chat and build 3D VR environments in a vast virtual space. As discussed earlier, it provides thousands of unique worlds for shopping, chatting, and playing games. In 1999, an educational community known as the Active Worlds Educational Universe (AWEDU) was developed (Dickey, 2003).

This is a unique educational community that makes the Active Worlds technology available to educational institutions. Through this community, educators can build their own educational environment using a library of customisable objects, and can then place relevant learning material in their environment. Through these environments, users are able to explore new concepts and learning theories and can communicate using text-chat. Users are represented in the environment by avatars which help them feel better immersed in the educational environment. Students from all over the world can be connected through this system, and it therefore aids cultural sharing and social learning. The AWEDU environment is extremely versatile and may be used for a number of types of learning. Dickey (2003) presents the use of the environment as a form of distance education within the university. Riedl, Barrett, Rowe, Smith and Vinson, (2000) provide a description of a class held within the Active Worlds environment. The course was designed for training teachers on the integration of technology into the classroom. Nine students took part in the class; their actions and group discussions were recorded during their online sessions and, along with results from questionnaires, are presented in the paper. While the majority of students were pleased with the freedom the virtual environment offered, not all adapted to this new form of learning. The evaluation discovered that one of the major benefits of this type of learning was that students were aware of the presence of others in the shared environment and this interaction with others kept students interested and motivated.

C-VISions was launched in 2000, and is a collaborative virtual learning environment that concentrates on supporting science learning. The system presents learning stimuli that help school children understand fundamental concepts from chemistry, biology and physics. C-VISions encourages active learners; students can run science experiments in the virtual world and view the outcomes as they change simulation parameters. Chee and Hooi (2002) describe their physics environment and in particular the Billiard World, a simulation to help students learn about mass, velocity, acceleration, conservation of momentum, friction, and the coefficient of restitution. This world contains a billiard table with two balls and a cue stick. Users can interact with a number of "live" objects that are provided within the world. For example, the cue stick can be aimed at a ball and then used to strike it. Students can replay the most recent simulation and can view the plotting of graphs of that event synchronously. This helps the students see the relation between their action and how it is plotted on a graph. It therefore helps them to understand the graph representations. Users can navigate around the world and change their viewpoints using buttons provided. The system is multi-user, and so events happening in one user's environment are propagated to all other connected users. Users may share video resources, and shared electronic whiteboards are also provided. The system provides a Social World where students can mingle and student-student communication is supported through text and audio chat. Chee (2001) describes a preliminary evaluation of the first prototype of this system. The study revealed that all students found the system "an enjoyable way to learn" and each felt they gained a better sense of understanding about the subject matter. Some problems using the collaboration tools were highlighted. For example, students found it difficult to work together on group tasks. This was put down to inexperience using the tools. While this study was small, involving only three students, the results proved encouraging that this type of 3D environment has something to offer students.

In April 2000, a consortium of companies and institutions began research into the design and development of a multi-user 3D collaborative environment for training. The goal of the environment was to support group learning, in particular on-the-job training, without the need for all those involved to be in the same location at the same time. Moving away from the traditional videoconferences, this system known as INVITE, the Intelligent Distributed Virtual Training Environment, had a fundamental objective of making people feel that they are working as a group rather than alone in front of a computer. The technologies required for such a system are described by Bouras, Triantafillou, and Tsiatsos (2001), along with implementation issues of the multi-user architecture. The project focuses on the importance of a social presence and the general sense of belonging within a learning environment, presenting the notion of photo-realistic avatars as a way to achieve this. The system design allows synchronous viewing of e-learning content within the 3D environment through a presentation table. Users can see pictures, presentations, 3D objects and prerecorded videos simultaneously, and collaboration is provided through application sharing. An initial prototype of the system was developed, and a first evaluation showed that INVITE could be a powerful tool for collaborative learning with test-users enjoying learning in the virtual environment. The INVITE project terminated prematurely, and so the main contribution it made to the area of virtual learning environments was a detailed system specification and outline of features that should be included in such a system.

The research group from the University of Patras in Greece who were involved in the development on the INVITE Project continued their work, leading to the development of EVE (Educational Virtual Environments). Like INVITE, EVE is a Web-based, multi-user environment that explores the use of shared virtual spaces for training. Their system addresses two main challenges. The first was a technological challenge to develop a learning environment that resembles the real world and that provides additional functionality to enhance the users' experience. Secondly, the pedagogical challenge of making an educational model that contributes in the most efficient way to the distribution of knowledge. EVE is organized into two types of place for each user, their personal desk space and the training area. The personal desk refers to a 2D place where all the asynchronous features of the system relating to that user can be accessed. Thus a user can access course and user information, upload and download files, view and reply to personal messages, and manage their profile. The training area is the virtual classroom where learning takes place, and consists of a presentation table, a whiteboard, and avatar representations for all connected students and a tutor. Features such as application sharing, brainstorming, and text and audio communication are also supported. The tutor has control over the course, learning material, and students. They decide what course content is displayed on the presentation board and when students may ask questions, and can also assign students to breakout session rooms during an e-learning class and monitor their text chat sessions. An evaluation of the system, provided by Bouras and Tsiatsos (2006), shows that test-users found the system interesting and promising for e-learning. The test users were chosen from a number of Greek schools and a teacher from each selected school also evaluated the system. The users' social presence and the intuitive virtual environment were highlighted as advantages of the system. Collaboration tools such as audio and text communication, application sharing, and visualisation on the presentation table also proved popular. Overall the feedback was positive, with both students and teachers seeing the appeal and usefulness of the 3D paradigm. Feedback was also taken from students about possible improvements that could be made to the system. The introduction of facial expressions, along with tool tips for assisting during navigation, are discussed. The future work of the EVE project therefore involves the implementation of these changes along with the addition of new rooms to the environment to support smaller groups for project work.

Mobile Learning Environments

The use of mobile devices for learning, termed m-learning, has been another area of interest for researchers of late. Their portable nature makes them convenient for many people to use while on the move. Therefore, the extension of e-learning to these devices seems a natural progression. While laptop computers are widely popular and capable of delivering large amounts of information efficiently, smaller mobile devices, such as PDAs, also show promise for learning. Oliver and Wright (2003) outline the main advantages of PDAs as their light weight and portability, their ease of use, and their low cost. Also, most are wireless enabled. Csete, Wong, and Vogel (2004) accredit the functionality provided on these devices as a reason for their growing popularity. Most mobile devices now include an address book, calendar, to-do list, and memo pad. Wireless enabled devices provide e-mail and Web browsing, and most support flash, audio, and movie files. Indeed, their functionality is continually increasing as companies are now developing versions of their software for these devices. Disadvantages of these devices, such as small screen size and limited processor power and memory, mean that applications for them must be lightweight and content needs to be adapted for this new platform. These drawbacks are, however, outweighed by their inexpensive and convenient nature, which makes them the ideal target for a learning application. The major advantage this mobile platform brings to e-learning is that students have "anytime-anywhere" access to course material.

Much research is now being carried out into providing services on these mobile devices for learning. The MOBIlearn project is a worldwide European-led research and development project exploring learning through a mobile environment (*www. mobilearn.org*). This project concentrates on creating pedagogy for learning in these environments, and looks at the adaptation of existing e-learning content for mobile devices. Their main objective is to enable content delivery for adult learning and professional development through collaborative spaces, context awareness, and adaptive human interfaces. M-learning is another European research and development programme that aims to deliver learning content to young adults who are no longer taking part in education or training (*www.m-learning.org*). In particular, they target those who are unemployed or homeless and those who do not enjoy traditional education. To engage the user in learning, themes of interest to young adults are used and are presented in the form of interactive quizzes and games. Modules include activities designed to develop aspects of literacy and numeracy. They have developed a number of learning tools ranging from interactive quizzes for teaching languages and driver theory test to giving the learners access to online Web page building and community tools.

Many researchers see games and interactive challenges as the way forward into mobile learning. Ketamo (2002) has designed a game for handheld devices that teaches geometry to 6-year-old kindergarten kids. The system proved effective and in particular helped low-skilled students understand geometry better. Göth, Hass, and Schwabe (2004) have developed a location-based game to help new university students become familiar with the university and its surroundings. Students are grouped into teams and have to carry out a number of tasks at certain locations on the campus. Pocket PiCoMap, as described in Luchini, Quintana, and Soloway (2003), is another interactive tool for mobile learning which helps students build concept maps (i.e., graphical representations of complex ideas and the relationships between them). Students draw a link between two concepts on their map and can then add a descriptive label to this linking edge. An English sentence describing the visual representation is dynamically created and displayed, thus helping the students understand how the relationship between the concepts is interpreted.

Some applications using 3D graphics on mobile devices are now also being developed offering a wide range of services to their users. For example, Lipman (2002) explored the use of 3D models on mobile devices for the visualisation of structural steelwork models on construction sites. Zimmerman, Barnes, and Leventhal (2003) designed an effective system for teaching mobile users the art of origami. A 3D model is provided showing the different steps involved in creating a particular shape. The user follows a set of instructions and uses the 3D model as a visual aid to gain a better understanding of the action they are to perform. This rendering of 3D graphics on mobile devices is an area of interest to us, and together with the potential of these devices to provide tools for collaboration, we feel a mobile learning system with these technologies could be very effective.

Above, we have outlined ways in which 3D graphics have been used for learning. Initially, 3D was used as a means of training within specific fields. For example, it proved popular for teaching medical students to perform surgery. More recently, 3D graphics have been amalgamated with multi-user technologies to form complete learning environments. A number of projects using this technology have been identified and discussed above. Within these environments, students take on the role of a character and navigate through a virtual on-screen location to access course notes and interact with each other. Each of the systems described have their own merits and limitations. Building on the strengths of the systems above and proposing a solution to their limitations, we have developed a system that recognises the importance of social learning as part of an individual's education. This aspect was not fully addressed by other systems. Many of the traditional text-based e-learning systems discussed previously are aimed at third level students, providing diploma and degree qualifications. To date, no collaborative VR learning environment has been developed to solely cater to this particular market. Our research investigates the benefits that a 3D learning environment can bring to this domain. As the prevalence of mobile devices increases, their use as a learning tool is now being researched. Above, we have presented some currently available m-learning systems, and we too are exploring this area. In the next section we discuss our research, as we develop both a desktop 3D collaborative learning environment and a mobile application to supplement this. In particular, our system examines the use of 3D graphics in conjunction with various collaborative tools to act as a medium for learning.

Collaborative Learning Environment with Virtual Reality (CLEV-R)

The system which we are developing is entitled collaborative learning environment with virtual reality (CLEV-R) and addresses problems with current e-learning systems. The main objectives of the research underlying the development of CLEV-R include:

- Exploring the use of a 3D multi-user environment for e-learning, both to supplement traditional learning and for use in distance education.
- Supporting both social interaction and collaboration among system users.
- Developing the system so that it is cost-effective and requires minimal software on the client side.
- Exploring the extension of 3D interfaces for learning to mobile devices.

- Evaluating the resulting systems in terms of usability and effectiveness as a learning solution.

The following scenario indicates some issues faced by people wishing to take part in online courses. It highlights how a system like CLEV-R can address many of the concerns which people experience when using distance learning tools online.

Sample Scenario

Mary has been working for several years as an administrator in a legal firm. She wishes to further her career by obtaining a professional qualification. As she is working full time, she is unable to attend a university. Her employer suggests that she takes an online course. She has reservations about doing this because she knows of others who have found it difficult to complete courses online. They found them to be challenging; the lack of contact with others was isolating and it was difficult to maintain motivation for the duration of the course. Her friend Rachel recommends CLEV-R, an e-learning system that she found very convenient. She completed a business course using this system and said it was an enjoyable way to learn. Rachel attended university once a month; however, the rest of the course took place in a 3D virtual environment online. CLEV-R is also available on mobile devices and so she often used her PDA to access course content and communication tools while on the move. She particularly liked the collaborative aspects of CLEV-R and used them for both learning and socialising with others. Mary is convinced that this is an ideal solution for her learning needs.

The problem that Mary faced is a typical one, encountered by many people wishing to take up online courses. The social isolation, ennui, and lack of support within e-learning applications are all issues which we are addressing through the development of an online collaborative learning environment that uses 3D graphics and VR to engage and motivate the user. Our VR environment for e-learning concentrates on providing collaborative tools so students can work, learn, and socialise together (Monahan, McArdle, Bertolotto, & Mangina, 2005). Mimicking a real university, it consists of a central common area surrounded by lecture rooms, meeting rooms, and social rooms. Learning materials are presented within the environment through various multimedia techniques and communication controls, such as text and audio chat, allow students and tutors to converse easily (Monahan, McArdle, & Bertolotto, 2005). The following paragraphs outline some of the most important features of the system and explain their use in an e-learning application.

User Representation

One of the main disadvantages people see with existing e-learning applications is the lack of social presence and the feeling of isolation that can be experienced while partaking in an online course. Thus, one of the primary objectives of our environment is to remove this sense of loneliness and create a greater sense of community within each online course. The basis for our online collaborative learning environment is to facilitate multi-user support, allowing many users to be present and navigate around the same environment simultaneously. It is also vitally important that users of the environment are aware of all other connected users at any one point in time. Users are represented within the system by avatars. Upon registering for a course, each student and tutor is required to select a character to represent him or her in the VR environment. This 3D character is the user's on-screen persona for the duration of a course. In order to create an effective learning community, it is imperative that these avatars are distinctive for each individual user. In this way, avatar representations allow users of the system to recognize others, and hence feel a social presence in the learning environment. Applying different clothing or hairstyles to each character can create unique avatars.

Communication Tools

In order to support collaboration, communication technologies are imperative. In fact, it is the lack of support for real-time communication that we feel is a major drawback in current e-learning systems. In any learning scenario, it is imperative that students have a lot of communication with course tutors and also with their fellow students. Much research has been carried out to determine the importance of communication in learning, and it been has shown that students often learn from each other in informal chats as well as from lecture content (Redfern et al., 2002; Laister et al., 2002). Communicating with others who are partaking in the same course makes students feel more involved in the learning environment and

Figure 6. The communication controls of CLEV-R

removes any sense of isolation that may occur in single-user learning environments. As such, a major aspect of CLEV-R is the provision of multiple communication methods. The communication controls for CLEV-R are provided in a graphical user interface (GUI), as shown in Figure 6. Text and audio chat communication is supported. Students can send both public and private messages via text-chat and can broadcast audio streams into specific areas of the VR environment. Also users may broadcast Web-cams into the 3D environment and so have real-time face-to-face conversations with other connected users. The avatars in our system are enabled with gesture animations, which are a further form of communication. For example, avatars can raise their hand if they wish to ask a question and can also nod or shake their head to show their level of understanding of a certain topic. Of course users can also communicate asynchronously with others via e-mail.

Interactive Tools

Another common problem with Web-based learning environments is that the learning content is primarily presented through various forms of text, including word files, PDF documents, HTML, and so forth. While these may be effective for presenting the learning material, they do not portray course content in a motivating or engaging way for the students. Thus, within the development of CLEV-R, we provide different multimedia methods for presenting course content within the learning environment. The system supports features such as PowerPoint slides, movies, audio,

Figure 7. Virtual university structure within CLEV-R

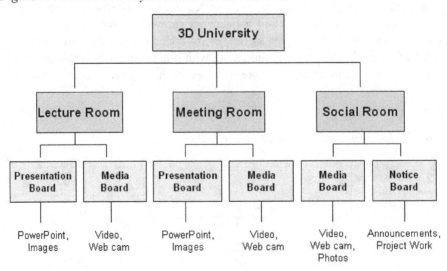

animations, and images. Rather than downloading these media files to the students' own PC, they can be experienced from within the virtual environment in real-time with other students. Many different features are available within the various virtual rooms of CLEV-R to support these file types. These are outlined in Figure 7, and the remainder of this section describes the different areas in our virtual university and the support for learning that each provides.

Lecture Room

The lecture room is the virtual space where most of the tutor-led synchronous learning occurs, and it supports a learning style similar to traditional classroom-based education. This room provides several features to enable a tutor to present learning material to a number of students simultaneously. An example of an online lecture can be seen in Figure 8. A media board is provided, where the lecturer can upload both audio and video files. Where appropriate, the lecturer also has the option of streaming live Web-cam feeds into the lecture room. This can be used for demonstrating more practical aspects of a course or as a video conferencing tool for guest speakers. Lecture slides, such as PowerPoint files, can be displayed on

Figure 8. An online lecture taking place within CLEV-R

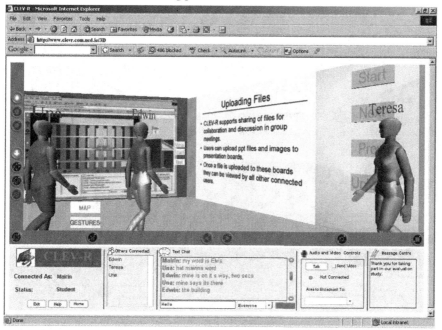

a presentation board, which also supports images files, including GIFs, JPGs, and PNGs. The tutor controls this presentation board and can progress through slide shows displayed here. Once the tutor changes the current slide, it is changed in the worlds of all connected students. In this way, students are continually kept up-to date about the state of the environment and are always aware what learning content is currently displayed. The tutor can also use the streaming audio facility to provide live audio commentary to accompany the presentation and address any questions raised by students.

Meeting Rooms

As one of the main focuses of CLEV-R is collaboration, it is very important to provide an area for this collaboration to take place. While the entire environment can be used for collaboration, designated areas of the environment provide additional functionality for groups of students to meet and work together. The meeting room as shown in Figure 9 provides a similar set of tools found in the lecture room. Students can use audio and text messages to communicate their ideas with each other. A presentation board allows students to upload their own material to the room for

Figure 9. Media board displaying a video within CLEV-R

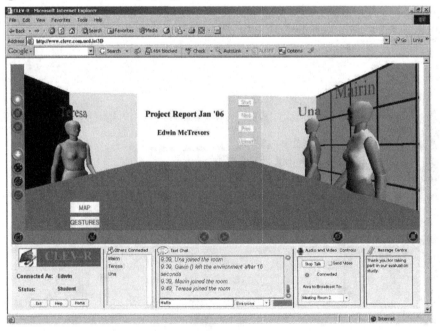

discussion. Each student can bring slideshows, animations, and media clips for discussion and viewing by the entire group. Live video can also be streamed into this room via a student's Web-cam to aid with the discussion.

Social Rooms

Social interaction is a key component of CLEV-R, and therefore nominated areas of the 3D university have been specifically created for users to mingle and partake in informal conversation with each other. While students can use these areas to discuss the course they are attending, they can also use them for social purposes. In a similar way to the meeting rooms, small numbers of students can gather together to share their experiences and stories as well as photos, pictures, and movies. Social rooms exist where a media board is available for students to upload images, videos, and Web-cam broadcasts. A centrally located lobby also serves as an informal setting, where students can chat and build rapports with others. Here users can talk informally about the course material. Students can display their project work on special notice boards provided; others can then peruse these posters at their own pace and in their own time. Students can also place advertisements for upcoming events and other general notices in this common area.

Library

As CLEV-R is primarily a learning environment, it provides easy access to learning material through a library. The library contains a bookcase and a number of desks. Lecture notes, which have been uploaded to the lecture room by the tutor, are automatically represented in the form of a book in the bookcase. When a student clicks on one of the books, the lecture notes associated with that book are displayed on a desk in the library. The student can then peruse the notes in situ within the 3D environment or download them to their own computer. The bookcase in the library also contains a number of links to external information sources such as online dictionaries and encyclopaedias.

Evaluation and Discussion

A usability study has been conducted to obtain user feedback on the CLEV-R system and also to ensure the standard of the functionality was adequate for users' needs. The test subjects took on the role of students within the 3D environment. They consisted of 7 postgraduate students, one secondary school teacher, and one college lecturer. The user trial was set up to ensure each user was exposed to all the features of CLEV-R. The test subjects registered for the system and choose an avatar to represent them in the 3D environment. Prior to the trial, each test subject received an image and a PowerPoint file via e-mail. They were also supplied with instructions for completing the user trial and an evaluation sheet. At an appointed time, those taking part in the trail attended a synchronous lecture in which a tutor presented slides and gave instructions on how to use CLEV-R. After a short class, the students were asked to complete a set of tasks, which involved exploring the 3D environment and the features it provides. For example, they were asked to access a set of notes from the library, view them, and download them to their own computer. Other tasks included uploading the supplied image. The participants were also required to test the text and audio communication features. Toward the end of the trial, all test subjects were instructed to attend a virtual meeting room where they had to upload their PowerPoint slides and discuss them. By assigning tasks in this way, each student experienced the facilities provided in CLEV-R and was able to supply feedback on both usability and the usefulness of the system for learning.

The results were encouraging and all test subjects were enthusiastic about the system.

As intuitive navigation within the 3D environment is a key aspect of the system, we were particularly interested in user-feedback on this matter. The feedback relating to navigation was mixed. While those who had prior experience of using 3D environments found manoeuvring easy, it took novice users some time to become familiar with the controls. Entering rooms proved particularly difficult and so we are improving the situation by removing doors and making the doorways wider. Test subjects found the communication controls easy to use, although some experienced an echo while using the audio controls. This can occur if speakers are too close in proximity to the microphone and so clearer instructions on this could resolve this issue. The lecture room was seen as an effective medium for teaching, and the participants particularly liked the real-time communication features. All users successfully uploaded files to the CLEV-R environment and collaborated on a task. Another key area of interest to us during this evaluation was the users' sense of immersion and presence within the 3D learning environment. Most of the test users felt part of a group and no one felt isolated during the evaluation. All of the subjects were engaged in the interactive environment and their interest in learning was maintained throughout the trial.

Test users with previous experience of e-learning systems were asked to comment further on CLEV-R, comparing its features to the e-learning systems previously encountered. The collaborative features of CLEV-R proved popular with these test subjects and they also liked their awareness of others during the online session. This is a feature they found lacking in other e-learning systems. Since the user trial, we have begun to address some of the technical issues that arose. We are also using the comments and feedback from the test subjects to improve the set of features CLEV-R provides. This preliminary user-trial paves the way for a more extensive trial with a larger number of test users in the near future.

mCLEV-R

We are developing a mobile version of CLEV-R that will provide "anytime-any-where" access to learning resources. This mobile version is called mCLEV-R and provides the opportunity for people on the move to work through course material and to communicate with course tutors and other users in real time when they cannot be stationed at a fixed location. Our research in this field has focused on the following aspects:

- Exploring the use of a 3D interface for m-learning.
- Examining the technical capabilities of small mobile devices with regard to 3D graphics. In particular, we are exploring the use of the Virtual Reality Modelling Language (VRML) on personal digital assistants (PDAs).
- Facilitating the use of PDAs as a collaboration tool for e-learning.
- Evaluating this ubiquitous and pervasive system for learning.

Mobile devices have certain limitations when it comes to developing any application for them. Small screen sizes with low resolution make it difficult to ensure an application looks well and displays all necessary information. Limited memory for running applications, and also for storage, means applications need to be light weight. Also, lack of software support is another concern. Their inexpensive and convenient nature, however, makes them the ideal target for a learning application, and once mCLEV-R has been developed, we feel it will be of great benefit to any mobile student.

Due to the device limitations mentioned above, the system needs to be greatly modified for this new platform. Firstly, the 3D environment provided in mCLEV-R is much simpler than that of the full-scale system. Only features absolutely necessary are downloaded to mobile devices, and even then may need to be simplified for more efficient rendering. For example, textures can be replaced with simple colours and complex shapes can be simplified or removed altogether depending on their importance in the environment. It is also necessary to reduce the functionality for the mobile system. Thus, we must prioritise the features of the system, carefully selecting those best suited to a mobile platform. The two most important features of our system are firstly to present learning content to users, and secondly to support social interaction among connected users. Thus mCLEV-R supports both these features.

Access to course content is supported through synchronisation with a desktop PC and by download from the 3D interface on the mobile device (see Figure 10). Due to small screen size and low resolution of the PDAs, course notes cannot be displayed clearly within the 3D environment. Therefore, we use external applications such as

Figure 10. The mCLEV-R interface on PDA

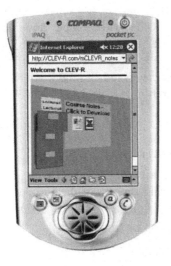 

Pocket Word, Pocket Slideshow, and Pocket Adobe Acrobat Reader to open course files on these devices. Technological limitations of these devices, including lack of software support, mean it is unfortunately not possible to ensure full consistency with the desktop version of CLEV-R. Thus students on mobile devices are not aware when a tutor changes a lecture slide and are not updated about other users' locations in the environment. They can, however, be notified about important changes in the environment through the communication techniques provided. Both text chat, as seen in Figure 7, and audio chat are available in the mobile system. Thus, mCLEV-R users are continually aware of other connected users and can converse via these communication modes in real time, making them feel part of the learning community.

We have introduced our system, CLEV-R, a collaborative learning environment with virtual reality that is used for e-learning. It takes a novel and modern approach to address some of the issues and problems with existing e-learning systems. A 3D university is provided where students can learn together with learning material delivered through the medium of VR. Online lectures are enhanced through the addition of multimedia, animations, and live video. These enhancements help to stimulate and motivate students. Recognising the importance of social learning, CLEV-R provides a social setting where students can interact with one another. Collaboration on group and project work is also possible using designated areas and special tools within the environment. CLEV-R promises to improve the usability of online learning and enhance the students' learning experience. The extension of the system to mobile devices is highly innovative and presents interesting research challenges. A subset of the functionality is provided on PDAs, and we feel mCLEV-R will be an invaluable accompaniment to the full-scale system, giving students the opportunities an ubiquitous learning environment provides. Once development is complete, we look forward to the results of an extensive evaluation determining their true value for online learning.

Future Trends for Collaborative Learning Environments with Virtual Reality

The e-learning domain is set to increase, as the focus in society shifts to life-long learning. People of all ages are now partaking in education courses, older generations are returning to the classroom to learn new skill sets, and younger generations are staying in education longer. E-learning is an ideal solution for the needs of life-long learning, allowing people to access course content, material, and help where and when they want. There is thus no doubt that research into the provision of e-learning courses will continue well into the future. But what exactly does the future have in store for e-learning?

Throughout this chapter, we have examined the use of collaborative virtual reality environments for online learning. 3D interfaces like this are already being developed in other domains, such as e-commerce and tourism, and we see them becoming much more widespread in the future. 3D environments for online education are very effective, as they are stimulating and motivating and so engage the student in their learning. They are made all the more amenable and inviting when combined with the multi-user and collaborative features discussed above. As more of these systems emerge, the advantages (such as better retention rates for online courses and more interaction, discussion, and cooperation between students) will be seen by educators. We feel this will ultimately lead to a general acceptance of VR and 3D as a medium for learning. Of course, it would be naïve for us to think that this concludes research into e-learning. E-learning and distance learning are continually evolving, adapting to new technologies and new requirements. We have no doubt that this will continue in the future and so, based on current state of the art technologies, we now surmise what the next milestones in e-learning will be.

There is great potential within these 3D learning environments to further enhance a user's learning experience. Firstly, the environment could be personalised to each user's individual preferences, thus making the environment even more welcoming to them. Personalisation and adaptive user interfaces are areas of high interest at the moment (Liu, Wong, & Hui, 2003; Ye & Herbert, 2004) and they could also be applied to these 3D learning environments. These techniques examine user profiles and preferences, and subsequently adjust system features for each user accordingly. Therefore, a user could alter the physical appearance of the virtual world and state how they wish course notes to be displayed, what format they want them to be in for download, whether they want them to appear online to other users, and so forth. Software agents could also be added to the system to remove some mundane tasks for the user and oversee the management of the environment (McArdle, Monahan, Bertolotto, & Mangina, 2005). They could be used to make recommendations to the users about course material and other similar users, and indeed to help tutors keep track of students' progress and results.

While the use of VR on desktop computers continues to grow in popularity, research is now being carried out on the possible uses of augmented reality (AR). This branch of computer science is concerned with augmenting a real world environment or scene with computer-generated objects. This is often achieved through the use of head mounted displays (HMDs); the user wears a special pair of glasses and as they look at objects in the real world, computer generated 3D objects and data are superimposed into their view via the glasses. While AR research has been taking place for some time, it is only now that hardware is able to deliver results which are satisfactory to the user. One of the driving forces behind this technology is the area of medical visualisation. An example of a system using a HMD to project a 3D model of a patient's liver is described by Bornik, Beichel, Reitinger, Sorantin, Werkgartner, Leberl, et al. (2003). This tool renders the patient's liver from an x-ray computed tomography (CT) scan and enables surgeons to measure the dimensions of the liver to locate a tumour prior to surgery. The surgeon can then manipulate this model to obtain different viewing angles and see features in more detail. One drawback of using head mounted displays is that they tend to be cumbersome to wear and do not feel very natural. Again, it is in the medical visualisation arena in which strides are being made to alleviate this issue. Schnaider, Schwald, Seibert, and Weller (2003) have developed MEDARPA, a tool to assist with minimal invasive surgery. It consists of the practitioner looking through a screen, which is placed over the patient. Based on information from previous scans, an internal view of the patient is displayed on the screen; sensors track the position of the screen and the doctor's tools and update the image accordingly. The doctor can then use the on screen image as a guide for the keyhole surgery.

These two examples from within the medical domain show where this technology is heading. As mentioned earlier, distance learning and learning in general, has always evolved with technology and there is no reason why it will not embrace this new AR technology. One can easily see how this technology could be adapted for education. The very fact that 3D models themselves can be projected into the real world provide a means for students to see for themselves things that may have been dealt with in a theoretical way within the traditional classroom. For example, complex chemical structures, human organs, computer components, and sophisticated machinery can be projected into the real world for students to interact with and manipulate, therefore increasing their understanding of a topic. We see the future of collaborative learning environments as discussed above adapting to augmented reality. A student, or indeed a teacher who is not able to attend the physical classroom setting, may have their representation projected into the classroom. They can then see the lecture taking place, and others are aware of their presence and can interact with them in a natural way. An alternative to this idea is for a holographic representation of the teacher to be projected to the location where the remote student is, in a similar style to that seen in the Star Wars movie series. Unfortunately, acceptance and widespread availability of this form of technology is a long way off.

Before the advent of AR technologies that offer truly ubiquitous and pervasive learning environments, the use of mobile computers as a supplement to e-learning will increase. As people lead busier and more hectic lives, the need to access learning content while on the move will become paramount, and m-learning will emerge as a solution to this. We envisage great improvements in mobile technologies that will allow people to access vast amounts of learning content from PDAs and mobile phones in the future. Improvements and growth in wireless networks will allow more sophisticated communication and collaborative techniques, and will also make it possible for mobile users to download large detailed virtual environments and fully partake in synchronous and interactive learning scenarios like the one CLEV-R permits. Systems like ours, with its collaborative tools supporting interaction between students, will be particularly beneficial and will play an important role in moulding the future of m-learning.

Conclusion

This chapter gives a brief insight into the history of distance learning, outlining how it is continually evolving and adapting to new technologies, and arguing that e-learning will embrace the current range of VR technologies now available. We particularly focus on the need for collaboration within e-learning systems. This chapter shows how 3D graphics, with its roots as a modelling tool for engineers, has been used in the past for computer games, and outlines how it is being used today in activities such as urban planning, tourism, and e-commerce. Online collaboration tools initially grew out of text-based fantasy computer games, and this chapter charts how they evolved, becoming conference tools and later acting as social aids. The use of 3D, combined with collaboration techniques, is a more recent phenomenon and several examples of such systems being developed have been discussed. These systems offer a new form of e-learning, addressing many of the issues, such as isolation and lack of motivation, which students often experience while using text-based e-learning environments. The benefits and weaknesses of these new VR e-learning systems are presented.

This chapter describes our efforts in developing a VR e-learning system called CLEV-R. Like some of the other systems, CLEV-R has the remit of providing a motivating and stimulating multi-user 3D environment; however, our research recognises the importance of social learning within groups of students, and so offers specific features to facilitate this. CLEV-R is an intuitive, multimedia rich Web-based environment, which can be used both as a complete distance learning solution and as an accompaniment to traditional classroom-based teaching. Unlike the other systems presented in this chapter, CLEV-R uniquely offers support for providing learning material and collaboration tools on mobile devices, such as PDAs. This addition provides anytime, anywhere access to course material and allows students to interact while they are away from their desktop computer. The use of mobile devices is a new avenue in the e-learning paradigm, which has recently been termed m-learning. As the need for pervasive learning environments comes to the forefront of the research community, the use of m-learning is sure to increase. We have also discussed some interesting future trends within 3D visualisations, particularly demonstrating how the need for improvements in medical visualisation is fuelling research in Augmented Reality. We conclude this chapter by proposing how AR can be adapted for use as a tool within e-learning to provide a truly pervasive and ubiquitous learning environment.

References

Bornik, A., Beichel, R., Reitinger, B., Sorantin, E., Werkgartner, G., Leberl, F., et al. (2003). Augmented reality based liver surgery planning. *Computer Graphics Forum, 22*(4), 795-796.

Bouras, C., Fotakis, D., Kapoulas, V., Koubek, A., Mayer, H., & Rehatscheck, H. (1999, June 7-11). In *Proceedings of the Virtual European School-VES, IEEE Multimedia Systems '99, Special Session on European Projects,* Florence, Italy (pp. 1055-1057).

Bouras, C., Philopoulos, A., & Tsiatsos, T. (2001, July). E-learning through distributed virtual environments. *Journal of Network and Computer Applications, 24*(3), 175-199.

Bouras, C., Triantafillou, V., & Tsiastsos, T. (2001, June 25-30). Aspects of collaborative environments using distributed virtual environments. In *Proceedings of the ED-MEDIA 2001 World Conference on Educational Multimedia, Hypermedia & Telecommunications* (pp. 173-178). Tampre, Finland.

Bouras, C., & Tsiatsos, T. (2006, June). Educational virtual environments: Design rationale and architecture. *Multimedia tools and applications, 29*(2), 153-173.

Burigat, S., & Chittaro, L. (2005, April). *Location-aware visualization of VRML models in GPS-based mobile guides. In Proceedings of the Web3D 2005: The 10th International Conference on 3D Web Technology* (pp. 57-64). New York.

Casher, O., Leach, C., Page, C., & Rzepa, H. (1998). Virtual reality modelling language (VRML) in Chemistry. *Chemistry in Britain* (pp 34-26).

Chee, Y.S. (2001). Networked virtual environments for collaborative learning. In *Proceedings of the Ninth International Conference on Computers in Education (ICCE/SchoolNet)* (pp. 3-11), Seoul, South Korea.

Chee, Y.S., & Hooi, C.M. (2002). C-VISions: Socialized learning through collaborative, virtual, interactive simulations. In *Proceedings of the Conference on Computer Support for Collaborative Learning (CSCL)* (pp. 687-696), Boulder, Colorado.

Chittaro, L., & Ranon, R. (2000). Virtual reality stores for 1-to-1 commerce. In *Proceedings of the CHI 2000 Workshop on Designing Interactive Systems for 1-to-1 E-Commerce,* The Hague, The Netherlands.

Chittaro, L., & Ranon, R. (2002, May). New directions for the design of virtual reality interfaces to e-commerce sites. In *Proceedings of the AVI 2002: 5th International Conference on Advanced Visual Interfaces* (pp. 308-315). New York: ACM Press.

Csete, J., Wong, Y.H., & Vogel, D. (2004). Mobile devices in and out of the classroom. In *Proceedings of the 16th World Conference on Educational Multimedia and Hypermedia & World Conference on Educational Telecommunications,* Lugano, Switzerland (pp. 4729-4736).

Daku, B.L.F., & Jeffrey, K. (2000, October 18-21). *An interactive computer-based tutorial for MATLAB.* In *Proceedings of the 30th ASEE/IEEE Frontiers in Education Conference* (pp. F2D:2-F2D:7). Kansas City, Missouri.

Dalgarno, B. (2002). The potential of 3D virtual learning environments: A constructivist analysis. *Electronic Journal of Instructional Science and Technology, 5*(2).

Dickey, M.D. (2003). 3D Virtual worlds: An emerging technology for traditional and distance learning. In *Proceedings of the Ohio Learning Network; The Convergence of Learning and Technology – Windows on the Future.*

Göth, C., Häss, U.P., & Schwabe, G. (2004). Requirements for mobile learning games shown on a mobile game prototype. *Mobile Learning Anytime Everywhere,* 95-100. Learning and Skills development agency (LSDA).

Hamill, J., & O'Sullivan, C. (2003, February). Virtual Dublin – A framework for real-time urban simulation. *Journal of the Winter School of Computer Graphics, 11,* 221-225.

Hudson-Smith, A. (2002, January). 30 days in active worlds – Community, design and terrorism in a virtual world. In *The social life of avatars*. Schroeder, Springer-Verlag.

Isbell, C.L., Jr., Kearns, M., Kormann D., Singh, S., & Stone, P. (2001, July 30-August 3). Cobot in LambdaMOO: A social statistics agent. In *Proceedings of the Seventeenth National Conference on Artificial Intelligence AAAI 2000* (pp. 36-41). Austin, Texas.

Johnson, C.A., Delhagen, K., & Yuen, E.H. (2003, July 25). H*ighlight: US e-commerce hits $230 billion in 2008*. (Business View Brief). Retrieved October 11, 2006, from Forester Research Incorporated at http://www.forrester.com

Ketamo, H. (2002). mLearning for kindergarten's mathematics teaching. In *Proceedings of IEEE International Workshop on Wireless and Mobile Technologies in Education* (pp. 167-170). Vaxjo, Sweden.

Kray, C., Elting, C., Laakso, K., & Coors, V. (2003). Presenting route instructions on mobile devices. In *Proceedings of the 8th International Conference on Intelligent User Interfaces* (pp. 117-124). Miami, Florida.

Laister, J., & Kober, S. (2002). Social aspects of collaborative learning in virtual learning environments. In *Proceedings of the Networked Learning Conference,* Sheffield, UK.

Lepouosas, G., Charitos, D., Vassilakis, C., Charissi, A., & Halatsi, L. (2001, May 16-18). Building a VR museum in a mueseum. In *Proceedings of Virtual Reality International Conference,* Laval Virtual, France.

Lipman, R.R. (2002, September 23-25). Mobile 3D visualization for construction. In *Proceedings of the 19th International Symposium on Automation and Robotics in Construction* (pp. 53-58). Gaithersburg, Maryland.

Liu, J.,Wong, C.K., & Hui, K.K. (2003). An adaptive user interface based on personalized learning intelligent systems. *IEEE Intelligent Systems, 18*(2), 52-57.

Luchini, K., Quintana, C., & Soloway, E. (2003, April 5-10). Pocket PiCoMap: A case study in designing and assessing a handheld concept mapping tool for learners. In *Proceedings of the ACM Computer-Human Interaction 2003, Human Factors in Computing Systems Conference* (pp. 321-328). Ft. Lauderdale, Florida.

McArdle, G., Monahan, T., Bertolotto, M., & Mangina, E. (2005). Analysis and design of conceptual agent models for a virtual reality e-learning environment. *International Journal on Advanced Technology for Learning, 2*(3), 167-177.

Monahan, T., McArdle, G., & Bertolotto, M. (2005, August 29-September 2). Using 3D graphics for learning and collaborating online. In *Proceedings of Eurographics 2005: Education Papers* (pp. 33-40). Dublin, Ireland.

Monahan, T., McArdle, G., Bertolotto, M., & Mangina, E. (2005, June 27- July 2). 3D user interfaces and multimedia in e-learning. In *Proceedings of the World Conference on Educational Multimedia, Hypermedia & Telecommunications (ED-MEDIA 2005)*, Montreal, Canada.

Nijholt, A. (2000). Agent-supported cooperative learning environments. In *Proceedings of the International Workshop on Advanced Learning Technologies* (pp. 17-18). Palmerston North, New Zealand.

O'Hare, G.M.P., & O'Grady, M.J. (2003). Gulliver's genie: A multi-agent system for ubiquitous and intelligent content delivery. *Computer Communications, 26*(11), 1177-1187.

Oliver, B., & Wright, F. (2003). E-learning to m-learning: What are the implications and possibilities for using mobile computing in and beyond the traditional classroom? In *Proceedings of the 4th International Conference on Information Communication Technologies in Education,* Samos, Greece.

Open University. (2005). *Media relations, fact sheet series, history of the open university*. Retrieved October 11, 2006, from http://www3.open.ac.uk/media/factsheets

O'Sullivan, C., Cassell, J., Vilhjálmsson, H., Dobbyn, S., Peters, C., Leeson W., et al. (2002). Crowd and group simulation with levels of detail for geometry, motion and behaviour. In *Proceedings of the Third Irish Workshop on Computer Graphics* (pp. 15-20).

Papagiannakis, G., Hoste, G.L., Foni, A., & Magnenat-Thalmann, N. (2001, October 25-27). Real-time photo realistic simulation of complex heritage edifices. In *Proceedings of the 7th International Conference on Virtual Systems and Multimedia VSMM01* (pp. 218-227). Berkeley, California.

Papagiannakis, G., Schertenleib, S., O'Kennedy, B., Poizat, M., Magnenat-Thalmann, N., Stoddart, A., et al. (2005, February). Mixing virtual and real scenes in the site of ancient Pompeii. *Computer Animation and Virtual Worlds, 16*(1), 11-24.

Raghupathiy, L., Grisoniz, L., Faurey, F., Marchalz, D., Caniy, M., & Chaillouz, C., (2004). An intestinal surgery simulator: Real-time collision processing and visualization. *IEEE Transactions on Visualization and Computer Graphics, 10*(6), 708-718.

Rakkolainen, I., & Vainio, T. (2001). A 3D city info for mobile users. *Computers & Graphics (Special Issue on Multimedia Appliances), 25*(4), 619-625.

Redfern, S., & Naughton, N. (2002). Collaborative virtual environments to support communication and community in Internet-based distance education. In *Proceedings of the Informing Science and IT Education, Joint International Conference* (pp. 1317-1327). Cork, Ireland.

Rickel, J., & Johnson, W.L. (1997). Integrating pedagogical capabilities in a virtual environment agent. In *Proceedings of the First International Conference on Autonomous Agents* (pp. 30-38). California.

Rickel, J., & Johnson, W.L. (1999). Virtual humans for team training in virtual reality. In *Proceedings of the Ninth International Conference on AI in Education* (pp. 578-585).

Riedl, R., Barrett, T., Rowe, J., Vinson, W., & Walker, S. (2001). Sequence independent structure in distance learning. In *Proceedings of Society for Information Technology and Teacher Education INternational Conference* (pp. 1191-1193)

Rischbeck, T., & Watson, P. (2002, March 24-28). A scalable, multi-user VRML server. In *Proceedings of the IEEE Virtual Reality Conference* (pp. 199-207). Orlando, Florida.

Ryan, J., O'Sullivan, C., Bell, C., & Mooney, R. (2004). A virtual reality electrocardiography teaching tool. In *Proceeding of the Second International Conference in Biomedical Engineering* (pp. 250-253), Innsbruck, Austria.

Schilling, A., & Coors, V. (2003, Septmeber). 3D maps on mobile devices. In *Proceedings from the Design Kartenbasierter Mobiler Dienste Workshop,* Stuttgart, Germany.

Schnaider, M., Schwald, B., Seibert, H., & Weller, T. (2003). MEDARPA - An augmented reality system for supporting minimally invasive interventions. In *Proceedings of Medicine Meets Virtual Reality 2003* (pp. 312-314). Amsterdam, The Netherlands.

UNESCO (2002). *Open and distance learning, trends policy and strategy consideration. United Nations Educational Scientific and Cultural Organisation (UNESCO)* Report 2002. Retrieved October 11, 2006, from http://unesdoc.unesco.org/images/0012/001284/128463e.pdf

Wikipedia Blackboard Incorporated. *In The Wikipedia Encyclopedia.* Retrieved October 11, 2006, from http://en.wikipedia.org/wiki/Blackboard_Inc

Ye, J.H., & Herbert, J. (2004, June 28-29). Framework for user interface adaptation. In *Proceedings from the 8th ERCIM Workshop on User Interfaces for All* (vol. 3196, pp. 167-174). Vienna, Austria: Springer Verlag.

Zara, J., Benes, B., & Rodarte, R.R. (2004, September 20-24). Virtual campeche: A Web based virtual three-dimensional tour. In *Proceeding of the 5th Mexican International Conference in Computer Science,* (pp. 133-140). Colima, Mexico.

Zimmerman, G., Barnes, J., & Leventhal, L.M. (2003). A comparison of the usability and effectiveness of Web-based delivery of instructions for inherently-3D construction tasks on handheld and desktop computers. In *Proceedings of Web3D 2003* (pp. 49-54). Saint Malo, France.

Appendix I: Internet Session

C-VISions: Collaborative Virtual Interactive Simulations

The C-VISions research group develop interactive simulations to help students learn (*http://yamsanchee.myplace.nie.edu.sg/NUSprojects/cvisions/cvisions.htm*). The Web site above provides details of their work along with relevant publications. Use this information to prepare a presentation, outlining the background to the research along with a synopsis of the systems they have developed.

Appendix II: Case Study

A university has been offering a virtual reality learning environment as an accompaniment to classes and as a distance learning solution for three years now. Students' acceptance of the technology has been high; however, faculty have been slow to adopt this new method of teaching.

Comp 4015 is a software engineering module offered by the university. The course involves the tutor giving a number of lectures detailing best practice methods for Java Programming; this generally takes the form of a PowerPoint presentation showing examples of poor coding. The tutor then asks individual pupils how they would fix the problem. This creates interaction and discussion within the class. Another aspect of the Comp 4015 module involves students working together on a group project, where each team must design a program to address a fictional company's needs. At the end of the course they must present their work to the class. The tutor is very reluctant to offer this course via the virtual reality environment. He feels the dialog in which the students engage in during the actual lectures will be lost. He is particularly worried that the group project will no longer be possible and it may have to become a project for individual students instead. Thirty percent of a student's final grade for this module comes from the final presentation, which students give, and the tutor is concerned that the student's presentations will no longer be possible if the module is offered via the virtual environment.

Taking the CLEV-R system described above, encourage the tutor to offer the Comp 4015 module in the virtual environment by offering advice on the following points and questions raised by the tutor:

1. The tutor has been teaching this module for many years and has all the lecture slides and material ready. He does not want to change the material in order to tailor it for the virtual environment.

2. How can the interaction, which his classes are well known for, be maintained when the module is offered in the virtual reality environment?

3. Can people who may never meet really partake in a group project and give a presentation at the end? What tools support this?

4. Students will just be anonymous, with no personality and no way for them to be distinguished or to get to know each other. Is there any way to address this?

5. Suggest how mCLEV-R, the mobile accompaniment to CLEV-R could be introduced and used on this course.

Appendix III: Useful Links

Human Computer Interaction Laboratory

http://hcilab.uniud.it/

MIRALab

http://www.miralab.unige.ch/

Research Unit 6

http://ru6.cti.gr/ru6/

M-Learning World

http://www.mlearningworld.com/

MOBIlearn

http://www.mobilearn.org/

TECFA

http://tecfa.unige.ch/

Augmented Reality

http://www.uni-weimar.de/~bimber/research.php

Appendix IV: Further Reading

Adelstein F., Gupta S., Richard G., III, & Schwiebert, L. (2004). *Fundamentals of mobile and pervasive computing.* McGraw-Hill Professional.

Bimber, O., & Raskar, R. (2005). *Spatial augmented reality: Merging real and virtual worlds.* A.K. Peters, Ltd.

Bowman, D.A., Kruijff, E., LaViola, J.J., & Poupyrev, I. (2004). *3D User interfaces: Theory and practice.* Addison-Wesley Professional.

Burdea, G.C., & Coiffer, P. (2003). *Virtual reality technology* (2nd ed.). Wiley-IEEE Press.

Comeaux, P. (2002). *Communication and collaboration in the online classroom: Examples and applications.* Anker Pub Co.

Mahgoub, I., & Ilyas, M. (2004). *Mobile computing handbook.* CRC Press.

McLennan, H. (1999). *Virtual reality: Case studies in design for collaboration and learning.* Information Today Inc.

Palloff, R.M., & Pratt, K. (2004). *Collaborating online: Learning together in community.* Jossey-Bass guides to online teaching and learning. Jossey-Bass.

Sherman, W.R., & Craig, A. (2002). *Understanding virtual reality: Interface, application and design.* The Morgan Kaufmann series in computer graphics. Morgan Kaufmann.

Appendix V: Possible Paper Titles/ Essays

- Issues with traditional text-based e-learning systems
- Combining collaborative tools and virtual reality
- Embracing new technologies to deliver learning material over the Internet
- Mobile technologies to offer ubiquitous learning environments
- Augmented Reality: The future for education?

Chapter VI

Using Emotional Intelligence in Personalized Adaptation

Violeta Damjanovic, Salzburg Research, Austria

Milos Kravcik, Open University Nederland, The Netherlands

Abstract

The process of training and learning in Web-based and ubiquitous environments brings a new sense of adaptation. With the development of more sophisticated environments, the need for them to take into account the user's traits, as well as the user's devices on which the training is executed, has become an important issue in the domain of building novel training and learning environments. This chapter introduces an approach to the realization of personalized adaptation. According to the fact that we are dealing with the stereotypes of e-learners, having in mind emotional intelligence concepts to help in adaptation to the e-learners real needs and known preferences, we have called this system eQ. It stands for the using of the emotional intelligence concepts on the Web.

Inside Chapter

The process of training and learning in Web-based and ubiquitous environments brings a new sense of adaptation. With the development of more sophisticated environments, the need for them to take into account the user's traits, as well as a user's devices on which the training is executed, and to place them within the context of the training activities, has become an important issue in the domain of building novel training and learning environments. Personalized adaptation represents a key aspect in technology enhanced learning and training communities. Different users could have different learning needs and preferences, and they could have different knowledge levels, as well as different opportunities to use certain training methods related to the fact that both users and theirs labs are placed in physical world. The chapter presents an approach to the realization of personalized adaptation according to the individual user's traits, such as: personality factors, cognitive factors, learning styles, and personality types (stereotypes) on one side, and user's devices on which the training is executed on the other side. At the same time, we are interested in how to manage teaching resources when the e-learners have different emotions, perceptions, and reactions. Because that we are dealing with the stereotypes of e-learners, having in mind emotional intelligence concepts to help in adaptation to the e-learners real needs and known preferences, we have named this system eQ, which stands for the using of emotional intelligence on the Web (electronic emotional intelligence). There are several key paradigms being used in the conceptual design of the eQ system: (1) this approach is based on using a multiagent system with the belief-design-intention agent rational model, (2) the eQ system is initially defined by considering component-based definition of the adaptive educational hypermedia system, (3) the eQ system uses the FOSP adaptive learning strategy, and (4) the main aim of the eQ system is to improve the adaptation processes in the Semantic Web and Grid environment.

Introduction

The history of learning can be followed back to ancient Greece, where Socrates used tutorial learning. Plato established one of the earliest known organized schools in Western civilization, the Academy in Athens, and further developed the form of live dialogue. Aristotle considered learning by doing as an efficient way of education. Already, in the 17th century Comenius wrote that learning has to be adjusted to the learner's abilities. Each person learns differently and needs to develop their own learning skills in their own way. Looking into the past we can see that ideas about how to learn are not new. However, what is new are the circumstances and opportunities. The existing school system is suitable for the industrial age, when manufacturing processes were performed in a routine way. The knowledge age demands higher skilled jobs based on critical thinking, creativity, collaboration, and interpretation abilities. Additionally, the percentage of "knowledge workers" is rapidly increasing and 50% of all employee skills become outdated in three to five years (Moe & Blodgett, 2000). Therefore, using only traditional methods cannot cover today's educational needs. Many relevant authorities have recognized the new demands on one hand and new potential on the other. In the following we mention some of them.

Peter Drucker sees new horizons. *"For the first time substantial and rapidly growing number of people have choices. For the first time, they will have to manage themselves. And society is totally unprepared for it."* He cites Plutarch in Drucker (1989), saying that education requires a focus on the strengths and talents of learners:

Any teacher of young artist—musicians, actors, painters—knows this. So does any teacher of young athletes. But schools do not do it. They focus instead on a learner's weaknesses. One cannot build performance on weaknesses, even corrected ones; one can build performance only on strengths. And these the schools traditionally ignore, in fact, consider more or less irrelevant. Strengths do not create problems—and schools are problem-focused.

Alfred Bork (2001) considers current and new paradigms concerning technology and learning. The current main learning paradigm, called *information transfer* or *classroom-teacher paradigm*, envisions the primary aim of learning as the acquisition of information. Its major auxiliary learning technology is the textbook. The author argues that we need much better learning for all and this learning has to be affordable for the individual and the world. Therefore, he predicts a future paradigm—*tutorial learning*. It sees learning as fully active, focusing on the student as learner rather than on authority figures giving information. *Tutorial learning* refers to the type of learning that takes place between a highly skilled tutor and the student, or a small group of students. The main problem related to this form of learning was that there were few good tutors, and it is a very expensive way of learning. But what makes the difference now is the available technology to rebuild learning and make it more interactive, individualized, and adaptive. *"For the first time we have the possibility of educating everyone on earth to each person's full potential."*

Wayne Hodgins (2005) presents the grand vision of *meLearning* that will provide personalized learning experiences to every person on the planet every day. When the learner is ready, the "teacher" will appear.

Roger C. Schank (2002) revises the concept *intelligence*. In the past, education and intelligence was built on accumulation of facts and ability to cite opinions of others. Today in school, pupils learn how to answer instead of how to query. The easier it is to get information, the lower its value. But the value of good questions increases. In a scenario from the future, when an issue arises, one can easily get related opinions of relevant authorities in a preferred form. If it is not enough, one can discuss the problem with other (suitable) people (all over the world) who are just dealing with a similar issue or with currently available instructors. In the future, intelligence will mean ability to reach the boundaries of the knowledge base.

Each person learns differently and needs to develop own learning skills in his or her own way. This is a reason why we explore using *emotional intelligence* (eQ) in learning on the Web (Web-based learning).

The main technological challenges and requirements for the next generation Web and Grid systems can be fulfilled by using emerging technologies, such as:

- **The Semantic Web:** This represents the idea of having data on the Web defined and linked in a way that can be used for more effective discovery, automation, semantic integration, metadata annotation, and reuse across various applications (W3C, 2001).

- **The Semantic Grid:** This attempts to extend the Semantic Web approaches and solutions to take into account Grid characteristics.

- **Knowledge Grid:** This offers high-level tools and techniques for distributed knowledge extraction from data repositories on the Grid.

- **Adaptive Web systems:** These are able to adjust to different user requirements and to manage sources of heterogeneity.

- **Peer-to-peer (P2P) architecture:** This considers a set of protocols, a computing model, and a design philosophy for distributed, decentralized, and self-organizing systems.

- **Ubiquitous computing (pervasive computing):** This describes distributed computing devices, such as personal devices, wearable computers, and sensors in the environment, as well as the software and hardware infrastructures needed to support applications on these computing devices.

Adaptation represents an important factor in building intelligent educational systems, with the aim to facilitate learning processes and to improve the learning efficiency through adjustment to real user needs. On one side, there are methods and techniques of adaptive hypermedia (AH) systems, as well as user modelling and personalization/adaptation methods, such as Brusilovsky (2001, 2003):

- **"pre-Web" generation of AH systems:** They explore adaptive presentation and adaptive navigation support and are concentrate on modelling user knowledge and goals.

- **"Web" generation of AH systems:** They explore adaptive content selection and adaptive recommendation based on modelling user interests.

- *"Mobile" generation of AH systems:* They explore using of known adaptation technologies with the aim to adapt to both an individual user and a context of his/her work.

On the other side, there is an opportunity for using new technologies and standards, such as metadata, Semantic Web, Web services, Semantic Web services, as well as the Semantic Grid. Development of the Semantic Grid has led to new achievements, such as OWL (Web Ontology Language) for expressing ontologies in a way that supports interoperability between systems. A key motivation for the semantic interoperability is the need to assemble new applications, as well as new tools and equipment for cooperation in order to provide the requisite global behaviour, without manual intervention (De Roure & Hendler, 2004).

In this chapter, we explore the impact of using AH systems in the Semantic Grid environment with the aim to point out certain potentials in further learning on the Web, as well as to show the way to increase learning efficiency. The Semantic Grid must be able to interoperate with a large-scale spectrum of current and emerging hardware and software technologies, on one side, and with a different user's profiles on the other side. Different users prefer different presentation forms: some prefer multimedia contents (graphical material and hypertext documents, simulations, presentations); others use traditional web pages (questionnaires, exercises, research study).

This chapter presents an approach to the realization of personalized adaptation according to the individual user's traits, such as: (1) personality factors, (2) cognitive factors, (3) learning style, and (4) personality types (stereotypes). Different users could have different learning needs and preferences, different knowledge levels, and different opportunities to use certain training methods and equipment.

The chapter first provides an overview of personalized adaptation and the adaptive educational hypermedia systems. In addition, this chapter explains the role of context, content, and adaptation management parts in building multiagent systems for personalized adaptation. Then, the key paradigms of the eQ agent system are discussed in detail. In the following section, implementation of our eQ agent system is presented. Chapter five explains fine art professional training, ACCADEMI@ VINCIANA, and two examples of using eQ agent system in improving the adaptation process in the Semantic Web and Grid environment: (1) e-learner is a preschool child, and (2) e-learner is an expert in the domain of painting technologies. The last section contains some conclusion remarks.

Using Personalized Adaptation in Learning

We can see certain similarities and parallels between the delivery processes in art and education, especially in their two forms, artefact and experience. This can illustrate the difference between learning objects and learning design, as well as the various degree of adaptation provided by different media.

In both areas artefacts are produced by authors—writers produce books, painters produce paintings, and composers produce compositions. On the other side, domain experts with pedagogical background write textbooks. These artefacts typically require active processing from their users, interpretation, and usually a require a higher degree of imaginative involvement to integrate the message into their minds.

Another form of delivery is experience—books and scenarios are interpreted by actors in plays and movies, and musicians interpret compositions in concerts. Also, traditional (*objectivist*) teaching is based mostly on the interpretation of textbooks by teachers and trainers. In these cases, the audience's mental processing is usually more passive as some abstract dimensions of the original artefact become concrete and therefore do not need so much imagination to be activated; typically the interpretation is more unambiguous.

In both art and education there is a transformation process between the artefact and experience. In art it is controlled by directors or conductors during rehearsals. Teachers are educated how to interpret textbooks during their pedagogical study. In modern (*constructivist*) forms of teaching they overtake the mediator or guide role and the performers are learners themselves instead of teachers, resulting in a very active participation, possibly fully embedded in the learning experience (e.g., field trips).

Personalized adaptation represents a key aspect in technology enhanced learning and training communities. This implies the requirement of a reactive and decentralized platform that can make informed decisions about how to respond to changes of the user's preferences, device capability, enterprise policy, and many other environmental factors. Roughly speaking, the main aim of personalized adaptation is to support ubiquitous, decentralized, agent-based systems and devices for learning, training, and doing well in different environments.

Development of a sharable digital library of learning and training resources can be useful in various systems, such as computer-based training systems, interactive learning environments, intelligent computer-aided instruction systems, distance learning systems, and collaborative learning environments. At the same time, there are different resources types, such as graphical material and hypertext documents, simulations, questionnaires, exercises, presentations, research study, experiments, and much more.

Figure 1. The process for developing eQ online

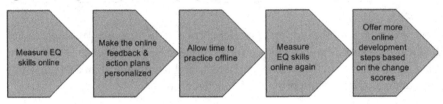

In this chapter, we propose using concepts of emotional intelligence (eQ) with the aim to achieve adaptivity in the domain that can be collectively referred to as a "context" in professional learning and training environments. More recently, the notion of eQ has attracted increased attention as one of the prerequisites for improving student's learning. Starting from the preliminary definition of eQ, originally proposed in Salovey and Mayer (2000), we describe eQ as *"a person's ability to understand learning emotions and to act appropriately based on this understanding."*

eQ represents an essential part of effective communication and adaptability, especially in the field of education, to support the user being more emotionally and socially intelligent, and to reduce negative behaviours. Web environment represents the perfect place to measure eQ skills and offer new suggestions for practicing these skills. The process for developing eQ online (Bradberry & Greaves, 2003) is shown in Figure 1, as well as in context management part of Figure 5.

The Role of Context, Content, and Adaptation Management

Based on experience from the development of adaptive educational hypermedia authoring tools (Kravcik, Specht, & Oppermann, 2004), the authors suggest that an efficient AH system should contains the following three parts:

- Context management
- Content management
- Adaptation management

Some of the more significant roles of each of these parts are discussed.

Context Management

Context management includes user modelling, enabling reusability, and sharing of the user model by various adaptive applications and user devices. In other words, context managers can be used to collect, collate, and process context information about users. The goal of this part is to design and implement a mechanism by which context information can be updated and distributed. Context management must be able to detect modification and addition of user's characteristics, and it must have location awareness module, as well as a component that provides data about enterprise policy (Robinson, 2000).

The approach represented here is based on modelling stereotypical models of user individual traits for adaptation. These individual traits include the following:

- Personality factors (extrovert, introvert)
- Cognitive factors (perceptual processing, phonological awareness, ability to maintain attentional focus)
- Learning styles (moving, touching, doing, auditory, visual)
- Personality types (conventional, social, investigative, artistic, realistic, and enterprising personality)
- Information about user's devices

All of these individual traits could be extracted by using specially designed psychological tests that perform multiagent systems represented as a distributed test-sensor system. The ontology for adaptation is made from context information about users,

Figure 2. An extension of the IEEE PAPI learner preference information (IEEE 1484.2.24)

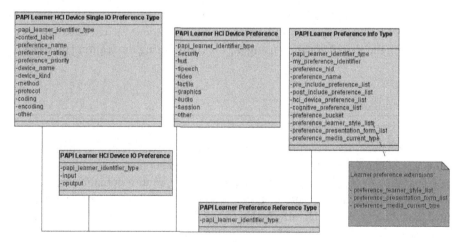

Figure 3. An extension of the IEEE PAPI learner portfolio information (IEEE 1484.2.26)

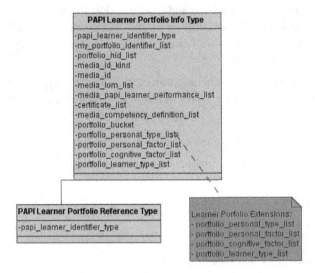

as well as about user's devices. This ontology is based on using the IEEE PAPI (Public and Private Information) Standard, which represents (IEEE PAPI, 2001):

A data interchange specification that describes learner information for communication among cooperating systems.

The IEEE PAPI Standard is extended to the parts that are related to the learner *preference information* (IEEE 1484.2.24), as well as the learner *portfolio information* (IEEE 1484.2.26) (shown in Figure 2, as well as Figure 3). These extensions are made with the aim of enabling using eQ concepts during the learning processes on the Web.

Content Management

The content management part maintains the domain model (learning objects with metadata, semantic concept networks/ontologies) and supports the authoring process (separation of content and layout, their reusability, semi-automatic annotation) (Kravcik, 2004). As an example of professional training domain, we have represented the ontology ACCADEMI@VINCIANA. This ontology involves solid team of experts from the area of fine art conservation and restoration, as well as physics and chemistry. It has three main parts, with the knowledge supporting the following (Damjanovic, Kravcik, & Devedzic, 2005):

- Learning about fine art painting methods and materials (education: painting methods and materials, conservation treatments, preventive conservation strategies, restoration, reproduction)
- Training on fine art painting methods and materials (education, classical painting technology analysis, painting damage diagnosis)
- Art Fraud E-detection (author identification, original expertise, fraud detection)

The ontology ACCADEMI@VINCIANA has several dimensions concerning professional training's intentions. First, this ontology describes three fundamental painting components, as well as their role in the construction of painting. These components could be explained as follows: colours (represent main artistic instrumentation), ground (represents the base, the underlay of painting), and binder (represents an important factor to firm adherence of colours to the ground). Second, this ontology observes fundamental aspects for analyzing painting methods and techniques. These aspects can be considered as follows (Kraigher-Hozo, 1991):

- **Purpose and usage:** icon, miniature, illumination, altar painting,
- **Ground material:** stone, tree, glass, ivory, parchment, canvas, paper, cardboard,
- **Binder and colours:** chalk, carbon, aquarelle, pastel, tempera, oil, encaustic,
- **Painting tools:** quill, cane, brush, air brush, artistic knife, aerograph,
- **Painting methods and techniques:** proplasmos, glykasmos, verdaccio, puntegiaro, trattegiaro, fa presto, impasto, alla prima, collage, frottage.

Third, ACCADEMI@VINCIANA ontology can be divided into the following two categories of trainings (Kraigher-Hozo, 1991) (shown in Figure 4):

- Trainings made by using physical methods
- Trainings made by using chemical methods

Figure 4. One part of the domain ontology - ACCADEMI@VINCIANA

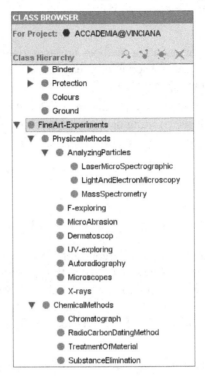

Trainings made by using Physical Methods

This includes trainings that could be performed by using (Kraigher-Hozo, 1991):

- **Dermatoscope:** For non-invasive diagnosis
- **Micro abrasion equipments:** For drilling micron level holes, and cutting or marking fragile or otherwise difficult materials
- **Microscopes:** For histological analyzing of paintings
- **Exploring the nanostructures of painting materials with X-rays:** This method show solid results in uncovering fraud, as well as in exploring the way of building paintings
- **UV exploring:** It can be used to learn the process of building paintings up to the identification of original
- **Fluorescent microscope (F-exploring):** It can be used to explore homogeneity of varnish and other transparent layers

- **Analyzing particles (protons, neurons):** ESA (Emission Spectral Analyze) (laser), Laser micro spectrographic analysis, Light and electron microscopy (scanning), Mass spectrometry, DBA (*Debye-Scherrer* Analyze) (analyzing small particles);
- **Autoradiography:** It can be useful for microscopic fluorescent measurements.

Trainings made by using Chemical Methods

This includes trainings that could be performed by using (Kraigher-Hozo, 1991):

- Microchemistry approach with pigments identification, emission spectral analysis, the iodine probe, DBA …
- **Chromatograph:** Substance that reacts on certain components (for example, if the reagent is protein, substance will be coloured red).
- **Exploring substance elimination:** Binders have different behaviours when they are heated in water (wax is smelted at 60°C, oil at 160°C).
- **Different treatments of certain material:** Burning samples, exposing samples to the rays of the sun or to the X-rays, high temperature, …
- **Radio carbon dating method:** One of the most widely used and best known absolute dating methods, based on the decay rate and half-time of C-14 (an unstable isotope of carbon).

All of these physical and chemical methods and devices could be used to explore and make artistic trainings with the aim to learn about painting methods and materials, as well as to explore and diagnose conservation strategies, originality, author identification, forgery, and much more (Damjanovic, Kravcik, & Devedzic, 2005).

Adaptation Management

Adaptation can be thought of as the behaviour of an entity in response to both changes in context management and needs in content management part. The adaptation manager could be used directly by an application that pushes relevant information to a user based on the user's stereotype and the user's learning and training needs. In this chapter, the adaptation manager decides to modify presentation content by using the FOSP (filter-order-select-present) adaptive learning strategy (Kravcik, 2004) that will be discussed in detail.

Figure 5 shows the conceptual design of the eQ agent system (Damjanovic, Kravcik, & Devedzic, 2005). *Context management part* is related to the first level of personalized adaptation in which using eQ concepts are made. The process for developing eQ online includes the following:

1. Measure eQ skills online
2. Make the online feedback and action plans personalized
3. Allow time to practice offline
4. Measure eQ skills online again
5. Offer more online development steps based on the change scores

Content management part includes learning objects (LOs), semantic metadata about learning materials, and training devices. *Adaptation management part* consists of the eQ agent system, which performs the proposed FOSP adaptive strategy.

Figure 5. Conceptual design of the eQ agent system

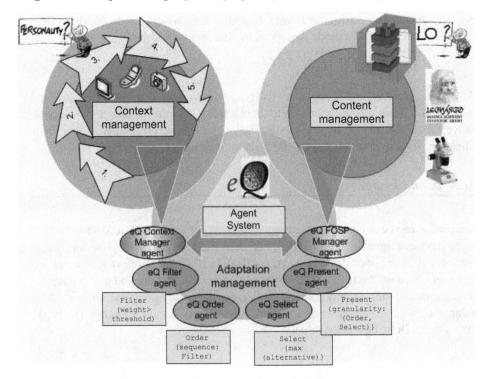

Adaptive Educational Hypermedia Systems

Development of the AH systems can be roughly divided into three generations of research (Brusilovsky, 2004):

- The first generation describes pre-Web hypertext and hypermedia (before 1996).
- The second generation is devoted to the Web-based AH systems (between 1996 and 2002).
- The third generation explores advanced developing technologies for "open corpus AH" and developing a component-based architecture for assembling adaptive Web-based educational systems (since 2002).

Recently, the impacts of many technology trends in further development of the AH systems can be noticed. These impacts can be considered as developing comprehensive frameworks for adaptive Web-based education, developing more intelligent educational material by using learning object metadata (LOM), and exploring the ideas of the Semantic Web for content representation and resource discovery.

The main characteristics of the AH system is their ability of adaptation to the following (Brusilovsky, 2001):

- **User characteristics:** User goals/tasks, knowledge, background, hyperspace experiences, preferences, interests, and individual traits. When we consider learning processes, we should observe some pedagogical attributes of learners, such as: teaching style, interaction style, grade level, and mastery level.
- **User environment:** Encompasses all aspects of the user environment that are not related to the users themselves, such as location, computing platform, bandwidth, and so on. Environment variables specify search paths for files, directories for temporary files, application-specific options, and other similar information.

The user characteristics might be determined by modelling users or by modelling groups of users with similar requirements (stereotypes). So, user models may be individual or stereotypical (Henze & Nejdl, 2003). In this chapter, we explore adaptation to the user's individual traits (personality factors, cognitive factors, learning styles, personality types). As it has been mentioned in Brusilovsky (2001), many researchers agree on the importance of modelling and using individual traits for adaptation, but there is little agreement on which features can and should be used, or how to use them.

One of the most popular kind of AH system is that one dedicated to the learning on the Web, known as the Adaptive Educational Hypermedia (AEH) system. Notable definitions of the AH, as well as AEH systems, could be mentioned:

AH system (Brusilovsky, 1996): *"By adaptive hypermedia systems we mean all hypertext and hypermedia systems which reflect some features of the user in the user model and apply this model to adapt various visible aspects of the system to the user."*

AEH system (Henze & Nejdl, 2003): *"An adaptive education hypermedia system is a quadruple."*

(DOCS, UM, OBS, AC)   (1)

Each component represented in (1) can be briefly described as follows (Henze & Nejdl, 2003):

- **DOCS** (**DOC**ument **S**pace): A finite set of first-order logic (FOL) sentences with constant symbols for describing documents (and knowledge concepts), and predicates for defining relations between these (and other) constant symbols.
- **UM** (**U**ser **M**odel): A finite set of FOL sentences with constant symbols for describing individual users (user groups), and user characteristics, as well as predicates and formulas for expressing whether a characteristic applies to the user.
- **OBS** (**OBS**ervation): A finite set of FOL sentences with constant symbols for describing observation, and predicates for relating users, documents/concepts, and observations.
- **AC** (**A**daptation **C**omponent): A finite set of FOL sentences with formulas for describing adaptive functionality (rules for adaptive functionality, rules for adaptive treatment)."

Our approach is based on modelling stereotypical models of user's individual traits for adaptation. We have used the *Jung/Briggs-Myers* typology of personality (Berens, 2002) in modelling the following basic personality types (stereotypes) (shown in Figure 6): (1) conventional personality, (2) social personality, (3) investigative personality, (4) artistic personality, (5) realistic personality, and (6) enterprising personality.

Figure 6. Personality types (stereotypes)

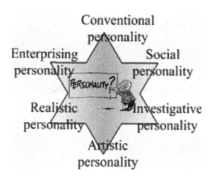

Individual traits can be extracted by using specially designed psychological tests. Moreover, several studies that have explored the use of individual traits in adaptation to the different user profiles (stereotypes) have concluded without finding any significant differences (Brusilovsky, 2001). As a possible solution, there is a need to have a certain relation between user traits on one side, and possible interface settings on the other side. It can be realized through building a repository of different metadata for adaptation that can be used, together with different catalogues of metadata, for education.

Current researches about the use of educational metadata are concentrated on applications of LOM standards (e.g., IEEE LOM). The main purpose of these standards is to improve reusability of LOs. LOM standards are supported by many LOs repositories (e.g., ARIADNE). LOs repositories represent an important research topic, which is connected through peer-to-peer (P2P) networks (e.g., Edutella). ELENA project is a closely related system that tries to employ ontology-based reasoning in adaptive Web-based systems (Dolog, Henze, Nejdl, & Sintek, 2003). This system uses user model ontology, and its purpose is to improve the level of personalization when a user searches for LO in open hypermedia space. However, none of those systems have explored the potentials of emotional intelligence in the Semantic Web environment.

We can start from the above explained definition of AEH system (definition 1). We will consider an artistic personality type with an introverted perception, with the aim to suggest users (learners) in which online experiments they could participate. The adaptive dimension of the eQ agent system will be discussed in the upcoming subsections (Damjanovic, Kravcik, & Gasevic, 2005).

eQ System: Document Space (DOCS)

The document space consists of:

- A set of n atoms (n corresponds to the number of online experiments)
- A set of m atoms (m corresponds to the equipment needed to execute an online experiment)

$$OE_1, OE_2, ., OE_n, EQP_1, EQP_2, ., EQP_m \tag{2}$$

In addition, the document space includes a set of predicates about specific equipment requirements for doing an online experiment:

$$e\_request1(EQPi, EQPj) \text{ for certain } EQPi \neq EQPj \tag{3}$$

Sometimes, the online experiments can be finished in different ways and by using different equipment. This kind of dependence between online experiments and equipment needed can be expressed by the needEquipment predicate:

$$\forall OE \, \exists EQP \, needEquipment(OE, EQP) \tag{4}$$

The above constraint (definition 4) is useful in the Semantic Grid environment for resource sharing among dynamic collections of individuals, institutions, and Web resources.

eQ System: Observation (OBS)

eQ has one atom for the observation of the participation of users in certain online experiments. It is based on using the user psychological facts, called facts. In addition, eQ has a predicate observe:

$$observe(OE, P, facts) \text{ for certain } OE, P \tag{5}$$

P represents user (learner) personality type.

eQ System: User Model (UM)

User model represents an important part of any AEH system. User model models user features and user preferences, which can be described as follows (Henze & Nejdl, 2003):

- User features describe the ability of user to exploit some of the effects. For example, it is a user's knowledge and experience about the effects they consider.
- User preferences describe to what extent the user is eager to make use of some effects. For example, it is a user's subjective mark of the effects they prefer or dislike.

User model characterizes a learner and learner's knowledge/abilities, so the other systems can access and update this information in a standard way. Participation of users (learners) in some online experiment can be convenient to the user when user personality type satisfies a set of psychological requests, such as: introverted, extroverted, and so on. For example, if we have an artistic personality with introverted perception, implying the usage of the keywords inner_world, ideas, images, memories, reflection, depth, then the rule for processing the above observation (definition 5) can be expressed in the following way:

$\forall OEi \ \forall Pj$

observe(OEi, Pj, inner_world) $\lor$

observe(OEi, Pj, ideas) $\lor$

observe(OEi, Pj, images) $\lor$

observe(OEi, Pj, memories) $\lor$

observe(OEi, Pj, reflection) $\lor$

observe(OEi, Pj, depth)

$\Rightarrow$ type(OEi, Pj, artistic_personality) (6)

eQ System: Adaptation Component (AC)

People with artistic personality and introverted perception are energized when they are involved with the ideas, images, memories, and reactions that are a part of their inner world. Introverts often prefer solitary activities and feel comfortable being alone, or spending time with one or two others with whom they feel an affinity. Based on these facts, the eQ adaptation component uses certain defined symbols to represent a suggestion to the user in order for their participations in certain online experiments. In addition, eQ adaptation component uses some keywords for representing a proposal about instruments needed in doing the experiment.

Now, we can explain the use of the following predicates of the eQ adaptation component: use_instrument and suggest_participant.

$\forall$OEi $\forall$Pj

$\forall$EQPk (observe(OEi, Pj, ideas)

$\Rightarrow$ type(OEi, Pj, artistic_personality)

$\Rightarrow$ EQPj e_request(EQPi, EQPj))

$\wedge$ ¬suggest_participant(Pj, OEi, big_experiment)

$\Rightarrow$ suggest_participant(Pj, OEi, small_experiment)   (7)

According to the fact about resource sharing on the Semantic Grid, we define a predicate called use_instrument:

$\forall$OEi $\exists$EQPk

$\forall$Pj (observe(OEi, Pj, ideas)

$\Rightarrow$ type(OEi, Pj, artistic_personality)

$\Rightarrow$ EQPj e_request(EQPi, EQPj))

$\wedge$ ¬use_ instrument (Pj, OEi, manual)

$\Rightarrow$ use_ instrument (Pj, OEi, digital)   (8)

Summary and Implications

One of the key challenges in today's Web environment is the need to deal with data and knowledge resources that are distributed, heterogeneous, and dynamic, based on using effective open, distributed, and knowledge-based solutions. This knowledge-oriented and semantics-based approach to the Web brings new paradigms to exploit techniques and methodologies from intelligent software agents and Web services representing components of the social networking and interacting in a ubiquitous and pervasive manner. These challenges are addressed in the eQ agent system we have proposed for dealing with personalized adaptation in the Semantic Web and Grid learning and training environment, which will be presented in the next section.

The Key Paradigms of the eQ Agent System

E-learning and training should provide advanced knowledge sharing and collaboration between both user profiles and user needs. This means that e-learning courses and trainings can be assembled dynamically from different repositories of LOs and tailored according to the user profiles and their learning needs.

In this chapter, we explore several key paradigms being used in conceptual design of proposed eQ agent system for personalized adaptation.

- First, this approach is based on using a multiagent system with the Belief-Desire-Intention (BDI) agent rational model.

- Second, this system is initially defined by considering the component-based definition of the AEH systems represented in Henze & Nejdl (2003).

- Third, this system uses the FOSP adaptive strategy proposed in Kravcik (2004).

- Finally, because we are dealing with the stereotypes of users, having in mind eQ concepts to help in adaptation to the user's real needs and known preferences, we have named this system eQ.

eQ stands for using eQ concepts on the Web, or using electronic eQ (Damjanovic, Kravcik, & Gasevic, 2005). In that way, we could determine the eQ agent system as a distributed test-sensor system, with the main aim to infer about user stereotypes, to recognize them, and to offer the personalized information and content wherever it happens, in online, offline, or virtual training labs.

eQ System: Multiagent System with the BDI Rational Model

Multiagent systems (MAS) are widely seen as the most promising technology for developing complex distributed software systems in the years to come. The most important reasons for using MAS when designing a system can be described as follows (Stone, 1997):

- Domains with different (possibly conflicting) goals and information, where MAS is needed to handle their interactions

- Having MAS could provide a method for parallel computation by assigning different tasks or abilities to different agents

- Full robustness of system and applications
- An easy way to add new agents (scalability)
- The modularity of MAS and simpler programming
- Exploring intelligence according to the need to deal with social interactions

eQ system represents MAS being developed to support a decentralized approach in both Web-oriented and ubiquitous environments. eQ uses embedded BDI rational model, in which the proposed FOSP adaptive learning strategy can be implemented. The BDI paradigm is based on the early philosophical work of Bratman regarding rational action theory (Bratman, 1987). Their primary contribution is the integration of the various aspects of BDI agent research, such as theoretical foundation from both a quantitative decision-theoretic perspective and a symbolic rational agency perspective, to the system implementation and building applications that are used as a practical BDI architecture.

eQ agents considers information about the user (user group), represented as instances from the ontology for adaptation, and according to the user stereotypes, user types (schoolchildren or experts), personality factors, cognitive factors, and learning styles, they find appropriate educational resources. Using the eQ agent system, personalized adaptation mechanisms pass by two phases: (1) personalized adaptation based on using contextual management, and (2) additional personalized adaptation based on using the proposed FOSP adaptive strategy.

eQ System: System Defined as an AEH System

A decentralized user model (UM) could be formed in continual following of the user's physical movements, as well as the user's history of preferences from the ontology for adaptation. For example, participation of user Pj in certain online training OEi could be done when the user's personality type satisfies a set of psychological requests, such as introverted, extroverted, and so forth An example is described in subsection 2.2.

eQ System: Using the FOSP Adaptive Strategy

Learning strategies represent techniques and methods that include techniques for accelerated learning, using certain environments for learning, graphic tools, emotional intelligence, and the other most widely implemented methods of helping learners to learn more successfully. These strategies are most successful when they are implemented and used in the collaborative learning environments in which each pair of learner/teacher is a part of a well-planned learning system. There must also be efficient methods of feeding that information back into the system so that there will be continued progress in teaching and learning. Nowadays, this process is well known as reusability of teaching resources that can be achieved at various levels. In addition, these strategies are most effective when they are applied in positive, supportive environments where there is recognition of the emotional, social, and physical needs of learners and where individual strengths are recognized, nurtured, and developed. This is one reason we explore use of eQ concepts in this chapter.

A novel method for specification of adaptation strategies in AH systems, which should support efficient collaborative authoring, is known as the FOSP method. The FOSP method is based on using a pattern identified in the adaptation process that consists of four operations (Kravcik, 2004):

1. Filter
2. Order
3. Select
4. Present

The main idea is to separate the partial results produced by different authors in such a way that they can be reused. FOSP method consists of the following three levels shown, in Figure 7:

Level 1 - Operations:

- Filter (selects just those components that have their weight greater than threshold)
- Order (sorts the selected components according to the sequence value)
- Select (chooses that one component with the highest alternative value)
- Present (displays the components, taking into account the granularity value)

Level 2 - Functions:

- Weight (the relevancy of the pedagogical role for the learning style)
- Sequence (the presentation order of the role for the learning style)
- Alternative (the relevancy of the media type for the learning style)
- Threshold (the threshold for the object display based on the learning style)
- Granularity (the max number of objects presented for the context)

Level 3 - Sets:

•   role, style, media, and context

This can be explained in the following way (Kravcik, 2004):

When a teacher wants to teach a learner certain new knowledge or skill, he usually first decides what types of learning resources are suitable for the particular user, for example for one learner it can be a definition and an example, for another a demonstration and an exercise. Then he should order the resources, that is decide whether to start with the definition or the example. Each learning resource can have alternative representations, so the teacher has to select the most suitable one—narrative explanation, image, animation, video, and so forth.

But, how to manage teaching resources when the learners have different emotions, perceptions, and reactions? In this chapter, we propose using the eQ agent system with the FOSP adaptation strategy, shown in Figure 7.

The aim of each of the above-mentioned levels in creating a flexible and ontology-powered agent system to support better adaptation and e-learning mechanisms will be discussed in detail. In order to explain the FOSP method, we define new document space that includes the sets of the following atoms (Damjanovic, Kravcik, & Gasevic, 2005):

•   A set of r atoms (the pedagogical role of the object [e.g., definition, example, demonstration]),

•   A set of t atoms (the media type [e.g., text, image, audio, video, animation]),

•   A set of c atoms (the usage context [e.g., multimedia desktop, mobile device]):

$R_1, R_2, .., R_r, MT_1, MT_2, .., MT_t, UC_1, UC_2, .., UC_c$ (2')

Figure 7. Introduction of the eQ agent system into the FOSP method

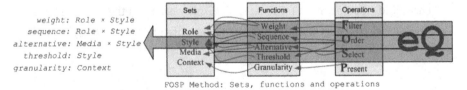

All of these atoms explained in (2') can be associated with those ones that are explained in (2). Further, the document space includes a set of predicates about media type and usage context need in e-learning (definitions 3' and 3'' can be also associated with predicate e_request1 explained in definition 3):

e_request2(MT$_k$, MT$_l$) for certain MT$_k$ ≠ MT$_l$ (3')

e_request3(UC$_e$, UC$_f$) for certain UC$_e$ ≠ UC$_f$ (3'')

Apart from the above explained pedagogical role, media type, and usage context, FOSP method considers one more type—the learner learning style (e.g., intuitive, sensitive, active, reflective). It can be represented as a set of l atoms (l corresponds to the learning style) (shown in 2''):

L$_1$,L$_2$,..,L$_l$ (2'')

Learning style can be: (1) haptic (moving, touching, and doing), (2) auditory (sound, music), and (3) visual (learning from pictures). Learning style is a subset of the learner personality type. At the same time, one personality type can use more learning styles. For example, if we have an artistic personality with introverted perception, the main motivation factor of this personality is in relation to her/his creativity. So, an artistic personality can use auditory or visual learning style. Now, the definition 6 can be extended in the following way:

∀Pj ∃Ll
observe_deep(observe, Ll, sound) ∨
observe_deep(observe, Ll, music)
⇒ person(observe, Li, auditory)   (6')

The definition 5 can be expressed in the following way:

observe_deep(OE, P, L, facts_style)
  for certain OE, P, L   (5')

This definition can be substituted with the following:

observe_deep(observe, L, facts_style)
  for certain OE, P, L   (5'')

Based on the adaptive strategy proposed in Kravcik (2004) we explain the FOSP functions (Damjanovic, Kravcik, & Gasevic, 2005):

- The weight function—it represents the relevancy of the pedagogical role for the learning style:

$$\text{weight: Role} \times \text{Style} \rightarrow \text{Integer} \tag{9}$$

$$\forall R \; \forall L$$
$$\text{observe\_deep(R, observe, L, facts\_style)}$$
$$\Rightarrow \text{weight(R, L, Relevancy)} \tag{10}$$

- The sequence function—it defines the presentation order of the role for the learning style:

$$\text{sequence: Role} \times \text{Style} \rightarrow \text{Integer} \tag{11}$$

$$\forall R \; \forall L$$
$$\text{observe\_deep(R, observe, L, facts\_style)}$$
$$\Rightarrow \text{sequence(R, L, Order)} \tag{12}$$

- The alternative function—it expresses the relevancy of the media type for the learning style:

$$\text{alternative: Media} \times \text{Style} \rightarrow \text{Integer} \tag{13}$$

$$\forall MT \; \forall L$$
$$\text{observe\_deep(MT, observe, L, facts\_style)}$$
$$\Rightarrow \text{alternative(MT, L, MT\_Relevancy)} \tag{14}$$

- The threshold function—it sets the threshold for the object display based on the learning style:

$$\text{threshold: Style} \rightarrow \text{Integer} \tag{15}$$

∀UC ∀L

observe_deep(UC, observe, L, facts_style)

⇒ threshold(UC, L, threshold_set)   (16)

- The granularity function—it specifies the max number of objects presented for the context:

granularity: Context → Integer   (17)

∀UC ∀L

observe_deep(UC, observe, L, facts_style)

⇒ granularity(R, L, max_number)   (18)

eQ System: New Adaptation Component

Specification of adaptation strategy by using the FOSP method consists of the following operations (Damjanovic, Kravcik, & Gasevic, 2005):

- Filter—for the current object it selects just those components that have their weight greater than threshold:

∀R ∀L observe_deep(R, observe, L, facts_style)

⇒ weight(R, L, Relevancy)

> (∀UC ∀L observe_deep(UC, observe, L, facts_style)

⇒ threshold(UC, L, threshold_set))

⇒Filter(component)   (19)

- Order—this sorts the selected components according to the sequence value:

∀R ∀L observe_deep(R, observe, L, facts_style)

⇒ sequence(R, L, Order)

⇒Order(component)   (20)

- Select—from the alternative components it chooses the one with the highest alternative value:

∀MT ∀L observe_deep(MT, observe, L, facts_style)

⇒ alternative(MT, L, MT_Relevancy)

∧ max(alternative)

⇒Select(component)   (21)

- Present—it displays the components, taking into account the granularity value:

∀UC ∀L

observe_deep(UC, observe, L, facts_style)

⇒ granularity(R, L, max_number)

⇒Present(component)   (22)

Summary

In practice, defining a pedagogic strategy for learners with a certain learning style means the instruction designer needs to specify the functional values of weight, sequence, alternative, threshold, and granularity for different types of LOs (i.e., content objects) (Kravcik, 2004). But it is not necessary to define all values. If no value is specified, a default one will be applied: 0 for weight, the minimum value for threshold and the maximum one for granularity. This approach is compliant with the established standards and recommendations, including the adaptive hypermedia application model (AHAM) reference model for adaptive hypermedia. Specification of adaptation strategies separating the content, declarative, and procedural knowledge in adaptive courses is quite natural, and similar approaches have been successfully applied in related areas, for instance in electronic documents generally.

Implementation of the eQ Agent System

Nowadays, there are different agent's methodologies and frameworks based on using the BDI rational model, such as JACK, Jason, Nuin, Jam, 3APL, SPARK, Gaia, and Jadex. Each of these methodologies/frameworks considers different types of goals: *query, perform, achieve, maintain, cease, avoid, optimize, test, preserve*. We have chosen to use the Jadex platform, which supports reasoning by exploiting the BDI model, and is realized as an extension to the widely used JADE middleware platform (Braubach, Pokahr, & Lamersdorf, 2004). Jadex supports the development of rational agents on top of the FIPA-compliant JADE platform, and supports

Figure 8. ADF belief-base

```
<beliefs>
<!-- FILTER agent -->
<beliefref name="eQFAgent" class="String"
      exported="true"><abstract/>
</beliefref>     <!-- ... -->   </beliefs>
<goals>
<!-- Perform filter operations -->
<performgoal name="filter_op" exported="true">
<dropcondition> $beliefbase.mission </dropcondition>
</performgoal> <!-- ... -->   </goals>
<plans>
<!-- Filter operation -->
<plan name="weight"> <body>new FilterPlan()</body>
<trigger> <goal ref="filter_op"/> </trigger>
</plan> <!-- ... -->   </plans>
```

achieve, maintain, query, and *perform* goal types (Braubach, Pokahr, Moldt, & Lamersdorf, 2004).

The Jadex BDI model considers three types of attitudes of agent rational behaviours: (1) belief (goals), (2) desire, and (3) intention. Beliefs represent the information about agent's internal, as well as external states, and provide domain-dependent abstraction of entities. The motivational attitudes of agents are captured by goals, which represent a central concept of the Jadex BDI architecture. And, last but not least, plans are the means by which agents achieve their goals.

All triggering events and beliefs must be specified in the agent definition file (ADF), whose role is to let the agents know what kind of event they must handle. Figure 8 shows one part of the eQ agent system's belief base defined in the ADF. All important agent startup properties, such as an agent name, agent implementation class, packages, and others, are possible to define in the ADF.

Fine Art Professional Training: ACCADEMI@VINCIANA

The main idea presented here is to implement a novel art academy based on using the Semantic Web and Grid possibilities, on one side, and better personalized adaptation methods based on using eQ concepts with the proposed adaptation strategy, on the other side.

Personalized Adaptation in Fine Art Professional Training

When the user starts application for fine art professional training and learning, this application automatically recognizes both user's individual traits and user's devices on which this application is executed (Damjanovic, Kravcik, & Devedzic, 2005). All information about the user's characteristics is contained within the ontology for adaptation (context information), extracted by distributed personality test-sensors. An eQ Context Manager Agent finds all context facts about observed user and sends these results to the eQ FOSP Manager Agent, with the aim to perform personalized adaptation and to present adapted content information to the user. eQ Context Manager Agent has a location awareness module whose role is to support changes in the user's device attribute values. For example, the user starts using training application on the laptop, and then migrates to a PDA. This means that the content information has to be additionally adapted, and the eQ FOSP Manager Agent has to perform some kind of filtering which shrinks the images to a size that fits nicely on the screen of the PDA.

Figure 9. eQ Agent System uses three levels of the FOSP method: Operations, functions, and sets

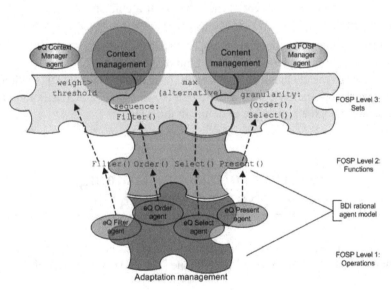

All points of the considered eQ agent system, which uses the FOSP method for personalized adaptation, are shown in Figure 9. Levels one and two can be directly implemented through the eQ BDI reasoning engine, as shown in Figure 9. This means all triggering events and beliefs must be specified in the Agent Definition File (ADF), whose role is to let the agents know what kinds of events they must handle.

Practical Results

We represent two examples of using the eQ agent system for improving the adaptation processes in the Semantic Web and Grid environment: (1) e-learner is a preschool child, and (2) e-learner is an expert in the domain of painting technologies. The main difference between both of these learner's profiles represents their ability to organize and use knowledge. Experts have a notable level of experience and knowledge, different from beginners (preschool child). Knowledge and experience of experts can be distinguished in the way they have organized knowledge, as well as the way they represent and interpret information about their environment. According to the way in which the knowledge is organized, experts remember information, infer about certain facts and categories from the organized knowledge, and solve different problems by using existing knowledge.

User identification means considering a huge number of criteria and characteristics from the ontology for personalized adaptation. In order to explain as simply as possible the role of the eQ agent system in achieving better personalized adaptation, we consider minimum criteria required from the FOSP adaptation method. That means joining both the ontology for personalized adaptation and the domain ontology - ACCADEMI@VINCIANA, based on finding the pair of values, such as: (1) learning

Table 1. Learner's characteristics at the FOSP Level 3 – Sets

Attribute name	A) e-learner is a preschool child		B) e-learner is an expert	
	Instance value - Ontology for adaptation	Instance value - Domain ontology	Instance value - Ontology for adaptation	Instance value - Domain ontology
Learner type (LT)	Beginner	Preschool child	Expert	Expert
Learning style (LS)	Visual	Visual	Visual	Video; Audio; Speech; Text
Media type (MT)	Computer	Computer	Computer; PDA; online experiments	Computer; PDA; online experiments
Presentation form (PF)	Video	Video	Video	Video; online experiments; docs + pictures

style – style, (2) learner type – role, (3) media type – media, (4) presentation form – form. The eQ BDI agent rational mechanism executes the FOSP adaptation method based on using all of these pairs of values from ontologies. As a result, different e-learners get adapted and personalized educational contents.

Firstly, we can define the FOSP Level 3 (Sets) for both examples (shown in Table 1).

The FOSP adaptive strategy is executed based on using the definitions (9 – 22). If we suppose that there are the following educational resources from the domain ontology ACCADEMI@VINCIANA, such as (1) *techniques*, (2) *materials*, (3) *fundamentals*, and (4) *experiments*, then the characteristics of the ontology resources could be represented. Therefore, we define the importance indexes of educative resources for both examples of e-learners (shown in Table 2).

Now, we execute the FOSP functions: weight, sequence, alternative, threshold, and granularity. This execution is based on using the component-based definition of the AEH system by using the values that came from both Table 1 and Table 2.

- **The FOSP weight function:** We can suppose that the user is a **beginner** with the **visual learning style**, which uses a **computer** to access the educational resources. The FOSP adaptive strategy executes weight function for different

Table 2. Characteristics of the educational resources

Instance name	A) e-Learner is a preschool child			B) e-Learner is an expert		
	Learner type (Role)	Learning style	Media type	Learner type (Role)	Learning style	Media type
Techniques	Beginner (5); Expert (5)	Video (5); Audio (5); Text (1)	Computer (5); Mobile (2)	Beginner (5); Expert (5)	Video (4); Audio (5); Text (5)	Computer (5); Mobile (2)
Materials	Beginner (3); Expert (5)	Video (3); Audio (2); Speech (1); Text (1)	Computer (5); Mobile (2)	Beginner (3); Expert (5)	Video (4); Audio (5); Speech (3); Text (5)	Computer (5); Mobile (3)
Fundamentals	Beginner (2); Expert (5)	Video (3); Audio (2); Speech (1); Text (1)	Computer (5)	Beginner (2); Expert (5)	Video (4); Audio (5); Speech (3); Text (5)	Computer (5)
Experiments	Beginner (1); Expert (5)	Video (3); Audio (2); Speech (1); Text (1)	Computer (5); PDA (3); Mobile (1)	Beginner (1); Expert (5)	Video (5); Audio (5); Speech (4); Text (4)	Computer (5); PDA (3); Mobile (2)

values of resources. For example, in the case that the educational resource is *techniques*, the value of weight function is:

weight: Role × Style → Integer, or

weight: (5 × 5 → 25)

In the case that the educational resource is *experiments*, the value of weight function is:

weight: (1 × 3 → 3)

If the educational resource is *materials*, the value of weight function is:

weight: (3 × 3 → 9)

And, if the educational resource is *fundamentals*, the value of weight function is:

weight: (2 × 3 → 6)

Based on these results, we conclude that the course about painting techniques that represent the best educational material fits in with the learner who is a beginner who uses a visual learning style and the computer as a device to access the educational materials. The next courses could be the following: the course about painting materials,or the course about fundamental elements of painting technology, while the course about painting experiments would not fit in with the beginner's profile.

- **The FOSP sequence function:** Using the definition (11) with the different values of the educational resources, the FOSP sequence function calculates the next order of these resources: (1) *techniques*, (2) *materials*. Now, the FOSP alternative function is executed.

- **The FOSP alternative function:** For example, in the case that the educational resource is *techniques*, the value of alternative function is:

alternative: Media × Style → Integer, or

alternative: (5 × 5 → 25)

In the case that the educational resource is *materials*, the value of alternative function is:

alternative: (5 × 3 → 15)

We conclude that the course about painting techniques represents the better solution for the beginning learner. At the same time, the course about painting materials represents an alternative solution for the beginner.

- **The FOSP threshold function:** Using the definition (15) with the different values of the educational resources, the FOSP threshold function calculates the next order of these resources: (1) *techniques*, (2) *materials*.

- **The FOSP granularity function:** The FOSP granularity function specifies the max number of objects presented for the context. For example, the course about painting techniques includes 8 sub courses, while the course about painting materials includes just 2 smaller sub courses.

All results of the FOSP functions are shown in Table 3.

Now, we execute the FOSP operations: Filter, Order, Select, and Present, based on the results of the FOSP functions shown in Table 3. The results of the FOSP operations are adapted to the specific user's profiles.

In a case when the e-learner is a preschool child, result of Present operation includes components of the educative resource – *techniques*: (1) Tempera, (2) Wash Paint-

Table 3. The results of the FOSP functions

Instance name	A) e-learner is a preschool child					B) e-learner is an expert				
	weight	sequence	alternative	threshold	granularity	weight	sequence	alternative	threshold	granularity
Techniques	25	1	25	5	8	20 / 25	2	20 / 25	4 / 5	8
Materials	9	2	15	3	2	20 / 25	3	20 / 25	4 / 5	2
Fundamentals	6	-	-	-	4	20 / 25	4	20 / 25	4 / 5	4
Experiments	3	-		-	2	25 / 25	1	25 / 25	5 / 5	2

ing, (3) Aquarelle, (4) Oil Painting, (5) Varnish Painting, (6) Encaustic, (7) Gilding, and (8) Drawing.

When the e-learner is an expert in the domain of painting technologies, the eQ agent system offers components of the educative resource—*experiments* that include the following components: (1) physical methods and (2) chemical methods.

Summary

The important characteristics for considering user stereotypes could be extended with the aim to give more precise and adapted results of the educational processes. It means that new instances from the ontology for personalized adaptation should be considered, including those instances made as a result of the IEEE PAPI Standard extension. Moreover, we could achieve usage of the eQ agent system in the Semantic Grid environment by introducing instances that represent instruments needed for doing online experiments. This kind of environment could be used to execute specialized experiments about painting technologies and materials. Then, the experts can use expensive, but distributed scientific devices, in an ubiquitous and pervasive manner. They can share the results with other practical scientists, remote colleagues, and students, as well as members of various online societies (physics, chemistry, government, police...).

Conclusion

The process of training and learning in Web-based and ubiquitous environments brings a new sense of adaptation. E-learning needs to use new technologies in order to provide advanced knowledge sharing and collaboration between different user's profiles and different user's needs. Thus, the Semantic Grid can be used for the creation of new scientific results, new business, and even new research disciplines.

With the development of more sophisticated environments, the need for them to take into account the user's traits and user's devices on which the training is executed, and to place them within the context of the training activities, has become an important issue in the domain of building novel training and learning environments. Hence, our approach for achieving adaptivity is based on using the eQ concepts, MAS, AEH systems, and the BDI rational agent's paradigm in the Semantic Web and Grid environment. The benefits of taking the proposed approach are numerous, and can be characterized as follows:

- **Collaboration** with other students, teachers, tutors, experts
- **Knowledge-based:** It includes domain knowledge representation in the form of ontologies, as well as knowledge about the learner and his/her social and emotional context.
- **Ubiquitous:** The capability to support multiple pedagogical models and to automatically adopt them.

In this chapter, an example of fine art professional training illustrates the potential benefits of using personalized adaptation in professional training environments. As the potential benefits, we can mention the following:

- Adaptation by focusing on the main subjects from the domain of artistic training (painters, conservators, restorers, technologists, fraud investigators)
- Using all available resources (learning materials, training devices) wherever the user is physically located
- Exploring ancient and current technologies with the aim of finding better solutions
- Analyzing generated results and deciding about using preventive painting strategies
- Collaboration with the aim of achieving the original expertise and art fraud investigation

In addition, we can stress the possibility to envisage Semantic Grid, which behaves like a constantly evolving organism, with ongoing, autonomous processing rather than on-demand processing (De Roure, Jennings, & Shadbolt, 2005). Thus, the Semantic Grid becomes an *organic Grid* which itself can generate new processes and new knowledge, manifest in the physical world through ambient intelligence vision.

Acknowledgments

This research is linked to the Network of Excellence (NoE) in Professional Learning – ProLearn, Work package WP1: Adaptive Personalized Learning.

References

Berens, L.V. (2002). Multiple models of personality types. *Australian Psychological Type Review, 4*(1-2), 9-14.

Bork, A. (2001). Tutorial learning for the new century. *Journal of Science Education and Technology, 10*(1), 57-71.

Bradberry, T., & Greaves, J. (2003). *Can you develop emotional intelligence online?* TalentSmart Inc. Retrieved October 15, 2006, from http://www.talentsmart. com/media/uploads/pdfs/Can%20You%20Develop%20Emotional%20Intell igence%20Online.pdf

Bratman, M.E. (1987). *Intentions, plans, and practical reason.* Cambridge, MA: Harvard University Press.

Braubach, L., Pokahr, A., & Lamersdorf, W. (2004). Jadex: A short overview. In *Proceedings of the Net.ObjectDays 2004 Conference, AgentExpo* (pp. 195-207).

Braubach, L., Pokahr, A., Moldt, D., & Lamersdorf, W. (2004). Goal representation for BDI agent systems. In *Proceeding of the Second International Workshop on Programming Multiagent Systems (PROMAS-2004)* (pp. 9-20).

Brusilovsky, P. (1996). Methods and techniques of adaptive hypermedia. *User Modelling and User-Adapted Interaction, 6*(2-3), 87-129.

Brusilovsky, P. (2001). Adaptive hypermedia. *User Modelling and User-Adapted Interaction, 11*(1-2), 87-110.

Brusilovsky, P. (2003). From adaptive hypermedia to the adaptive Web. In J. Ziegler & G. Szwillus (Eds.), *Proceedings of Mensch & Computer 2003: Interaktion in Bewegung* (pp. 30-33). Stuttgart, Germany.

Brusilovsky, P. (2004). Adaptive educational hypermedia: From generation to generation. In M. Grigoriadou et al. (Eds.), *Proceedings of the 4th Hellenic Conference with International Participation in Information and Communication Technologies in Education* (pp. 19-33). New Technologies Publications.

Damjanovic, V., Kravcik, M., & Devedzic, V. (2005). An approach to the realization of personalized adaptation by using eQ agent system. In *Proceedings of UM'2005 Workshop on Personalized Adaptation on the Semantic Web (PerSWeb'05)* (pp. 116-125).

Damjanovic, V., Kravcik, M., & Gasevic, D. (2005). eQ through the FOSP method. In *Proceedings of the ED-MEDIA 2005 World Conference on Educational Multimedia, Hypermedia and Telecommunications* (pp. 3080-3088). Montreal, Canada.

De Roure, D., & Hendler, J.A. (2004). E-science: The grid and the Semantic Web. *IEEE Intelligent Systems, 19*(1), 65-71.

De Roure, D., Jennings, N.R., & Shadbolt, N.R. (2005). The semantic grid: Past, present and future. *Proceedings of the IEEE, 93*(3), 669-681.

Dolog, P., Henze, N., Nejdl, W., & Sintek, M. (2003). Towards the adaptive semantic Web. In *Proceedings of Principles and Practice of Semantic Web Reasoning, International Workshop, PPSWR 2003,* Mumbai, India.

Drucker, P. (1989). *New realities.* New York: Harper & Row.

Henze, N., & Nejdl, W. (2003). *Logically characterizing adaptive educational hypermedia systems.* In *Proceeding of the International Workshop of Adaptive Hypermedia and Adaptive Web-based Systems (AH 2003),* Budapest, Hungary.

Hodgins, W. (2005). *Grand challenges for learning objects.* Presentation at Learntec, Karlsruhe, Germany.

IEEE PAPI. (2001). IEEE 1484.2.1, Standard for Learning Technology - Public and Private Information (PAPI) for Learners (PAPI Learner) - Core Features.

Kraigher-Hozo, M. (1991). *Painting / Painting methods / Materials.* Sarajevo: Svjetlost Publications.

Kravcik, M. (2004). The specification of adaptation strategy by FOSP method. In *Proceedings of AH2004 Conference,* Eidhoven, The Netherlands.

Kravcik, M., Specht, M., & Oppermann, R. (2004). Evaluation of WINDS authoring environment. In *Proceedings of the Adaptive Hypermedia 2004 Conference* (pp. 166-175). Eidhoven, The Netherlands.

Moe, M., & Blodgett, H. (2000). *The knowledge Web.* Merrill Lynch.

Robinson, R. (2000). *Context management in mobile environments.* PhD thesis, University of Queensland, Australia.

Salovey, P., & Mayer, J.D. (2000). Emotional intelligence. *Imagination, Cognition and Personality, 9*(3), 185-911.

Schank, R.C. (2002). Are we going to get smarter? In J. Brockman (Ed.), *The next fifty years: Science in the first half of the twenty-first century* (pp. 206-215). New York: Vintage.

Stone, P. (1997). *Multiagent systems.* Retrieved October 15, 2006, from http://www-2.cs.cmu.edu/afs/cs/usr/pstone/public/papers/97MAS-survey/node2.html

W3C. (2001). *Semantic Web.* Retrieved October 15, 2006, from http://www.w3.org/2001/sw/

Appendix I: Case Study

Fine Art Professional Training

The application for fine art professional training recognizes the user with the "artistic personality" (personality type), "introverted perception" (personality factor), "visual" learning style, in which the user type is an "expert" that explores "art fraud" and uses a "PDA" (user device). Thus, the first level of *contextual* personalized adaptation is finished. Now, the content is adapted for that user, which is the task of the eQ FOSP Manager Agent. This agent supervises four other eQ agents, who, one after the other, performs the main operations of the FOSP adaptive strategy (Filter, Order, Select, and Present). The eQ Filter Agent starts to perform Filter operation by selecting just those components that have their weight function greater than threshold function. Both of these functions are related to the semantically annotated FOSP sets that represent content from both the ontology for personalized adaptation and the domain ontology. The eQ Filter Agent sends the filtered components as results to the next agent—eQ Order Agent, which performs Order operation by sorting the selected (filtered) components according to the sequence value. It sends a sequence of the selected components to both the eQ Select Agent and the eQ FOSP Manager Agent. The eQ Select Agent performs Select operation by selecting the component with the highest alternative value, and finally, the eQ Present Agent performs Present operation according to having the granularity value from the sets of the selected or the alternative components. All values of considered FOSP functions, such as threshold, weight, alternative, sequence, and granularity, are related to the ontology concepts, such as Role, Style, Media, and Context (FOSP sets).

Fine art professional trainings based on the use of physical methods could be realized with different optical tools (microscopes, dermatoscopes, micro-abrasion equipment, equipment for UV and F exploring, cameras). In the case of the above explained user, the eQ Present Agent brings some physical methods as a result. Actually, it means that the eQ Present Agent offers trainings by using X-ray, UV exploring, and F-exploring as training methods that could be used to achieve art fraud investigation.

Questions

1. How can the results of the eQ agent system be executed in the case of using different typology of personality in modelling user stereotypes than *Jung/Briggs-Myers* typology?

2. What kind of typology of personality would you use in modelling user stereotypes?

Appendix II: Useful URLs

Pervasive Computing Reading Group – Papers, Related Conferences, & Journals

http://www.cs.utah.edu/~sgoyal/pervasive/

IEEE Pervasive Computing - A catalyst for advancing research and practice in ubiquitous computing

http://www.computer.org/portal/site/pervasive//

Emotional Intelligence – White Papers, Case Studies

http://jobfunctions.bnet.com/search.aspx?scname=Emotional+Intelligence&dtid=1

Web site on Emotions, Emotional Intelligence, Learning & more

http://eqi.org/toc2.htm

IEEE PAPI Standards – PAPI Learner, Drafts, and Specifications

http://edutool.com/papi/

Jadex – BDI Agent System

http://vsis-www.informatik.uni-hamburg.de/projects/jadex/

W3C Workshop on Metadata for Content Adaptation

http://www.w3.org/2004/06/DI-MCA-WS/

ProLearn Project (Professional Learning) Research Activities

http://www.prolearn-project.org/index.html

Appendix III: Further Reading

De Roure, D., & Hendler, J.A. (2004). E-science: The grid and the Semantic Web. *IEEE Intelligent Systems, 19*(1), 65-71.

De Roure, D., Jennings, N.R., & Shadbolt, N.R. (2005). The semantic Grid: Past, present and future. *Proceedings of the IEEE, 93*(3), 669-681.

Dolog, P., Henze, N., Nejdl, W., & Sintek, M. (2003). *Towards the adaptive semantic Web*. Proceedings of the PPSWR 2003 Workshop, Mumbai, India.

Henze, N., & Nejdl, W. (2003). Logically characterizing adaptive educational hypermedia systems. In *Proceedings of the International AH 2003 Workshop*, (pp. 15-28). Budapest, Hungary.

Salovey, P., & Mayer, J.D. (2000). Emotional intelligence. *Imagination, Cognition and Personality, 9*(3), 185-911.

Chapter VII

Accessing Learning Content in a Mobile System:
Does Mobile Mean Always Connected?

Anna Trifonova, University of Trento, Italy

Abstract

This chapter has the aim to point out an important functionality of a ubiquitous mobile system, and more specifically, its application in the learning domain. This functionality is the possibility to access the learning material from mobile devices, like PDAs (personal digital assistants) during their off-line periods and the technique to approach it, called hoarding. The chapter starts with the overview of a concrete mobile learning system—Mobile ELDIT, so as to give a clear idea of when and how this problem appears and why it is important to pay attention to it. Later, a description of the development approaches for both general and concrete solutions are discussed, followed by more detailed description of the important hoarding steps.

Introduction

The use of mobile devices for educational purposes was explored for the first time quite a long time ago, but the term mobile learning can be more and more often found in the literature of recent years. This is due to the fast advances of the mobile devices industry. On the market a large variety of devices with already reasonably powerful characteristics is available. The prices also allow almost everyone to be in possession of such a toy. Of course, this leads to the growing desire to use mobile devices more widely in our everyday activities.

At the same time, in the learning domain the research on the use of those mobile devices and technologies for educational purposes is also growing. Learning happens at every time and in every place of our life and the concept of ubiquitous computing overlaps very well the ways we would like to support the learning processes.

As mobile becomes so important, we should consider what makes a mobile learning system different from what we are used to having in an e-learning system, and how we should adapt to the coming changes. One of these differences is the possibility to become disconnected, and in order to allow the user to continue using the system without disturbance, a technique called hoarding might be used. Here we will define what hoarding is, when it will be needed, and how to integrate it into a mobile learning system.

While mobile learning is mainly discussed within universities and research organizations, there are also commercial m-learning products that appear on the market. They include downloadable m-learning modules, online access to learning material especially designed for mobile devices, supportive tools, and complex frameworks for mobile content creation and management. Some examples are given in Table 1 at the end of the chapter.

Figure 1. Chapter content

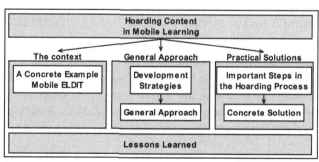

Background

The field of mobile learning is growing with every passing day. New ideas, approaches, and solutions are continuously appearing, involving different mobile devices, different target groups, and having different pedagogical or technology-testing goals. A review of the literature (Trifonova & Ronchetti, 2003b) shows that there are as many common points researched as there are differences.

Mobile devices, including cell phones, PDAs, and even notebooks, are used for different purposes in different m-learning projects. In certain cases, content is accessed online through the local area network or by using the Internet. In other cases, the devices are used for communication between students and teachers or for cooperation with other students for completing common tasks. Voice or SMS might be used for receiving important educational information, images might be interchanged for sharing experiences, or common spaces might be used for collaborative work. Some of the important research directions are the following:

- The adoption to context, in particular providing location-aware learning
- The pedagogical side of m-learning – new approaches to teaching and studying
- Integration to e-learning and reuse of learning materials
- Usability issues, like facilitation of the input and output
- Provisioning of supportive to learning services
- and so forth

Nevertheless, two things are often overlooked—the support of the user during off-line periods and the possibility to access the study content even if the device is not connected at the moment. The problem appears when the learning material is of large size, especially compared to the available memory of the device, and cannot be fully loaded locally. Generally, the issue is dealt with in two ways: in some cases, the researchers/developers rely that the devices' limitations, like small memory and intermittent connection, will soon disappear. The other alternative often used is that the full content is packed in small predefined modules that fit into the local memory of the device.

Our approach aims to provide a more flexible and adaptable solution. We would like to allow dynamic selection of the "portion" of learning material needed by the current user that should be loaded in the device memory. In order to discuss this problem, we should start from the architecture approaches for building a mobile learning system and the functionalities it includes.

Mobile ELDIT: A Real Mobile Learning System

The project that will be described here is called Mobile ELDIT. It aims at development of a mobile version of an online language learning system, so that the content of the e-learning platform is available to the mobile users in a ubiquitous way. Here, some details about the system will be given, as this system is the example for the architectural approaches and the working solutions described throughout the following sections. The system should be seen as a proof-of-concept, rather than a model to follow.

Mobile ELDIT (or m-ELDIT) is a mobile version of an existing innovative e-learning platform (Gamper & Knapp, 2003). From the users' point of view, ELDIT consists of two types of data—a searchable dictionary of words, both in German and Italian, and a set of texts, also in German and Italian, divided thematically into groups. The texts are especially designed for the preparation for the exam in bilingualism that is required in the South Tyrol region in Italy as a precondition for employment in the public sector. The content is prepared in such a way that will allow the user to optimally acquire needed lexical set, work on texts that had appeared on previous exams, and practice with the questions which might be asked for every single text. Though this system is especially suitable for people preparing for the bilingual exams, it can be used also by anyone interested in learning and practicing the Italian and German languages. The user might use the system as a normal electronic dictionary and search for unknown words or might browse the texts for more systematic studying. Currently, in Mobile ELDIT, only one of these two parts is included—the part comprising texts and associated to them words, which allow the users to switch, or at least to shift part of, their methodical study from a PC to a PDA device and to do it "on the go."

Here is a possible scenario of usage of Mobile ELDIT:

Scenario 1: A girl form Germany found nice work in the South Tyrol parts of Italy. In order to keep this work she needs in short time to pass a special exam and acquire a certificate of bilingualism. She starts to prepare herself for the exam by using the especially designed online e-learning system from her desktop PC. For her Christmas holidays she plans to go by train back home to Germany. On the last work day, she synchronizes her PDA with her desktop PC. The next day she gets on the train and, as her travel will be few hours, takes out her PDA device to continue her systematic study. She starts reading an Italian text, which comes next in her study plan, and clicks on *unknown word* to see its meaning. As she is preparing for the exam, she needs to have deep knowledge on every word, different forms, and senses, so she also reads a few examples and other cases of usage of the same word. She also takes a look at the list of words that derive from the chosen one, and later continues reading the text. Continuously, she takes notes on the words she is learning, so that she can re-read them again later. At home she connects the PDA to her PC and some synchronization happens in the background while the device battery charges. On her way back, she continues reading other texts that are needed for her preparation.

This scenario has the goal to give a concrete example for a way to present learning content to the user in a ubiquitous way. It also has to show a few important points that we will discuss further.

1.   How is the learning content presented to a mobile device and to a desktop PC?

2.   What differs in these two cases?

3.   If the content is Web-based, do we always need Internet connection to access it?

In the next section, a description will be given of the architecture that sits behind Mobile ELDIT and the concrete technological solutions to every module.

General Mobile Learning Architecture and its Application in Practice

In general, e-learning systems have a wide spectrum of functionalities and responsibilities (Aggarwal, 2000). Maybe the distribution of didactic material stays in first place, but other important functionalities include, but are not limited to, the management of the learning resources, the support of different user roles and thus the identification of users and authorization of their access to the system, and often also the personalization of the learning experience based on the knowledge about the user collected during the system usage or through questionnaires and assessments, the support of collaboration between the participants, and so forth.

Let's imagine another simple scenario where a mobile device is used:

Scenario 2: A user at the university requests an interaction with the mobile learning system from her PDA. The system shows to the user the services which it can provide, and the user selects to request more information about a seminar. The system provides to the user the data about the subject, speaker, and location of the seminar, and asks the user if he is interested. When the user responds positively, the system also creates a reminder, which is triggered depending on what time the user needs to get to the seminar room. Later, the systems give the user directions for how to get to the seminar room. Though in the seminar room no Internet connection is available during the seminar, the user is able to watch the slideshow of the presentation on the PDA display. The student takes notes and later is able to see them from the desktop PC in the library from a standard Web browser.

Confronting the scenario of the first section and the one above with common e-learning functionalities (for details see Trifonova & Ronchetti, 2003a), we reveal three main differences, namely the context, device hardware, and software characteristics and connectivity.

- **Context:** In the mobile scenario, it is important to obtain the context information that might be dynamically changing and that might influence different behaviour of the user to which the system should react accordingly. By contextual information we mean, for example, the spatial data (i.e., the location in the scenario given previously), other environmental information which might be obtained with special sensors, like surrounding noise level or changes in the available light, availability of resources, like parameters of the infrastructure or the battery condition of the device, and so forth.

- **Device hardware and software characteristics:** The most obvious difference between e-learning and m-learning is the usage of "mobile devices for learning." There is often a discussion about exactly what devices might be considered "mobile devices for learning." Should we stress the size of the device, or underline the fact that the device is mobile (not fixed)? Should laptops be considered "mobile devices for learning?" To be more clear, we define a "mobile device for learning" as "*any device that is small, autonomous and unobtrusive enough to be carried in everyday life with the user and that will be used to support the educational processes, teaching or studying*" (Trifonova & Ronchetti, 2003b). Typically compared with a desktop PC, these devices are much smaller; for example, PDAs with a 16 bit colour 240x320 pixels screen. And the screens are not the only hardware difference. Some devices have touch screens instead of keyboard. Other, like mobile phones, do have keyboard, but with a different layout, and in this case the input speed is much more limited. It is visible that the input sometimes could be difficult, but in all cases it is different from the PC. Another very important difference is in the available software, both in sense of existing programs and difference in versions. Even if a mobile version of an application exists, most often it is very limited. For example, most e-learning systems strongly depend on frames to present their content, but the current Internet Explorer version of the Pocket PC has no support for frames.

- **Connectivity:** The connectivity is one of the main prerequisites for any e-learning system. Recently, the high bandwidth requirements are quite strong. Nowadays, there are lots of technological ways to access Internet from a mobile device: WAP, GPRS, UMTS, WiFi, Bluetooth. Though the options grow fast, still very often the bandwidth is comparatively smaller, and the user often gets disconnected, either because the infrastructure is not provided or because the expenses are still high and the user prefers to connect when a cheap connection is again available. We can distinguish disconnected periods that are intentional or not.

Depending on the concrete application that is being created, it is possible that only some of these differences will appear between the desktop and a mobile version of a system. For example, if the mobile devices that will be used are laptops, then the software and hardware characteristics are practically the same as in e-learning. Still, the connectivity is not guaranteed, and the environment of the user might be changing periodically.

To support the described differences, we proposed a general mobile learning architecture (Trifonova & Ronchetti, 2003a) that, if needed, sits on the top of an e-learning system, thus reusing some of the e-learning system functionalities, like, for example, the repository with the study materials, or in other cases the authorization of the user and assigning of proper access rights.

The so-called mobile learning management system (mLMS) consists of three modules that map the three main differences we talked about. The modules are called: (1) "Context Discovery" – the module responsible for finding out the context data, (2) "Mobile Content Management and Presentation Adaptation" – the module where the presented data should be especially adapted to fit the devices limitations (hardware or software), and finally, (3) "Packaging and Synchronization" – the module which should prepare the system for the periods of disconnection, such that the user can study even in those circumstances. The modules should communicate between themselves for optimal performance. The architecture is presented in Figure 2. On the left, you can see the e-learning system and the user with a desktop computer, which receives Web pages, possibly with multimedia content. On the server (see the lower part of the figure) different modules exist (not limited to what is shown on the picture) and interact between themselves. On the right, the mobile user connects to the m-learning system, and receives specially designed pages, the content of which the mobile server might request form the e-learning server. The functionalities of the mLMS modules will be described better with a deeper look at *Scenario 2,* previously described.

Figure 2. Mobile learning: General view

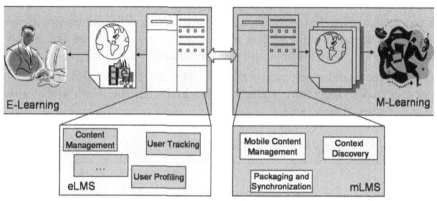

Scenario 2 explanation: Considering the previously introduced scenario, here is how it will be supported by the proposed architecture. First, the user request is captured and, in order to proceed, the system needs to know who the user is and what device is being used. This is done automatically by the "Context Discovery" module, which (based on the first request or additional interaction) already holds the information about the user id and the capabilities and limitations of the device (both software and hardware). Based on this data, the system can check the user role (student, teacher, guest, etc.) and access rights in the eLMS to decide what services can be offered at this moment, and propose a list to the user. After the next interaction with the user, the m-learning system requests information about the seminar from the eLMS and triggers the "mobile content management and presentation adaptation" module. Knowing the capabilities of the device (from the "context Discovery" module), the data is redesigned and returned to the user. Afterward, the user requests a reminder be set up for her. The system needs additional context information, namely the user location, in order to calculate the needed time to get to the seminar room. Once again, the "context discovery" module is triggered to track the user current position. Meanwhile, as the system "knows" that the network is not accessible in the seminar room, it activates the "packaging and synchronization" module. The eLMS might contain a large amount of materials concerning the seminar—the presentation itself, including explanations from the lecturer, related links, additional papers and examples, and so forth. As the system already knows the limitations of the device, the "packaging" module selects (with certain confidence) what part will be more useful and important during the seminar (for example, only the presentation). In order to fit the device memory, the system also "asks" the "presentation adaptation" module to resize the images used. Afterward, the presentation is seamlessly uploaded to the user's PDA and is accessible when needed. During the presentation, user's notes are saved locally on the device, but on next connection to the Internet, synchronization is done and the notes are uploaded to the server in device independent format. The system also saves the interesting and important parts of the presented material together with the notes in the student's personal folder on the server, so that they are accessible later from the desktop PC in the library.

Here is how the modules proposed in this general architecture and described in the above map work to meet the needs of mobile ELDIT, and the solutions that were used in its technical development.

Context Discovery

For the adaptation needs of Mobile ELDIT, the only context information that has to be discovered is the device hardware and software limitation. Knowing the screen size, the browser type and the device's browser support for scripts and frames will allow the "Adaptation" module to create the proper "look" for the Mobile ELDIT pages. As a first step, we chose the easiest way to discover the context—through the device browser's HTTP request that is captured on the server side.

As shown in Figure 3, the HTTP request contains what we needed, that is, what the device is (Windows CE device), what the screen is (240×320), the colour resolution (colour 16), what the browser is (Mozilla/2.0), and so forth. In other mobile learning systems, or in a more complicated version of Mobile ELDIT, it is possible to use other context discovery methods. There are quite a lot of technological solutions nowadays (for example, the device independence initiative *www.w3.org/2001/di/*).

Figure 3. HTTP request from a mobile device (iPAQ Pocket PC)

```
GET http://science.unitn.it/mELDIT/text.056 HTTP/1.1
Accept: application/vnd.wap.xhtml+xml, application/xhtml+xml;
  profile="http://www.wapforum.org/xhtml", text/vnd.wap.wml, image/vnd.wap.wbmp, */*
UA-OS: Windows CE (POCKET PC) - Version 3.0
UA-color: color16
UA-pixels: 240x320
UA-CPU: ARM SA1110
UA-Voice: FALSE
UA-Language: JavaScript
Accept-Encoding: gzip, deflate
User-Agent: Mozilla/2.0 (compatible; MSIE 3.02; Windows CE; PPC; 240x320)
Host: science.unitn.it
Proxy-Connection: Keep-Alive
```

One can imagine also other scenarios where adaptation can be used to show to the user context-dependant (e.g., location-dependant) language learning material, like, for example, the system proposed by Jung (2004). Thus, other methods of context discovery will be also needed, but it is out of the scope of our current work.

Content Adaptation

In order to keep the Mobile ELDIT users' experiences as close to the experiences with the online ELDIT system, we chose to use a browser as an interface to the learning material. Most of the browsers on the mobile devices nowadays still do not support frames, and support only limited versions of script languages. This leads to the need of specific adaptation of the content. The adaptation is also needed because, commonly, Web pages are designed for screen size at least 800x600, and in most cases are hard to read and navigate from devices with a smaller screen. ELDIT is not an exception. Different adaptation techniques can be used to attack this problem (see Butler, 2001). The adaptation can be server-side, or can be done in a proxy between the server and the client, or can be done on the client side. All of these solutions have their pros and cons.

The data of the ELDIT system consists of XML files, both for the texts and for the word entries. For displaying the data to a desktop PC, on the server side on every user request (on the fly), HTML pages are produced containing frames and Java scripts. The data is mainly text, but the entries are highly interlinked. For the Mobile ELDIT, we have decided to use server-side adaptation, namely XSLT transformations of the XML data on a Cocoon server (for more details, see *http://cocoon.apache. org*). Our decision was pushed by two facts—first, our data was already in XML format, which allowed us to easily create the adaptation rules using XSLT; second, the adaptation on the server side is a much better solution in the mobile context, as the adaptation process consumes quite a lot of computational power and will not fit well on a mobile device, as the devices are limited in CPU speed, operational memory, and battery.

Figure 4 shows a screenshot of a word entry from the ELDIT system (Figure 4a), displayed in a desktop PC browser. One can see that it is made out of three frames that contain the main information about the selected word in the left-hand frame, and additional information in the right-hand frame. The frame above is dedicated to the searching functionality of the system. In the mobile version, we do not support searching. This decision is because the row data of ELDIT is a much larger amount than the available memory of standard mobile devices. Thus, we are not able to provide the entire dictionary on the device anytime (see next section about packaging and synchronization). It is also impossible to predict what word a user might be searching for. Thus, we have "converted" the screen on the left (4a) into a series of interconnected screens on the mobile device (4b and 4c). When a user

Figure 4. M-ELDIT content adaptation. 4a (on the left): Browser view of ELDIT word entry with three frames; 4b (right top): m-ELDIT additional information (idiomatic expressions) for a word entry; 4c (right bottom) m-ELDIT basic word entry screen

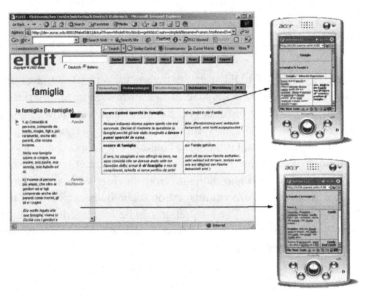

wants to see a word entry, first, the main screen is displayed and the user might select to view more detailed information by clicking the links that were added during the XLST transformations on the server.

Packaging and Synchronization

The last functionality in our architecture is called "Packaging and synchronization" and it will be discussed in detail separately in the following section.

Hoarding: What is it and Why do We Need it?

In the literature, one can see that quite a lot of years pass, but the supposition that "very soon" every device will always have connection has still not come true. In the fall of 2000, Clark Quinn says:

The vision of mobile computing is that of portable *(even wearable) computation: rich interactivity,* total connectivity, *and powerful processing. A small device that is* always networked, *allowing easy input through pens and/or speech or even a keyboard when necessary (though it may be something completely different like a chord keyboard), and the ability to see high resolution images and hear quality sound.*

In the above citation, we have italicized few words in order to focus your attention on the key expectations about the future of mobile computing and, as a result, also about m-learning. Though this sooner or later will happen, the current situation is not like we would like it to be. The devices had really become mobile in the sense of light and small for an impressively short period of time and, though there are quite a lot of technological ways to connect to the Internet, through WAP, GPRS, Wi-Fi, and so forth, still users have long periods of disconnection. These periods might be intentional or not—because of the lack of proper infrastructure or because the connection has high costs. Nevertheless, it is obvious that the vision of ubiquitous learning comprises the importance to give the user the possibility to access the learning materials that he/she wants to study even when the connection is not presented. Moreover, a good situation would be developed in such a way that the user does not bother and does not even understand whether connection exists or not.

To solve the problem described above, there comes to play a technique called hoarding (Trifonova & Ronchetti, 2005). Hoarding in practice is a procedure for automatic selection and caching of the data that the user will need during his off-line periods. Generally, hoarding is needed whenever the full data set of a certain application is bigger than the device's available memory; that is, it is not possible to have all the data on the device all the time. In such a case, it is necessary to select only the most relevant information and to consider how much memory is available. In our mobile learning context the data is the learning material that the user intends to study during the next off-line session. We should emphasis that, in the context of ubiquitous scenario, our interest is in the automation of the process. In other words, we do not want the learner to explicitly say what he/she wants to study, but on the contrary, the system should be able to predict this. The fact that the process is automatic is good for two main reasons. First, we will free the user from tedious operations, and second, often we can not even trust the user in his/her own judgment for his/her knowledge and future needs.

The hoarding process should consist of few steps that we can formalize as follows:

1. **Predict the "starting point":** The algorithm should start by finding the entry point of the current user for the next learning session.

2. **Create a candidate set:** All related documents (objects) should be found and a "candidate for caching" set of objects should be created.

3. **Predict the most probable session path:** The algorithm should discover the most probable sequence of LO the user will be following.

4. **Prune the set:** The candidate set should be pruned; that is, the objects that will not be needed by the user should be excluded from the candidate set, thus making it smaller. This should be done based on user behaviour observations and domain knowledge.

5. **Find the priority to all objects still in the hoarding set:** When the candidate set is pruned, using all the knowledge available about the user and the current learning domain, every object left in the hoarding set should be assigned a priority value. The priority depends on how important the object is for the next user session, and should be higher if we suppose that there is a higher probability that an object will be used sooner.

6. **Sort the objects, based on their priority:** The hoarding algorithm produces an ordered list of objects.

7. **Cache, starting from the beginning of the list (thus putting in the device cache those objects with bigger priority):** and continue with the ones with smaller weights, until available memory is filled in.

As one can see, the hoarding process and its predictions should be based on the system knowledge about the learner style, preferences, and previous experience. Very useful knowledge can be extracted from the students' previous interactions with the system. These interactions are usually written and saved in log files that can be analyzed. For Mobile ELDIT, such log files are gathered by a local proxy on the mobile device that captures the browsers requests, and is also responsible for the system's cache. Some preprocessing of the log files is needed for doing analysis. The preprocessing is commonly one of the most time and computationally consuming processes, though in our context, this process will most likely be performed on the server, and not when the user is interacting with the online system, and thus it will not be disturbing for the user.

In the context of hoarding, we recognize two groups of characteristics that should be "known" to the system about the user. We schematically call the first "user behaviour," which will be kept in "usage patterns" profiles. The second is "user knowledge," which will be kept in an individual user's profile. The two groups of characteristics will be used differently by the hoarding algorithm. The user behaviour can be described in terms of browsing styles (e.g., consecutive, random, interest driven, etc.), preferred type of educational media (e.g., prefers video to combination of text and pictures), and so forth. Based on the user behaviour, we can group the learners and analyze the similarities and differences between the groups and between the members of the same group. This should help us predict what will be needed; that is, this data will be used to fill in the hoarding set. On the other hand, the user knowledge profile should consist of everything that the system knows about what the user already knows. An example is the system awareness of the user's competence in a certain subject (i.e., beginner, intermediate, advanced) or a list of all the topics already covered by the user previously. In contrast of the user behaviour, the profile of the user knowledge will be used for pruning the entries from the "candidates for hoarding" set; that is, for excluding objects in order to decrease the size of the hoard.

For the Mobile ELDIT application, we tried a few different strategies for hoarding (Trifonova & Ronchetti, 2005), which include the generation of the candidate set, pruning, and prioritizing of the learning objects. First, we discovered that in our scenario the users have often very consecutive browsing behaviour. In other words, when shown a list of texts to be reviewed, the learners almost always read the texts in the order they are listed. This seems to be logical behaviour for students accessing other types of learning materials, where to understand the information presented later in the material there is a prerequisite that they have a good understanding of the information that preceded it. This consecutive behaviour is a concrete usage pattern that helps to decide the inclusion of material into the candidate hoarding set. Some of the parameters that should be discovered for every user are the depth of the browsing, the number and types of learning objects requested, the time usually spent, and so forth. As far as the pruning is concerned, in the Mobile ELDIT we wanted to test the possibility for fully automatic hoarding, and also the automatic discovery of "user knowledge." A special feature of m-ELDIT is that the learning content is divided into small chunks (texts and connected words) and some of them are repeatedly shown to the user. Because of this fact, we used as a pruning rule the following logic: if the user had the option to review a chunk of the material, but decided not to do it, there is a big probability that the learner knows this chunk and will not need it in the future, and thus it will be pruned next time. Even this simple rule made the hoarding set decrease in size quite fast. However, its simplicity has a negative side also. In certain cases the deduction made with this rule that the user "knows" a certain word is not correct, but the word gets excluded from the hoarding set in the next iteration. This leads to an increased miss rate; that is, the number of unsatisfied user requests. A more sophisticated rule might take into consideration also the time the users spent for reviewing certain content chunks, or the number of times the same chunk was requested.

Possible further improvements in the hoarding might be done by grouping the users by similarity in their behaviour or knowledge. Predictions on what actions will be taken by a user, and thus decisions on what to include or exclude from the hoard might be taken based on the behaviour or the knowledge of another user that previously had shown very big similarity with the current one. Note that the best similarity measure will differ from one application to another—one case might be the type of reviewed learning material, in another its quantity, in a third the time spent on every portion.

As the learning material and the users of every specific mobile learning system will differ, all these processes, and the decisions taken, will be based often on a big number of parameters that should be defined based on analyzes of the tracking data collected of the specific system. For example, the size of the hoarding set should be a function of the available memory on the mobile device and the size of the learning content chunks. The behaviour of the user might differ based on the learning tasks, and thus things like grouping of the users might be done based on specific classification strategies. Also, the discovering of the user knowledge might be done in various ways—our strategy was automatic discovering, but also other methods are possible, like questionnaires or tests.

Details on the results of the experimentations with hoarding strategies and parameters can be found in Trifonova (2006).

Conclusion

Mobile learning seems to be an integral part for the future of learning. And it is a step further on the road from e-learning to ubiquitous learning. Ubiquitous access to learning material supposes that, regardless of whether Internet connection is available or not, the user will have access to the learning material needed at the moment from the device used at the moment. Throughout this chapter it was shown that the technology needed for realizing a ubiquitous learning system, the pieces of the puzzle, are already available. Possibilities are wide and waiting to be explored. Often, applications would be developed in such a way as to utilize the newly appearing fast Internet connections from the mobile device. But when such an option is not possible or is not sufficient, the needed piece of the puzzle is called hoarding.

Hoarding should be based on deep understanding of user behaviour, both specifics of the concrete user and the common patterns in the behaviour of all users of a concrete system. We have shown a possible approach used in a real mobile learning system, which showed us the viability of hoarding in practice. Nevertheless, specific parameters should be extracted in every specific case, as the user behaviour might differ drastically based on the proposed study material and connections between chunks.

Additional Sources

Here we give ideas of the existing commercial m-learning tools and systems. We do not intend to give a complete list of available products, but rather examples of available possibilities and starting points for future work. The entries are grouped by provided functionality and are supported with URL and short description.

References

Aggarwal, A. (2000). *Web-based learning and teaching technologies: Opportunities and challenges*. Hershey, PA: Idea Group.

Butler, M.H. (2001). *Current technologies for device independence* (HP Labs Tech. Rep. HPL-2001-83).

Table 1. Commercial m-learning examples

Downloadable content modules
http://hotlavasoftware.com
Hot Lava Software provides offline course modules for Palm and PocketPC. A number of modules can be downloaded for free, while others are commercial. Some examples are Cisco® mobile learning (example: CCNA® Prep 4-PACK: Networking, TCP/IP, Ethernet), Kids Mobile Learning; (example: 1st Grade Language Arts: Standardized Practice Test), Microsoft mobile learning (example: MCSE Prep Data Networking), COMPTIA A+ mobile learning, English as a Second Language, Business and Sales Skills Mobile Learning, and so forth.
http://www.italyguides.it
Italy Guides provides small audio tourist guides that can be downloaded and listened to with iPod. Information is available for some of the most interesting Italian cities – Rome, Florence, and Venice.
http://www.ipreppress.com
- Merriam-Webster Inc., in collaboration with iPREPpress, offers its learning material on iPod. The commercial 2006 Edition Pocket Dictionary is already available on the site. The 2006 Pocket Thesaurus and the Pocket Atlas are expected soon. Free modules are available also in subjects like the Declaration of Independence (1776), the Constitution of the United States, (1787); the Social Security Act (1935), etc.
Online accessible content
http://en.wapedia.org/
The popular lately Wikipedia provides a cell phone accessible version of its materials.
http://www.alc.co.jp/eow/pocket/
Japan is one of the leading places offering m-learning. Examples are many of the services offered by DoCoMo to i-mode enabled mobile phones. Pocket Eijiro is an English language learning site provided by ALC, where also small multi-choice quizzes can be used to test users' knowledge.

Table 1. continued

Content creation and management platforms
http://www.axmor.com
AXMOR provides the tools to deliver mobile learning content to PocketPC and Palm devices. The platform consists of .Net-based Web site and Pocket PC part. Content maintenance, user management and reporting of different activities is done online. On the other hand, locally on the mobile device the purchased content is managed and played. The modules are in Macromedia Flash.
http://hotlavasoftware.com
Hot Lava Software, mentioned above, also offers mobile content authoring, publishing, delivery, and tracking for many mobile devices types, including PDAs and cell phones.
http://www.symexuk.com/
Symex offers to teachers a mobile system to facilitate teaching activities, like planning teaching, collecting students data, and managing their results. The system is available for PDAs and can be synchronized by connecting the device to the PC or via the Wi-Fi network.
Other tools
www.macromedia.com
Macromedia provides a Lite version of Flash for creating multimedia movies on mobile devices, including cell phones.
http://www.pocketmobility.com
Different free and commercial tools for mobile education and learning are provided by Pocket Mobility Inc., like Quizzler Maker, to create easily quizzes for any platform. The bundle allows the teacher to collect the average scores in the class, to see which questions were missed the most, and so forth.
http://classinhand.wfu.edu/
DataInHand, created at Wake Forest University, allows from a PDA with wireless connection to control presentations, to receive feedback from classroom answers, and see the distribution of the answers.

Gamper J., & Knapp, J. (2003). A data model and its implementation for a Web-based language learning system. In *Proceedings of the Twelfth International World Wide Web Conference (WWW2003)*.

Jung, L. (2004). Context-aware support for computer-supported ubiquitous learning. In *Proceedings of the 2nd IEEE International Workshop on Wireless and Mobile Technologies in Education (WMTE'04)*.

Quinn, C. (2001). *Mobile, wireless, in-your-pocket learning. LiNE Zine: Learning in the new economy*. Retrieved October 16, 2006, from http://www.linezine.com/2.1/features/cqmmwiyp.htm

Trifonova, A., & Ronchetti, M. (2003a, August 30-September 1). A general architecture to support mobility in learning. In *Proceedings of the 4th IEEE International Conference on Advanced Learning Technologies (ICALT 2004 - Crafting Learning within Context)*, Joensuu, Finland.

Trifonova, A., & Ronchetti, M. (2003b, November 7-11). Where is mobile learning going? In *Proceedings of The World Conference on E-learning in Corporate, Government, Healthcare, & Higher Education (E-Learn 2003)*, Phoenix, Arizona.

Trifonova, A., & Ronchetti, M. (2005, June 27- July 2). Hoarding content in an m-learning system. In *Proceedings of the World Conference on Educational Multimedia, Hypermedia and Telecommunications (ED-Media 2005)* (pp. 4786-4794). Montreal, Canada.

Trifonova, A. (2006, March 21). *Towards hoarding content in m-learning context.* PhD thesis, University of Trento, Italy.

Chapter VIII

A Choreographed Approach to Ubiquitous and Pervasive Learning

Sinuhé Arroyo, Digital Enterprise Research Institute, Innsbruck, Austria

Reto Krummenacher, Digital Enterprise Research Institute, Innsbruck, Austria

Abstract

*This chapter introduces a conceptual choreography framework and shows its tremendous interest for ubiquitous and pervasive applications. Choreography is the concept of describing the externally visible behavior of systems in the form of message exchanges. As information of various sensors, services, and user applications have to be integrated in ubiquitous and pervasive environments to provide seamless assistance to users, it is indispensable that means to map heterogeneous message exchange patterns and vocabularies are provided. The authors aim at giving the reader an understanding of the principles and technologies underlying the choreography framework of **SOPHIE**. Semantic descriptions of message exchange patterns are used to overcome heterogeneity in communication, regardless of the concrete application domain.*

Introduction

In a highly mobile and active society, ubiquitous access to information and services is an observable desire. Due to the fast improvement and wider use of information and communications technology, the amount of information accessible has become much greater than only a few years ago. Adaptive and pervasive systems allow humans accessing user-tailored information spaces to filter the overwhelming flow of data and extract the knowledge that is relevant and needed. To do so, these applications have to be able to identify where, and under what context, a user is engaged with a given process. The context is of high importance for an application to adapt automatically to changing situations and to provide relevant information. Context is a very general term comprising information not only about the human user and the environment, but also about the devices and services involved. In general, context information consists of highly heterogeneous data from various data sources delivered and received following various protocols. There are only two solutions to the problem of accessing ubiquitous services and extracting knowledge from manifold information sources. Either there are ways to standardize the description and the communication protocol to agree on the processes and data format in forehand for all information sources and services (which is on a global scale an impossible endeavor) or, there have to be means to map and align related information and communication patterns.

For example, one information provider might use the term "painter," while another might use the term "creator" to describe an artist. In order to search for a painting by Picasso in both their data repositories using the same query, it is necessary—in the case of paintings—to connect the terms "painter" and "creator" so that a machine can figure out that they refer to the same concept. Furthermore, it can be the case that one of them expects an "ack" confirming the reception of the information, while the other one does not, thus also requiring alignment, as far as message exchange patterns (MEPs) are concerned.

The requirements in the design of ubiquitous and pervasive software systems call for well decoupled approaches, where devices interoperate by exchanging self-contained messages. These systems realize their functionality by defining from a high-level point of view their dynamics, control flow, and the message interface that allows others to consume their functionality by making or responding to requests.

Choreography deals with describing the external visible behavior of systems as message exchanges. In order to allow interoperation among systems exposing different visible behaviors, the means to map heterogeneous message exchanges is required.

The Semantic Web provides the technology for aligning related descriptions on a machine level, allowing—by semantically annotating data—communication, system coordination, and information exchange among heterogeneous applications.

By combining both approaches and by semantically describing the conversational patterns and message contents used by interacting parties, communication among heterogeneous ubiquitous nodes can be achieved and resumed in an ontology mapping task. Based on the output of such a task, intermediate services can be defined to put in place the logics required to map and convert the sequence, cardinality, and content terminology of the messages sent by one device, to the sequence and cardinality expected by another, regardless of the behavioural and structural model used by each party.

Applying these technologies to educational applications enables a new and wider range of possible learning procedures:

- Globally distributed resources can be interlinked and combined.
- Learning resources can be personally annotated.
- Knowledge can be tailored to a student's cultural background and needs.
- Collaborative and distributed learning becomes much simpler, thanks to the modularity of the information.

In consequence, the reuse of material by cross-fertilization suddenly becomes a reality, creating important synergy effects. The internationalization of education, and thus the creation of global learning objects repositories (Arroyo & López Cabo, 2006) can be further advanced without failing due to cultural barriers and without fighting the natural reform resistance of many national boards.

The remainder of this chapter is structured as follows. the second section details a use case to exemplify the use of semantic-driven choreographies in a ubiquitous setting. The third section introduces the general principles that drive the construction of a choreography service. The fourth section presents **SOPHIE,** a choreography service specially suited for the fine-grained interaction requirements of ubiquitous and pervasive applications. The fifth section depicts how the different concepts and ideas presented in the previous section are put to work in order to provide a technical solution to the use case. Finally, the sixth section concludes the chapter by summarizing the most relevant issues tackled in the chapter.

Case Study

To illustrate how a choreography engine integrates and interoperates with ubiquitous user applications and services, a hypothetical use case is presented: a mobile application supporting educational travel. The application guides users through a city and some of their museums, presenting information about the environment and important sights, interacting with information systems that use different data conceptualizations and conversational protocols.

Walking around Barcelona's Old Town

Our expedition starts at the tourist office on Placa de Sant Jaume in the middle of the old town. A friendly guide behind the counter tells us that Barcelona's tourist guide system is accessible from a small SiSTA[1]-application. She promises that the application will assist us in finding our way and that it is able to gather information tailored to our interests and needs. So, before leaving the tourist office, we fill out a simple form to define our personal profiles (interests and preferences) and store it on the user information server run by the tourist board. Among other things we choose to get information about Catalonian restaurants, including opening hours, the price of the daily menus, and access for people with limited mobility, as one member of our group is traveling with a wheel chair. We believe it is part of such a trip to enjoy lunch in a local restaurant.

From the Placa de Sant Jaume, it is only a short walk into the medieval heart of the city, the Barri Gòtic. Hence, we chose to first have a look at the gothic buildings and the remains of the old Roman walls. The application communicates with the local servers of the quarter and provides messages with maps that guide us optimally through the neighborhood, so that we eventually end up at the cathedral. We marked in the profile that we definitely do not want to miss that impressive gothic edifice. Whenever we stop on our way or pass an important sight, the application connects with the surrounding access points to receive new messages that automatically pop up information about buildings, places, and people. Just around the corner from Placa de la Catedral, the application points us to a little family owned tapas bar with a small back yard. Perfect!

After our hourly lunch break we continue on to visit the Catedral de Barcelona. From the mobile application we learn that the construction of the cathedral began in 1298, during the bishopric of Bernat Pelegrí and the reign of King Jaume II, but that the construction continued on until the 20th century. Resumes about the initiators and about the architects, Josep Oriol Mestres and August Font i Carreras, who completed the present-day facade and detailed images of the edifice and its interior, are shown to us one by one to perfectly fit the small screen of our smart phones.

Suddenly, there appears a warning message on the screen that we need to hurry to reach the Picasso Museum on time, as rain is announced to start pretty soon. We decide, therefore, to bookmark the information about the crypt of Santa Eulàlià to have a look at it in the evening.

In the Picasso Museum

As we enter the medieval palaces hosting the Museo Picasso, our application pays the admission by sending a message to the museum's information system. After leaving our coats at the wardrobe, as it will be pretty warm inside, we select from a set of proposed permanent and temporary exhibitions the ones we are mostly interested in. The application keeps on receiving new messages and provides us with an optimal route through the museum, so that we avoid temporarily crowded rooms. This allows us to easily enjoy the wonderful work of art displayed. On the way to the exhibition room on the second floor, we get to take a glance through the window and see how badly it is raining outside. Luckily, we managed to get to the museum before the thunderstorm began.

Despite the quality of the whole collection, we fall particularly for Picasso's series of paintings about Las Meninas, by Velàzquez. Thanks to the perfect time at which the application leads us to Las Meninas, there are barely any other visitors blocking the view and disturbing our experience. As we tarry around these marvelous paintings, the application informs us that Velázquez' unique masterpiece was the inspiration for 58 oil paintings that were created between August and December 1957 while Picasso was living in Cannes. In addition, the application provides us with resumes and background information about the artists and the period, and about the paintings, their interpretation, history and technical details, as well as about the building history and the architect of the room the exhibition is in. All this information, including images and multimedia elements (video sequences, audio

Figure 1. Ubiquitous device: Picasso Museum

descriptions, and interviews), are again issued one by one and well-tailored to our mobile device.

After more than five hours and many new acquirements about Pablo Ruiz Picasso and his life and friends, we decide to leave the museum and head back to the city centre. As we make our way to the exit, the application reminds us of several paintings and sculptures that we have not enjoyed in detail yet: Portrait of Aunt Pepa (1896), Portrait of Señora Canals (1905), a magnificent example from the rose period, and Blanquita Suárez (1917), to only name a few.

Before leaving the museum, we pass at the gift shop, as the application indicates that there are currently special offers for big-size posters. We simply cannot resist and ask for a replica of Las Meninas. At the exit of the store, the poster is already wrapped and waiting for us, and the payment was automatically taken care of by the electronic cash support. Out on the street the application informs us about an open-air concert in Antoni Gaudi's Park Guell. As we have not yet been there, we agree to go, and the travel guide suggests taking the metro at Jaume I, and to change to the green line to get to the station Lesseps. As we leave the metro, a map pops up and shows us the way to the park. We arrive easily at the entrance and right on time to finish off the evening with a wonderful summer night concert.

Choreography Service

A necessary building block of every message-based system is a choreography service or engine. A choreography service is a mediator that receives messages from other systems, adapting them to fulfill the requirements of the addressee. Due to the fact that the content, conceptualization, structure, semantics, sequence, and cardinality of interacting systems is wide, the idea of abstracting mapping details from interacting parties and overall application design seems to be promising.

The idea of overcoming the heterogeneity among messages using a choreography service is thought to have a lot of potential. On the one hand, as the number of accessible services increases, as well as the number of structural and behavioural styles, the use of some intermediate layer is required to overcome heterogeneity. On the other hand, the development of new applications and the cumbersome integration of existing ones can be greatly decreased, as off-the-shelf services can be readily used to build bigger and more complex software systems minimizing integration efforts. In a nutshell, the design of modern applications requires a compromise among interoperation and decoupling that is sometimes hard to realize due to the heterogeneous nature of services. If services communicate by exchanging messages, a choreography engine is a good mediation layer that could speed up the development and interoperation of new and existing software functionality.

In the following, a choreography service is understood as a necessary building block to realize the message-based interactions among ubiquitous and pervasive systems.

Driving Principles

When designing a choreography service for the interaction of a wide variety of systems, regardless of the concrete application domain, a number of driving principles need to be taken into consideration. The remainder of this section discusses these aspects.

Conceptual Framework

The first step in analyzing choreographies is to identify the different entities that partake in the interaction. A choreography service defines terms and roles for these entities.

Separation of Models

The definition of a choreography service requires that the models that build it are clearly differentiated. As a result, a modular framework should be designed, where different formalism can be readily added, extended, or replaced in order to allocate the most suitable one, depending on the target application and application domain.

Semantic-Driven and Mediation

Due to the natural heterogeneity of the open environment where services reside, the interoperation of heterogeneous message exchanges requires the production of intermediate structures—mediators—that allow overcoming mismatches. By semantically describing the different entities that characterize the choreography service, such structures can be produced as a result of a mediation task. In doing so, mediation allows any party to speak with any other (Fensel & Bussler, 2002), facilitating an intermediate layer that provides a generalized solution to resolve communication mismatches.

Technological Independence

The design of a fully extensible choreography service should not make any assumptions about underlying technologies. In particular, the details regarding transport and communication frameworks should be left aside. In doing so, a choreography service should rely on such underlying technologies, defining a clear border, which allows separating the particular communication details from the conceptual model used. In addition, as new ontological languages based on different logical formalisms are developed, independence from existing and emerging specifications should be obliged. In consequence, the conceptual model is driven by the semantic description of its constituent entities, not making any constraint or assumption on the ontological language used to model such descriptions.

Separation of Internal and External Behaviour

Choreographies deal with the externally visible behaviour of parties. The internal details should be clearly separated from the external ones, allowing its independent definition. Deeply in this direction, the description of collaborative processes is out of the scope of this work, as is orchestration in general.

Global View vs. Decentralized Approach

Many traditional models call for centralized approaches where the interaction among parties is controlled by a unique point. In contrast, the nature of ubiquitous systems is decentralized. While a decentralized approach is preferred due to its flexibility to adapt to different application domains, eventually, a global point of view is chosen to control the message exchange. A choreography service should take both approaches into consideration, allowing parties to choose the most suitable one at any time.

Pattern-Driven

Particular types of interactions among services, such as negotiation or interactive information gathering, follow well-established and researched message exchange patterns (MEPs). The choreography service should allow the usage of such conversational protocols as the main building block that can be used to overcome heterogeneities among services.

SOA-Based

A realization of all these basic principles, especially regarding semantic-driveness and technological independence, the choreography service should be realized as a SOA with support for semantics.

Semantic Services chOreograPHi engInE

SOPHIE [(Arroyo & López-Cobo, 2005), (Arroyo & Duke, 2005), (Arroyo & Siclia, 2005), (Arroyo & López-Cobo, 2006), (Watkins, Arroyo, Duke, Richardson, Schreder, Wahler et al., 2005)] is a conceptual framework for a choreography service realized as a semantic service oriented architecture (SSOA) that follows precisely the principles detailed in *Driving Principles*. The framework does not make any assumptions about the underlying communication framework (Chinnici, Moreau, Ryman, & Weerawarana, 2005; Mitra, 2003), ontological language (Dean & Schreiber, 2004; de Brujin, 2005; Klyne & Carrol, 2004), or behavioural paradigm (Abstract State Machines (ASMs), Petri nets, temporal logic, etc).

SOPHIE is especially suitable for supporting the fine grained interaction among ubiquitous applications following different structural, behavioural, or operational models. **SOPHIE** elaborates on current existing initiatives (Andrews, Curbera, Dholakia, Goland, Klein, Leymann et al., 2003; Arkin, Askary, Fordin, Jekeli, Kawaguchi, Orchard et al., 2002; Kavantzas, Burdett, & Ritzinger, 2004), trying to overcome their limitations with the addition of a layered syntactical model, support for semantics, and technological independence. Also, the use of MEPs as the core building block to describe the skeleton of messages has been introduced.

Models

The conceptual model of **SOPHIE** makes a clear distinction between semantic and syntactic models. The semantic model details the support for semantics, while the latter details the syntax of the framework. The syntactic model depicts three different complementary models: structural, behavioural, and operational. The structural model provides the grounding pillars of the framework. The behavioural model affects the conduct of the structural model, and the operational model facilitates the means to allow the interoperation of different behavioural models. This layered approach enables a straight mechanism to extend the different models. The work presented here defines the behavioural model as abstract state machines (ASMs). Petri nets, temporal logic, or transaction logic can, however, also be used instead of ASMs and are plugged in easily. The semantic model is currently based on WSML. Nonetheless, the design allows easily extending the grammar and ontology of *SOPHIE* to accommodate any other ontology language.

Structural Model

A *conversation* represents the logical entity that permits a set of related message exchanges among parties to be grouped together. Conversations are composed of a set of building blocks. *Elements* represent units of data that build up documents. *Documents* are complete, self-contained groups of elements that are transmitted over the wire within messages. *Messages* characterize the primitive piece of data that can be exchanged among parties. As messages are exchanged, a variety of recurrent scenarios can be played out. *Message exchange patterns* identify placeholders for messages that allow sequence and cardinality to be modeled, defining the order in which parties send and receive messages. A set of messages sent and received among parties optionally following a MEP that account for a well defined part of a conversation are referred to as a *message exchange*. A conversation can be thus defined as a set of message exchanges among parties, with the aim of fulfilling some goal. Every conversation is carried out over a communication facility, referred to as a communication network by the involved parties. The specification differentiates among two types of parties, *initiating parties* and *answering services*. Both parties produce and consume messages, and, additionally, initiating parties take care of starting the message exchange.

Behavioural Model

A *choreography* describes the behaviour of the answering service from the initiating party's point of view (Roman, Scicluna, & Feier, 2005). It governs the message exchanges among parties in a conversation. Normally, ASMs or Petri Nets are used to model the sequences of states the choreography goes through during its lifetime, together with its responses to events.

Operational Model

The atomic building blocks that permit a number of mismatches among interacting parties to be resolved are logic boxes. A *logic box* facilitates the reorganization of the content of documents, its mapping to messages, and the order and cardinality of messages, thus enabling the interoperation among parties following different message exchange patterns. Additionally, and depending on the type of box, the differences in the vocabulary used to describe the application domain can be overcome. Currently, the specification defines five different types of logic boxes, namely *refiner box*, *merge box*, *split box*, *select box*, and *add box*.

Semantic Model

Ontologies define the semantics of the engine. They provide a vocabulary that can be mediated for the understanding of interacting parties. *Domain ontologies* facilitate the general vocabulary to describe the application domain of the answering service and the initiating party. The *choreography ontology* provides the conceptual framework and vocabulary required to describe choreographies. In doing so, it defines and allows for the reuse of a common vocabulary for the definition of the structural and behavioural models. Its aim is, as a result of a reasoning task, to generate the operational model. Additionally, *ontology mappings* put in place the mechanisms to link similar ontological concepts and instances.

Ubiquitous SOPHIE

Even though the application running on our smart phones conforms (fictively) to the standardized framework for traveling services, the MEPs, the messages, and the message contents used differ in the case of Barcelona's old town and the Picasso Museum. While in the first case the system is fully compatible with our SiSTA application, in the second, the developers opted for a more cumbersome mechanism of receiving and delivering information based on proprietary non-standardized terminology and message protocols.

Normally, such a situation would completely prevent us from using our smart phones to get information during the whole visit to Barcelona, as naming conventions and MEPs differ greatly. Fortunately, science moves along very fast and provides us with solutions that allow us to overcome this awkward situation.

Figure 2. SOPHIE models

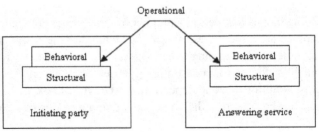

In case the conceptual framework provided by **SOPHIE** is used to describe the message exchanges of the SiSTA application on our smart phone and of the one in the Picasso Museum, interoperation among these would be possible.

Technical Solution

In the following, the technical solution is presented. The work focuses on a small section of the message exchange between our smart phone and the system in the Picasso Museum.

Domain Ontology

As a first step, the domain ontologies used by our SiSTA (SiSTAOnt) application and the Piccasso Museum (PicMusOnt) are partially depicted in Table 1.

The SiSTA domain ontology (SiSTAPOnt) contains the generic concept Creator with two properties called *name* and *birth*. The Picasso Museum domain ontology (PicMusOnt) contains an equivalent concept Artist with three properties called *firstName, surname,* and *birthDate*. By applying the appropriate mediation techniques, it is straightforward to express *PicMusOnt:Artist* as an equivalent concept to SiSTAOnt:Ceator, as name is linked to *firstName* and *surename*, and *birth* to *birthDate*. *SiSTAOnt:Object* and *PicMusOnt:ArtWork* are similarly related.

SOPHIE provides the paradigm used to define the choreographies of the SiSTA and the Picasso Museum applications. By importing from the sketched domain ontologies and the choreography ontology model as defined in (Arroyo, forthcoming), it

Table 1. Example of the domain ontologies SiSTAOnt (a) and PicMusOnt (b)

(a)	*(b)*
concept *Creator*	**concept** *Artist*
name **ofType** _string	firstName **ofType** _string
birth **ofType** _date	surname **ofType** _string
	birthDate **ofType** _date
concept *Object*	**concept** *ArtWork*
name **ofType** _string	workOfArtName **ofType** _string
date **ofType** _date	workOfArtDate **ofType** _date
description **ofType** _string	workOfArtDescription **ofType** _string
createdBy **ofType** Creator	workOfArtCreator **ofType** Artist

is possible to detail the structural and behavioural aspects of the message interfaces of both applications.

Behavioural Aspects

Figure 3 shows a simplified message exchange pattern for information requests among both applications. The SiSTA application sends an *infoRequest* message to the Picasso Museum application. The requested information is searched in the database and a resulting *info* message is sent in return to the SiSTA system.

If the Picasso Museum and the SiSTA application were to use different MEPs, the operational model of **SOPHIE** can be applied. Figure 4 shows the MEPs followed

Figure 3. Request-response message exchange pattern

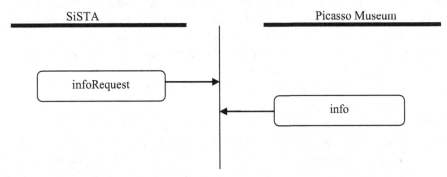

Figure 4. Request-response and multi-in-out message exchange pattern

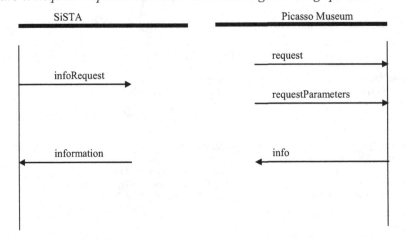

by both interacting parties. In this case, the SiSTA application follows the request-response MEP, while the Picasso Museum applies the In-Multi-Out (Arroyo, forth-comng; Arroyo & López-Cobo, 2005) MEP. Thus, the later requires two message (request and requestParameters) to indicate the nature of the information required, while the SiSTA application uses a single one (infoRequest).

Structual Aspects

In the following, the different core building blocks of the structural models of both applications are described.

The SiSTA application uses the following structural model:

- **Elements:** requestName, requestedObject (name, date, description, creator (name and birth))
- **Documents:** dRequest, dInformation
- **Messages:** infoRequest, information
- **Mapping among documents and elements:**
  - ◦ dRequest.{ requestName, requestedObject }
  - ◦ dInformation.{ requestName, requestedObject }
- **Mapping among messages and documents:**
  - ◦ infoRequest.{ dRequest }
  - ◦ information.{ dInformation }

The Picasso Museum applies the following structural model:

- **Elements:** requestId, artwork (name, date, description, artist (firstName, surname and birthDate))
- **Documents:** documentRequest, documentParameters, documentInfo
- **Messages:** request, requestParameters, info
- **Mapping among elements and documents:**
  - ◦ documentRequest.{ requestId }
  - ◦ documentParameters.{ artWork }
  - ◦ documentInfo.{ artWork }
- **Mapping among documents and messages:**
  - ◦ request.{ documentRequest }

Table 2. Example of the choreography ontologies SiSTAOntChor (a) and PicMu-sOntChort (b)

(a)	(b)

concept creator
  subconceptOf { Λ#element, SiSTAOnt#Creator }
	concept artist
	  subconceptOf { Λ#element, PicMusOnt#Artist }

concept objectName
  subconceptOf { Λ#element, SiSTAOnt#Object }
	concept artWork
	  subconceptOf { Λ#element, PicMusOnt#ArtWork }

concept dRequest
  subconceptOf { Λ#document}
	concept documentRrequest
	  subconceptOf { Λ#message }

concept infoRequest
  subconceptOf { Λ#message}
	concept request
	  subconceptOf { Λ#message }

concept information
  subconceptOf { Λ#message }
	concept info
	  subconceptOf { Λ#message }

Figure 5. Split box for infoRequest message

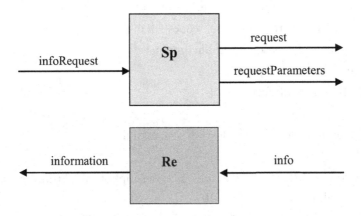

- ◦ requestParameters { documentParameters }
- ◦ info.{ documentInfo }

Table 2 shows a fraction of the choreography ontologies *SiSTAOntChor* and *PicMu-sOntChort* and depicts some elements, documents, messages, and their mappings as used by the parties to model their message exchange. Notice that the concepts detailed are inherited from the domain ontology of each party and the choreography model ontology (Λ) defined by **SOPHIE** (Arroyo, forthcoming).

Operational Aspects

Once a suitable mapping between the concepts of both choreographies has been found, it is straightforward to define the operational model. Figure 5 provides an example of a split and a refiner box.

The split box permits the mapping of the types and names of elements and documents, dividing their content between the *infoRequest* message and request and *requestParameters* in order to suit both MEPs. The refiner box takes care of converting the names of the incoming message and its contents to the ones expected by the addressee, according to the specified mappings.

Conclusion

This chapter has given detailed insight into how to apply the conceptual choreography model of **SOPHIE** to improve and integrate ubiquitous applications. It presented a use case revolving around an educational trip to Barcelona involving interactive knowledge exchange by use of smart phone applications. The basic principles desired for the conceptualization of a semantic-based choreography framework were detailed. Based on these basic concepts, **SOPHIE**, a conceptual framework for a model driven choreography engine, was introduced. The choreography engine makes use of semantic descriptions of MEPs to overcome heterogeneity in communication. Finally, the different models of **SOPHIE** were applied to the use case, exemplifying how to overcome heterogeneity at various levels in a ubiquitous learning and knowledge exchange environment.

References

Andrews, T., Curbera, F., Dholakia, H., Goland, Y., Klein, J., Leymann, F., et al. (2003). *Business process execution language for Web services.* Retrieved October 17, 2006, from http://www6.software.ibm.com/software/developer/library/ws-bpel.pdf

Arkin, A., Askary, S., Fordin, S., Jekeli, W., Kawaguchi, K., Orchard, D., et al. (2002). *Web service choreography interface* (WSCI) 1.0. Retrieved October 17, 2006, from http://www.w3.org/TR/wsci/

Arroyo, S. (forthcoming). *SOPHIE: Semantic services chOreograPHi Engine.* PhD thesis.

Arroyo, S., & Duke, A. (2005). SOPHIE: A conceptual model for a semantic chore-ography framework. In *Proceedings of the Workshop on Semantic and Dynamic Web Process (SDWP'05) in conjunction with the International Conference on Web Services ICWS'05, EEUU,* Orlando, Florida.

Arroyo, S., & López Cobo, J. M. (2005 November). SOPHIE: Architecture and overall algorithm of a choreography service. In *Proceeding of First Online Metadata and Semantics Research Conference (MTSR'05)* (pp. 21-30).

Arroyo, S., López Cobo, J. M., & Sicilia, M. (2005, September 6-9). Structural models of patterns of message interchange in decoupled hypermedia systems. In *Proceedings of the International Workshop on Peer to Peer and Service Oriented Hypermedia: Techniques and Systems in conjunction with the Sixteenth ACM Conference on Hyertext and Hypermedia (HT'05),* Salzburg, Austria.

Arroyo, S., López Cobo, J. M., Sicilia, M., & Sánchez-Alonso, S. (2005). A Semantic Web service architecture for learning object repositories. *Advances in electronic business: Semantic Web and intelligent Web services* (vol. 2). Idea Group Inc.

Arroyo, S., & López Cobo, J. M. (2006). Describing Web services with semantic metadata. *International Journal on Metadata, Semantics and Ontologies, 1*(1), 76-82.

Arroyo, S., & Sicilia, M.A. (2005, November). SOPHIE: Architecture and overall algorithm of a choreography service. In *Proceedings of the First Online Metadata and Semantics Research Conference.*

Chinnici, R., Moreau, J-J., Ryman, A., & Weerawarana, S. (Eds.). (2005). *Web services description language* (WSDL) version 2.0, Part 1: Core language. Retrieved October 19, 2006, from http://www.w3.org/TR/wsdl20

Dean, M., & Schreiber, G. (Eds.). (2004). *OWL Web ontology language reference. W3C recommendation.* Retrieved October 19, 2006, from http://www.w3.org/TR/owl-ref/

de Brujin, J. (2005). *The Web service modeling language WMSL: An overview.* (Tech. Rep. No. DERI-TR-2005-06-16). DERI Innsbruck.

Fensel, D., & Bussler, C. (2002). The Web service modeling framework WSMF. *Electronic Commerce Research and Applications, 1*(2), 113-137.

Kavantzas, N., Burdett, D., & Ritzinger, G. (2004). *Web services choreography description language* version 1.0. Retrieved October 19, 2006, from http://www.w3.org/TR/2004/WD-ws-cdl-10-20040427/

Klyne, G., & Carrol, J.J. (Eds.). (2004). *Resource description framework (RDF): Concepts and abstract syntax. W3C recommendation.* Retrieved October 19, 2006, from http://www.w3.org/TR/rdf-concepts/

Mitra, N. (Ed.). (2003). *SOAP* version 1.2, Part 0: Primer. Retrieved October 19, 2006, from http://www.w3.org/TR/soap12-part0/

Roman, D., Scicluna, J., & Feier, C. (2005). *D14v0.1: Ontology-based choreography and orchestration of WSMO services*. In M. Stollberg & D. Fensel (Eds.). Retrieved October 19, 2006, from http://www.wsmo.org/TR/d14/v0.1/

Watkins, S., Arroyo, S., Duke, A., Richardson, M., Schreder, B., & Wahler, A. (2005). *D8.3: WP 8: Case study B2B in telecommunications, DIP (data, information and processes) project, WP8 B2B in telecommunications*. Retrieved October 19, 2006, from http://dip.semanticweb.org/

Endnote

[1] Simple Standardized Travel Agent: a fictional European framework for travel guides.

Appendix I: Useful Links

Business Process Execution Language for Web Services version 1.1

http://www-128.ibm.com/developerworks/library/specification/ws-bpel/

WSMO Web Service Modeling Ontology

http://www.wsmo.org/

W3C Web Services Choreography Working Group

http://www.w3.org/2002/ws/chor/

Jay Lyman (TechNewsWorld): W3C Publishes Web Services Choreography Language

http://www.technewsworld.com/story/33574.html

Tim Finin & Joel Sachs: Will the Semantic Web Change Science?

http://nextwave.sciencemag.org/cgi/content/full/2004/09/09/3

Knowledge Media Institute (The Open University): Cashew, Composition and Semantic enHancEment of Web-services

http://kmi.open.ac.uk/projects/cashew/

David Burdett: Using Web Services for Business, Part II - Making yourself understood

http://webservices.sys-con.com/read/39932.htm

Andre Everts: An Architecture for Web Knowledge Mediation

http://www.ics.forth.gr/isl/SemWeb/proceedings/session1-3/html_version/node2.html

Semantic Web Services Initiative Architecture Committee (SWSA): SWSA Use Cases

http://www.daml.org/services/use-cases/architecture/

Appendix II: Further Reading

Andrews, T., Curbera, F., Dholakia, H., Goland, Y., Klein, J., Leymann, F., et al. (2003). *Business process execution language for Web services*. Retrieved October 17, 2006, from http://www6.software.ibm.com/software/developer/library/ws-bpel.pdf

Arkin, A., Askary, S., Fordin, S., Jekeli, W., Kawaguchi, K., Orchard, D., et al. (2002). *Web service choreography interface (WSCI)* 1.0. Retrieved October 17, 2006, from http://www.w3.org/TR/wsci/

Arroyo, S. (forthcoming). *SOPHIE: Semantic services chOreograPHi engine*. PhD thesis.

Barros, A., Dumas, M., & Oaks, P. (2005, March). A critical overview of the Web services choreography description language (WS-CDL). *BPTrends*. Available from http://www.bptrends.com/

Caituiro-Monge, H., & Rodriguez-Martinez, M. (2004). Net traveler: A framework for autonomic Web services collaboration, orchestration and choreography in e-government information systems. In *Proceedings of the IEEE International Conference on Web Services (ICWS'04)* (pp. 2-10).

Kavantzas, N., Burdett, D., & Ritzinger, G. (2004, April). *Web services choreography description language version 1.0.* Retrieved October 17, 2006, from http://www.w3.org/TR/2004/WD-ws-cdl-10-20040427/

Khalaf, R., Mukhi, N., & Weerawarana, S. (2003, May 20-24). Service-oriented composition in BPEL4WS. In *Proceedings of the 12th International World Wide Web Conference,* Budapest, Hungary.

Malucelli, A., & Oliveira, E. (2004). Ontology-services agent to help in the structural and semantic heterogeneity. In *Proceedings of 5th Working Conference on Virtual Enterprises,* Toulouse (pp. 175-182).

Milanovic, N., & Malek, M. (2004, November-December). Current solutions for Web service composition. *Internet Computing, IEEE, 8*(6), 51-59.

Paolucci, M., Srinivasan, N., Sycara, K.P., & Nishimura, T. (2003). Towards a semantic choreography of Web services: From WSDL to DAML-S. In *Proceedings of the IEEE Int. Conference on Web Services (ICWS'03)* (pp. 22-26).

Peltz, C. (2003, October). Web services orchestration and choreography. *Computer, 36*(10), 46-52.

Roman, D., Scicluna, J., & Feier, C. (2005, March). In M. Stollberg & D. Fensel (Eds.), *D14v0.1.: Ontology-based choreography and orchestration of WSMO services.* http://www.wsmo.org/TR/d14/v0.1/

Simon, B., Miklós, Z., Nejdl, W., Sintek, M., & Salvachua, J. (2003, May 20-24). Smart space for learning: A mediation infrastructure for learning services. In *Proceedings of the 12th International World Wide Web Conference,* Budapest, Hungary.

Appendix III: Possible Paper Titles/ Essays

- Globalization of education: Can/shall machines surpass human cultural boundaries?

- Service choreography as means to overcome data and communication heterogeneity implied by ubiquitous applications.

- The difference of human and computer communication: Do the basic principles of a semantic-based choreography framework differ from how humans communicate?

- Benefits/drawbacks subsumed by the usage of conceptual choreography models in ubiquitous computing and their relation to underlying technology.

- Value added of using MEP to describe semantic interactions (choreography) in a ubiquitous and context aware environment.

Chapter IX

Semantic Knowledge Mining Techniques for Ubiquitous Access Media Usage Analysis

John Garofalakis, University of Patras, Greece

Theodoula Giannakoudi, University of Patras, Greece

Yannis Panagis, University of Patras, Greece

Evangelos Sakkopoulos, University of Patras, Greece

Athanasios Tsakalidis, University of Patras, Greece

Abstract

In this chapter, an information acquisition system is proposed which aims to provide log analysis, dealing with ubiquitous access media, by use of semantic knowledge. The lately emerging figure of the semantic Web, the ontologies, may be used to exalt the Web trails to a semantic level so as to reveal their deeper usage information. The proposed architecture, which is presented in detail, intends to overcome mobile devices' trail duplicates problems and detect semantic operations similarity of server

Web services, which are often composed to provide a function. The references that supplement the chapter provide publications that discuss mainly log file mining and analysis and semantic similarity. Useful technology-used URL resources are also provided.

Introduction

User driven access to information and services has become more complicated, and can sometimes be tedious for users with different goals, interests, levels of expertise, abilities, and preferences. The Boston Consulting Group announced that a full of 28% of online purchasing transactions failed and 1/3 of them stopped shopping online due to usability difficulties (Boston Consulting Group, 2000). This problem is crucial in online sales systems with thousands of products of different kinds and categories. It is obvious that typical search methods are becoming less favourable as information increases, resulting in money losses.

In user-centred applications, two parameters affect usability:

- **Orientation and navigation strategy:** Users are frequently uncertain as how to reach their goals. Because users have different states of knowledge and experience, information presentation may be too redundant for some of them and too detailed for others.

- **Quality of search results:** Users cannot locate efficiently the information they need (results must be relevant and be presented quickly).

Moreover, with the unprecedented growth of the Internet usage, Web sites are being developed in an uncontrollable, ad-hoc manner, a fact frequently reflected to unpredictable visit patterns. Thus, a critical task for a Web site maintainer is to use enumerable metrics in order to identify substructures of the site that are objectively popular.

Web usage knowledge acquisition has emerged as a method to assist such a task. The fundamental basis for all knowledge manipulation operations entails processing Web server access log files. In its most simplified approach, usage trails' management entails registering absolute page visits or identifying popular paths of information inside a Web site, by the means of log file analysing software solutions such as Web trends (*http://www.webtrends.com*), and Analog (*http://www.analog.cx*). When the goal is to detect popular structural Web site elements, more elaborate techniques have been devised. Some representative work is presented hereafter.

In this work we propose knowledge acquisition techniques and annotation procedures of knowledge objects deriving from the Web usage through any kind of infrastructure, typical browsers, or new media (handheld devices and mobile phones). The key aim of our work is to enhance business intelligence by manipulation and collection of knowledge from ubiquitous access to Web data.

In this chapter we are going to analyze techniques to acquire and manage knowledge emanating from three different sources and corresponding categories:

- Web site business/academic context
- Academic ontologies forming educational Semantic Web sites
- (Semantic) Web usage objects

The proposed novel mechanisms enable bilateral knowledge acquisition from any source of the above to any resulting knowledge category.

We will present a promising prototype that validates our approach as effective. The evaluation of our study is quite encouraging, thus enabling efficient knowledge acquisition.

Background

Significant work on converting server log files to valuable sources of access patterns has been conducted by Cooley (2000). Apart from analysing log files, it is important to use analysis as input, and determine which changes, if any, to bring to the Web site structure. Chen, Park, and Yu (1998) describe efficient algorithms to infer access patterns corresponding to frequently traversed Web site paths. Srikant and Yang (2002) infer path traversal patterns and use them to indicate structural changes that maximize (or minimize) certain site-dependent criteria. Finally, Christopoulou, Garofalakis, Makris, Panagis, Sakkopoulos, and Tsakalidis (2002, 2003), and Makris, Panagis, Sakkopoulos, and Tsakalidis (2005) define techniques to assess the actual value of Web pages and experiment on techniques and mechanisms to reorganise Web sites.

Motivation

A log file is a record of Web activity that automatically records use and information such as the date, time, IP address, HTTP status, bytes sent, and bytes received. The format of the entries in the log files is predefined and its common fields are:

Remotehost	rfc931	authuser	[date]	"request"	status	byte

where remotehost is the remote hostname or the IP address if the DNS hostname is not available, rfc931 is the remote login name of the user, authuser is username as which the user has authenticated himself (only in the case of using password protected WWW page), [date] is the date and time of the request, "request" is the request line exactly as it came from the client (i.e., the file name, and the method used to retrieve it [typically GET]), status is the HTTP response code returned to the client, which indicates whether or not the file was successfully retrieved, and if not, what error message was returned, and bytes is the number of bytes transferred.

A typical line of a log file with common log format is like the following:

151.99.190.27 - - [01/Jan/1997:13:06:51 -0600] "GET /index.htm HTTP/1.0" 301 -4

A variant of the common log format has been lately proposed by W3C [1], which is called the "extended" log file format. This format permits a wider range of data to be captured. This proposal was motivated by the need to capture a wider range of data for demographic analysis and also the needs of proxy caches. Some new fields are added, the most important of which are the "referrer," which is the URL the client was on before requesting the current URL, the "user_agent" which is the software the client claims to be using and the "cookie," in the case where the site visited uses cookies.

In general, extended log format consists of a list of prefixes such as c (client), s (server), r (remote), cs (client to server), sc (server to client), sr (server to remote server, used by proxies), rs (remote server to server, used by proxies), x (application-specific identifier), and a list of identifiers such as date, time, ip, dns, bytes, cached (records whether a cache hit occurred), status, comment (comment returned with status code), method, uri, uri-stem, and uri-query. Using a combination of some of the aforementioned prefixes and identifiers, additional information such as referrers' IPs, or keywords used in search engines, can be stored.

A typical line of a log file with extended log format is like the following:

195.251.240.89 - - [17/Jan/2005:09:56:31 +0200] "GET /images/im_meta.gif HTTP/1.1" 200 669
"http://www.ceid.upatras.gr/" "Mozilla/4.0 (compatible; MSIE 6.0; Windows 98)"

Although the Web log files consist of rows with common fields, each row record may be a result of a different logic of Web browsing. The crucial point where this differentiation is located concerns the variety of devices through which a user accesses a Web site and the use of the new upcoming technology, the Web services. Since most Web sites nowadays give the possibility of mobile access, and a significant number of them use composite Web services to implement complicated functionalities, it is not a trivial task to mine sessions and extract conclusions about how individual users are accessing the site.

The most common case of log data deals with the trails blazed from navigation by regular Web browsers. The user visits consecutive Web pages through her Web browser, and HTTP requests are sent to the Web server for all the files that comprise the page view of a certain page. These files include graphic images, stylesheet definitions, scripts, frames, and texts. The user's request recording process is presented diagrammatically in the following figure.

Additionally, there is the case of log trails that come from user browsing from mobile devices. The particularity of this navigation style arises from the different screen size of those devices. The small screen quickly renders Web pages confusing and cumbersome to peruse. A possible solution to this problem could be the creation of special Web pages for the small screens of mobile devices, but then the

Figure 1. Recording of user requests to the Web server through a PC device

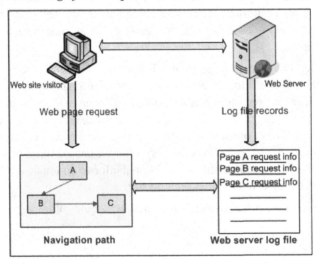

administrators should double their labour when adding new content to their Web sites or modifying old content. A pretty convenient solution is the one proposed by Buyukkokten, Kalijuvee, Garcia-Molina, Paepcke, and Winograd (2002), where the Web page content is being summarized and semantically grouped in units, offering to the user multi-layer navigation to a page body. Similar solutions are followed by the majority of Web site administrators. In this special case, the log file records a large number of hits, which all concern the same page. For example, when the user first accesses a Web page through his mobile device, he parses a summary of the content with links to more detailed presentations of each semantic subject group. After clicking a link, a new entry will be added in the log file, although the same Web page will be accessed. The following figure presents an instance of the described case.

Another special case which accounts for the existence of log file records deriving from substantially differentiated browsing is the use of composite Web services.

Figure 2. Recording of user requests to the Web server through a small-screen device

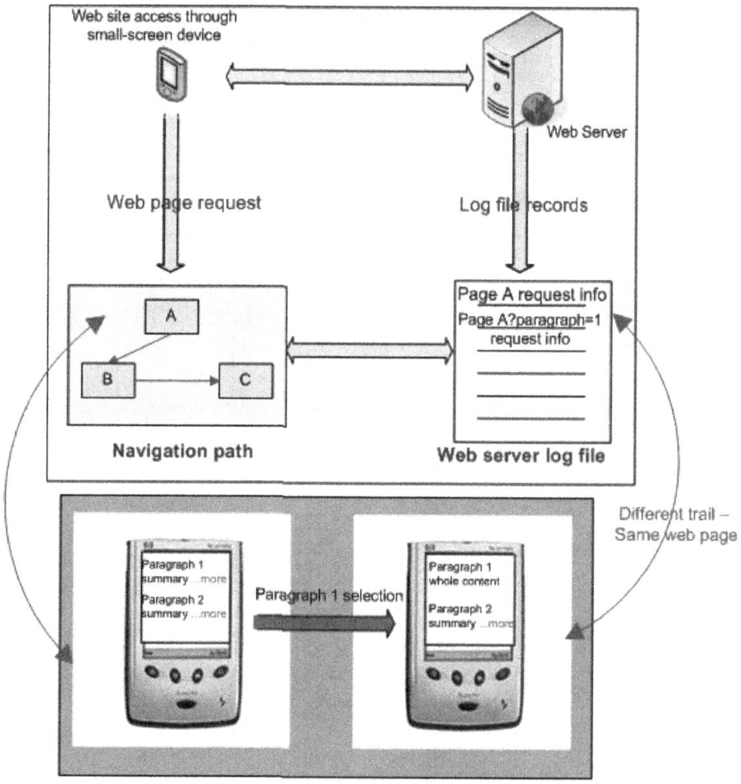

In this occasion, when a user requests a service, the requested URI automatically calls a method from another URI and, as a result, multiple lines of HTTP requests are recorded to the log file, although the client has submitted just a single request (Figure 3). All these lines represent the provision of a functionality which is formed as an integrated service. The specific functionality may be assigned to a representative notion through a (semi) automatic approach.

In general, there is a variety of instances for the large amount of different handheld devices where a specific design approach is followed. All these cases lead to the recording of Web trails with the same type of fields, but with a fundamentally different concept. The great diversity of trails complicates the procedure of session mining at the stage of usage analysis. It is essential to characterize these pages in a way that it will be perceptible, whether multiple log records involve a specific Web access. The lately emerging figure of the semantic Web, the ontologies, may be used to exalt the Web trails to a semantic level so as to reveal their deeper usage info. Semantically, characterized Web pages will have the same meaning, whether they are accessed though a PC browser, or a mobile device browser, and multiple hits to the same page due to the size of small-screen devices will be avoided. Furthermore, requests for services with relevant operations will be located through their semantic annotation, allowing for easier information extraction about the usage of Web server's services, as well as for possible compositions of these services.

Figure 3. Recording of composite Web services requests

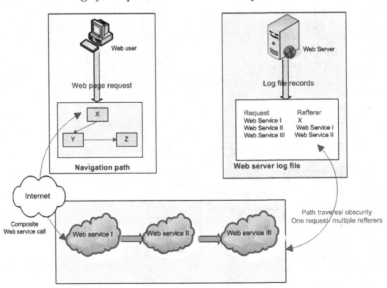

The Prototype System Architecture

In this work, a prototype system of information acquisition is proposed, which overcomes the problem of different navigation trails because of different access device, assigning semantic meaning to the Web pages and the Web services. The proposed system aims to enhance and ease log analysis by use of semantic knowledge. Traditional Web usage analysis is assisted by a well-known domain ontology for the Web site in order to answer combined, semantically enhanced queries about the Web site and the Web server's services usage.

The proposed system analyses the usage of a Web site with linchpin, the Web site's semantic features, as they are expressed through an OWL ontology, which is relevant to the thematic field of the Web site. Knowledge was mined from three different data resources: (a) the Web site content, (b) the usage data, (c) an ontology representative of the Web site notions.

The Web site content provides the semantics of its Web pages and its structure. The usage data contain information about the average number of hits from individual users' visits to every Web page in proportion to the whole set of distinct users' visits. The notions ontology is used for the assignment of Web site content and Web services to standard attributes of the specific field, so as to ensure homogeneous annotation of the Web pages. In addition, this ontology provides adequate apprehension of the correlations between the classes and, by extension, the instances which the site pertains to. Thereby, it offers the possibility to the end-user to form queries relevant to the subject Web pages with combinative and sophisticated criteria.

Our system consists of five distinct functional parts: (1) keyword extraction from the Web site content, (2) keyword extraction for the Web services from WSDL files, (3) the exalting from keywords to semantic characterizations, (4) the usage data preprocessing, and (5) the system front-end to the end-user. The first four parts deal with the pre-processing of the input data (Web site content, Web services descriptions files, and log files), so as to build the appropriate knowledge base that will be used from the query mechanism of the fifth part, as a repository. Web site content is parsed; keywords are extracted and assigned to ontology classes and instances. Web service description files are parsed, descriptive text is anchored and indexed, and keywords are assigned to ontology classes. Different approaches are used for the content and services semantic annotation that will be explained in the next section. The log files' manipulation involves log file cleaning and the session extraction, where mobile access sessions are identified and further processed, in order to deal with special features of those records. The last part constitutes the system interface to the end-user. This is used by the end-user in order to form his query to the information base acquiring knowledge about the Web pages visit ratio through PCs or mobile devices, and the Web services request ratio, based on their semantic attributes.

We have implemented a prototype system based on the architecture that has been described with C# [8] in the Microsoft Visual Studio .NET environment [3] with a CPAN module, which applies semantic similarity measures on the WordNet lexical database.

Web services [9] play an important role to the system implementation. The translation procedure is performed through a Web service, using an online translation engine. Furthermore, the semantic similarity measures may be applied through a Web service, in case the CPAN module is not locally available or updated information on WordNet lexicon may be sought through the Web service.

The system architecture is presented in Figure 4.

As it is shown in the figure above, before executing semantic queries for knowledge mining about the Web site and services usage, there are specific functional components that have to be performed in a specific order.

Concerning keyword extraction from the Web site content, two distinct modules are used, and they are subsequently performed:

1. The first process extracts keywords from the Web page body and from the URLs outside the Web site's domain to which this page provides links.

2. The second process extracts keywords from the most popular links to the specific Web page.

In the case of non English pages, the translation module is utilized. In our experiments we utilized it to translate the Greek words to English in order to be able to perform further automated lexical analysis. Furthermore, this module ensures that all the cases and forms of a word will be expressed through their stem.

In parallel, the extraction of keywords describing the Web services provided may be carried out. The keywords that describe each Web service functionality and operations are extracted from specific <documentation> tags embedded in the <wsdl: operation> and <wsdl:service> tags that the WSDL file [10] contains. The most frequent keywords are kept and stemmed.

After having created the appropriate sets of keywords for the site pages and services, there is one additional module that needs to be implemented in order to complete the Web site data processing, the metadata assignment module. This module applies appropriate mechanisms of word and phrases assignment, so as to semantically characterize the Web site pages with ontology terms, and to categorize the Web services to semantic classes.

In the following, when the Web site semantic annotation has been completed, the log file processing module processes raw usage data and extracts user sessions by also performing extra manipulation for the mobile accesses.

Figure 4. Proposed system architecture

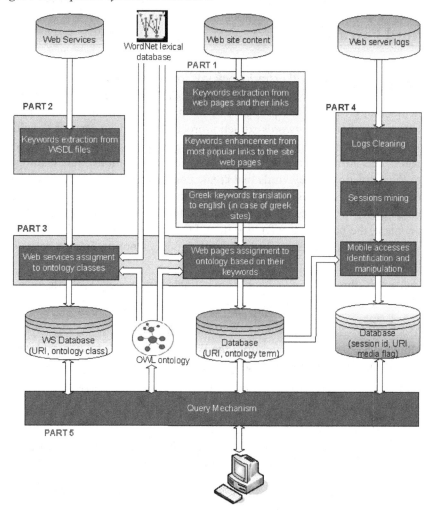

Finally, after all the appropriate modules are completed, the information analyzing module may be used for query submission to produce site usage analysis from a variety of devices using specific semantics. It enables a combined analysis of semantically enriched statistical queries on the preprocessed raw data, overcoming the distinctiveness of log records for ubiquitous media access. This module is further enhanced with a reporting function to produce graphic results (pies, bars, etc.).

Next, the different modules that constitute the system are discussed in detail.

Web Site Preprocessing

Keyword Extraction

As already mentioned, we will extract keywords for every Web page from the Web page body itself, the Web pages it references, and the Web pages that reference it. This methodology was initially proposed by Eirinaki, Vazirgiannis, and Varlamis (2003). Here, we refine the keywords extraction procedure, taking under consideration the structure of contemporary Web sites, which present high connectivity between their pages. This attribute, in combination with the aforementioned methodology, leads to the extraction of keywords that create conflict about the specific content of a Web site's page, although they characterize the whole site's content. In order to avoid conflicts, we utilize for the characterization of a specific page, the Web page's content, the pages that reference it, and the relative content of Web pages out of the site domain that are linked by the Web page, ignoring links to pages of the same domain.

More concretely, three sets of keywords are extracted from every Web site page.

1. Keywords are extracted from the Web page's content.
2. More keywords are extracted from the Web pages that are referenced by the certain page and do not belong to the Web site's domain.
3. Additional keywords are extracted from the pages, which cross-reference the specific page.

After experimentation, we concluded that using 50 keywords for each set extracted is adequate for the content characterization purpose and leads to the creation of normal size sets that will ensure faster manipulation in the semantic annotation process that follows. Further fine-tuning can be performed and the system can be reconfigured at any keyword list length.

The specific tasks undertaken for the Web site indexing process are described below.

Initially, the Web site is parsed, and for every Web page the HTML tags are cleaned, the stop-words (very common words, numbers, symbols, articles) are removed, since they are considered not to contribute to the semantic denotation of the Web page's content, and at last, the top 50 most frequent keywords are extracted. The set of 50 keywords that represent a Web page is complemented by 50 more keywords which are extracted from the Web pages that are cross-referenced by the specific page.

Next, the most popular pages that reference each Web site page are sought using Web searching and the logged external referrers. In the case of Web reference searching,

Google (*www.google.com.gr/apis*) was utilized, mainly because of its Web service programming interface. The first 10 most popular Web sites, which reference the specific page, are considered. The HTML code of each of these pages is parsed and the area around the certain link is spotted. The margins of this area are anchored 100 bytes before the link and 100 bytes after the link. Halkidi, Nguyen, Varlamis, and Vazirgiannis (2003) report the text included in that character/byte window as representative of the referenced Web page subject, which was successfully verified in our case, too. After removing the HTML tags (and broken HTML tags from the edges) and the stop-words, the most frequent words are extracted. A set of the top 50 most frequent keywords is again kept for each Web site page from the set of keywords extracted from the set of 10 Web pages. Overall, after the compilation of these steps, appropriate keyword sets annotate every Web page of the Web site under analysis.

Translation/Stemming

Web page keywords should be translated in order to facilitate lexical processing in non-English sites. For the purposes of translation automation, we have developed a Web service, which posts the keywords to the Babel Fish translation engine (*http://babelfish.altavista.com*) and receives the translation results. We have leveraged the functionality of the WordNet lexical database (Miller, 1995), for words of the English vocabulary only, in order to stem Web page keywords. Other WordNet-like solutions can be also easily incorporated, such as the EuroWordNet (*http://www.illc.uva.nl/EuroWordNet/*) in order to natively achieve lexical analysis in other languages, via a Web service interface.

Manipulation of Web Service Description

Concerning the initial manipulation of Web services, we assume that no Web services discovery tasks have to be undertaken, since the Web site administrator or analyst that will make use of our system will definitely be aware of the Web services available on that Web server. Consequently, the steps performed deal with the extraction of keywords that characterize Web service functionality and methods.

In order to extract keywords that represent the available Web services, their WSDL file is used, since it provides a formal and well-structured presentation of the particular Web service aspects. WSDL is an XML format for describing network services as a set of endpoints operating on messages containing either document-oriented or procedure-oriented information. A WSDL document uses the following elements in the definition of network services:

- **Types:** A container for data type definitions using some type system (such as XSD).

- **Message:** An abstract, typed definition of the data being communicated.

- **Operation:** An abstract description of an action supported by the service.

- **Port Type:** An abstract set of operations supported by one or more end-points.

- **Binding:** A concrete protocol and data format specification for a particular port type.

- **Port:** A single endpoint defined as a combination of a binding and a network address.

- **Service**: A collection of related endpoints.

For the purpose of our system, only the <PortType> tags, particularly the <Opera-tion> tags which are embedded in them (Figure 5), and the <Service> tag (Figure 6) are considered of interest, since they provide information about the tasks that are performed by the specific Web service and its methods. The other tags describe definitions and specification about the format of the data, the bindings, and the protocol for the communication. This information will not be processed, since we don't need to fully annotate the Web services in a semantic level, but to determine their representative notions.

In order to extract keywords set from the WSDL files for the Web services available, we identify two cases: (a) the <Operation> and <Services> tags contain <documenta-tion> tags, which describe in natural language the Web services and their methods or (b) no <documentation> tag is available. Thus, every WSDL file is parsed and its <Operation> and <Services> tags are anchored. Every node's sub-trees are checked for the existence of <documentation> tags. In the case where this tag is located, its content is indexed, possible HTML tags in it are removed, and finally, very common words and symbols are ignored in order to extract the words that carry the meaning of the specific Web services. These words are stemmed through the WordNet lexical database, in order to ensure that all the cases and forms of a word will be expressed through their stem. As before in the Web site content processing, 50 keywords are kept from every WSDL, according to their appearance frequency in the set of ex-tracted words, representing the specific Web service functionality.

In cases that the <documentation> tag is not located, the only data available that may put information about the specific method or the service is its name. Particu-larly for the Web methods, the element names that the method may take as input may be also used to complement the dataset that describes the Web service. These elements tags are located under the <types> tag. According to the specific Web method name, the corresponding element type tags may be easily found and used for Web service description. Since these words (service name, methods names, and

Figure 5. Part of WSDL file presenting methods of a Web service

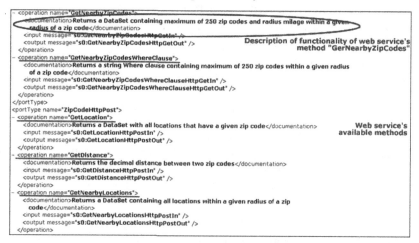

Figure 6. Part of WSDL file presenting description of a Web service

elements) usually comprise strings that may be semantically apprehensible by the human, but not by a lexicon, the WordNet functionality is used in order to lexically analyze these strings to distinct words of the vocabulary. Hence, for instance, the Web service called "ZipCode," if no documentation is provided, will be checked by the WordNet for its ability to be recognized as a vocabulary word. No lexicon contains a word "zipcode," although the phrase "zip code" will explain in general the notion of the certain Web service. Thus, the initial string is split, indicating a new string whenever a capital letter is met. In the following, the set of these strings is checked using the WordNet to test whether they are recognized as a phrase. If not, every single string is checked for whether it constitutes a vocabulary word. The strings that are recognized as words or phrases are kept as the representative keywords of the service and its methods.

Exalting to Semantic Characterization

In this step, the content of the Web site pages is related to classes and instances of an OWL ontology (*www.w3.org/TR/owl-ref/*) and the Web services provided are classified to the relevant ontology classes. The OWL Web Ontology Language is intended to provide a language that can be used to describe the classes and relations between them that are inherent in Web documents and applications.

A basic factor for the accomplishment of the metadata assignment to Web site pages and services constitutes the use of semantic similarity measures between the keywords and the ontology terms with WordNet lexical database. In WordNet, English nouns, verbs, adjectives, and adverbs are organized into synonym sets, each representing one underlying lexical concept. The specific measure that was applied in this system is the Wu and Palmer one (1994). This measure calculates relatedness by considering the depths of the two sets of synonyms in the WordNet taxonomies, along with the depth of the LCS, where LCS is the root taxonomy.

$$score = \frac{2*depth(lcs)}{(depth(s_1) + depth(s_2))}$$

This means: $score \in (0,1]$.

The score can never be zero because the depth of the LCS is never zero (the depth of the root of a taxonomy is one). The score is one if the two input synonym sets are exactly the same.

Before describing the functionalities that are carried out at this point, an example OWL ontology, which was used for the prototype system testing, is described.

The OWL Ontology

The ontology that was used in the system implementation derived from a DAML ontology (*www.daml.org/ontologies/64*) that describes a computer science university department. We transformed this ontology to the OWL format and instantiated it in Protégé (*http://protoge.stanford.edu/*) for the Computer Engineering and Informatics

Figure 7. Portion of the OWL ontology

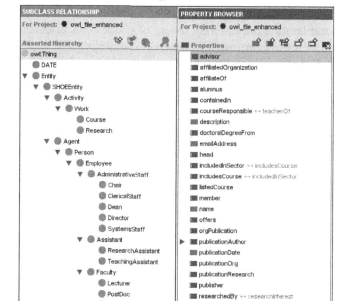

Department (CEID) of the University of Patras. Portion of the ontology classes and properties, as they are displayed in Protégé, is presented in Figure 7.

Metadata Assignment

Making use of this semantic similarity measure, in order to exalt from the keywords set representing each Web page or service to semantic characterizations through smaller sets of ontology terms, we use as criteria the average semantic similarity score of each ontology term (class or instance) with the whole set of keywords of the page. As a result of the metadata assignment, the knowledge that derives for a random URI is that it is semantically classified in specific ontology classes and assigned to certain ontology instances. In the case of Web services, they are only classified to classes, since their assignment to specific instances, such as "Internet

Technologies Course," would probably be neither feasible nor essential for the information acquisition tool that exploits these assignments.

Taking under consideration the different nature of classes and instances, two approaches are used for the assignment of Web pages to ontology classes and instances, correspondingly. The primary aspects that affected the choice of our approaches are the hierarchical structure of the ontology and the particularity of instances context in contrast with the generality of class notions.

Algorithm RecognizeClasses (Given_Ontology)

For each ontology_class

1. **Check whether class ID is recognizable by WordNet**

    If recognized => Class_Represenative = class ID;

    Else

2. **Check "label" existence**

    If exists

    3. **Check whether label id recognizable by WordNet**

        If recognized => Class_Represenative = class "label;"

        Else go to step 4;

    Else

    4. **Check "equivalentClass" existence**

    If exists

        5. **Repeat steps 1,2,3 for the equivalent class**

        If class recognized, break();

         Else go to step 6;

    Else

        6. **Repeat steps 1,2,3,4 for the parent class of class under examination**

            If class recognized, break();

        Else

             REPEAT step 6 for the parent class of the current class UNTIL

             Class recognized OR root class reached

Regarding the ontology classes, we first follow a words/phrases recognition methodology (as previously done during keyword extraction from the Web services and method names and elements), in case their documentation was not provided. Correspondingly, to the services names and elements, the ontology classes' IDs are processed in order to identify the appropriate strings that will describe the class. The classes incorporate a representative ID, which is either a word recognizable by WordNet, or a string semantically comprehensible by the human, but not by a lexicon. In the second case, the existence of the attribute <rdfs:label> is checked, which constitutes a description of the meaning of the specific class. In the case that the class carries a label, it is checked against the WordNet lexical, whether it is recognized as a phrase. If recognized, the label as a whole will be semantically compared with Web site pages/services keywords instead of the class itself. If not, each of the label words will represent the class for the semantic comparisons. If the class does not have a "label" attribute, it is examined whether the attribute <rdfs:equivalentClass> exists. If it is found, the equivalent class is acquired for its ID/label recognition. In the case that the class has not been recognized at all yet, the previous procedure is followed for its parent class considering it as the closest semantically related one. The process will continue for the classes that are located on the path to the root-class, until a class is found that incorporates an ID or a «label» recognized by WordNet.

When all the classes have been recognized, the Web pages and services are classified to them through their keywords. The similarity measure is calculated between every meaning of a keyword and a class, under the constraint that only identical word parts of speech are compared. For instance, it is not possible to calculate the semantic similarity measure between a verb and an adverb, or a verb and adjective, and so on. The greatest similarity measure of all the class meanings with all the meanings of a specific keyword is kept. All the keywords representing a page are compared with a specific ontology class, and the average of their similarity scores is considered the overall similarity score of the specific Web page/service to the specific class. After experimentation, we concluded that a threshold of 0.7 should be satisfied by the overall similarity score, in order to classify the Web page/service to the instance. This process is performed for every Web page and service and its semantic similarity with every ontology class is calculated and compared with the predefined threshold.

Class instances are handled using a slightly different approach, and deal only with the Web page keywords. The assignment of a Web page to an instance requires the existence of keywords in the set of the page's keywords that are semantically very close to the specific instance. Since instances may consist of one word, such as "Databases," or a phrase, such as "Introduction to theory of signal processing," they are tokenized for further examination. In the case of phrases, tokens do not include common vocabulary words, which would never be used as a single-word query in a search engine, such as "to," "of," "the," and so forth. For every Web page, every instance's token is semantically compared with every Web page's keywords, and the highest semantic score is kept as the similarity score of the token to the Web page. The average of the similarity score of every instance's token to a page is considered as the overall semantic relatedness between the instance and the page. During our experiments, we found that this semantic relatedness should satisfy at least the threshold of 0.8, in order to consider that the page relevant with the specific instance. The new terms set derives after the examination of every set of instances and Web pages.

To handle exception cases, the instance tokens, which are not recognized in Word-Net at all, are specially marked by the system as high importance. Such tokens are mainly entities, which can be found among the Web pages' keywords. In this event, all the Web pages, which are characterized by the certain keywords set, will be assigned to the specific instance.

As a result, the Web site pages will have been assigned to relevant classes and instances of the ontology after the completion of this process. All assignments will be recorded in the local database. In the following section, we present the necessary log files pre-processing procedure.

Log Files Processing

In this step, the Web server log files are cleaned, sessions are identified, and the paths are completed, according to the way Cooley (2003) identifies them. The log files are initially cleaned from records of requests for images, requests for non informational files, such as D-HTML parts (i.e., cascade stylesheets (css) and scripting code), and requests that were not successfully responded to or were submitted by search spiders and robots.

In the following, the log files are parsed and user sessions are extracted. In our case, sessions include the set of distinct URIs that were requested in certain order. In order to determine individual sessions, we use three fields of the log files: the user IP, the user agent, and the time interval between consecutive requests. Thus, the pair IP-agent defines a user. However, if time between hits exceeds half an hour, it is considered that a new session started. As a next step, path completion is performed and the page references that are missed due to caching mechanisms of local browsing are filled in.

The agent field is further utilized here to determine whether a session extracted has been recorded for an access through a PC or a mobile device, because different operating systems can be used for these kinds of devices. For the sessions identified as mobile users' navigations, further processing tasks are undertaken in order to detect different trails of the same Web pages through semantic annotations of the aforementioned pages. This step intends to face the problem emerging from the screen size of mobile devices, where the entire page content cannot be displayed at once, as previously explained. Thus, although different URIs will have been recorded, their semantics will be identical or very close. Exploiting the semantic characterizations of the total of the Web site URIs, we calculate the similarity of pages parsed together by mobile devices. We denote the page having the lesser assignments as A, the page with more assignments as B, the sequence of classes and instances assigned to page A as A_s, the sequence of classes and instances assigned to page B as B_s, and the number of semantic assignments of page A as a. The similarity, sim, between pages A and B, is defined through the following relation:

$$sim = \frac{|\{A_s \cap B_s\}|}{a}$$

We concluded after extended experimentation that when the ratio sim satisfies at least the threshold of 90%, the two URIs under examination involve the same page. When meeting such URIs, we keep only the one having the greater number of assignments in the session, considering that we will end up including the URI that will better characterize the set of URIs that concern the same page. Finally, the user sessions that are extracted are stored in the local database accompanied by a flag indicating their media derivation.

Knowledge Acquisition

The proposed system is complemented with a query interface, which is used to analyze the knowledge derived from: (a) Web server log files, (b) metadata information about the Web site and services, (c) OWL ontology representative of the domain. This last module comprises a query builder that performs log file mining based on site/services semantics and the access media used.

The possibilities that our prototype system's interface (Figure 8) provides to the analyst are distinguished in two cases of analysis, whether knowledge acquisition is performed for Web pages or Web services. These two groups of URIs have already been differentiated during the metadata assignment, where the pages are assigned to ontology classes and instances, whereas the Web services are assigned just to ontology classes, leading to the building of a Web services semantic catalogue. Therefore, in the case of Web pages, queries about usage of pages with strictly-defined semantic content may be performed. This attribute would cause inefficiencies in the Web services case. In regard to the Web services, we consider as useful for the site administrator or just the analyst, queries that concern the average number of requests for Web services related to a specific notion, and queries about the common semantic notions of Web services that are called as composite Web service as well. The last type of Web service usage query may help the analyst understand what functionality was aimed by the designer who uses the available Web services together, so as to redesign or enhance them.

The system's possibilities for the most complicated case of Web sites pages querying are:

- Forming of a semantic query where three query parts have to be determined.
  - **Statistical part:** Selection of the statistical question from a list of pre-defined questions.

Figure 8. Knowledge acquisition interface part

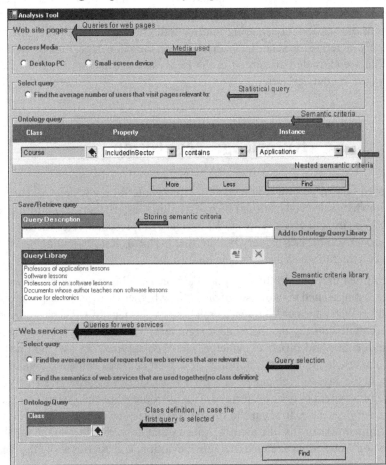

○ **Semantic part:** Description of the semantic criteria that have to be satisfied. This query part may either be formed through the available form or it may be selected from a library storing favourite queries, and it is executed on the ontology.

○ **Access media part:** Determination of the device used to access the Web site under analysis for the specified query. The contribution of this part is to provide individual analysis for trails from different kind of devices.

- Storing of queries with a representative.

- Recall of stored query as a condition during the building of a new query, achieving in this way the creation of a chain of nested queries.

- Creation of union queries. As a result, the user may define one or two groups of pages as criteria for the individual user visits' hits. This feature leads to the extraction of useful conclusions for the visitors' preferences. Via queries, such as "What user ratio visits Web pages relevant to hardware courses and pages relevant to software courses, as well?", the analyst may detect the pages that do not interrelate superficially, but are interesting for some user groups.

The tasks performed when the user submits a query are:

- Ontology querying through the Protégé programmatic interface in order to retrieve instances defined by user-provided semantic criteria (in the case of Web pages-related queries).

- Metadata database to retrieve URIs assigned to specific instances/classes.

- Logs database to retrieve answer to the statistical part of the query.

In order to facilitate ontology querying, we have utilized a very popular ontology management tool, Protégé. Although any other ontology management tool could be used, some basic aspects of this tool were critical for our decision to build upon it. Protégé is a free, open source ontology editor and knowledge-base framework. It provides a foundation for customized knowledge-based applications. Protégé supports XML Schema, RDF(S), and OWL. Furthermore, its API makes it possible for other applications to use, access, and display knowledge bases created with Protégé. We exploited this programmatic interface in order to allow the analysts to specify semantics on the Web site that interests them.

The system interface is complemented by a results pane, where final query results and intermediate results of the involved modules are displayed.

Conclusion and Future Work

In this chapter, we presented a prototype system which provides log analysis for ubiquitous access media, taking advantage of site content metadata characterization. Knowledge about the preferences of Web site visitors, distinguished to mobile users or not, for the Web site subjects and the utilization of available Web services based on their semantics, may be acquired, contributing to the administrator's decision-making for site reorganization or services redesign.

The proposed architecture delivers new functionality to the log analysis systems, taking advantage of the semantics underlying the pages content and the services description. We integrated these semantics with the Web trails in order to provide a new system that excels in three distinct axes: (a) it offers the possibility of semantic queries about site usage, leading to the extraction of conclusions about the preferences of visitors to the Web sites' subjects as they are expressed through its pages, (b) it manipulates the log trails that result from mobile devices more effectively, taking under consideration their specificity (many records of Web pages for one page navigation) and overcoming it by exploiting the pages semantics, and (c) it gives the option of extracting knowledge about the way other developers use a server's Web services, grouping them to semantic classes and detecting common semantics of Web services that are used together, so as to help the administrator's effort to understand the desirable functionality.

Future steps include works for a number of different directions. First of all, the semantic annotation process of the Web site content and services may be enhanced, applying more sophisticated linguistic rules and patterns, which detect word with special semantic weight. Furthermore, the Web pages content and the Web services descriptions could lead to enrichment of the architecture's efficiency, if dealt as a whole, instead of isolated keywords. To this direction, automatic annotation mechanisms could be integrated to the proposed system to further facilitate the administrative purposes.

Furthermore, future work includes research on enhancing log file processing. We consider the impact of taking into account structural information, such as the Web pages depth, during the discovery of the most popular pages. The integration of different structural metrics for log file analysis (Christopoulou et al., 2003) and session building methods could ameliorate the computational part of Web page value calculation. Moreover, system expansions in order to support Web site reorganization tasks are particularly interesting. Nonetheless, we hope that our system will help researchers to acquire deeper understanding of user behavior over a particular Web application.

References

Boston Consulting Group. (2000). *Online shopping promises consumers more than it delivers.* Boston Consulting Group Study.

Buyukkokten, O., Kaljuvee, O., Garcia-Molina, H., Paepcke, A., & Winograd, T. (2002). Efficient Web browsing on handheld devices using page and form summarization. *ACM Transactions on Information Systems, 20*(1), 82-115.

Chen, M. S., Park, J. S., & Yu, P. S. (1998). Efficient data mining for path traversal patterns. *IEEE Transactions on Knowledge and Data Engineering, 10*(2), 209-221.

Christopoulou, E., Garofalakis, J., Makris, C., Panagis, Y., Sakkopoulos, E., & Tsakalidis, A. (2002, June 11-15). *Automating restructuring of Web applications.* (ACM Hypertext 1-58113-477-0/02/0006). College Park, MD.

Christopoulou, E., Garofalakis, J., Makris, C., Panagis, Y., Sakkopoulos, E., & Tsakalidis, A. (2003). Techniques and metrics for improving Web site structure. *Journal of Web Engineering, 2*(1-2), 90-104.

Cooley, R. (2000). *Web usage mining: Discovery and application of interesting patterns from Web data.* PhD thesis, University of Minnesota.

Cooley, R. (2003). The use of Web structure and content to identify subjectively interesting Web usage patterns. *ACM Transactions on Internet Technology.* Retrieved October 19, 2006, from http://portal.acm.org

Eirinaki, M., Vazirgiannis, M., & Varlamis, I. (2003). SEWeP: Using site semantics and a taxonomy to enhance the Web personalization process. In *Proceedings of the 9th SIGKDD International Conference on Data Mining and Knowledge Discovery (KDD'03)* (pp. 99-108).

Halkidi, M., Nguyen, B., Varlamis, I., & Vazirgiannis, M. (2003). THESUS: Organizing Web document collections based on link semantics (special issue on Semantic Web). *VLDB Journal, 12*(4), 320-332.

Makris, C., Panagis, Y., Sakkopoulos, E., & Tsakalidis, A. (2005). An algorithmic framework for adaptive Web content. In *Proceedings of the International Workshop on Adaptive and Personalized Semantic Web ACM HyperText 2005,* (Studies in Computational Intelligence 14, pp. 1-10). Springer Verlag.

Miller, G. A. (1995). WordNet: A lexical database for English. *Communications of the ACM, 38*(11), 39-41.

Srikant, R., & Yang, Y. (2001). *Mining Web logs to improve Web site organization.* In *Proc. of the 10th Int. Conference on World Wide Web* (pp. 430-437).

Wu, Z., & Palmer, M. (1994). Verb semantics and lexical selection. In *Proceedings of the 32nd Annual Meeting of the Association for Computational Linguistics* (pp. 133-138), Las Cruces, New Mexico.

Appendix I: Case Study – Semantic Analysis of the Log Files of the Web Site of Computer Science and Informatics Department of the University of Patras

This site constitutes the official Web site of the Computer Science Department in Patras (*http://www.ceid.upatras.gr*). It has four levels and publishes a number of 253 Web pages. Its content provides information about department administration, undergraduate and postgraduate studies, staff, research projects, news and interests, and the university campus. It was designed with HTML, apart from some dynamic pages implemented with PHP. There are two available versions (the Greek and the English versions). The Web site's structure graph may be considered coherent. This department also provides, through the same server that hosts the site, three Web services: a Web service that provides information about students' diplomas, a Web service providing info about students themselves, and a Web service providing the bookings of a specific student to the department library. Furthermore, part of the Web site content exhibits mobility. We have collected a Web log covering 6 months (January 2005-May 2005). We have at our disposal the ontology described in the chapter.

Our goal is to extract knowledge about the average number of users that visit both hardware and software courses and how these rates differ from mobile devices. Furthermore, we aim at detecting the desired functionality from the developers that use the aforementioned Web services (or two of them) together (if any).

Questions

1. What will be the steps that we will perform to prepare our resources for the final goal?

2. How will the knowledge acquisition form be used to serve our purpose?

3. Could we succeed our goal without the use of the ontology? What difficulties/obstacles would we meet?

Appendix II: Useful URLs

Extended Log File Format Specification

http://www.w3.org/TR/WD-log file.html

Google Web Apis Home Page

http://www.google.com.gr/apis/

Microsoft Visual Studio

http://msdn.microsoft.com/vstudio/

OWL Web Ontology Language Reference

http://www.w3.org/TR/owl-ref/

Pfizer Glossary

www.pfizer.com/pfizer/privacy/mn_privacy_glossary.jsp

The DARPA Agent Markup Language Web Site

http://www.daml.org/ontologies/64

The Protégé Ontology Editor and Knowledge Acquisition System

http://protege.stanford.edu/

Visual C# Developer Center

http://msdn.microsoft.com/vcsharp/

Web Services Activity

http://www.w3.org/2002/ws/

Web Services Description Language (WSDL)

http://www.w3.org/TR/wsdl

Appendix III: Further Reading

Personalised applications and services for a mobile user

http://ieeexplore.ieee.org/iel5/9846/31027/01452113.pdf?tp=&arnumber=145211
3&isnumber=31027

Semantic Web for mobiles

http://www.nokia.com/nokia/0,,5176,00.html

Towards know-when technology in the mobile information space: long-term user trace log analysis in the mobile Internet

http://ieeexplore.ieee.org/iel5/8792/27823/01241263.pdf?tp=&arnumber=124126 3&isnumber=27823

U-Commerce & U-Business: Towards ubiquitous tourist service coordination and integration – A multi-agent and Semantic Web approach
http://portal.acm.org/ft_gateway.cfm?id=1089656&type=pdf&coll=portal&dl=AC M&CFID=59696675&CFTOKEN=65594825

Appendix IV: Possible Paper Titles/ Essays

- Knowledge learning processes for usage of every electronic media anywhere
- Re-engineering business logic with the Semantic Web service usage analysis techniques
- Ubiquitous media: Can they be more than mobiles and how soon?

Chapter X

To Ease the Dilemma of Help Desk:
The Application of Knowledge Management Techniques in Manipulating Help Desk Knowledge

Nelson Leung, University of Wollongong, Australia

Sim Kim Lau, University of Wollongong, Australia

Abstract

Information technology has changed the way organizations function. This resulted in the reliance of help desks to deal with information technology related areas such as hardware, software, and telecommunication. Besides, the adoption of business process reengineering and downsizing has led to the shrinkage of the sizes of help desks. Consequently, the help desks have to cover more information technology products and resolute more technical enquiries with less staff. Thus, the outcome is clear that users have to wait comparably longer before the help desk staff are available to offer assistance. This chapter describes the development of help desk, ranging from help desk structures to support tools. This chapter also discusses the application of knowledge management techniques in the development of a proposed conceptual knowledge management framework and a proposed redistributed knowledge management framework. While the conceptual knowledge management framework proposes a standard methodology to manage help desk knowledge, the proposed redistributed knowledge management framework allows simple and routine enquiries to be rerouted to a user self-help knowledge management system. The proposed system also enables help desk to provide technical knowledge to users 24 hours a day, 7 days a week. Regardless of time and geographical restrictions, users can solve their simple problems without help desk intervention simply by accessing the proposed system through portable electronic devices.

Introduction

In the past two decades, the emergence of information technology (IT) has converted a large part of organizational activities from manual- and paper-based to automatic- and electronic-based. Such a conversion not only increases the complexity of IT infrastructure, but also increases the coverage of help desk on software, hardware, network, and other IT related areas. It is quite common for a single help desk to cover hundreds of thousands of software, hardware, application programs, and network connections, and sometimes it is difficult even to memorize all those names. What exacerbates the situation is the wide adoption of management methodology such as business process reengineering and downsizing. This leads to the shrinkage of the size of help desk because the overall budget has been reduced. This also leads to the loss of priceless knowledge considered crucial for the daily operation within the help desk boundary, because a significant number of experienced help desk staff has been reduced. The consequence for more service with less staff is quite obvious: a user has to wait comparably longer before a first level operator is available. In addition, the help desk staff are no longer available for high-level and proactive support activity or training. According to a research conducted by the Help Desk Institute (Broome & Streitwieser, 2002), most respondents in the help desk industry have reported that their call volume has been increasing every year for the past 10 years. Heckman and Guskey (1998) confirm that "help unavailable when needed" is the major reason for service delivery failure in the help desk, which in turn leads to user dissatisfaction.

Help desk experts and academic researchers continue to look for ways to relieve the above burden, and the effort includes development of systems, support structures, and models, but the hard work seems in vain. What goes wrong? Humans always use reflective design concepts as a method to develop a system; in other words, we tend to solve a problem based on past experience and conscious reflection without local adaptation. For example, the New South Wales (NSW) Government in Australia tries to improve access to the Sydney Airport, Port Botany, and the city for people living in the west and southwest of Sydney by building M5 East. But M5 East itself is actually creating congestion problem, as more than 100,000 vehicles a day travel on the M5 East. This almost doubles the Roads and Traffic Authority's calculation in its environment impact statement, predicting that 55,000 vehicles would be using the tunnel by 2011 (Smith, 2005). Rather than alleviate congestion, M5 East itself encourages more people to drive more often, which in turn carries 7.1% of passengers away from the East Hill Rail Lines (Smith, 2004). Similarly, various support models, structures, and technologies are designed to ease high volume of enquiries within the help desk environment; however, such actions actually create more trouble in the real world if the problem domain and user's need have not been investigated thoroughly.

This chapter describes the development of help desk, ranging from help desk structures to support tools. This chapter also discusses the application of knowledge management techniques in the development of the proposed conceptual knowledge management framework and redistributed knowledge management framework. While the conceptual knowledge management framework proposes a standard methodology to manage help desk knowledge, the proposed knowledge management framework allows simple and routine enquiries to be rerouted to the user self-help

Figure 1. Chapter overview

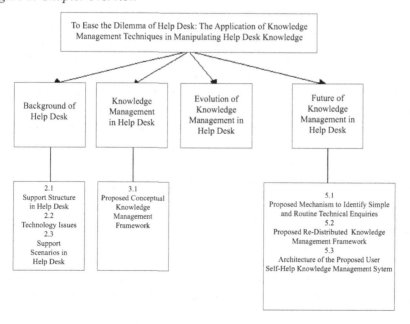

knowledge management system so that users can fix their problems without help desk intervention. Figure 1 illustrates the overview of this chapter.

Background of Help Desk

Organizations have been investing heavily in IT and information systems (IS) development to solve business problems, to gain competitive advantage, and to sustain organizational improvement. Consequently, the variety and complexity of software, hardware, and network technology have greatly increased. This leads to the establishment of help desk to provide technical support to users. Help desk, also known as computer call centre, contact centre, IT assist centre, or support centre, is an access point to provide IT-related advice, information, or troubleshooting action to user. Its responsibilities include first line incident support in case of IT failure, day-to-day communication between IT department and user, business system support, and service quality report generating (Central Computer and Telecommunications Agency, 1989). In short, it is a user's first contact place for all issues relating to IT support. The help desk also acts as a facilitator to collect and analyse its data to help itself in a more proactive role (Marcella & Middleton, 1996).

Before help desk emerged, users either called whomever they knew, or a so-called "computer expert," in the IT Department when they required technical support (Smith, 1996). However, this ad-hoc support framework has some shortcomings. Firstly, the IT staff might not be available for immediate assistance because they were usually occupied by other crucial projects. Secondly, excess amount of support duty would lead to high level of frustration within the IT department because they were not able to spend time on their tasks or projects. Thirdly, users usually called the wrong person, workgroup, or even department for support. In this case, users were often required to make another call or be transferred to the person who was responsible for solving the problem (Middleton, 1999; Smith, 1996). This not only delayed the support process but also interrupted the development and deployment of new services and systems in the IT department. Thus the idea of help desk emerges with the purpose to minimize the above problems and to meet user expectation.

Support Structure in Help Desk

Although each help desk is unique according to the organization's strategic investments, support doctrine, business it supports, and customer expectations, generally help desk can be divided into front line (first level), second level, and third level support, as illustrated in Figure 2 (Czegel, 1999). Basically, enquiries come into the front line (first level) support from various sources. At this level, first level operators will attempt to provide answers for simple questions. Users can choose to access

Figure 2. Three level support structure

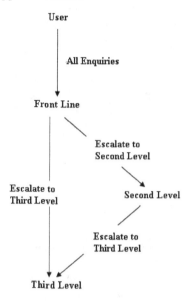

Figure 3. Two level support structure

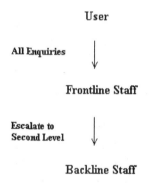

Figure 4. One level structure support

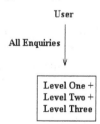

help desk through various channels, which include telephone, Web forms, e-mail, fax, or walk-in. If the first level operator cannot resolve the problem, it will be escalated to second or third level support. Second level analysts, who possess in-depth IT knowledge, will conduct a series of research and testing to solve the problem. If it involves on-site support, such as hardware installation, a second level engineer usually takes over the job. If the second level support staff still cannot handle the problem, then the case will be passed to a third level specialist, such as a database administrator, Web site developer, or vendor, to resolve the problem. Kajko-Mattsson (2003) reports that the three level concept currently dominates a large segment in help desk support structures, but some organisations choose to simplify it into two levels, or even one level support, as illustrated in Figures 3 and 4, respectively.

Technology Issues

To support different users, help desk should be equipped with high technology equipments to ensure efficient and effective troubleshooting. Fully loaded help desk is never a by-product of sudden universal explosion; rather the transformation takes a long time, with a lot of resources and efforts. According to Kendall (2002), help desk in mid-late 1980s only contained a desk, a phone, and a pen. At that time, senior management executives never recognized a help desk's value. On the other hand, help desk was viewed as a non-profit-generating function that always showed up as a cost on the ledgers (Czegel, 1999). When the organization realizes IT malfunction will hinder individual user or sometimes the whole organization from working at optimal productivity, senior managements start to invest strategically on help desk technologies. In addition, modern technology has also accelerated the delivery of the help desk evolution. High technology tools have been used to support, stimulate, and accelerate the consolidation of multiple help desks.

Automatic call distribution systems play an important role in promoting help desk consolidation because it can handle a large number of calls simultaneously on a single phone number. Automatic call distribution is a system that helps to manage the flow of phone calls, record historical data, and generate call statistic report (Underwood, Hegdahl, & Gimbel, 2003). When a user calls, the automatic call distribution system that interconnects a finite number of help desk operators will distribute the call to the first available operator. If all the staff members are busy, the call will be placed in a queue. Most of the systems will then play a recorded message to inform the user that *"all lines are currently busy and the first available help desk operator will answer the call as soon as possible."* At the same time, the automatic call distribution system keeps monitoring the queue, sending "the first user in the queue" to the next available operator, and makes sure the calls are evenly distributed among the help desk operators. An Interactive Voice Response system is widely installed as a front end for the automatic call distribution system. The

Interactive Voice Response system is an automated answering system that allows users to interface with other technology, such as a mainframe, database, and fax machine. It also allows the users to get information or to perform a specific function simply by selecting the required options from the menu via the telephone pad (Czegel, 1999). Additionally, the automatic call distribution system that possesses supervisory functions enables help desk supervisors to monitor the workload, listen in on calls, monitor queue status, reroute calls, and reconfigure automatic call distribution system settings to fit different call patterns. Supervisory and management reports, that include total incoming, outgoing plus abandoned calls, call answered, average talk time, and average hold time, can be generated by the automatic call distribution system (Underwood et al., 2003; Czegel, 1999). These reports allow the help desk to continuously enhance its performance by rearranging manpower, purchasing or developing new technologies, or changing automatic call distribution system configurations. For example, if the statistics show that there is an enormous number of abandoned calls in the morning, then more staff should be added to the morning shift.

The emergence of help desk management systems is a major step for help desk automation (Middleton, 1999). Czegel (1999) depicts four basic functions of help desk management systems as call information logging, ticket escalating, ticket storing, and reporting. Call logging function enables the help desk operator to record user's personal detail, computer setting, and problem description in a ticket storing function or ticket repository. The help desk operator always refers to that piece of record as a ticket. As soon as the user calls to request technical support, the help desk operator has to open a ticket, fill in the details and then save it in the storing function. If the problem requires further escalation, the operator can forward or assign the ticket to a particular analyst or workgroup by the ticket escalating function. An analyst or workgroup who holds the ticket is responsible for updating all follow-up action, progress, and resolution method into the ticket repository. When the problem is resolved, the ticket will be closed. The reporting function allows help desk supervisors or managers to generate report with difference parameters, such as high priority ticket, outstanding ticket, problem types and so forth (Underwood et al., 2003). Reporting is a very powerful function to manage the daily operation of help desk. For example, if there are too many outstanding tickets waiting to be resolved, it may be an indication to hire more staff. If there is a huge number of tickets related to a software or hardware problem, then it may require a thorough check up on the system concerned.

Help desk expert systems have been highlighted as a feasible application in the help desk industry due to the scarceness, diverseness, and expensiveness of expertise (Goker, Roth-Berghofer, Bergmann, Pantleon, Traphoner, Wess, & Wilke, 1998). The ever and fast expansions of IT often result in the help desk staff requiring specific knowledge and expertise to understand and handle enterprise-wide systems. Consequently, it makes the help desk staff unable to offer immediate assistance if one of the experts with a particular knowledge is unavailable. Expert systems or knowledge-based systems are a subset of artificial intelligence, which imitates human reasoning processes to solve specific problems (Turban & Aronson, 2001). If an expert system is developed, the first level operator is able to provide recommendation and solution for a routine or even complex problem simply by entering its description and symptom into the system. Then, the embedded inference engine will try to find the best diagnostic method from the knowledge-based system. This way, the second and third level support staff can be freed for more important duty. However, Middleton (1999) argues that expert systems and other artificial intelligence-related systems are not as widely used as expected. Some of the problems in developing help desk expert system are high cost and time consumption in knowledge acquisition and knowledge base maintenance, high complexity of problem domains, and difficulties in help desk expert system development (Czegel, 1999).

Remote control software is a help desk software that makes use of modern data communication technology to view, access, or even take control of computers to carry out troubleshooting over the network (Underwood et al., 2003). There are two types of remote control software: client-based and Web-based. The difference is that the client-based one requires installing a small program called client, whereas Web-based simply connects through the Internet. Compared to traditional on-site support methods, remote control provides a quicker way for problem solving, as long as the target computer has Internet access and also encourages user involvement in fixing a problem, by watching and learning the required process through the technician's demonstration. However, security is always an important issue with remote access. Auspiciously, most of the software can be configured so that the technician must gain permission from the user before viewing and controlling the target computer. Additionally, users can retake control or even terminate the session at any time. At Griffith University, the help desk is able to solve 75% to 85% of problems remotely, whereas the resolution rate drops to 53% without the aid of remote control software (Scullen, 2001).

Support Scenarios in Help Desk

The effectiveness and efficiency of a help desk support process requires harmony among support staff, users, support structure, and inherent technologies. To demonstrate the roles of the above, let us consider two support scenarios.

In the first scenario, Michael has difficulty in creating a table of contents when he is using Microsoft Word for his financial report. Without too much consideration, he decides to call the HD hotline for assistance. Subsequently, an automatic call distribution system picks up the call and starts to look for the first available staff member within first level support. The automatic call distribution system soon realizes that Mary's phone is idle, and therefore it decides to direct Michael's call to Mary. Since creating a table of contents is a fairly easy task, Mary possesses enough knowledge to walk John through the entire creation procedure without further escalation. Michael, satisfied with the new creation, hangs up, but Mary is still required to open a ticket, fill in troubleshooting details, and close the ticket within the help desk management system. The support process in this scenario is fast and smooth, but that is not always the case—some incoming enquiries may require in-depth expertise on a particular IT-related area. In the second scenario, Jack calls the help desk hotline because he wants to set up a virtual private network between the Sydney and Melbourne office. His call is directed to Mary by the automatic call distribution system. Mary soon realizes that she does not have enough knowledge to provide assistance, so she decides to escalate this enquiry to Nicole, who is a network analyst in second level support. Before transferring the call, Mary quickly briefs Nicole about the enquiry and assigns an open ticket to Nicole. Since setting up a virtual private network is very complicated to general users, Nicole makes a suggestion to Jack about using remote control software to establish the network. By using the remote control software, Jack can sit back, watch, learn, or even take notes on what Nicole has done during the setup process. In this way, Jack may be capable of establishing his own virtual private network in the future if need be. After Jack agrees with Nicole's approach, she takes about 30 minutes to complete the whole setup process, and another five minutes to fill in the support details for the opening ticket. As mentioned earlier, the delivery of satisfactory HD service depends on support staff, users, support structure, and technologies. However, the knowledge required to walk a user through the support process should be rated as important as other factors. Very often, HD fails to provide speedy and effective solutions, simply because the knowledge is not available, either temporary or permanently.

Knowledge Management in Help Desk

Help desk experts use both tacit and explicit knowledge to solve a user's problem. Tacit knowledge refers to skills, perceptions, assumptions, and experiences that reside in a staff member's brain, whereas explicit knowledge refers to written documents, such as technical manuals and guide books. One way to manipulate tacit and explicit knowledge is to apply the concept of knowledge management in the workplace. To examine whether the contribution of knowledge management can be extended to help desk, it is critical to review the background of knowledge management.

Back to the mid-1980s, management tools and techniques such as total quality management, downsizing, and business process reengineering were developed by western companies to aid in regaining market shares occupied by the Japanese company. However, both input and improvement are short-term, because these solution approaches are generic and easily available to all rival companies. Once an approach is proven successful, the rival company duplicates and adopts the same practice (Sharkie, 2003). The practices of downsizing, business process reengineering, and outsourcing, which aims for process optimization, as well as cost and time saving, have resulted in a loss of many experienced employees, along with their capability and knowledge, which in turn has "drained" away organizations' inspiration and creativity (Coulson-Thomas, 1997). Thus, organizations have to repay high, severe, and long-term prices in return for transient benefit. The worst aspect, however, is that, after several years of downsizing and business process reengineering, companies in the western world are now competing with each other on equal cost, quality, and delivery performance levels. This means that the company has difficulties in differentiating with other challengers. What intensifies the already fierce battlefield is the availability of cheap labour in Asian and other developing countries. Thus, the concept of knowledge management has emerged to sustain long term competitive advantage by preserving organizational knowledge (Turban & Aronson, 2001). Knowledge is now recognized as one of the most important management assets because knowledge enables organizations to utilize and develop resources, enhance their fundamental competitive ability, and develop sustainable competitive advantage (Sharkie, 2003). In other words, knowledge allows an organization to do better than rivals.

Knowledge management is designed to manage and capitalise on knowledge that accumulates in the workplace (Martensson, 2000). This is achieved by organizing formal and direct processes to create, store, and retain knowledge for the benefit of the organization (Dawson, 2000; Smith, 2001). The entire process of knowledge management (as illustrated in Figure 5) is divided into five stages: create, store, make available, use, and evaluate knowledge (Chait, 1999; Wiig, 1997). There are four methods to create organizational knowledge by means of the interaction between explicit and tacit knowledge (Nonaka, Toyama, & Konno, 2001). The first method is socialization. It is the process of developing tacit knowledge from tacit knowledge embedded in human or organization through experience sharing, observation, and traditional apprenticeship. The second method is called externalization. This is the process of turning tacit knowledge into new explicit knowledge simply by transforming tacit knowledge in the form of a document, such as manual and report. The third method is combination. This is the process of merging and editing "explicit knowledge from multiple sources" into a new set of more comprehensive and systematic explicit knowledge. The last method is internalization. This is the process of embodying explicit knowledge as tacit knowledge by learning, absorbing, and integrating explicit knowledge into individual's tacit knowledge base.

The second and third stages of knowledge management, store and make available, are often linked with technologies. Explicit knowledge created is collected and stored in some form of the database or knowledge base, in which the users have the right to access by using "search and retrieve" tools, intranets, Web access and applications, groupware, and so forth (Alavi & Leidner, 1999; Prusak, 1999; Smith,

Figure 5. Five stages of knowledge management

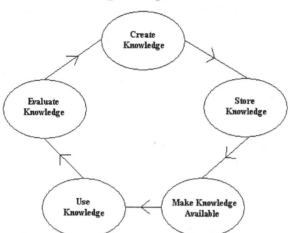

2001). Whether knowledge can create value or not, it is directly connected to the fourth stage of knowledge management because knowledge has little value without use (Dawson, 2000). Though the application of knowledge is varied in accordance with the business nature, the focus is still on how to make use of knowledge to improve the current value chains. The fifth stage of knowledge management is knowledge evaluation. This phrase eliminates incorrect or outdated knowledge (Alavi & Leidner, 1999). In other words, organization must keep creating new knowledge and replace any knowledge that has become invalid (Dawson, 2000).

Knowledge management, unlike other generic solutions, is capable of sustaining long term competitive advantage, but how can this be achieved? Sharkie (2003) indicates that a rival company still can duplicate and imitate the process of knowledge management or even its technology, but they can never copy the knowledge and skills of employees. The spirit of knowledge management encourages organizations to create and use knowledge continuously, and also enables them to take initiative in innovating and enhancing service, product, and operation. To promote knowledge management, organizations should exploit the advantages of modern data communication techniques and computerized devices, as well as other forms of IT software and hardware. On one hand, advanced technology is able to streamline the process of knowledge management, but on the other hand, it enables knowledge management to be performed pervasively and ubiquitously. For instance, Internet and mobile phone technology allow two or more parties to exchange knowledge through text message, e-mail, phone conversation, or even video conferencing (Poston & Speier, 2005). In another instance, portable devices, such as laptop computers and personal digital assistants (PDAs), also provide a medium for individuals to store and access knowledge from anywhere in the world, at anytime.

Though knowledge management is a fundamental factor behind a company's success, several issues must be handled carefully. A minority view knowledge management as another repackaging of IT projects (Lueg, 2001). However, IT tools are merely designed to fit into the knowledge management process, rather than to add value to knowledge. For example, a knowledge management system is just an IT-based system used to store and disseminate knowledge (Alavi & Leidner, 1999; Smith, 2001). To add value to knowledge, groups, individuals, and leaders should be encouraged to cooperate and collaborate in knowledge transfer and sharing (Goh, 2002). Unfortunately, not all potential knowledge contributors are willing to share their knowledge in an organization. Since knowledge is perceived as a source of power, some of the potential contributors may be scared of losing their power or value if they do not retain enough propriety knowledge, thus making them more replaceable in the organization (Kankanhilli, Tan, & Wei, 2005). To encourage knowledge contribution, various forms of monetary and non-monetary rewards can be offered to contributors. Level of trust, time availability, leaders' participation, environment setting, and organizational structure are also keys to motivate knowledge transfer and sharing (Coulson-Thomas, 1997; Goh, 2002; Martensson, 2000).

Proposed Conceptual Knowledge Management Framework

Although help desks are composed of help desk support staff and technical equipment, the actual axis of the overall support process in help desk is knowledge. When users require technical support, this means they lack sufficient IT-related knowledge to carry on their duty. The help desk staff is responsible for assisting users in solving the problem by using knowledge residing in some sort of repository, such as a human's brain, a database, or a technical manual. To standardize the process in managing knowledge within a help desk's environment, we propose a conceptual knowledge management framework (see Figure 6). The proposed conceptual knowledge management framework makes use of the fives stages of knowledge management and knowledge management systems to manipulate help desk knowledge. The technical knowledge is converted by both externalization and combination. Externalization is used to convert skill, technique, experience, and perception from experts into explicit knowledge, and combination is used to combine and revise explicit knowledge from manual, guidebook, and training documentation into a more systematic and organized knowledge. In this way, both types of knowledge are converted to a form that can be stored in the electronic repository. Structure Query Language (SQL) can be applied to allow the help desk staff to retrieve the required knowledge from the repository. More advanced techniques, such as search engines, agent technology, and artificial intelligence, can also be applied to retrieve this knowledge. The retrieved knowledge is used to resolve a user's problem. The shorter product life cycle in IT also means the knowledge residing in the repository

Figure 6. Proposed conceptual knowledge management framework

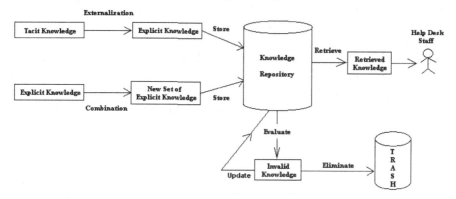

is required to be evaluated regularly in order to maintain its validity. The invalid knowledge is either renewed and stored in the repository or removed permanently from the repository.

Evolution of Knowledge Management in Help Desk

The proposed conceptual knowledge management framework has provided a methodology for manipulating help desk knowledge. In order to maximize its effect, a certain degree of customization may be required, depending on the organizations. Although literature has shown that research has been conducted on the application of knowledge management in help desk, most of them are focused on the technical aspect of how to store and retrieve knowledge, and only a handful cover the entire knowledge management process in help desk (Chan, Chen, & Geng, 2000; Czegel, 1999; Davis, 2002). To effectively customize the conceptual knowledge management framework, it is essential to have a thorough understanding of how knowledge is managed along with the evolution of help desk. Thus, a brief overview on the development of knowledge handling techniques in the help desk is given in the following section.

At the early stage, a decentralized help desk model was very popular. Organizations often had more than one help desk in the 1980s. Various help desks were established by departments, branches, and IT work groups. For example, there were nine different help desks in Western Kentucky University, in which users had to determine which help desks to call, depending on where the problem was, what the problem was, and when the problem occurred (Kirchmeyer, 2002). The decentralized help desk model shares the belief that diverse support issues could be referred to related help desks easily so that a timely response could be acquired. At that time, each help desk had its own collection of training manuals, guidebooks, technical manuals, and other paper-based documentations in which computer knowledge was stored and organized. In the very beginning, decentralized help desks worked well together with this primeval knowledge handling technique because computer systems were simple and straightforward. So it was quite easy for the help desk staff to locate the right piece of knowledge from the low-quantity paper-based manuals. On the other hand, the effort required to update the paper-based documentation was light because computer life cycles were relatively longer.

As IT infrastructure grew more complicated, and organization-wide information systems were interconnected with a large number of hardware and software, the classification of problem domains became not so distinct. Users started to confuse multiple help desks, and they were often being directed from one help desk to another before obtaining a correct solution. Then, organizations started adopting the centralized help desk model (Marcella & Middleton, 1996). The idea was to merge various help desks into one, in which the user only needs to memorize a single telephone number for all IT-related enquiries. This makes help desk the first and single point of contact. Nevertheless, the adoption of help desk consolidation also challenged the traditional way of managing IT knowledge. Rather than allowing IT knowledge to be scattered in multiple collections of paper-based documentations, a centralized help desk was required to merge all of them into one. Obviously, the conventional paper-based manipulation method could not afford the sudden burst of knowledge from various help desks. One can easily imagine the clumsiness of the combined paper-based documents. Moreover, IT knowledge residing in the combined paper-based version would be extremely hard to search and update. As long as help desk staff realized that electronic repositories could provide assistance, they started migrating IT knowledge into a computer file system that has the capability of accommodating huge amounts of IT expertise. However, it has its disadvantage, in which there is a lack of flexibility in handling knowledge. Very often, a programmer is required to implement complicated programs even in the simplest knowledge retrieval and storing tasks. Then, the emergence of database technology overcomes the shortcomings in the file system. Database technology not only provides a more structured way to manage knowledge, but the simplicity and easy-to-learn ability of SQL also allow the help desk staff to create, store, retrieve, use, and review knowledge effectively and efficiently. Because of these advantages, database technology has assisted the development and standardization of information and knowledge in the help desk industry.

Nowadays, some global corporations with offices all over the world implement another model, called the distributed or virtual help desk model. This model promotes help desks of multiple physical locations. Users can still keep in touch with them by using one contact number through the modern call routing technology (Tischler

& Trachtenberg, 1998). In this way, help desks are able to operate 24 hours a day, 7 days a week, regardless of the location. For example, Morgan Stanley, one of the largest investment banks in the world, consists of four help desks in different sites (United States, England, Japan, and Hong Kong), which enable them to provide enterprise-wide 24-hour help desk service. Though distributed help desks may only have one electronic knowledge repository located in one particular office, the innovative data communication technology allows the help desk staff to store, retrieve, and update knowledge regardless of geographical and time limitation.

E-support is another innovative support model that is believed to lead to a new revolution in the help desk industry in the near future. It can be achieved due to its ability to provide better, faster, and cheaper service. Broome and Streittwieser (2002) specify that all support actions that use Internet or Web as the primary communication channel should be included as e-support. One of the key stimuli in promoting e-support is the emergence of Web-based tools. Users can make use of e-mail or Web form to contact the help desk, ignoring its actual service hours, or users can access online resources, such as knowledge base and frequently asked question lists (FAQ), to look for information that is useful in resolving their existing difficulties.

Table 1. Evolution of help desk support models and technologies

Year	Help Desk Model	Technologies
1980s	Decentralized Help Desk Model	1) Stored knowledge in form of paper-based documentations 2) Retrieved knowledge manually (by help desk staff only)
1990 -1995	Centralized Help Desk Model	1) Merged and stored knowledge from different help desks in computer file system 2) Used computer program to retrieve knowledge (by help desk staff only)
1995 - now		1) Store knowledge in electronic database 2) Help desk staff can retrieve knowledge by SQL
1997 - now	Distributed/Virtual Help Desk Model	1) User from different geographic location can use one contact number to call help desk through modern call routing technology 2) Data communication technology allows help desk staff to store, retrieve, and update knowledge regardless of geographical and time limitation
2000 - now	E-support Help Desk Model	1) User can make use of e-mail or Web form to contact help desk 2) Both user and help desk staff can access online resources 3) Conduct Web training 4) Exploit remote control technology

Furthermore, the help desk staff is capable of conducting Web training or using remote control technology to help users resolve their problems. The concept of e-support breaks through the customary knowledge management border by expanding the third and fourth stages of knowledge management (make knowledge available and use knowledge) to the user. The evolution of the help desk support models, and the involved technologies, is summarized in Table 1.

Future of Knowledge Management in Help Desk

The proposed concept knowledge management framework has standardized the process of manipulating knowledge in the help desk. What is more, the combination of knowledge management and database technology enables the help desk to manipulate enormous amounts of knowledge in a structured way. Both tacit and explicit knowledge are converted in a form that can be stored in a knowledge base. The knowledge can later be retrieved and used by help desk staff and users. Is that all the contribution that knowledge management can make to the help desk industry? Nonetheless, the potential of knowledge management is far beyond that: effective customization in knowledge management has the capability to aid help desks in controlling the continuous increase of incoming enquiries. To ease overloaded help desks, one way is to develop a trouble-free system, but it is technically impossible up to this moment. Another way is to stop users from calling help desk. Researches conducted by Knapp and Woch (2002), as well as Dawson and Lewis (2001) have provided a clue in resolving help desk challenges. The former indicates that 80% of enquiries require no specialized knowledge, whereas the latter points out that close to 50% of calls to the ITS help desk at Deakin University are related to login name and password. Both researches confirm that the majority of incoming technical enquiries are simple and routine. Rather than calling help desk, users are capable of solving simple and routine technical problems themselves if sufficient knowledge and guideline are provided. The concept of e-support sustains the idea of transferring part of the troubleshooting duty from the help desk to users. When the users have problems, they can solve their problems by searching related solutions from an online knowledge base or FAQ. However, online user knowledge bases normally share the same design as the one accessed by the help desk staff. If the knowledge base is designed to support "keywords search," in which users have to locate the most appropriate solutions by entering a few keywords that best describe the problems, users often do not know how to use the right jargon to explain the problems. Although they may successfully use their own words to depict the problems, the "keyword search" may return 10 or even more solutions, which will deepen users' frustration. The complexness of the user interface can drive away novice users, or even users classified as medium-skilled. Similarly, FAQ is always overlooked by users because its mechanism lacks the ability to support users in dynamic and flexible manners. To relieve the overloaded help desk, we propose a new framework to redistribute simple and routine enquiries within the help desk environment. We also propose development of the user self-help knowledge management system as a replacement to the legacy online knowledge base and FAQ, in order to improve the support process at the help desk.

Proposed Mechanism to Identify Simple and Routine Technical Enquiries

Let us first define the phrase "simple and routine technical enquiries." Simple and routine technical enquiries in this research refer to technical problems that can be solved by users if adequate relevant information is provided without direct or indirect intervention from the help desk staff. Based on the help desk support areas defined by Sundrud (2002), these enquiries can be categorized into four types: IT administrative enquiries, hardware enquiries, software enquiries, and miscellaneous enquiries. The IT administrative enquiries include account setup, account termination, account maintenance, account login, account suspension, password retrieval, password reset, password syntax information, password invalid, software installation and purchasing, and hardware installation and purchasing, as well as service purchasing. The hardware and software enquiries include performance and functional concerns in relation to various types of hardware and software. The miscellaneous enquiries include queries on missing and corrupted files and unreachable Web sites and servers, in addition to their performances. Such categorization not only provides a structured way to further identify and elaborate simple and routine enquiries, but it also helps associate and retrieve solutions for the related enquiries. For example, software functional enquiry can be further categorized into functional enquiries of Microsoft products, Adobe products, Oracle products, and so forth. Thus, solutions for functional enquiries of Adobe PDF reader and Photoshop can be grouped under the Adobe products category. When the user has functional enquiry on Adobe products, the associated solutions of PDF Reader and Photoshop can be retrieved.

The above categories may vary depending on the types of software and hardware, users, users' skill sets, and business processes. To identify routine and simple enquiries, we propose using the reports generated by the help desk management system and the automatic call distribution system. These reports provide data and information on problem type, resolution method, call duration (time required to solve the problem), and so forth. By inspecting the reports in a regular manner, the help desk manager can work out which enquiries are routine and simple. For example, the help desk management report may have indicated that there were many enquiries about "e-mail login failure," in which most of them were related to "password invalid," and the required resolution method was merely to "reset password." Thus, by matching

Figure 7. Proposed mechanism to identify simple and routine technical enquiries

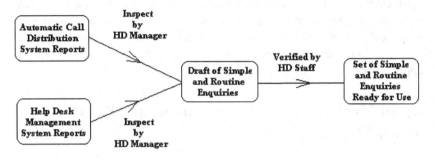

the above information with call duration in the automatic call distribution system report, the help desk manager could confirm the enquiries as simple and routine, because the duration for each call was short. However, the advice of the help desk staff can never be overlooked. Hence, the classifications of the enquiries that have been deduced by the help desk manager must be verified by the help desk staff to ensure their accuracy. The proposed mechanism of identifying simple and routine enquiries is illustrated in Figure 7.

Proposed Redistributed Knowledge Management Framework

The proposed mechanism of identifying simple and routine enquiries will be added to the conceptual knowledge management framework to allow the simple and routine enquiries to be redistributed in an effectively manner. The resulting redistributed knowledge management framework is shown in Figure 8. Rather than storing explicit knowledge into repositories straightaway after externalization and combination, the proposed mechanism will be applied after externalization and combination, with the aim of distinguishing the knowledge into two categories: (1) simple and routine and (2) complex. While simple and routine knowledge is stored in the proposed user self-help knowledge management system, the complex one is resided in the general knowledge repository. Consequently, users can first access the proposed user self-help knowledge management system and look for the most appropriate solution in accordance with the associated IT problems. If the solution is not available in the proposed self-help knowledge management system, then the user will contact the help desk for assistance. The repository where complex IT knowledge resides will be used by the help desk staff to answer complicated technical enquiries. This framework also allows the proposed system to be tailor-made in accordance with a user's skill sets. Because IT knowledge often contains a lot of technical terms

Figure 8. Proposed redistributed knowledge management framework

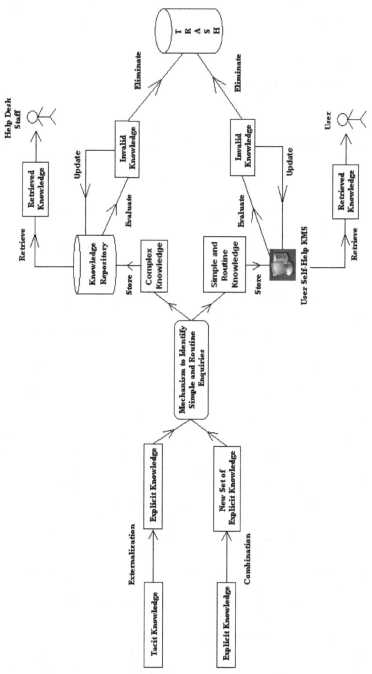

and jargons, the help desk staff can rephrase and simplify the resolutions stored in the self-help knowledge management system to ensure users can understand the resolution methods.

Architecture of the Proposed User Self-Help Knowledge Management System

The basic architecture of the proposed user self-help knowledge management system is shown in Figure 9. There are five basic components within the architecture: the user's browser, two software agents (interface and search agent), a resolution knowledge base that stores solutions for simple and routine enquiries, and the interface database that stores information required to facilitate user communication. A software agent is a computer program that behaves like human and is capable of autonomous actions in pursuit of specific goals (Liu, Zeng, & Lin, 1999; Nienaber & Cloete, 2003). Software agent technology can be used to free users from onerous search duty by dedicating itself to looking for the most suitable solution in the extensive knowledge base based on user's requirement. Moreover, it is also capable of facilitating user communication and description of problems.

Though a traditional programming approach is able to develop a similar system, using a software agent approach to develop the proposed user self-help knowledge management system tends to (1) be more natural in depicting and modeling the complexity reality; (2) reduce problems associated with coupling of components, and (3) reduce difficulties associated with managing relationships between software components (Jennings, 2001). In practice, systems developers can customize the system based on the actual needs of both users and the organizations by inserting different attributes into software agents. Examples of agent characteristics include autonomy, reactivity, proactiveness, collaborativeness, mobility, adaptability, personality, temporal continuity, communication ability, flexibility, learning ability, and intelligence (Jennings, 2001; Liu et al., 1999; Nienaber & Cloete, 2003). The agent approach also minimizes the re-programming effort for system updating and maintenance because adding, converting, removing, or replacing an agent is relatively easier than any other existing approach (Jennings, 2001). The unique characteristics in software agent technology enable the help desk to customize its own user self-help knowledge management system based on this architecture. This architecture can be modified to suit different help desk's criteria: (1) by adding extra software agents; (2) by removing software agents; (3) by inserting additional attributes into software agents, and (4) by removing existing attributes from software agents. For example, if it is decided that additional feature in which the user can choose to conduct an online consultation with the help desk staff is needed (in case the user cannot find any suitable solution), then the system can add an additional communication agent

Figure 9. Proposed architecture of user self-help knowledge management system

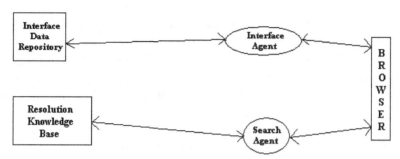

which possesses the ability to facilitate online consultation. This type of customization is straightforward and does not require major changes to the system.

The proposed user self-help knowledge management system also makes use of modern Web technology as a mean to deliver the system. The system is delivered by the World Wide Web (WWW) and appears on the browser to facilitate the interaction with user and delivering the user request for resolution. The WWW is originally designed to allow people to retrieve or browse information on static Web pages by clicking on the related URL, but the potential of Web is far from that. Nowadays, Web technology is exploited to accommodate a wide variety of flexible, dynamic, and interactive activities that range from simple applications and multimedia Web pages to sophisticated business systems and complex software applications. The rapid development of data communication techniques, such as wireless local area network (WLAN) and 3G mobile network, further breaks down the traditional boundaries of desktop computers to be the only Web-accessed device. Currently, mobile devices such as laptop computers, 3G mobile phones, and personal digital assistants are capable of taking part in Web activities (Menkhaus, 2001). As a result, users can access the proposed user self-help knowledge management system through portable electronic devices with Internet connectivity. The following steps describe how the system will be deployed.

- To activate the system, the user simply clicks on the target URL. Subsequently, the interface agent that possesses communication capability will deliver a dynamic user interface to the browser, based on the information stored in the interface database. The dynamic and interactive communication capabilities of the interface agent provide an "easy to use" user interface in helping users present and identify the problems. A simple implementation of the dynamic user interface is shown in Figure 10. Firstly, the interface agent interacts with users by asking them to select a problem type on the user interface. Based on the input, the interface agent will generate the next category of possible problem scenarios. This type of interaction will continue until the agent has gathered sufficient information to process the query.

- When the problem is described through the deployment of the interface agent, the search agent will be deployed to search for possible solutions. The search agent which possesses "the ability to act autonomy" is responsible for this task. Here, "the ability to act autonomy" refers to the capability of an agent to perform its task without direct control from the user or with only minimum supervision and direction. To achieve the preset goal of finding the most appropriate resolution, the search agent will be deployed as soon as the agent is able to "sense" sufficient information has been gathered. The search agent will then examine the contents in the knowledge base, make its own decision to select a solution according to user's problem description, and return the solution to the user.

Figure 10. Simple implementation of dynamic user interface

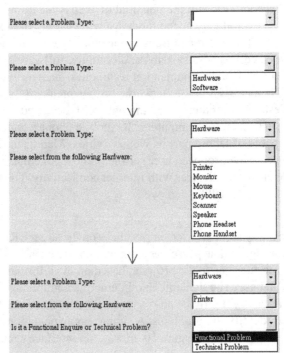

Conclusion

The proposed conceptual knowledge management framework enables help desks to create, store, make available, use, and evaluate both tacit and explicit knowledge. By adding the proposed simple and routine technical enquiries identifying mechanism and user self-help knowledge management system to the conceptual knowledge management framework, simple and routine technical enquiries are redistributed in a way that users can look for their own solutions instead of calling help desk. Since a sizeable amount of enquiries are now rerouted to the user self-help knowledge management system, help desk staff can be freed up to handle high level support issues, to participate in proactive support activities, and to attend regular trainings. From the user perspective, rather than waiting in a long queue for a simple resolution, users can look for the most appropriate solution simply by accessing the system through mobile electronic devices, regardless of time and geographical restrictions. Alternatively, for those who have complicated enquiries, the waiting and troubleshooting durations will now be shorter because more staff are available and fewer users are in the queue. This means the user can now enjoy a better, quicker, and more direct service. Economically speaking, the proposed user self-help knowledge management system is an extremely cost-effective support method because the average cost for a Web self-help transaction is 400 times less than a telephone transaction and 80 times less than an e-mail transaction (Broome & Streitwieser, 2002). The proposed user self-help knowledge management system has the potential to convert the radical habit of a user's dependence upon the help desk, as well as to promote the ubiquity and pervasion of a self-learning atmosphere. This potential cannot be overlooked, as an old Chinese proverb says "Give a man a fish and you feed him for a day. Teach a man to fish and you feed him for a lifetime."

References

Alavi, M., & Leidner, D.E. (1999). Knowledge management systems: Issues, challenges, and benefits. *Communications of the Association for Information Systems, 7*(1), 1-37.

Broome, C., & Streitwieser, J. (2002). What is e-support? *Service and support handbook* (pp. 31-40). Help Desk Institute.

Central Computer and Telecommunications Agency (1989). *IT infrastructure library: Help desk*. HMSO Publication Centre.

Chait, L.P. (1999). Creating a successful knowledge management system. *Journal of Business Strategy, 20*(2), 23-26.

286   Leung & Lau

Chan, C.W., Chen, L., & Geng, L. (2000). Knowledge engineering for an intelligent case-based system for help desk operations. *Expert Systems with Applications, 18*, 125-132.

Coulson-Thomas, C.J. (1997). The future of the organization: Selected knowledge management issues. *Journal of Knowledge Management, 1*(1), 15-26.

Czegel, B. (1999). *Help desk practitioner's handbook.* Wiley.

Davis, K. (2002). Charting a knowledge base solution: Empowering student-employees and delivering expert answers. In *Proceedings of the 30th SIGUCCS Conference on User Services,* Providence, Rhode Island.

Dawson, E., & Lewis, T. (2001). *Deakin university ITS help desk: Co-operative partnership as the solution.* Paper Presented at the 2001 Australasia Educause Conference on the Power of 3, Gold Coast, Queensland, Australia.

Dawson, R. (2000). Knowledge capabilities as the focus of organisational development and strategy. *Journal of Knowledge Management, 4*(4), 320-327.

Goh, S.C. (2002). Managing effective knowledge transfer: An integrative framework and some practice implications. *Journal of Knowledge Management, 6*(1), 23-30.

Goker, M., Roth-Berghofer, T., Bergmann, R., Pantleon, T, Traphoner, R., Wess, S., & Wilke, W. (1998). The development of Homer: A case-based CAD/CAM help-desk support tool. In *Proceedings of the 4th EWCBR European Workshop on Case-Based Reasoning,* Dublin, Ireland.

Heckman, R., & Guskey, A. (1998). Sources of customer satisfaction and dissatisfaction with information technology help desks. *Journal of Market Focused Management, 3*(1), 59-89.

Jennings, N.R. (2001). An agent-based approach for building complex software-systems. *Communications of the ACM, 44*(4), 35-41.

Kajiko-Mattsson, M. (2003). Infrastructures of virtual IT enterprises. In *Proceedings of the 2003 IEEE International Conference on Software Maintenance,* Los Alamitos, California.

Kankanhilli, A., & Tan, B.C.Y. (2005). Contributing knowledge to electronic knowledge repositories: An empirical investigation. *MIS Quarterly, 29*(1), 113-143.

Kendall, H. (2002). *Prehistoric help desk!! Support world.* Help Desk Institute.

Kirchmeyer, R. (2002). The consolidated help desk. In *Proceedings of the 30th Annual ACM SIGUCCS Conference on User Services,* Providence, Rhode Island.

Knapp, M., & Woch, J. (2002). Towards a natural language driven automated help desk. In *Proceedings of the Third International Conference on Computational Linguistics and Intelligent Text Processing* (pp. 96-105).

Copyright © 2007, Idea Group Inc. Copying or distributing in print or electronic forms without written permission of Idea Group Inc. is prohibited.

Liu, H., Zeng, G., & Lin, Z. (1999). A construction approach for software agents using components. *ACM SIGSOFT Software Engineering Notes, 24*(3), 76-79.

Lueg, C. (2001). Information, knowledge, and networked minds. *Journal of Knowledge Management, 5*(2), 151-159.

Marcella, R., & Middleton, I. (1996). The role of the help desk in the strategic management of information systems. *OCLC Systems and Services, 12*(4), 4-19.

Martensson, M. (2000). A critical review of knowledge management as a management tool. *Journal of Knowledge Management, 4*(3), 204-206.

Menkhaus, G. (2001). Architecture for client-independent Web-based applications. In *Proceedings of the Technology of Object-Oriented Languages and Systems.*

Middleton, I. (1999). *The evolution of the IT help desk: From crisis centre to business manager in the public and private sectors.* MSc thesis, The Robert Gordon University, Faculty of Management, School of Information and Media, Aberdeen, UK.

Nienaber, R., & Cloete, E. (2003). A software agent framework for the support of software project management. In *Proceedings of the 2003 Annual Research Conference of the South African Institute of Computer Scientists and Information Technologists on Enablement through Technology* (pp. 16-23).

Nonaka, I., Toyama, R., & Konno, N. (2001). SECI, Ba and leadership: A unified model of dynamic knowledge creation. *Managing industrial knowledge creation, transfer and utilization.* Sage Publications.

Poston, R.S., & Speier, C. (2005). Effective use of knowledge management systems: A process model of content ratings and credibility indicators. *MIS Quarterly, 29*(2), 221-244.

Prusak, L. (1999). The nature of knowledge and its management. *The knowledge management yearbook 1999-2000.* Butterworth-Heinemann.

Scullen, J. (2001). *Re-engineering desktop support at Griffith University.* Paper Presented at the 2001 Australasia Educause Conference on the Power of 3, Gold Coast, Queensland, Australia.

Sharkie, R. (2003). Knowledge creation and its place in the development of sustainable competitive advantage. *Journal of Knowledge Management, 7*(1), 20-31.

Smith, A. (2004, August 24). Motorway design must learn from past mistake. *The Sydney Morning Herald*, p. 4.

Smith, A. (2005, March 12). Traffic levels far outstrip predictions. *The Sydney Morning Herald*, p. 13.

Smith, C.L. (1996). Building a help desk from scratch, with no staff, no equipment and no money: Moulding novice student consultants into seasoned help desk operators. In *Proceedings of the 24th annual ACM SIGUCCS Conference on User Services,* Chicago.

Smith, E.A. (2001). The role of tacit and explicit knowledge in the workplace. *Journal of Knowledge Management, 5*(4), 311-321.

Sundrud, R. (2002). *Computer help desk services: A case study of three comunity colleges in Pennsylvania.* Doctor of Education thesis, College of Education, Tempe University, AZ.

Tischler, F., & Trachtenberg, D. (1998). *The emergency of the distributed help desk.*

Telemarketing and Call Center Solutions.

Turban, E., & Aronson, J.E. (2001). *Decision support systems and intelligent systems.* Prentice Hall.

Underwood, J., Hegdahl, D., & Gimbel, J. (2003). To corral support, a proper set of tools are needed. In *Proceedings of the 31st Annual ACM SIGUCCS Conference on User services,* San Antonio, Texas.

Wiig, K.M. (1997). Knowledge management: An introduction and perspective. *Journal of Knowledge Management, 1*(1), 6-14.

Appendix I: Internet Session – Formulating a Knowledge Management Framework Using Knowledge Management Technique and Technology

Interaction

Review the information presentation in the Web sites on knowledge management strategy, technique, and technology *http://www.cio.com/research/knowledge.* Then develop a knowledge management framework or process to allow your organization to manipulate knowledge in an effective and efficient manner based on its actual needs.

Appendix II: Case Study

Title of Case

Freeman is a Hong Kong financial institution providing financial services and products to individuals, as well as medium and large-size businesses, corporations, and governments across Hong Kong and around the world. There are 18,000 employees in Freeman and almost 95% of the employees are required to use computers in their daily operation. To ensure IT support can be provided to the employees in a timely manner, a help desk with 30 support staff was established by the Department of IT in 1993. Unfortunately, the adoption of downsizing in Freeman has reduced the support team to 15 staff that includes 5 first level support staff. In other words, a single first level support staff has to service 3,600 users. One can easily imagine the predicament of this help desk if there is a sudden outage on one of the essential systems. More than 18,000 users call at the same time, but only a few are available to pick up the calls. After the shrinkage of the size of the help desk, many users start to complain that they have to wait for more than 15 minutes before help desk staff is available to pick up their calls.

On one Monday morning, John is very frustrated because he cannot log in to his e-mail account with his usual password. He decides to call the help desk right away. Monday morning is considered to be peak hours for help desk because quite a number of users had changed their e-mail passwords the previous Friday and most users cannot remember the new passwords after they return to work on Monday morning. He waits on the phone queue for about fifteen minutes, and Mary, who works as the first level operator in the help desk, is finally available to pick up his call. Mary carefully listens to John's problem and asks him to make sure the "Num Lock" on the keyboard is on. She also reminds him to disable the "Caps Lock" on the keyboard because e-mail password is case sensitive. Then Mary asks John to try the password again. John still cannot get into his e-mail account and receives the same error message, "password invalid," as before. Suddenly, John remembers that he had changed his e-mail password last Friday before he finished his work, but he is unable to remember that password now. Not wasting any time, Mary quickly walks the user through to access the password reset Web page, where John can reset his password to the default. Subsequently, John is successfully logged in to his e-mail account using the default password. Before hanging up the phone, Mary reminds John to change the default password because of security reasons. Afterwards, Mary needs another five minutes to open a ticket, fill in troubleshooting details and close the ticket in the help desk management system. John takes approximately twenty-5 minutes to solve this extremely simple enquiry, while Mary requires 15 minutes to complete the whole support process.

Questions

1. What is your comment about the support process of the help desk at Freeman?

2. Can the proposed redistributed knowledge management framework be applied to the help desk at Freeman? Why?

3. Did you ever call help desk or any other form of call centre regarding simple and routine enquires? Can the proposed redistributed knowledge management framework be applied to that help desk or call centre? If so, what improvement would you expect?

Appendix III: Useful URLs

Help Desk Institute – The world's largest membership association for the service and support industry

http://www.helpdeskinst.com/about/

Help Desk FAQ – The definitive global resource for helpdesks, customer relationship management, and technical support

http://www.philverghis.com/helpdesk.html

Iain Middleton, Key Factors in Help Desk Success

http://www.abdn.ac.uk/~ltu008/imiddleton/?page=helpdesk

Cornell University Information Technology Help Desk

http://www.cit.cornell.edu/helpdesk/

The Knowledge Management Resource Center

http://www.kmresource.com/

Inside Knowledge Magazine – A knowledge management publication

http://www.ikmagazine.com/

Knowledge Management Benchmarking Association

http://kmba.org/

Knowledge Management Consortium International

http://www.kmci.org/

Australian Public Service Knowledge Management Case Studies

http://www.agimo.gov.au/practice/km_case_studies

Knowledge Management Papers and Case Studies

http://www.steptwo.com.au/papers/index.php?subject=km

Appendix IV: Further Reading

Alavim, M., & Leidner, D.E. (2001, March). Review: Knowledge management and knowledge management systems: Conceptual foundations and research issues. *MIS Quarterly, 25*(1), 107-136.

Laszlo, K.C., & Laszlo, A. (2002). Evolving knowledge for development: The role of knowledge management in a changing world. *Journal of Knowledge Management, 6*(4), 400-412.

Chait, L.P. (1999, March-April). Creating a successful knowledge management system. *Journal of Business Strategy,* 23-26.

Cooper, V., Lichtenstein, S., & Smith, R. (2005, July 7-10). *Toward successful knowledge transfer in Web-based self-service for information technology services* (PACIS 2005). Bangkok, Thailand. Retrieved October 19, 2006, from http://www.pacis-net.org/file/2005/291.pdf

Eales, J. R. T. (2004). A knowledge management approach to user support. *Proceedings of the 2004 Australasian User Interface Conference (AUIC 2004),* Dunedin.

Appendix V: Possible Paper Titles/ Essays

- Knowledge management in Help Desk
- The customization of knowledge management techniques in Help Desk
- The application of knowledge management techniques in manipulating Help Desk knowledge
- The development of knowledge management framework in Help Desk

Chapter XI

Discursive Context-Aware Knowledge and Learning Management Systems

Caoimhín O'Nualláin, DERI Galway, Ireland

Adam Westerski, DERI Galway, Ireland

Sebastian Kruk, DERI Galway, Ireland

Abstract

In this chapter, we look at the research area of discursion and context-aware information as it relates to the user. Much research has been done in the area of effective learning, active learning, and in developing frameworks through which learning can be said to be achieved and have some possibility of being measured (i.e., Networked Learning and Bloom's Taxonomy) (Bloom, 1956). Having examined many such frameworks, we have found that dialogue plays a large part, and in this chapter we specifically examine dialogue in context of the user's background and social context. This always plays a critical role, and it is around this that we want to dig deeper. We aim to provide a quality discourse analysis model which will achieve in more detail a picture of the users actual level of knowledge. Problem solving skills, together with the critical thinking capability as part of a team, and individually, in the following chapter.

Background

Over the past 20 years, we have had many and varied computer-based and Web-based packages which aim to teach the user some skills. But most of these packages fail to achieve their design goals for one of many reasons, for example:

1.   Lack of user driven focus
2.   Lack of engagement
3.   Poor navigation system
4.   No eductational theory used or involved
5.   Lack of challenge or testing of lessons learned
6.   No assessment whatsoever
7.   No feedback on any assessments covered
8.   Lack of contact with anyone else doing the course

Figure 1. Hierarchy of topics

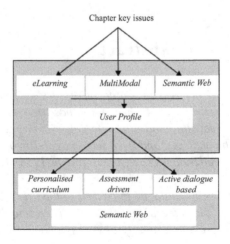

9.   No followup in relation to a future path or career

10.   No credits built up for future courses in work

These, through our research, tend to be the main reasons why computer-based training and Web-based training courses are not being completed. In this body of work we have taken these results and aimed to counteract them by developing a new direction, emphasis, and structure in how courses are created. Our initial aim is to greatly reduce the retention issues and to make courses more personally engaging and worthwhile. In so doing, new technology, which in the past had been used for the sake of being used and not to help in making courses more effective or useful, must be used effectively. These aspects are considered to be the failings of e-learning over the years (Badger, 2000; Crichton, 2003; Greenagel, 2002). In the next version of the Web, that is, Web 2.0, we will see far more powerful and useful Web-based applications based around the semantic information community. We will examine some applications which exibit some semantic options in the education area and in other areas later in this chapter.

Very important to this chapter and to learning utilities is the area of pedagogy, and the initial pedagogy frameworks examined was based on Goodyear (2001) and Salmon (2000), which deal with encouraging asynchronous methods of collaboration, but do not attempt to take into consideration the context of the user (i.e., gender, context, age group, or background). In fact, the collection of action verbs put together to aid evaluation of user input is very much based on language more likely to be used by middle aged academics rather than most of the student population (Figure 1).

Figure 2. Accepted active verbs from Bloom's Taxonomy

TCD Action Verbs for expressing Learning Outcomes (Bloom's Taxonomy)

			Critical Thinking		
			Analysis	Synthesis	Evaluation
Knowledge	Comprehension	Application			
					adapt
				arrange	appraise
			analyse	assemble	assess
		apply	appraise	associate	associate
	classify	choose	calculate	collect	compare
Knowledge	describe	demonstrate	categorise	compose	connect
arrange	discuss	dramatise	compare	conceptualise	consider possibilities
define	explain	employ	contrast	connect	create
duplicate	express	illustrate	criticise	construct	criticise
identify	indicate	interpret	differentiate	create	design
label	locate	operate	discriminate	develop	discriminate
list	observe	practice	distinguish	distil	estimate
memorise	recognise	schedule	examine	elaborate	evaluate
name	report	sketch	experiment	formulate	generate ideas
order	restate	solve	plan	initiate	hypothesise
recall	review	use	question	manage	imagine
record	select	write	test	organise	judge
recognise	translate			prepare	measure
relate				plan	visualise
repeat				produce	
reproduce				propose	
state				synthesise	
				write	
Remembering previously learned information	*Grasping the meaning of information*	*Applying knowledge to actual situations*	*Breaking down objects or ideas into simpler parts and seeing how the parts relate and are organized*	*Rearranging component ideas into a new whole*	*Making judgments based on internal evidence or external criteria*

Added to that was Socratic method (Hwee, 2000), in which the dialogue was based on the teacher-student dialogues with a high level of questioning involved to get the student engaged, develop their learning, and reinforce what they know, especially in terms of developing problem solving in an open discursive manner with the student's work group. Another body of research which we examined (Gee, 2003; Goldman, 2004; Money, 2005; Noriko Hara & Chaloula, 1998) paves the way to extending, to a much greater degree, what is possible and what we in this body of research aim to extend and adapt to an even greater extent and which we will illustrate later in the chapter and see in future years, the development of Web2. Ultimately, as a fundamental requirement for learning, constructivist principles, and more precisely, social constructivism, was applied in this model (Pask, 1997), very much building

Figure 3. Literature review

Issue	References	Main contribution
E-learning & Learning	Reigeluth, C..M., 1996	What is the new paradigm of instructional theory?
	Britain & Liber, 1999	Framework for evaluation of VLE s
	Salmon, G.,2000	E-moderating: The key to teaching and learning online
	Goodyear, P. , 2001	Effective networked learning in higher education: Notes and guidelines
	Pask, G., 1997	An idiosyncratic history of conversation theory in software, and its progenitor
	Oviatt, S., 2004	When do we interact multimodally? Cognitive load and multi modal communication patterns
Semantics for E-learning	Quesada, J., & Kinsch, W., 2000	A computational theory of complex problem solving using latent semantic analysis
	Dodds, L., 2004	An introduction to FOAF
	Kruk, S.R., 2004	FOAF-Realm - control your friends' access to resource. In Proceedings of the 1st Workshop on Friend of a Friend, Social Networking and the (Semantic) Web (FOAF Galway), Galway, Ireland, pages 1–9.
Profiling and Personalisation	Talaveral, L., & Gaudioso, E., 2004	Mining student data to characterise similar behaviour or groups in unstructured collaborative space
	Nuallain, C.O., & Redfern, S., 2005	Providing more effective curriculum through building dynamic profiles and tracking user behaviour
	Britain, S., & Liber , O., 2004	A framework for the pedagogical evaluation of virtual learning environments

on the work of Piaget (activity is central to learning), Vygotsky (we learn from social contact), and Bruner (the concept of scaffolding). It is the research of these individuals that we use as the foundation to go forward and advance the argument or hypothesis for a more discursive, context-aware environment. It has already been clearly illustrated in Reigeluth (1996) where the quote "one size does not fit all" came from, which further justified and reinforced our aims at providing a unique user experience for each student based on their needs and requirements.

Main Thrust of the Chapter

With that in mind, we have captured much data about the user and body of users so as to learn more about the student and, in so doing, allow us to dynamically create screens which appeal to the learning style of the user and reinforce this with knowledge of the device type. It also allows the student to relate and feel very comfortable in the environment presented to the user. One of the aspects of this, which we can clearly illustrate, is the use of language, which can be either selected by the user or picked up from the student profile.

The effect of this will be that all material will be presented in the language the student is most familiar with, without having to buy additional versions. Similarly, with learning disabilities, such as dyxlexia, if the student indicates in the pre-test that they have this learning disability, the screens the student uses automatically alter so as to be presented in a mint green, and limited text will be displayed on the screens and icons appear on buttons rather than text, which research has indicated is an aid to usability and readability for dyslexic students .

As part of this flexability and collaborative interface, we have adapted and utilised technology for the sake of learning, to provide the user with more ways of interacting with the curriculum, both asynchronously and synchronously. Through the methods provided, we can increase the level of engagement, as indicated in Figure

Figure 4. Language options for the user

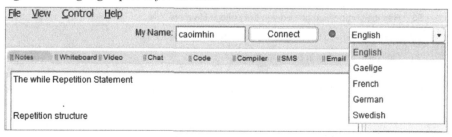

5, which provided student survey results of environment, but also allow the tutors, teachers, and moderators the opportunity to capture and give valuable feedback, which was not possible in other environments. All of this is captured and stored in the users profile.

The survey relates to aspects of test versions of the current application, which show aspects of satisfaction the users indicated from using the application as part of a computer programming course. The programming course and some of the difficult concepts really challenged and tested us severely.

Figure 5. Survey results of aspects the students liked

%	STUDENT REPLY'S TO USAGE
53	competed for the practice
53	competed for the fun
53	said this helped their programming a lot
60	Said they would like to see this type of collaborative environment online
93	would like to get involved in another one like this one next year
60	Internet surfing
60	e-mail
13	24 X 7 access
67	Solutions online
73	Your team score online
53	Online chat
60	Live audio with class and tutor
47	Marking scheme online
60	Hints and tips online
55	Texting
50	Live video with classmates
40	Notes online
40	Compiler
53	Has the competition helped you like college life more Y/N
53	Has it helped you to be able to look for help if you needed it?
20	Outline of mistakes in better feedback

The Profile

The profile in place is made up of 25 categories which cover all user significant features, including personal data about age, background, whether they are town dwellers or city dwellers, type of work, and hours of work. Added to this is assessment and tracking information on how the user navigates the course. Altogether, 150 fields are used to collect user data, which for the most part help build up a picture and allow the course to change so as to suit the learners needs and specific requirements. This can be a stand-alone package or a corporate package, which can inform the boss as to the user's ability and aptitudes. The assessment module which forms part of this package is designed specifically for the user taking part in the course, as it reacts to replies to questions in the pre test and to the way the user uses the course which maps to their learning style and changing learning style. This user profile ultimately has as its core options to produce reports which inform us as to many different aspects of the user's ability and attentiveness, even which aspects of the course users do not like while completing or taking part in the course. The assessment aspects are very thorough and again adapt to the user's style and options selected and the input or contribution they make to the course. The assessment model is outlined in the diagram below.

This assessment framework is very thorough and is both formative and summative. But as a result of the problem solving nature of the package, it is also very interro-

Figure 6. Model of the assessment carried out as part of our framework

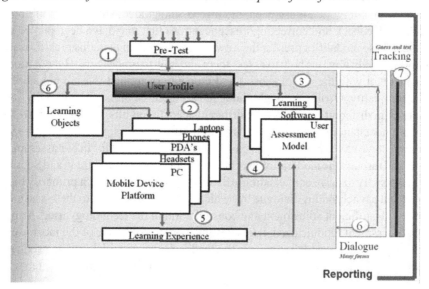

gative and tries to probe into how a user went about solving a problem and why, and then establishes if problem solving skills are being learned or if "test and click" is being used so as to get through the course as quickly as possible. This aspect is best achieved through the tracking and dialogue aspects of the assessment framework. To further reinforce the learning, there are several dialogue aspects where users are encouraged to discuss problems and material with their work group or tutor so as to build and correct scaffolding that may be forming. It is the brainstorming and dialogue which has proved itself as being most effective in tests carried out over the 3-year duration of experiments. We have also found, as a result of the collaboration aspects, that we have established a 98% retention level, with students asking for more events like this one in other subject domains. Overall, this environment, which engages students in programming and problem solving after several permutations, has found the right mix and is now very successful, and both engaging and motivating through building on success and meeting and talking with classmates or study groups to work through problems online.

The online aspects, just like the users, are varied and diverse. There are several ways of collaborating both synchronously and asynchronously within the model currently being user tested. The methods and features were those specifically requested by users. The example of SMS messaging came about from data indicating that 100% of students had mobile phones, which was much higher than the numbers with personal computers and personal computers with Internet connectivity. With the subsequent selection on dialogue methods and richness, we facilitate dialogue or discursion and, as far as is possible, reflect the context of the user and their learning preference. With most of these collaboration features we allow archiving of student conversation and tutor conversation so as to provide a very good reflective tool which can be reviewed in the user's own time and place. The dialogue, as can be seen from our model, is assessed, monitored, and graded, with the aim of giving beneficial feedback and correcting misconceptions that may have been picked up. Many of these modalities present their own specific challenge in this regard, as it is not immediately obvious how to assess them and how to grade them. But our model does just that with the use of rubrics and moderators applied to each modality to maintain quality. Quality through dialogue can often be an issue, especially with people from different locations with different accents and lilts, which can make the level of understanding difficult, and as a result difficult to assign marks and grades. This aspect we have also taken into consideration and catered for in our assessment model and through the moderation aspect. The moderators in the Salmon and Socratic method also try to drive conversations (Salmon, 2000, 2002), which primarily build up skills in asynchronous dialogue but which can also be applied to the assessment model with sufficient adjustment and consideration of the technology used. As part of the assessment module used, it has become apparent that one of the most useful features for the users and the tutors is the feedback aspect, which can be used very much for multiple purposes. Firstly, the users can get answers to queries which were hindering their progress. Furthermore, through presenting more problems to the user, the level of understanding and feedback uptake can be measured. This in itself can be used to illustrate how effective a learner is at applying knowledge, learning, and ultimately aiming to achieve high order learning. If these goals are not being achieved and the user is somewhat frustrated, another modality may be suggested by the moderator following usage patterns displayed as a result of pre test data or tracking data, which may indicate the user has selected the wrong learning style or modality in which to learn and, although their learning ability will not be stopped, it may not be their preferred environment to use.

Interoperability, or cross platform usage, is a major hindrance to uptake and investment in a package or e-learning package, and questions may exist like *"Is it going to be compatible with the new and old system?"* and *"Can the data in the old system be integrated into this one?"* Quite often packages are created with no consideration to compatibility with other products or old systems and future proofing. With passing years has come about standardisation, taken place in different forms. Firstly, with better ability to interoperability comes better compatibility. From the point of view of the changing Internet world, this has brought about great change, and the creation of object libraries that can be used and reused and altered without requiring whole course rebuilding. It also means great cost savings as object libraries can be bought and exchanged as needed. This has in turn changed the e-learning market to one of course creation, object creating, and adaptability. This again has cost savings for the developer and will allow the user greater flexibility in terms of the style of object they use, based on their personal preference, and give a different perspective and greater understanding of the context. It is this standardisation that is driving the next version of the Web and allowing material to be adapted for other device types very quickly and cheaply in comparison to past development life cycles. These approaches in terms of future proofing are far more sustainable and have driven the development of the Semantic Web, as outlined in the following pages.

In this section, we will be discussing our research in the broad area of "Discursion" and "Context-aware" information. There is a growing body of research into learning collaboration, and we have related this research to our body of work that investigates the effectiveness of our collaborative model (Nuallain, 2004, 2005) and the importance of all aspects of discursion, fundamentally asserting that knowledge of context is essential to provide a quality discourse analysis.

Semantic Web 2.0

When Tim Berners-Lee invented the World Wide Web, it was a mere collection of HTML documents. Soon, and rapidly, it grew to the stage we have at the moment. Internet has become more than just a source of information. It has become a source of entertainment, communication, and last but not least, business opportunities.

However, with the search engines as robust as Google, everyone has the feeling that we cannot grow the Internet the way we did so far. Even now, many people just cannot efficiently search for information. Our B2B systems suffer from hard-to-overcome heterogeneity.

Second-generation Internet is currently the hot topic, both in industry and academia. It is perceived as a remedy for all problems we know from the current Internet. However, academia and industry define the future Web in different ways.

Future Trends

Research centres around the world work on the Semantic Web. In their vision, the future Internet will be more than just human-understandable text. The idea is to add machine-processable meaning to current and future information. Future search engines on the Semantic Web will be able to understand both the information they index and users' queries they process. B2B systems will be able to cross the boundaries of heterogeneity and find better deals with partners they cannot communicate with at the moment. However, there are a couple of concerns with respect to the Semantic Web, such as who should provide the machine-processable descriptions, that are still to be answered.

Web 2.0 is the Holly Grail of the contemporary Internet companies. Instead of making the information machine-understandable, Web 2.0 brings whole communities of users to interact with the information and each other. Wikis allow groups of people to edit the information in truly collaborative fashion. Endeavours like *http://www.wikipedia.org/* (wiki-based Internet encyclopaedia edited by an open community) proved the immense potential of community impact. Web 2.0 is also about the tagging. In services like deli.cio.us or Flickr, community users annotate bookmarks or photos they share with a simple set of keywords. As opposed to the old Web, everyone can annotate each resource. And in contrast to the Semantic Web, there is no meaning applied to each keyword (no disambiguation); however it is much easier to edit the information.

Semantic Web also aims to grasp the potential of online communities by initiatives like FOAF (Dodds, 2004) (friend of a friend), that describes online communities in a semantic fashion. FOAFRealm (*http://www.foafrealm.org/*) is one of the projects based on FOAF metadata, with its flag product, distributed profile management system (D-FOAF). One of the interesting features of the D-FOAF is the social semantic collaborative filtering (SSCF) [1] that incorporates solutions known from collaborative filtering, the Semantic Web, and Web 2.0. Other projects, like semantic wikis, also aim to utilize social semantic information sources defined by emerging Semantic Web 2.0.

The Potential of Semantic Web in E-Learning

In the early 1990s, e-learning was pushed as the "killer application" of our time, as it was to allow the delivery of education to everyone, everywhere. It was also promised to allow a high level of flexibility, as the users could log on at any time and continue their learning when it suited them best. This led to a high degree of popularity for the concept of e-learning and the potential that could be achieved through it in terms of learning. The development of e-learning had associated with it the big advantage of cost efficiency over instructor-led training. However, much of the promise was just as much a gloss as the material available. The material lacked instructional design, educational potential, engagement, and any feedback to the user. Despite the use of the Internet, the courses are very static and flat. Further enhancing of acceptability of courses is limited by the lack of bandwidth and limited access of people to computers and the Internet.

Due to the big growth of the popularity of e-learning, it quickly became much more then just delivering courses in order to provide electronic equivalence of academic-like courses. Companies that consider themselves to provide e-learning services have very diversified areas of interest. The scope of delivering or using e-learning services can be understood as broadly as the very meaning of concepts like learning and knowledge transfer. The level of competition between contemporary solutions is pushing e-learning into new areas that could bring additional profits and attract new users. One of the domains that can offer a lot is Semantic Web.

Applying the idea of Semantic Web in the e-learning domain can lead to better understanding of user requirements or needs, and therefore delivering content that suits him best. This can be achieved by providing extensive metadata descriptions for various e-learning content and mechanisms to reason about those annotations. One of the aims of Semantic Web is to provide machine understandable content. As far as e-learning is concerned, this can be understood in many ways. One is creating systems that support users with some feedback based on automatic recognition of their needs and correlating it with the best possible learning paths. On the other hand, user interaction and activity carry a lot of useful information, which can be used in a variety of ways to improve the quality of learning experiences. To utilize this potential as much as possible, the information from all learners should be gathered, shared, and reused. Moreover, the learners should be able to adjust and refine the process of instruction and make their own annotations and bookmarks.

Choices made by a particular learner can indicate what the prerequisites for a given learning object are. We know the user profile: capabilities, preferences, history, courses taken, and so forth, and we can assume with some probability that these properties are needed to start this course. Collecting similar information from other learners, we provide more and more accurate assumptions. After reaching a particular line of certainty, a metadata of the considered learning object can be updated, and new information reused in the future to better suit the learner abilities.

The same can be applied to acquire information about learning unit objectives. Observing the choices of the learners after they have finished a given learning object gives us clues and hints about new skills gained by the user.

Moreover, the choices made by a learner during a course can be stored and reused to propose a similar path for another similar person interested in the same topic. This way, experiences of other people can help to teach new pupils in better, more adjusted fashion.

Bookmarks and annotations of individuals also carry important information [17]. People create their own classifications and hierarchies, which are of use for others who try to find interesting materials from particular domains of interest. We believe that learners should form a more collaborative, open community and share their knowledge. This improves acquiring new information.

To facilitate searching, discovering, and learning, bookmarks and annotations of other people are freely available. Intersecting Semantic Web with social aspects introduces this feature with the possibility of making some restrictions. Various personal ontologyies can be used, like Distributed Friend of a Friend network [18, 19], to store and manage user profiles. It enables exchange of the bookmarks and other information between different people. Moreover, groups of friends who share more data (e.g., their entire user profiles) can be created. This additional advantage that semantics provides is supplying new users with the possibility to add their friends to the list of known people. Using this information in the profile, we can conclude some initial knowledge about these new learners.

Semantic Web also provides a means to deal with a wide diversity of metadata formats for describing learning objects and user profiles. To address this problem an ontology approach for modelling problem domains is proposed.

Architecture of Semantic E-learning Systems

As noted before, the key element of Semantic Web is annotation resources. In order to address previously described benefits, the following should be concerned:

- Ontology for e-learning content
- Ontology for user profile
- Composition of learning objects

These are the basis of the architecture of an e-learning system based on the social semantic information sources (see Figure 7).

Figure 7. Architecture of the future e-learning system

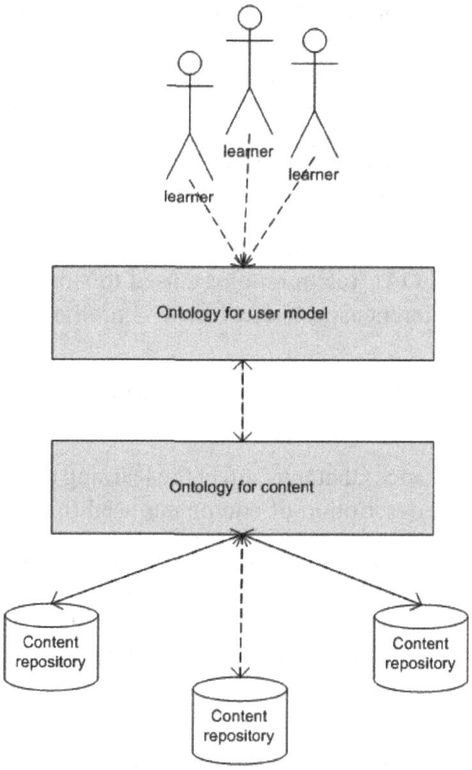

Ontology for Legacy Content Description

Contemporary learning systems describe their resources using mainly Learning Object Metadata, Dublin Core, BibTeX, and many of their own formats, which are created to fulfil the needs of particular product or company. Although those specifications are mature and exist for a long time, they miss some key concepts needed to utilize our ideas.

We distinguish two goals for resource description.

- Express common concepts in different formats
- Preserve the information acquired from user actions (e.g., prerequisites, objectives)

To address the first problem, we propose using an ontology approach. Common conceptual level will preserve the semantics of different descriptions and ease the mediation between them. This will ensure cooperation of heterogeneous environments, which use different formats to accomplish their tasks [20,21].

Ontology for User Learning Profile

In order to deliver a personalised content, the system gathers as much information about the user as possible. FOAFRealm ontology used to store this information, will cover a wide area of different aspects of a learner's profile:

- **Resume:** Personal description of a user, including education, areas of expertise, work experience, career level, and so forth
- **Capabilities:** Circumstances that may affect the learning process (e.g., user's disabilities) and also a description of equipment used (e.g., a mobile phone with a limited display).
- **Actions:** History of user's choices about courses and learning objects (e.g., which of given alternative course parts were picked). This part of the ontology will cover all different paths and scenarios chosen by the user. Such information will be used to help the user with his future choices and also as advice to other people who have similar preferences.
- **SSCF (social semantic collaborative filtering):** Bookmarks with courses and objects that users find valuable or interesting. This information will be reused as suggestions for their friends and people with similar interests.
- **Friends:** Data about friendships from FOAF profiles. If there is not enough detailed information about the users (for example the users have not fully filled their profiles), preferences of their friends might be used for personalisation (assuming that generally friends have common interests).

Information from each of these parts of the ontology will influence the learning process and materials composition in different ways. Resume will provide a hint on user's interests and will help to decide which materials are inappropriate for a particular user (a seasoned engineer should not be taught basic math, etc.). The Capabilities section obviously determines presentation techniques which might be used and the device to be used to convey the information.

Information deduced from user actions has to be stored in the resource description. Contemporary metadata formats do not provide sufficient vocabulary for such purposes and thus have to be extended. We need to express information about prerequisites and learning objectives more precisely. Learner choices will help to determine exact abilities that are needed to start a certain learning object and which are gained after finishing it. New vocabulary to describe these two aspects will be added to the user model ontology.

Learning Objects Composition

This section describes the usage of ontologies discussed previously in order to create user-oriented courses. E-learning object ontology and user profile description are key elements for a mechanism that composes courses according to individual user abilities and preferences.

The subject of various objects orchestration can be examined from many points of view. The one that is reasoned and researched often is composing based on workflow of specific information. Such techniques can be very clearly seen in research concerning Web services composition. During searching for components that will fulfil the users' task, the most important goal for the system is to match compatible services within the flow in a way that will enable the transfer of data from one service to another in the chain. The solution of this problem allows the reusing of previously processed data and composing a bigger functionality from smaller parts. Although similar attempts have been made in the e-learning domain by introducing tailoring of an object's size and level basing on some input parameters [22], this chapter takes into account user requirements concerning e-learning products, and extends the discussed meaning of composition. In order to bring users greater satisfaction from the system on-the-fly, proposed courses' composition techniques consider proper object ordering within the flow. They are not only based on technical aspects of connectivity of one object with another, they but also deliver various descriptions of object content and their relation to user description.

The main idea which could lead to achieving our goal is by taking advantage of benefits brought by initiatives like FOAF user profiling [17, 18, 19]. Collaborative filtering technologies allow the finding of people with similar interests and extracting data about their choices while composing courses for their needs. In the final solution, the users will interactively select the track that they want to follow, choosing components suggested by the system. Recommendations will aim to user requirements. In general, to prepare a course, some pre and post conditions for each object are needed.

According to our current research, there are two main sources of preconditions. The first source is based on user profiling, as mentioned previously. While creating a course, the system should dynamically create a list of possible objects that the users could select from; the contents of the list should be based on choices of people of similar interests. The definition of the similar interests concept can be understood in various ways depending on the amount of knowledge the system has about current users. In the best case, the system would be up to analysing choices of people that the users themselves declared of similar interest (e.g., by utilizing functionality of previously mentioned FOAF technology). If we are dealing with totally new users who has not described by themselves people of similar interests or assigned themselves to some kind of user group, system reason can be used based on information like nationality, occupation, and so forth.

The second source of preconditions is a less innovative idea, but also very important, especially when prior information about the user is not available. The ultimate goal of composing the course can be aided by analyzing definitions found in objects description ontology that contains some suggested predefined user's experience and level and specifies the context of the object in a given domain. The predefined descriptions of a required user level are a good guide for the system at its bootstrapping. Taking notice of object context is far more important even when the system has wide knowledge about users and their learning choices. By analyzing the paths users have taken during the course, the compassion system can find objects that are popular at some point of learning in a given subject but do not necessarily concern the subject directly. For example, while learning Spanish, at some point many foreign users might have chosen to learn about Spanish history. That fact should result with the system proposing Spanish history lessons to a new foreign user that is only interested in learning the language and grammar. By comparing object context with user expectations, automatic course generation can be controlled in a way to give better results and to satisfy users more.

In order to maintain the quality of proposed courses, while the user selects one of the given options, the system should be able to track post conditions of the user-selected object and modify further parts of the course. Post conditions are information defining what benefits the user gains by completing an e-learning object and what level he will hold after. At this point of the research, to achieve the goals described at the beginning, we assume to extract this information only from fixed descriptions stored in object ontology. Ideally, this information could also be created dynamically on-demand by analyzing what similar users have learned after completing the course. This solution, however, assumes some additional input from the user to rate objects and is rather meant for future research.

Sample Application Description

Storage and sharing of educational information is a crucial element of e-learning. A social semantic digital library called JeromeDL is an example of a system that can be applied in e-learning as a user orientated knowledge repository. It is one of the first systems that bind together the preciously described Semantic Web and Web 2.0 efforts.

The idea of social semantic information sources has been implemented in a 2-layer metadata enrichment architecture. The lower layer is responsible for lifting up enriching concepts of legacy metadata like MARC21, BibTeX, or DublinCore to the semantic level. This allows the interoperability with already existing legacy digital library systems. However, the legacy metadata (especially MARC21) is usually hard to understand by an average user of a digital library. Therefore, JeromeDL delivers a second layer of metadata enrichment that is community oriented. Communities of users (and authors) can interact in the Web 2.0 fashion by tagging resources through the Social Semantic Collaborative Filtering (SSCF) interface. SSCF allows users to annotate resources (and share those annotations with their friends) according to the way they perceive the world. Semantic information managed by both layers of metadata enrichment is later used by the semantic query expansion algorithm that takes user interests into account. Ongoing research is looking into using social semantic DL as a source of future LOs.

Conclusion

As has been indicated, much of the wrongs that have taken place in e-learning can now be rectified with the framework outlined in the research in this chapter and through the use of the current research being carried out in the Semantic Web, which in conjunction with the collaborative aspects, can overcome and drive a new, exciting, and engaging learning future on the Web. We have indicated some ideal current developments in the e-learning area, the semantic potential and its possible impact on learning through profiling, and the complicated assessment model. The semantic technology can deliver all aspects of the model outlined in our research.

References

Badger, A. (2000). *Keeping it fun and relevant: Using active learning.*

Bloom, B.S.E. (1956). *Taxonomy of educational objectives: The classification of educational goals: Handbook of, cognitive domain.*

Crichton, S. (2003). Innovative practices for innovators: Walking the talk. *Online training for online teachers.*

Dodds, L. (2004, February). *An introduction to foaf.*

Gee, J.P. (2003). *An introduction to discourse analysis: Theory and method.* London: Routledge.

Goldman, R. (2004). *Speech interaction for mobile devices: A natural solution to a contextual conumdrum.*

Goodyear, P. (2001). *Effective networked learning in higher education: Notes and guidelines.*

Greenagel, F.L. (2002). *The illusion of e-learning: Why we are missing out on the promise of technology.*

Hwee, Y. (2000). *Assessing critical thinking through scaffolded asynchronous online discussion.*

Money, A.G. (2005). Once more with feeling: An emotional approach to multimedia context analysis. *IASTED05.*

Noriko Hara, C.J.B., & Charoula, A. (1998). *Content analysis of online discussion in an applied education psychology. 2*(28), 115-152.

O'Nuallain, C., & A.B. (2004). How can one effectively assess students working in a collaborative mobile environment on an individual basis? *MLearn04.*

O'Nuallain, C., & Redfern, S. (2005). The promotion of effective learning through collaborative methods in a wireless ubiquitous environment. *CAL05.*

Pask, G. (1997). *An idiosyncratic history of conversation theory in software, and its progenitor, gordon pask.*

Reigeluth, C.M. (1996). What is the new paradigm of instructional theory.

Salmon, G. (2000). *E-moderating: The key to teaching and learning online.* Sterling, USA: Kogan Page.

Salmon, G. (2002). *E-tivities: The key to active online learning*: RoutledgeFalmer.

About the Authors

Miltiadis D. Lytras (PhD, Department of Management Science and Technology, Athens University of Economics and Business-AUEB, "An ontological approach to the specification of advanced semantics for learning content: The convergence of Knowledge Management and Pedagogy in E-Learning," MBA AUEB, BSc Informatics AUEB) is the editor-in-chief of the *International Journal of Knowledge and Learning* (http://www.inderscience.com/ijkl) as well as the editor-in-chief of the *International Journal of Teaching and Case Studies* (http://www.inderscience.com/ijtcs). He is a faculty member in the Computer Engineering and Informatics Department-CEID (University of Patras), and in the Department of Business Administration-BMA (University of Patras). His research focuses on semantic web, knowledge management and e-learning, with more than 80 publications in these areas. He has co-edited/co-edits 20 special issues in international journals and has authored/edited ten books. He is the founder and officer of the Semantic Web and Information Systems Special Interest Group in the Association for Information Systems (http://www.sigsemis.org) as well as the co-founder of AIS SIG on Reusable Learning Objects and Learning Design (http://www.sigrlo.org). He serves as the editor-in-chief of six international journals while he is associate editor or editorial board member in seven more. He has participated in 20 R&D projects and currently he serves as member of the Scientific Advisory Board of ELEGI Project (http://www.elegi.org).

Ambjörn Naeve (www.nada.kth.se/~amb) has a background in both mathematics and computer science and received his PhD in computer science from KTH in 1993. With his *Garden of Knowledge* project (1996-98) he initiated the research on interactive learning environments at KTH, where he presently heads the Knowledge Management Research group (http://kmr.nada.kth.se). He is also the coordinator of research on interactive learning environments at the Uppsala Learning Lab at Uppsala University. The KMR-group has been involved in Semantic Web research and development since 1999. The work of the KMR-group focuses on how to make use of Semantic Web technology in order to enable more efficient forms of technology-enhanced learning and administration, and support the emergence of a *public knowledge and learning management environment*. Prominent among the KMR tools are the frameworks *SCAM* (http://scam.sourceforge.net) and *SHAME* (http://kmr.nada.kth.se/shame), the concept browser *Conzilla* (www.conzilla.org) and the electronic portfolio system *Confolio* (www.confolio.org). The KMR-group is active within several international networks in technology-enhanced learning and Semantic Web, notably, *Prolearn* (www.prolearn.eu), *SIGSEMIS* (www.sigsemis.org) and *Sakai* (http://sakaiproject.org). Naeve is also a well-known industry consultant with extensive experience in conceptual modeling for software engineering and business applications. He is the inventor of Conzilla and has developed a conceptual modeling technique called *unified language modeling* (http://kmr.nada.kth.se/cm), which is specially designed to depict conceptual relationships in a linguistically coherent way (i.e., to "draw how we talk about things").

* * *

Hyggo Almeida is an electrical engineer PhD candidate at the Electrical Engineering Department (DEE), Federal University of Campina Grande (UFCG) since 2004. He has a master's in computer science with focus in software engineering for multiagent systems from Federal University of Campina Grande in 2004. He is currently an assistant professor at the Computer and Systems Department at the Federal University of Campina Grande. He is leading activities related to component based development and pervasive computing. He has more than 70 papers published in conferences and journals.

Sinuhé Arroyo is a PhD researcher in the area of semantic services. He has success-fully managed the DERI partner contribution in the EU-funded projects (http://www.esperonto.net) and DIP (http://dip.semanticweb.org/). Sinuhé has been very active in EU-framework 6, participating on the elaboration of two IP accepted propos-als in call five, DIP and SEKT, and one accepted STREP, LUISA in the sixth call. Previous to his current position he was Project leader at iSOCO in Madrid, Spain, responsible for the architecture and development of various applications in the field of the B2B applying Semantic Web technology; earlier to this roll he was software engineer senior at the same company, responsible for the design and implementa-tion of various B2B applications also applying Semantic Web technology. While at Ermestel S.L in Madrid, Spain, he was responsible for the design and implementa-tion of various database centric applications with the role of Software Engineer Junior. Sinuhé obtained his MS in computer science from Universidad de Malaga (UMA), Malaga, Spain in 2000. He also holds a BS in software engineering from University Complutense de Madrid (UCM), Madrid, Spain in 1997. Currently he is undergoing the review process of his PhD thesis.

Michela Bertolotto received a BSc and a PhD degree (1998) in computer science from the University of Genova. Subsequently she held a postdoctoral position at the National Center for Geographic Information and Analysis at the University of Maine (1998-2000). Since 2000, she has been a college lecturer in the Department of Computer Science at University College Dublin. Her research interests include spatial data handling, virtual reality and geometric modelling for GIS.

Violeta Damjanovic is a member of the GOOD OLD AI research group and a PhD candidate at the Department for Electronic Business, University of Belgrade, Serbia and Montenegro. She received her BSc in information systems, degree as a specialist in Internet technologies, and MSc in electronic business from the University of Bel-grade, in 1998, 2003, and 2005, respectively. Her interests mostly include Semantic Web, semantic grid, Web intelligence, ambient intelligence, multi-agent systems, adaptive hypermedia systems, and applications of artificial intelligence techniques to education. She can be reached at vdamjanovic@gmail.com.

Chris Dede is the Timothy E. Wirth professor in learning technologies at Harvard's Graduate School of Education. His fields of scholarship include emerging tech-nologies, policy, and leadership. His funded research includes a grant from the National Science Foundation to aid middle school students learning science via shared virtual environments and a Star Schools grant from the U.S. Department of Education to help middle students with math and literacy skills through augmented reality simulations. Chris has served as a member of the National Academy of Sci-ences Committee on Foundations of Educational and Psychological Assessment, a member of the U.S. Department of Education's Expert Panel on Technology, and International Steering Committee member for the Second International Technology in Education Study. Among others, he serves on Advisory Boards and Commissions for PBS TeacherLine, the Partnership for 21st Century Skills, and the Pittsburgh Science of Learning Center.

Edward Dieterle is an advanced doctoral candidate in Learning and Teaching at the Harvard Graduate School of Education (HGSE). Prior to coming to HGSE, he worked as a high school science teacher in Prince George's County, Maryland and as an instructor at Johns Hopkins University and Trinity College. Dieterle served on the National Academy of Sciences Committee on Improving Learning with Information Technology and has written extensively on integrating technology and inquiry-based science into classroom instruction for Maryland Public Television and the National Park Service. His primary research interests focus on media-based learning styles made possible by multiuser virtual environments and augmented realities, which support the situational and distributional nature of cognition with respect to thinking, learning, and doing.

Glauber Ferreira is an MSc student at the Federal University of Campina Grande. He received a BS in computer science from the Federal University of Alagoas, at Maceió, Brazil, in 2004. His research areas include multi-agent systems interaction protocols, pervasive computing, and software components for building mobile virtual communities applications.

John Garofalakis, born in 1959, obtained his PhD from the Department of Computer Engineering and Informatics (CEID), University of Patras, Greece, in 1990, and his Diploma on Electrical Engineering from the National Technical University of Athens, Greece, in 1983. He is currently associate professor in CEID and manager of the Telematics Center Department at the Research and Academic Computer Technology Institute of Greece. His research interests include performance evaluation, distributed systems and algorithms, Internet technologies and applications. He has published over 65 papers in various journals and refereed conferences and is author of several books and lecture notes in the Greek language.

Theodoula Giannakoudi was born in Greece. She is currently a postgraduate student at the Computer Engineering and Informatics Department at the University of Patras, Greece, and a member of the Telematics Center Department at the Research and Academic Computer Technology Institute of Greece (RACTI). Theodoula holds an MSc from the same department, where she has also completed his undergraduate studies. Her interests span the areas of Web usage mining and Semantic Web.

Kostas Kolomvatsos is a postgraduate student at the Department of Informatics & Telecommunications, National & Kapodistrian University of Athens, Greece. He received his Bsc in informatics from the Athens University of Economics and Business (Department of Informatics) in 1995 and his Msc in new technologies in informatics and telecommunications from the National & Kapodistrian University of Athens (Department of Informatics and Telecommunications) in 2005. His interests include Semantic Web, ambient intelligence, intelligent agents systems and intelligence techniques to education.

Milos Kravcik received his diploma in informatics and PhD in applied informatics from the Comenius University in Bratislava, Slovakia. He has worked as a research fellow at the Faculty of Mathematics, Physics and Informatics of this university and later at the Fraunhofer Institute for Applied Information Technology FIT, Sankt Augustin, Germany. His main research interests include adaptive hypermedia systems, e-learning and mobile learning. Currently he is working at the Open University Nederland in Heerlen and can be reached at milos.kravcik@ou.nl.

Sebastian Kruk is a lead researcher in eLITE (e-learning project and project manager of Corrib.org affiliated with DERI Galway and Gdansk University of Technology (GUT). The main area of interest covers Semantic Web technologies, digital libraries, information retrieval, security and distributed computing. He works on the semantic digital library system called JeromeDL (based on the research originally initiated with Henryk Krawczyk). Other projects related to digital libraries covered by Corrib.org are MarcOnt Initiative, FOAFRealm and HyperCuP. He contributes to the open source community with a number of other projects like ResourcePocket and Questionnaire Application, or JOnto (unified Java API for taxonomies). He invented the Virtual Desktop implemented in MetadITo e-learning project and DigiMe—a ubiquitous, next stage of evolution of FOAFRealm identity management framework. He is recently working on the Didaskon that will deliver a framework for semantically-empowered based on user's profile, dynamic curriculum assembling of learning objects.

Reto Krummenacher received his engineering degree in communication systems from the Swiss Federal Institute of Technology (EPFL) in Lausanne, Switzerland in 2004. His master thesis on location-aware prefetching was written in collaboration with the Fraunhofer Institute IPSI in Darmstadt, Germany. Since Fall 2004 he is a PhD student with the Digital Enterprise Research Institute (DERI) at the University of Innsbruck, Austria. He is currently involved in national and European projects on Semantic Web service technologies. The focus is set on communication and coordination of services with emphasize on the use of these technologies in ubiquitous computing.

Sim Kim Lau is a senior lecturer in the Information Systems Discipline, School of Economics and Information Systems at the University of Wollongong. She has published widely in refereed information systems journals and international conferences. Her research interest is in the area of application of artificial intelligence and optimization techniques to business problems, and more recently in the area of semantic web and ontology. Her teaching covers knowledge-based information systems and decision support systems.

Nelson Leung received a Bachelor of Information Technology from the Queensland University of Technology, Master of Information Systems from the Griffith University and Master of Information Systems (Research) from the University of Wollongong. He is now a PhD student in the Information Systems Discipline, School of Economics and Information Systems at the University of Wollongong. Prior to that, he was a customer service manager for Hong Kong Broadband and Network and was responsible for overseeing the call centre and the support staff. Before Hong Kong Broadband and Network, Leung worked as an IT help desk supervisor for Getronics which provides help desk outsourcing service for Morgan Stanley Dean Witter.

Emerson Loureiro received an MSc in informatics from the Federal University of Campina Grande, at Campina Grande, Brazil, in 2006, and a BS in computer science from the Federal University of Alagoas, at Maceió, Brazil, in 2004. His current research activities are focused on pervasive computing, mainly on the aspects of middleware, software engineering, adaptation, context awareness, and service provision.

Gavin McArdle received a BSc (Hons) degree (2003) in computer science from University College Dublin (UCD). He has subsequently undertaken a PhD degree in UCD. His research involves the development of a virtual reality environment for collaborating, learning and socialising online. McArdle's research interests include visualisation techniques, virtual reality along with learning methods and pedagogy. Gavin has presented work at a number of international and European conferences, including Eurographics and Ed-Media.

Teresa Monahan received a BSc (Hons) degree in computer science from University College Dublin (UCD) in 2003. She is currently studying for her PhD, also in UCD, where her studies involve research into online learning environments, 3D interfaces and mobile learning. Her research interests include collaborative e-learning systems, virtual reality and mobile applications. Teresa has presented work at several international conferences including Eurographics, the IASTED conference on Web-based education and Siggraph.

Holger Nösekabel received his PhD in business computing from the University of Regensburg, Germany, in 2005. His research interests include mobile computing, specifically mobile education, and he actively participated in national and EU funded research projects related to mobile computing. Other related areas of interest encompass usability aspects and multimedia content for mobile devices.

Caoimhín O'Nualláin is a lead researcher in the ELITE research project in Digital Enterprise Research Institute (DERI) in Galway. His main area of interest covers e-learning, pedagogy, technologies, instructional design, usability testing of media for different devices, assessment planning and designing resources for special needs students. Nearly four years ago he put together the new framework for his e-learning model for ubiquitous devices which would enhance learning and extend the audience for learning to include mobile users, life long learners and special needs users. This same framework can also be used for many other applications and uses which I am pushing as possible commercialisations in the future.

Yannis Panagis was born in Greece, in 1978. He is currently a PhD candidate at the Computer Engineering and Informatics Department at the University of Patras and a member of the Research Unit 5 of the Research Academic Computer Technology Institute (RACTI). Yannis holds an MSc from the same Department, where he has also completed his undergraduate studies. His interests span the areas of data structures, string processing algorithms and Web engineering, where he has published papers in international journals and conferences. He has also co-authored two book chapters.

Angelo Perkusich received a PhD and MSc in electrical engineering from the Federal University of Paraíba, at Campina Grande, Brazil, in 1994 and 1987, respectively. In 1982 he received a BS in electrical engineering from the Engineering Faculty of Barretos. From 1988 to 1990 he was an assistant professor of the Electronic and Systems Department at the Federal University of Pernambuco. From 1992 to 1993 he was a visiting researcher at the University of Pittsburgh, USA. From 1991 to 1994 he was an assistant professor of the Electrical Engineering Department at the Federal University of Paraíba. Since 1994 he is an adjunct professor at such department. He is a project leader/consultant at the affiliated Nokia project for the development of embedded systems applications for mobile devices. His research interest include software engineering for embedded systems, dynamic software composition, formal methods, and pervasive computing.

Evangelos Sakkopoulos was born in Greece, in 1977. He is currently a PhD candidate at the Computer Engineering and Informatics Department, University of Patras, Greece and a member of the Research Unit 5 of the Research Academic Computer Technology Institute (RACTI). He has received the MSc degree with honours and the Diploma of Computer Engineering and Informatics at the same institution. His research interests include Web searching, large data set handling, data mining, Web services, Web engineering, Web usage mining, Web-based education and intranets. He has more than 30 publications in international journals and conferences at these areas.

Karen Schrier recently finished MIT's Comparative Media Studies program, where she completed her graduate thesis, "Revolutionizing History Education: Using Augmented Reality (AR) Games to Teach Histories." Prior to MIT, she worked at an educational media company, where she produced numerous published academic guides for K-12 and college students. Karen has presented internationally on mobile storytelling, educational media, and AR games. She recently published a book chapter on designing AR games and presented a paper at ACM IGGRAPH 2006. She is currently living and working in New York City, where she creates educational animations and games for college students.

Anna Trifonova has graduated at New Bulgarian University (Sofia, Bulgaria) in 1999. Her specialty was information systems and technologies—applications in business and office. She finished her PhD at the International Graduate School of Information and Communication Technologies at the University of Trento, Italy in March 2006. Her research topic was "Mobile Learning: Wireless and Mobile Technologies in Education." Her scientific interests and publications to that time are mainly in the mobile learning domain, and starting from year 2003 she has more than 15 articles in international pear-reviewed conferences and workshops on this topic.

Athanasios K. Tsakalidis, computer-scientist, professor of the University of Patras. He was born in 1950, in Katerini, Greece. Studies include: Diploma of Mathematics, University of Thessaloniki in 1973; Diploma of Informatics in 1980; and PhD in informatics in 1983, University of Saarland, Germany. From 1983 to 1989 he was a researcher in the University of Saarland. Tsakalidis has been student and cooperator (12 years) of Prof. Kurt Mehlhorn (Director of Max-Planck Institute of Informatics in Germany). From 1989 to 1993 he has served as associate professor and since 1993 professor in the Department of Computer Engineering and Informatics of the University of Patras. From 1993 to 1997 and from 2001 to present, he serves as chairman of the same department. He is currently a member of the board of directors of the Research Academic Computer Technology Institute (RACTI), coordinator of research and development of RACTI, and vice-director of RACTI. He is one of the contributors to the writing of the "Handbook of Theoretical Computer Science"

(Elsevier and MIT-Press 1990). He has published many scientific articles, having especially contributed to the solution of elementary problems in the area of data structures. Scientific interests include: data structures, computational geometry, information retrieval, computer graphics, data bases, and bio-informatics

Adam Westerski.is currently is a student on Gdansk University of Technology (GUT), Poland. He is pursuing his degree in computer science with specialization in systems engineering and databases. Westerski is writing his master's thesis on the "Usage of Semantic Web Mechanisms for Supporting Web Services Composition in E-Learning Solution." Areas of interest includes: Semantic Web, Web services, and their composition and appliances of those technologies in e-learning. He was a researcher at the Digital Enterprise Research Institute (DERI), and has been involved in many research projects and currently still maintains cooperation with DERI researchers. At the beginning of his research carrier he wrote a few articles concerning Semantic Web usage in the domains of digital libraries and e-learning. Preceding his research interests he has worked for a couple of years in the industry focusing on java development.

Index

community support 97
component-based software 14
computed tomography (CT) 148
Computer Engineering and Informatics
        Department (C.E.I.D.) 250
computing context 11–12
constructivist 163
consumer 17
content standards 97
context 6, 11
  -aware 301
  acquisition 12
  aware applications 12
  discovery 204
  management part 170
  reasoning 12
  representation 12
contracts 14
cost 105
curriculum resources 97

D

dermatoscope 168
desire 185
digital
  divide 104
  literacy 1, 67, 94, 198, 263
discovery messages 10
discursion 301
distributed profile management system (D-
        FOAF) 302
document space (DOCS) 172, 174
domain-specific ontologies 21
dynamic host configuration protocol
        (DHCP) 8

E

e-learner 158
e-learning 68
educational tasks 71
elements 229
emotional intelligence (EQ) 161, 164
energy restrictions 8
enhanced messages service (EMS) 81
environmental detectives 56

eQ
  context manager agent 186
  FOSP manager agent 186
equipment damage 106
event service 17
EVE project 135
experiments 188
external 11

F

file transfer 87
filter 179, 183
first-order logic (FOL) 172
FOSP weight function 188
frequently asked question lists (FAQs) 278
friends 306
fundamentals 188

G

general
  event notification architecture (GENA)
        19
  packet radio system (GPRS) 9
global positioning system (GPS) 37, 128
granularity 179
  function 183
graphical user interface (GUI) 140
  GUI design 84

H

handheld devices for ubiquitous learning
        (HDUL) 35, 37, 41
haptic 181
Harvard
  Extension School (HES) 41
  Graduate School of Education (HGSE)
        41
head mounted displays (HMDs) 148
Hyper Text Mark-up Language (HTML)
        124
hysical context 11

I

i-mode 83
inappropriate use of technology 106

V

virtual
  European schools (VES) 132
  reality (VR) 119, 126, 129
visual 181

W

Web site content 243
Weight 179
Wi-Fi 5
wireless
  handheld
    computing devices (WHDs) 35
    devices (WHDs) 37
  local area network (WLAN 283
  telephony application interface (WTAI)
      77
World Wide Web (WWW) 283
WSDL files 248

Z

ZipCode 249